Free expression in America

# Free Expression
# in America

ADVISORY BOARD

Mary Fortney
Social Studies Consultant
Indiana Department of Education

Rosemarie Kuntz
Government Teacher
Perry Meridian High School, Indianapolis

Karl E. Schneider
Teacher
Arsenal Technical High School, Indianapolis

J. Alexander Tanford
Professor of Law
Indiana University

Richard A. Waples
Attorney at Law
Indiana Civil Liberties Union

# FREE EXPRESSION IN AMERICA

*A Documentary History*

Edited by SHEILA SUESS KENNEDY

Primary Documents in American History and Contemporary Issues

GREENWOOD PRESS
Westport, Connecticut • London

**Library of Congress Cataloging-in-Publication Data**

Free expression in America : a documentary history / edited by Sheila
   Suess Kennedy.
        p.   cm.—(Primary documents in American history and
   contemporary issues, ISSN 1069–5605)
     Includes bibliographical references and index.
     ISBN 0–313–30241–3 (alk. paper)
     1. Freedom of speech—United States.   2. Freedom of the press—
   United States.   I. Kennedy, Sheila Suess.   II. Series.
   KF4770.F738   1999
   342.73'0853—dc21          99–21789

British Library Cataloguing in Publication Data is available.

Library of Congress Catalog Card Number: 99–21789
ISBN: 0–313–30241–3
ISSN: 1069–5605

First published in 1999

Greenwood Press, 88 Post Road West, Westport, CT 06881
An imprint of Greenwood Publishing Group, Inc.
www.greenwood.com

Printed in the United States of America

The paper used in this book complies with the
Permanent Paper Standard issued by the National
Information Standards Organization (Z39.48–1984).

10 9 8 7 6 5 4 3 2 1

# Contents

# Series Foreword

This series is designed to meet the research needs of high school and college students by making available in one volume the key primary documents on a given historical event or contemporary issue. Documents include speeches and letters, congressional testimony, Supreme Court and lower court decisions, government reports, biographical accounts, position papers, statutes, and news stories.

The purpose of the series is twofold: (1) to provide substantive and background material on an event or issue through the texts of pivotal primary documents that shaped policy or law, raised controversy, or influenced the course of events, and (2) to trace the controversial aspects of the event or issue through documents that represent a variety of viewpoints. Documents for each volume have been selected by a recognized specialist in that subject with the advice of a board of other subject specialists, school librarians, and teachers.

To place the subject in historical perspective, the volume editor has prepared an introductory overview. Documents are organized either chronologically or topically. The documents are full text or, if unusually long, have been excerpted by the volume editor. To facilitate understanding, each document is accompanied by an explanatory introduction. Suggestions for further reading follow the document or the chapter.

It is the hope of Greenwood Press that this series will enable students and other readers to use primary documents more easily in their research, to exercise critical thinking skills by examining the key documents in American history and public policy, and to critique the variety of viewpoints represented by this selection of documents.

# Acknowledgments

Compilation of this volume of resources would not have been possible without the assistance of Jon Donovan and Dhiann Kinsworthy, students at Indiana University–Purdue University at Indianapolis, whose persistence and skill made the tedious job of obtaining permissions and tracking down obscure sources far less daunting.

Thanks must also go to Jane Hostetler, whose formatting and computer skills were an essential part of the project.

# Introduction

The purpose of this volume is to demonstrate the extraordinary importance of free expression to the American constitutional system and to detail the social and political tensions that have accompanied the decision of the founders of the United States to restrain the government's authority over the communication of ideas.

Those who constructed the American system did not work in a vacuum. While the Constitution and especially the Bill of Rights were truly revolutionary as governing instruments, the ideas and ideals that influenced and shaped these documents came out of a rich intellectual tradition. This country's founders built upon the philosophy of the Enlightenment to create a nation where individual rights would enjoy unprecedented protection. Central to their notion of liberty was a belief that the free exchange of ideas is the bedrock upon which all other freedoms depend. They were formed by the Western intellectual tradition, with its emphasis upon science, empiricism, and rationality. It should come as no surprise that a worldview that placed so high a value upon reason would insist upon protecting the intellectual process from state interference. It is truly impossible to understand American constitutional law without first understanding the meaning and importance of the Free Speech Clause of the First Amendment and the relationship of that clause to the rest of the First Amendment and indeed the rest of the Bill of Rights.

Taken as a whole, the First Amendment to the United States Constitution is nothing less than a celebration of the value of intellectual and moral autonomy. By forbidding government interference with the beliefs of individuals—religious, political, or personal—the First Amendment protects the right of citizens to form opinions freely, to exchange those opinions voluntarily, and to attempt to persuade others of their value.

The founders considered this process essential to the formation of an educated and thoughtful citizenry. They believed that self-government would be possible only for those who enjoyed the widest possible access to information. In order to protect that access, in order to safeguard the "marketplace of ideas" that they envisioned, they incorporated within the First Amendment broad protections for speech and assembly as well as explicit freedom for the press.

While scholars and historians understand the First Amendment as an organic whole that protects freedom of individual conscience from government interference, the public has rarely seen free-speech protection in that way. State and federal legislatures have responded to public sentiment by passing laws to "protect" Americans from the expression of ideas they believe to be dangerous or immoral. Courts are not immune from public passion, and depending upon the political temper of the times, the context of the issue, and the composition of the particular court involved, these attempts have met with varying success.

The documents chosen for this volume are a reflection of the ongoing conflict between individual liberty and the passions of the majority, as played out in the context of the First Amendment. If there is any doubt that the urge to censor is as deeply rooted in the American psyche as our stubborn insistence on our rights to "do our own thing," these selections should dispel it. In the pages that follow, the conflict is between those who read the First Amendment's free-speech protections expansively and those who would apply protection only to political expression narrowly defined. While it would be impossible to discuss that conflict without frequent reference to court decisions, an effort has been made to include other contemporaneous materials—magazine articles, newspaper coverage, statutes, and treatises—that reflect popular opinion and provide a context for the legal battles.

Americans did not invent liberty, but we were the first to premise a government on the notion that states derive their power from the consent of the governed. We were the first to expressly limit the ability of government to infringe the "natural rights" of the individual, even when a majority of citizens might agree that the infringement was justified. This volume traces the evolution of that experiment in government in one area: the right to free expression. It has been a fascinating journey, and it is far from over.

# Part I

# Foundations of Liberty

## DOCUMENT 1: Magna Carta (1215)

The concept of liberty, the notion that individuals have rights that should be secure even against the state, did not emerge overnight. The development of our Western idea of liberty has been chronicled elsewhere and is not the proper sphere of this discussion. But certain documents provide crucial insight into the evolution of our legal system and can shed light upon the progression from English feudal monarchy to the system created by our Constitution and Bill of Rights.

The great charter of English liberty was decreed (under pressure) by King John at Runnymede on June 15, 1215 A.D. None of its provisions directly concerned free speech; that should not be surprising, since the nobles who forced its adoption were an elite possessed of properties and privileges that they wished, above all, to protect from arbitrary and capricious action by the Crown and others. Thus the document deals most forcefully with what we might today call due-process issues: requirements of notice, hearing, and proportionality of fines and impositions. The Magna Carta established certain property and inheritance rights; it also obligated government to enforce certain contracts and protected a (limited) right to travel.

As significant as these matters were to the evolution of later law, what is most striking is the document's basic premise: that the power of the Crown should not be unlimited. Implicit in the articles is the notion that would later find expression in our Declaration of Independence, that government rests on the consent of those it governs. While the liberties enumerated in the Magna Carta may seem minimal to us today, the concept of limited sovereign power became the foundation of modern libertarian theory.

\* \* \*

THE GREAT CHARTER OF KING JOHN, GRANTED JUNE 15, A.D. 1215.

John, by the grace of God, king of England, lord of Ireland, duke of Normandy and Aquitaine, and count of Anjou, to the archbishops, bishops, abbots, earls, barons, justiciars, foresters, sheriffs, stewards, servants, and to all his bailiffs and faithful subjects, greeting. Know that we,

1. RIGHTS OF THE CHURCH

In the first place have granted to God, and by this our present charter confirmed for us and our heirs for ever that the English church shall be free, and shall have its rights undiminished and its liberties unimpaired; and it is our will that it be thus observed; which is evident from the fact that, before the quarrel between us and our barons began, we willingly and spontaneously granted and by our charter confirmed the freedom of elections which is reckoned most important and very essential to the English church, and obtained confirmation of it from the lord pope Innocent III; the which we will observe and we wish our heirs to observe it in good faith for ever. We have also granted to all free men of our kingdom, for ourselves and our heirs for ever, all the liberties written below, to be had and held by them and their heirs of us and our heirs.

2. GRANT OF LIBERTY TO FREEMEN

If any one of our earls or barons, or of others holding from us in chief through military service, shall die; and if, at the time of his death, his heir to be of full age and owe a relief: he shall have his inheritance by paying the old relief;—the heir, namely, or the heirs of an earl, by paying one hundred pounds for the whole barony of an earl; the heir or heirs of a baron, by paying one hundred pounds for the whole barony; the heir or heirs of a knight, by paying one hundred shillings at most for a whole knight's fee; and he who shall owe less shall give less, according to the ancient custom of fees. . . .

12. NO TAX (SCUTAGE) EXCEPT BY THE GENERAL COUNCIL

No scutage or aid shall be imposed in our kingdom unless by the common counsel of our kingdom; except for ransoming our person, for making our eldest son a knight, and for once marrying our eldest daughter; and for these only a reasonable aid shall be levied. Be it done in like manner concerning aids from the city of London.

13. LIBERTIES OF LONDON, AND OTHER TOWNS

And the city of London shall have all its ancient liberties and free customs as well by land as by water. Furthermore, we will and grant that all other cities, burroughs, towns, and ports shall have all their liberties and free customs.

### 14. GENERAL COUNCIL SHALL CONSENT TO ASSESSMENT OF TAXES

And for holding the general council of the kingdom concerning the assessment of aids, except in the three cases aforesaid, and for the assessing of scutages, we shall cause to be summoned the archbishops, bishops, abbots, earls, and greater barons of the realm, singly by our letters, and furthermore, we shall cause to be summoned generally, by our sheriffs and bailiffs, all others who hold of us in chief, for a certain day, that is to say, forty days before their meeting at least, and to a certain place; and in all letters of such summons we will declare the cause of such summons, and, summons being thus made the business shall proceed on the day appointed, according to the advice of such as shall be present, although all that were summoned come not. . . .

### 17. COURTS SHALL ADMINISTER JUSTICE IN A FIXED PLACE

Common pleas shall not follow our court but shall be held in some place certain.

### 18. LAND DISPUTES SHALL BE TRIED IN THEIR PROPER COUNTIES

Recognitions of novel [newly made] disseisin [to recover seized property], of mort d'ancester [deaths of family], and of darrein presentment [secret formal statement], shall not be held elsewhere than in the counties to which they relate, and in this manner—we, or, if we should be out of the realm, our chief justiciar, will send two justices through each county four times a year, who, with four knights of each county chosen by the county, shall hold the said assizes in the county and on the day and in the place of meeting of the county court.

### 19. KEEPING THE ASSIZE COURTS OPEN

And if the said assizes cannot all be held on the day of the county court, there shall stay behind as many of the knights and freeholders who were present at the county court on that day as are necessary for the sufficient making of judgments, according to the amount of business to be done.

### 20. FINES AGAINST FREEMAN TO BE MEASURED BY THE OFFENSE

A free man shall not be amerced [fined] for a trivial offence except in accordance with the degree of the offence, and for a grave offence he shall be amerced in accordance with its gravity, yet saving his way of living; and a merchant in the same way, saving his stock-in-trade; and a villein shall be amerced in the same way, saving his means of livelihood—if they have fallen into our mercy; and none of the aforesaid amercements shall be imposed except by the oath of good men of the neighbourhood. . . .

23. Neither a town nor any tenant shall be distrained to make bridges or embankments, unless that anciently and of right they are bound to do it.

24. No sheriff, constable, coroner, or other of our bailiffs, shall hold "Pleas of the Crown." ...

26. If any one holding from us a lay fee shall die, and our sheriff or bailiff can show our letters patent containing our summons for the debt which the dead man owed to us,—our sheriff or bailiff may be allowed to attach and enroll the chattels of the dead man to the value of that debt, through view of lawful men; in such way, however, that nothing shall be removed thence until the debt is paid which was plainly owed to us. And the residue shall be left to the executors that they may carry out the will of the dead man. And if nothing is owed to us by him, all the chattels shall go to the use prescribed by the deceased, saving their reasonable portions to his wife and children.

27. If any freeman shall have died intestate his chattels shall be distributed through the hands of his near relatives and friends, by view of the church; saving to any one the debts which the dead man owed him.

28. COMPENSATION FOR THE TAKING OF PRIVATE PROPERTY

No constable or other bailiff of ours shall take anyone's corn or other chattels unless he pays on the spot in cash for them or can delay payment by arrangement with the seller.

29. No constable shall force any knight to pay money for castle-guard if he be willing to perform that ward in person, or—he for a reasonable cause not being able to perform it himself—through another proper man. And if we shall have led or sent him on a military expedition, he shall be quit of ward according to the amount of time during which, through us, he shall have been in military service.

30. NO TAKING OF HORSES OR CARTS WITHOUT CONSENT

No sheriff nor bailiff of ours, nor any one else, shall take the horses or carts of any freeman for transport, unless by the will of that freeman.

31. NO TAKING OF TREES FOR TIMBER WITHOUT CONSENT

Neither we nor our bailiffs shall take another's wood for castles or for other private uses, unless by the will of him to whom the wood belongs.

32. We will retain the lands of those convicted of felony only one year and a day, and then they shall be delivered to the lord of the fee. ...

35. UNIFORM WEIGHTS AND MEASURES

There shall be one measure for wine throughout our kingdom, and one measure for ale, and one measure for corn, namely "the London quarter"; and one width for cloths whether dyed, russet or halberget, namely two ells within the selvages. Let it be the same with weights as with measures.

36. NOTHING FROM HENCEFORTH SHALL BE GIVEN OR TAKEN FOR A WRIT OF INQUISITION OF LIFE OR LIMB, BUT IT SHALL BE GRANTED FREELY, AND NOT DENIED. ...

38. No bailiff shall in future put anyone to trial upon his own bare word, without reliable witnesses produced for this purpose.

39. GUARANTEE OF JUDGMENT BY ONE'S PEERS AND OF PROCEEDINGS ACCORDING TO THE "LAW OF THE LAND."

No free man shall be taken or imprisoned or disseised or outlawed or exiled or in any way victimised, neither will we attack him or send any-one to attack him, except by the lawful judgment of his peers or by the law of the land.

40. GUARANTEE OF EQUAL JUSTICE (EQUALITY BEFORE THE LAW)

We will sell to no man, we will not deny or delay to any man, either justice or right.

41. FREEDOM OF MOVEMENT FOR MERCHANTS

All merchants shall be able to go out of and come into England safely and securely and stay and travel throughout England, as well by land as by water, for buying and selling by the ancient and right customs free from all evil tolls, except in time of war and if they are of the land that is at war with us. And if such are found in our land at the beginning of a war, they shall be attached, without injury to their persons or goods, until we, or our chief justiciar, know how merchants of our land are treated who were found in the land at war with us when war broke out, and if ours are safe there, the others shall be safe in our land.

42. FREEDOM TO LEAVE AND REENTER THE KINGDOM

It shall be lawful in future for anyone, without prejudicing the alle-giance due to us, to leave our kingdom and return safely and securely by land and water, save, in the public interest, for a short period in time of war—except for those imprisoned or outlawed in accordance with the law of the kingdom and natives of a land that is at war with us and merchants (who shall be treated as aforesaid). . . .

45. APPOINTMENT OF THOSE WHO KNOW THE LAW

We will not make justices, constables, sheriffs or bailiffs save of such as know the law of the kingdom and mean to observe it well. . . .

54. No man shall be taken or imprisoned upon the appeal of a woman for the death of anyone except her husband.

55. All fines imposed by us unjustly and contrary to the law of the land, and all amercements made unjustly and contrary to the law of the land, shall be altogether remitted, or it shall be done with regard to them according to the judgment of the twenty five barons mentioned below as sureties for the peace, or according to the judgment of the majority of them together with the aforesaid Stephen archbishop of Canterbury, if he can be present, and with others whom he may wish to associate with himself for this purpose. And if he can not be present, the affair shall

nevertheless proceed without him; in such way that, if one or more of the said twenty five barons shall be concerned in a similar complaint, they shall be removed as to this particular decision, and in their place, for this purpose alone, others shall be substituted who shall be chosen and sworn by the remainder of those twenty five.

56. If we have disseized or dispossessed Welshmen of their lands or liberties or other things without legal judgment of their peers, in England or in Wales,—they shall straightway be restored to them. And if a dispute shall arise concerning this, then action shall be taken upon it in the March through judgment of their peers—concerning English holdings according to the law of England, concerning Welsh holdings according to the law of Wales, concerning holdings in the March according to the law of the March. The Welsh shall do likewise with regard to us and our subjects.

57. But with regard to all those things of which any one of the Welsh was, by king Henry our father or king Richard our brother, disseized or dispossessed without legal judgment of his peers, which we have in our hand or which others hold, and for which we ought to give a guarantee: we shall have respite until the common term for crusaders. Except with regard to those concerning which a plea was moved, or an inquest made by our order, before we took the cross. But when we return from our pilgrimage, or if, by chance, we desist from our pilgrimage, we shall straightway then show full justice regarding them, according to the laws of Wales and the aforesaid districts. . . .

60. Liberties to be granted to all subjects

All the foresaid customs and liberties, which we have granted to be holden in our kingdom, as much as it belongs to us, all people of our kingdom, as well clergy as laity, shall observe, as far as they are concerned, towards their dependents.

61. Oath to observe rights of the church and the people

Inasmuch as for the sake of God, and for the bettering of our realm, and for the more ready healing of the discord which has arisen between us and our barons, we have made all these aforesaid concessions,—wishing them to enjoy for ever entire and firm stability, we make and grant to them the following security: that the barons, namely, may elect at their pleasure twenty five barons from the realm, who ought, with all their strength, to observe, maintain and cause to be observed, the peace and privileges which we have granted to them and confirmed by this our present charter, in such wise, namely, that if we, our justice, or our bailiffs, or any one of our servants shall have transgressed against any one in any respect, or shall have broken some one of the articles of peace or security, and our transgression shall have been shown to four barons of the aforesaid twenty five: those four barons shall come to us, or, if we are abroad, to our justice, showing to us our error; and they shall ask us to cause that error to be amended without delay. And if we do not amend that error, or, we being abroad, if our justice do not amend it within a term of forty days from the time when it was shown to us or, we being abroad, to our justice: the aforesaid four barons shall refer the matter to the remainder of the twenty five barons, and those twenty five barons, with the whole land in common, shall distrain and oppress us in every way in their power,—namely, by taking our castles, lands and possessions, and in every other way that they can, until amends shall have been made according to their judgment. Saving the persons of ourselves, our queen and our children. And when amends shall have been made they shall be in accord with us as they had been previously. And whoever of the land wishes to do so, shall swear that in carrying out all the aforesaid measures he will obey the mandates of the aforesaid twenty five barons, and that, with them, he will oppress us to the extent of his power. And, to any one who wishes to do so, we publicly and freely give permission to swear; and we will never prevent any one from swearing. Morever, all those in the land who shall be unwilling, themselves and of their own accord, to swear to the twenty five barons as to distraining and oppressing us with them: such ones we shall make to swear by our mandate, as has been said. And if any one of the twenty five barons shall die, or leave the country, or in any other way be prevented from carrying out the aforesaid measures,—the remainder of the aforesaid twenty five barons shall choose another in his place, according to their judgment, who shall be sworn in the same way as the others. Moreover, in all things entrusted to those twenty five barons to be carried out, if those twenty five shall be present and chance to disagree among themselves with regard to some matter, or if some of them, having been summoned, shall be unwilling or unable to be present: that which the majority of those present shall decide or decree shall be considered binding and valid, just as if all the twenty five had consented to it. And the aforesaid twenty five shall swear that they will faithfully observe all the foregoing, and will cause them to be observed to the extent of their power. And we shall obtain nothing from any one, either through ourselves or through another, by which any of those concessions and liberties may be revoked or diminished. And if any such thing shall have been obtained, it shall be vain and invalid, and we shall never make use of it either through ourselves or through another.

*Source*: James McClellan, *Liberty, Order, and Justice: An Introduction to the Constitutional Principles of American Government*, 2d ed. (Richmond, VA: James River Press, 1991), 36–42.

## DOCUMENT 2: *Areopagitica* (John Milton, 1644)

*Areopagitica*, subtitled *A Speech for the Liberty of Unlicenc'd Printing*, is considered one of the seminal defenses of freedom of speech and publication in English history. Although John Milton is known to students today primarily as a great poet, he was also an essayist; in *Areopagitica* he used his considerable prose talents to address the English Parliament, which was considering the imposition of a license to be required before books or pamphlets might be printed. Milton characterized this essay as his testimony against such a measure and systematically demolished the purported purposes of such a licensing measure. The essay is considered a classic document in the history of libertarian thought.

\* \* \*

*This is true Liberty, when free-born men*
*Having to advise the public may speak free,*
*Which he who can, and will, deserv's high praise,*
*Who neither can nor will, may hold his peace;*
*What can be juster in a State then this?*
                         Euripid. Hicetid.

. . . this whole Discourse propos'd will be a certaine testimony, if not a Trophey. For this is not the liberty which wee can hope, that no grievance ever should arise in the Commonwealth, that let no man in this World expect; but when complaints are freely heard, deeply consider'd, and speedily reform'd, then is the utmost bound of civill liberty attain'd, that wise men looke for. To which if I now manifest by the very sound of this which I shall utter, that wee are already in good part arriv'd, and yet from such a steepe disadvantage of tyranny and superstition grounded into our principles as was beyond the manhood of a *Roman* recovery, it will bee attributed first, as is most due, to the strong assistance of God our deliverer, next to your faithfull guidance and undaunted Wisdome, Lords and Commons of *England*. . . .

. . . I know not what should withhold me from presenting ye with a fit instance wherein to shew both that love of truth which ye eminently professe, and that uprightnesse of your judgement which is not wont to be partiall to your selves; by judging over again that Order which ye have ordain'd *to regulate Printing. That no Book, pamphlet, or paper shall be henceforth Printed, unless the same be first approv'd and licenc't by such,* or at least one of such as shall be thereto appointed. For that part which preserves justly every man's Copy to himselfe, or provides for the poor, I touch not, only wish they be not made pretenses to abuse and persecute honest and painfull Men, who offend not in either of these particulars. But that other clause of Licencing Books, . . . I shall now attend with such a Homily, as shall lay before ye, first the inventors of it to bee those whom ye will be loath to own; next what is to be thought in generall of reading, what ever sort the Books be; and that this Order avails nothing to the suppressing of scandalous, seditious, and libellous Books, which were mainly intended to be supprest. Last, that it will be primely to the discouragement of all learning, and the stop of Truth, not only by dis-exercising and blunting our abilities in what we know already, but by hindring and cropping the discovery that might bee yet further made both in religious and civill Wisdom.

I deny not, but that it is of greatest concernment in the Church and Commonwealth, to have a vigilant eye how Bookes demeane themselves, as well as men; and thereafter to confine, imprison, and do sharpest justice on them as malefactors: For Books are not absolutely dead things, but doe contain a potencie of life in them to be as active as that soule was whose progeny they are; nay they do preserve as in a violl the purest efficacie and extraction of that living intellect that bred them. I know they are as lively, and as vigorously productive, as those fabulous Drag-ons teeth; and being sown up and down, may chance to spring up armed men. And yet on the other hand unlesse warinesse be us'd, as good almost kill a Man as kill a good Book; who kills a Man kills a reasonable creature, Gods Image; but hee who destroyes a good Booke, kills reason it selfe, kills the Image of God, as it were in the eye. Many a man lives a burden to the Earth; but a good Booke is the pretious life-blood of a master spirit, imbalm'd and treasur'd up on purpose to a life beyond life. . . .

. . . For those actions which enter into a man, rather than issue out of him, and therefore defile not, God uses not to captivat under a perpetuall childhood of prescription, but trusts him with the gift of reason to be his own chooser; there were but little work left for preaching, if law and compulsion should grow so fast upon those things which hertofore were govern'd only by exhortation. . . . As for the burning of those Ephesian books by St. *Pauls* converts, 'tis reply'd the books were magick, the Syriack so renders them. It was a privat act, a voluntary act, and leaves us to a voluntary imitation: the men in remorse burnt those books which were their own; the Magistrat by this example is not appointed: these men practiz'd the books, another might perhaps have read them in some sort usefully. Good and evill we know in the field of this world grow up together almost inseparably; and the knowledge of good is so involv'd and interwoven with the knowledge of evill, and in so many cunning resemblances hardly to be discern'd, that those confused seeds which were impos'd on *Psyche* as an incessant labour to cull out, and sort asunder, were not more intermixt. It was from out the rinde of one apple tasted, that the knowledge of good and evill, as two twins cleaving together leapt forth into the World. And perhaps this is that doom which *Adam* fell into of knowing good and evill, that is to say of knowing good by evill. As therefore the state of man now is; what wisdome can there be to choose, what continence to forbeare without the knowledge of evill? He that can apprehend and consider vice with all her baits and seeming pleasures, and yet abstain, and yet distinguish, and yet prefer that which is truly better, he is the true wayfaring Christian. . . . Since therefore the knowledge and survay of vice is in this world so necessary to the constituting of human vertue, and the scanning of error to the confirmation of truth, how can we more safely, and with lesse danger scout into the regions of sin and falsity then by reading all manner of tractats, and hearing all manner of reason? . . . of the harm that may result hence three kinds are usually reckon'd. First, is fear'd the infection that may spread; but then all human learning and controversie in religious points must remove out of the world, yea the Bible it selfe; for that oft times relates blasphemy not nicely, it describes the carnall sense of wicked men not unelegantly, it brings in holiest men passionately murmuring against providence through all the arguments of *Epicurcus*: in other great disputes it answers dubiously and darkly to the common reader. . . . For these causes we all know the Bible it selfe put by the Papist into the first rank of prohibited books. . . . if learned men be the first receivers out of books, and dispredders both of vice and error, how shall the licencers themselves be confided in, unlesse we can conferr upon them, or they assume to themselves to be above all others in the Land, the grace of infallibility, and uncorruptednesse? And again, if it be true, that a wise man like a good refiner can gather gold out of the drossiest volume, and that a fool will be a fool with the best book, yea or without book, there is no reason that we should deprive a wise man of any advantage to his wisdome, while we seek to restrain from a fool, that which being restrain'd will be no hindrance to his folly. . . . 'Tis next alleg'd we must not expose our selves to temptations without necessity, and next to that, not imploy our time in vain things. To both these objections one answer will serve, out of the grounds already laid, that to all men such books are not temptations, nor vanities; but usefull drugs and materialls wherewith to temper and compose effective and strong med'cins, which mans life cannot want. The rest, as children and childish men, who have not the art to qualifie and prepare these working mineralls, well may be exhorted to forbear, but hinder'd forcibly they cannot be by all the licencing that Sainted Inquisition could ever yet contrive; ... this order of licencing conduces nothing to the end for which it was fram'd; ... unlesse their care were equall to regulat all other things of like aptnes to corrupt the mind, that single endeavour they knew would be but a fond labour; to shut and fortifie one gate against corruption, and be necessitated to leave others round about wide open. ...

... I know nothing of the licencer, but that I have his own hand here for his arrogance; who shall warrant me his judgement? The State, Sir, replies the Stationer, but has a quick return, The State shall be my governours, but not my criticks; they may be mistak'n in the choice of a licencer, as easily as this licencer may be mistak'n in an author: This is some common stuffe; and he might adde from Sir *Francis Bacon*, That *such authoriz'd books are but the language of the times*. For though a licencer should happ'n to be judicious more than ordnary, which will be a great jeopardy of the next succession, yet his very office, and his commission enjoyns him to let passe nothing but what is vulgarly receiv'd already. ...

... Truth and understanding are not such wares as to be monopoliz'd and traded in by tickets and statutes, and standards. We must not think to make a staple commodity of all the knowledge in the Land, to mark and licence it like our broad cloth, and our wool packs. ... Nor is it to the common people lesse then a reproach; for if we be so jealous over them, as that we dare not trust them with an English pamphlet, what doe we but censure them for a giddy, vitious, and ungrounded people; in such a sick and weak estate of faith and discretion, as to be able to take nothing down but through the pipe of a licencer. That this is care or love of them, we cannot pretend. ...

Well knows he who uses to consider, that our faith and knowledge thrives by exercise, as well as our limbs and complexion. Truth is compar'd in Scripture to a streaming fountain; if her waters flow not in a perpetuall progression, they sick'n into a muddy pool of conformity and tradition. A man may be a heretick in the truth; and if he beleeve things only because his Pastor sayes so, or the Assembly so determins, without knowing other reason, though his belief be true, yet the very truth he holds, becomes his heresie. ...

... This I know, that errors in a good government and in a bad are equally almost incident; for what Magistrate may not be mis-inform'd, and much the sooner, if liberty of Printing be reduc'd into the power of a few? But to redresse willingly and speedily what hath bin err'd, and in highest authority to esteem a plain advertisement more than others have done a sumptuous bribe, is a vertue (honour'd Lords and Commons) answerable to Your highest actions, and wherof none can participat but greatest and wisest men.

*Source*: John Milton, *Complete Poetry and Selected Prose of John Milton* (New York: Modern Library, 1950), 677–724.

---

## DOCUMENT 3: *Cato's Letters* (1720)

---

Between 1720 and 1723, John Trenchard and Thomas Gordon, writing in the American colonies under the pseudonym Cato, produced and distributed numerous essays on the nature of freedom. Issued as *Cato's Letters*, the essays were tremendously popular and influential, shaping much of the public debate over the relationship of the colonies with England and the principles that should guide any government with claims to legitimacy. One of the most widely quoted of the *Letters*, then and since, is number 15, entitled "Of Freedom of Speech: That the Same Is Inseparable from Publick Liberty." Those who argue that the First Amendment comes first in the Bill of Rights because it forms the basis for all of our other rights can find support in "Of Freedom of Speech," which the authors argue that our other liberties depend upon freedom of speech for their realization.

The continued relevance of *Cato's Letters* can be seen in the testimony of a citizen from South Miami, addressing a proposal before the Florida legislature to restrict anonymous Internet remailer services. "Will the traditional right of the people to anonymous and pseudonymous speech (such as the pseudonymously authored Cato's Letters and several of the Federalist papers) still be permitted under the proposed legislation?" he asked, in a message posted on the Internet in 1997. Just the year before, a federal court invalidated an Ohio statute that had banned distribution of pamphlets and political flyers unless the real name of the author appeared on the publication. Had a similar law been in effect in the colonies in the 1720s, one of the most eloquent and persuasive voices of the times would have been silenced.

\* \* \*

SIR,

Without Freedom of Thought, there can be no such Thing as Wisdom; and no such Thing as publick Liberty, without Freedom of Speech: Which is the Right of every Man, as far as by it he does not hurt and control the Right of another, and this is the only Check which it ought to suffer, the only Bounds which it ought to know.

This sacred Privilege is so essential to free Government, that the Security of Property, and the Freedom of Speech, always go together; and in those wretched Countries where a Man cannot call his Tongue his own, he can scarce call any Thing else his own. Whoever would overthrow the Liberty of the Nation, must begin by subduing the Freedom of Speech; a Thing terrible to publick Traytors.

This Secret was so well known to the Court of King Charles I, that his wicked Ministry procured a Proclamation to forbid the People to talk of Parliaments, which those Traytors had laid aside. To assert the undoubted Right of the Subject, and defend his Majesty's Legal Prerogative, was called disaffection, and punished as Sedition. Nay, People were forbid to talk of Religion in their Families: For the Priests had combined with the Ministers to cook up Tyranny, and suppress Truth and the Law. While the late King *James*, when Duke of York, went avowedly to Mass; Men were fined, imprisoned, and undone, for saying that he was a Papist: And, that King *Charles* II, might live more securely a Papist, there was an Act of Parliament made, declaring it Treason to say that he was one.

That Men ought to speak well of their Governors, is true, while their Governors deserve to be well spoken of; but to do publick Mischief, without hearing of it, is only the Prerogative and Felicity of Tyranny: A free People will be shewing that they are so, by their Freedom of Speech.

The Administration of Government is nothing else, but the Attendance of the Trustees of the People upon the Interest and Affairs of the People. And as it is the Part and Business of the People, for whose Sake alone all publick Matters are, or ought to be, transacted, to see whether they be will or ill transacted; so it is the Interest, and ought to be the Ambition, of all honest Magistrates, to have their Deeds openly examined, and publickly scanned: Only the wicked Governors of Men dread what is said of them; *Audivit Tiberius probra queis lacerabitur, atque perculsus est.* The publick Censure was true, else he had not felt it bitter.

Freedom of Speech is ever the Symptom, as well as the Effect, of good Government. In old Rome, all was left to the Judgement and Pleasure of the People; who examined the publick Proceedings with such Discretion, and censured those who administered them with such Equity and Mildness, that in the Space of Three Hundred Years, not Five publick Ministers suffered unjustly. Indeed, whenever the Commons proceeded to Violence, the Great Ones had been the Aggressors.

Guilt only dreads Liberty of Speech, which drags it out of its lurking Holes, and exposes its Deformity and Horror to Day-light. *Horatius, Valerius, Cincinnatus,* and other virtuous and undesigning Magistrates of the *Roman* Commonwealth, had nothing to fear from Liberty of Speech. Their virtuous Administration, the more it was examined, the more it brightened and gained by Enquiry. When *Valerius*, in particular, was accused, upon some slight Grounds, of affecting the Diadem; he, who was the first Minister of Rome, did not accuse the People for examining his Conduct, but approved his Innocence in a Speech to them; he gave such Satisfaction to them, and gained such Popularity to himself, that they gave him a new Name; *inde cognomen factum Publicolae est*; to denote that he was their Favourite and their Friend. . . .

But Things afterward took another Turn: Rome, with the Loss of its Liberty, lost also the Freedom of its Speech; then Mens Words began to be feared and watched; then first began the poisonous Race of Informers, banished indeed under the righteous Administration of *Titus, Nerva, Trajan, Aurelius* &c. but encouraged and enriched by the vile Ministry of *Sejanus, Tigellinus, Pallas*, and *Cleander*. . . .

The best Princes have ever encouraged and promoted Freedom of Speech; they knew that upright Measures would defend themselves, and that all upright Men would defend them. *Tacitus*, speaking of the Reigns of some of the Princes above-mention'd, says with Extasy, *Rara temporum felicitate, ubi sentire quae velis & quae sentias dicere liceat*: A blessed Time, when you might think what you would, and speak what you thought!

The same was the Opinion and Practice of the wise and virtuous *Timoleon*, the Deliverer of the great City of *Syracuse* from Slavery. He being accused by *Demoenetus*, a popular Orator, in a full Assembly of the People, of several Misdemeanors committed by him while he was General, gave no other Answer, than that *He was highly obliged to the Gods for granting him a Request that he had often made to them*; namely, *That he might live to see the* Syracusians *enjoy that Liberty of Speech which they now seemed to be Masters of.*

And that great Commander, *M. Marcellus*, who won more Battles than any *Roman* Captain of his Age, being accused by the *Syracusians*, while he was now a fourth Time Consul, of having done them Indignities and hostile Wrongs, contrary to the League, rose from his Seat in the Senate, as soon as the Charge against him was opened, and passing (as a private Man) into the Place where the Accused were wont to make their Defence, gave free Liberty to the *Syracusians* to impeach him: Which, when they had done, he and they went out of the Court together to attend the Issue of the Cause: Nor did he express the least Ill-will or Resentment towards these his Accusers; but being acquitted, received their City into his Protection. Had he been guilty, he would neither have shewn such Temper nor Courage.

I doubt not but old *Spencer* and his Son, who were the chief Ministers and Betrayers of *Edward* II would have been very glad to have stopped the Mouths of all the honest Men in England. They dreaded to be called Traytors, because they were Traytors. And I dare say, Queen *Elizabeth's Walsingham*, who deserved no Reproaches, feared none. Misrepresentation of publick Measures is easily overthrown, by representing publick Measures truly: When they are honest, they ought to be publick known, that they may be publickly commended; but if they be knavish or pernicious, they ought to be publickly exposed, in order to be publickly detested.

To assert, that King *James* was a Papist and a Tyrant, was only so far hurtful to him, as it was true of him; and if the Earl of *Strafford* had not deserved to be impeached, he need not have feared a Bill of Attainder. If our Directors and their Confederates be not such Knaves as the World thinks them, let them prove to all the World, that the World thinks wrong, and that they are guilty of none of those Villainies which all the World lays to their Charge. Others too, who would be thought to have no Part of their Guilt, must, before they are thought innocent, shew that they did all that was in their Power to prevent that Guilt and to check their Proceedings.

Freedom of Speech is the great Bulwark of Liberty; they prosper and die together: And it is the Terror of Traytors and Oppressors, and a Barrier against them. It produces excellent Writers, and encourages Men of fine Genius. *Tacitus* tells us, that the *Roman* Commonwealth bred great and numerous Authors, who writ with equal Boldness and Elloquence: But when it was enslaved, those great Wits were no more. . . . Tyranny had usurped the Place of Equality, which is the Soul of Liberty, and destroyed publick Courage. The Minds of Men, terrified by unjust Power, degenerated into all the Vileness and Methods of Servitude: Abject Sycophancy and blind Submission grew the only means of Preferment, and indeed of Safety; Men durst not open their Mouths, but to flatter.

*Pliny* the Younger observes, that this Dread of Tyranny had such Effect, that the Senate, the great *Roman* Senate, became at last stupid and dumb. . . . Hence, says he, our Spirit and Genius are stupified, broken, and sunk for ever. And in one of his Epistles, speaking of the Works of his Uncle, he makes an Apology for eight of them, as not written with the same Vigour which was to be found in the rest; for that these eight were written in the Reign of *Nero*, when the Spirit of Writing was cramped by Fear. . . .

All Ministers, therefore, who were Oppressors, or intended to be Oppressors, have been loud in their Complaints against Freedom of Speech, and the Licence of the Press; and always restrained, or endeavoured to restrain, both. In consequence of this, they have brow-beaten Writers, punished them violently, and against Law, and burnt their Works. By all which they shewed how much Truth alarmed them, and how much they were at Enmity with Truth.

There is a famous Instance of this in *Tacitus*: He tells us, that *Cremutius Cordus*, having in his Annals praised *Brutus* and *Cassius*, gave Offence to *Sejanus*, First Minister, and to some inferior Sycophants in the Court of *Tiberius*; who, conscious of their own Characters, took the Praise bestowed on every worthy *Roman*, to be so many Reproaches pointed at themselves: They therefore complain of the Book to the Senate; which, being now only the Machine of Tyranny, condemned it to be burnt. But this did not prevent its spreading. . . . Being censured, it was the more sought after. *From hence*, says *Tacitus, we may wonder at the Stupidity of those Statesmen, who hope to extinguish, by the Terror of their Power, the Memory of their Action*; for quite otherwise, *the Punishment of good Writers gains Credit to their Writings*. . . . Nor did ever any Government, who practised impolitick Severity, get any thing by it, but Infamy to themselves, and Renown to those who suffered under it. . . .

Freedom of Speech, therefore, being of such infinite Importance to the Preservation of Liberty, everyone who loves Liberty ought to encourage Freedom of Speech. . . .

*Valerius Maximus* tells us, that *Lentulus Marcellinus*, the *Roman* Consul, having complained, in a popular Assembly, of the overgrown Power of *Pompey*; the whole People answered him with a Shout of Approbation: Upon which the Consul told them, *Shout on, Gentlemen, shout on, and use those bold Signs of Liberty while you may; for I do not know who long they will be allowed you.*

God be thanked, we *Englishmen* have neither lost our Liberties, nor are in Danger of losing them. Let us always cherish this matchless Blessing, almost peculiar to ourselves; that our Posterity may, many Ages hence, ascribe their Freedom to our Zeal. The Defence of Liberty is a noble, a heavenly Office; which can only be performed where Liberty is. . . .

*Source*: "Of Freedom of Speech: That the Same Is Inseparable from Publick Liberty," Number 15, Saturday, February 4, 1720, *Cato's Letters* (New York: De Capo Press, 1971), 96–103.

# Part II

# The Concept of Free Speech and the Role of Government during the Founding and Early History of the United States

Beginning with the American Revolution, those who have believed in free expression have engaged in debate with those who would justify curbs on speech in the service of other goals. In one sense, the documents in Parts II through V can be seen as a reflection of that very basic debate.

Of course, if the issue could be defined so simply, the debate would not be so acrimonious nor so prolonged. Indeed, it has been difficult to achieve agreement on the most basic question: even today, the definition of "speech" for purposes of the First Amendment is not completely settled. Over the years, courts have grappled with a number of definitional issues. Does "speech" include symbolic behavior, like marching or flag burning? Is art speech? Are political contributions? When can the state properly interfere with acts that are clearly intended to convey a message? Can it do so when a hate crime is committed? When a rally is held?

The inquiry does not stop with the definition of speech. The Bill of Rights restrains only government. (Initially, it restrained only the federal government.) Any discussion about the constitutional right to free speech must begin with the question of state action, because if government is not involved, neither is the First Amendment. How involved must government be in order to find state action? How has the growth of government's influence over our everyday lives changed our understanding of the reach of the First Amendment? Why has the Supreme Court "incorporated" First Amendment protections into the Fourteenth Amendment, so that state and local governments are also prohibited from infringing our right to free expression? Have we strayed from the original intent of the founders by enlarging the reach of the Bill of Rights, and how is original intent to be defined? All of these questions have given rise to continuing public debate.

Once a court determines that the state is acting to regulate speech, its inquiry turns to the propriety of that action. Is the law too broad? Too vague? Can government ever regulate speech based upon the ideas being transmitted, or are "content-based" restrictions inherently unconstitutional? Should the rules be different when the speech occurs in a special environment—a school, for example, or a place of employment?

The principle underlying the free-speech provisions of the First Amendment is clear: government must be prevented from interfering with the marketplace of ideas. As the foregoing questions illustrate, however, the application of that principle to specific situations is a great deal more difficult. As technology provides new methods of communication, changing the nature of the press and other media and allowing far wider dissemination of ideas by more and more people, our understanding of the First Amendment necessarily evolves as well. James Madison and Thomas Jefferson did not anticipate radio and television, and certainly not the Internet; they and their colleagues enunciated principles concerning the proper role of government and the importance of the free exchange of ideas. As technology has advanced and we have developed media unthinkable in 1776, courts must look carefully at the principles underlying the First Amendment and must apply them to a very different reality.

Finally, even those who consider the First Amendment the cornerstone and sine qua non of individual liberty must acknowledge the existence and importance of other rights. Increasingly, the courts are faced with allegations that speech must be curbed in order to protect other fundamental rights like equality, free exercise of religion, or a woman's right to choose an abortion. Whether these cases present a true conflict or a seeming one, the pervasiveness of government increases their incidence.

The materials that follow are offered chronologically, so that the evolution of the law can be put in historical context. We begin with seminal writings like Thomas Paine's Common Sense and John Stuart

Mill's *On Liberty*. Almost immediately, however, the new nation enacted laws that seemingly ignored the principles of free speech, beginning with the Alien and Sedition Acts, and later, the so-called Comstock Laws, the Tennessee law that prohibited teaching of the theory of evolution, made famous in the trial of John Scopes, and a wide variety of other restrictions, which were frequently upheld by the courts. In the 1950s, with the rise of the Soviet Union, documents reflect the times. McCarthyism and the Legion of Decency define the decade.

Part V traces the evolution of free-speech doctrine through the turbulent 1960s, through the feminist "porn wars," and up to and including contemporary attempts to censor the Internet.

The documents provide a fascinating look at the social and cultural context within which these issues arose. A society that tolerates all ideas demands a great deal of its citizens, and the pages that follow bear witness to the fact that Americans have not always measured up. The chronological approach, although it has its drawbacks, paints a vivid picture of the evolution of a supremely important principle: that in order for societies to flourish, the individual mind and conscience must be free of restraints imposed either by government or by majority passions.

## DOCUMENT 4: *Common Sense* (Thomas Paine, 1776)

The development of a Western intellectual tradition valuing individuality and liberty found expression during the conflicts between England and the American colonies. While the tensions leading up to the Revolutionary War were not solely, or even primarily, ideological (indeed, some historians would argue that economic issues were at the heart of the drive for independence), leading polemicists of the time nevertheless argued for the libertarian philosophy with energy and passion.

Antigovernment rhetoric is not an invention of the late twentieth century. One of the most influential and fiery revolutionary pamphleteers was Thomas Paine, who had a great deal to say about society and government. In *Common Sense*, Paine addressed at some length the institutions of the monarchy and hereditary succession; he followed that discussion with an analysis of America's relationship with England, methodically rebutting the most common arguments against revolution. In the process, he suggested the form a new government might take. While *Common Sense* does not concern itself directly with freedom of speech, it is a classic example of the sort of political expression that the founders meant to protect. Paine is nothing if not a superb advocate for a cause; even today, *Common Sense* has the power to convince and engage the reader. We can only speculate about its effect on those who originally read and debated it in the midst of the passions then sweeping the colonies.

\* \* \*

## THOUGHTS OF THE PRESENT STATE OF AMERICAN AFFAIRS

In the following pages I offer nothing more than simple facts, plain arguments, and common sense; and have no other preliminaries to settle with the reader, than that he will divest himself of prejudice and prepossession, and suffer his reason and his feelings to determine for themselves; that he will put *on*, or rather that he will not put *off* the true character of a man, and generously enlarge his views beyond the present day.

Volumes have been written on the subject of the struggle between England and America. Men of all ranks have embarked in the controversy, from different motives, and with various designs; but all have been ineffectual, and the period of debate is closed. Arms, as the last resource, decide the contest; the appeal was the choice of the king, and the continent hath accepted the challenge. . . .

As much hath been said of the advantages of reconciliation, which, like an agreeable dream, hath passed away and left us as we were, it is but right, that we should examine the contrary side of the argument, and inquire into some of the many material injuries which these colonies sustain, and always will sustain, by being connected with, and dependant on Great Britain. . . .

I have heard it asserted by some, that as America hath flourished under her former connection with Great Britain, that the same connection is necessary towards her future happiness, and will always have the same effect. Nothing can be more fallacious than this kind of argument. We may as well assert, that because a child has thrived upon milk, that it is never to have meat; or that the first twenty years of our lives is to become a precedent for the next twenty. But even this is admitting more than is true, for I answer roundly, that America would have flourished as much, and probably much more, had no European power had any thing to do with her. The commerce by which she hath enriched herself are the necessaries of life, and will always have a market while eating is the custom of Europe.

But she has protected us, say some. That she hath engrossed us is true, and defended the continent at our expense as well as her own is admitted, and she would have defended Turkey from the same motive, viz., the sake of trade and domination.

Alas! we have been long led away by ancient prejudices and made large sacrifices to superstition. We have boasted the protection of Great Britain, without considering, that her motive was interest not attachment; that she did not protect us from our enemies on our account, but from her enemies on her own account, from those who had no quarrel with us on any other account, and who will always be our enemies on the same account. Let Britain wave her pretensions to the continent, or the continent throw off the dependance, and we should be at peace with France and Spain were they at war with Britain. The miseries of Hanover last war, ought to warn us against connections. . . .

But Britain is the parent country, say some. Then the more shame upon her conduct. Even brutes do not devour their young; nor savages make war upon their families; wherefore the assertion, if true, turns to her reproach; but it happens not to be true, or only partly so, and the phrase parent or mother country hath been jesuitically adopted by the king and his parasites, with a low papistical design of gaining an unfair bias on the credulous weakness of our minds. Europe, and not England, is the parent country of America. This new world hath been the asylum for the persecuted lovers of civil and religious liberty from every Part of Europe. Hither have they fled, not from the tender embraces of the mother, but from the cruelty of the monster; and it is so far true of England, that the same tyranny which drove the first emigrants from home pursues their descendants still. . . .

But admitting that we were all of English descent, what does it amount to? Nothing. Britain, being now an open enemy, extinguishes every other name and title: And to say that reconciliation is our duty, is truly farcical. The first king of England, of the present line (William the Conqueror) was a Frenchman, and half the peers of England are descendants from the same country; wherefore by the same method of reasoning, England are descendants from the same country; wherefore by the same method of reasoning, England ought to be governed by France. . . .

I challenge the warmest advocate for reconciliation, to show, a single advantage that this continent can reap, by being connected with Great Britain. . . . Our corn will fetch its price in any market in Europe, and our imported goods must be paid for buy them where we will.

But the injuries and disadvantages we sustain by that connection, are without number; and our duty to mankind at large, as well as to ourselves, instructs us to renounce the alliance: Because, any submission to, or dependance on Great Britain, tends directly to involve this continent in European wars and quarrels; and sets us at variance with nations, who would otherwise seek our friendship, and against whom, we have neither anger nor complaint. As Europe is our market for trade, we ought to form no partial connection with any part of it. It is the true interest of America to steer clear of European contentions, which she never can do, while by her dependance on Britain, she is made the make-weight in the scale of British politics. . . .

Though I would carefully avoid giving unnecessary offence, yet I am inclined to believe, that all those who espouse the doctrine of reconciliation, may be included within the following descriptions:

Interested men, who are not to be trusted; weak men who cannot see; prejudiced men who will not see; and a certain set of moderate men, who think better of the European world than it deserves; and this last class by an ill-judged deliberation, will be the cause of more calamities to this continent than all the other three.

It is the good fortune of many to live distant from the scene of sorrow; the evil is not sufficiently brought to their doors to make them feel the precariousness with which all American property is possessed. But let our imaginations transport us for a few moments to Boston, that seat of wretchedness will teach us wisdom, and instruct us for ever to renounce a power in whom we can have no trust. The inhabitants of that unfortunate city, who but a few months ago were in ease and affluence, have now no other alternative than to stay and starve, or turn out to beg. Endangered by the fire of their friends if they continue within the city, and plundered by the soldiery if they leave it. In their present condition they are prisoners without the hope of redemption, and in a general attack for their relief, they would be exposed to the fury of both armies.

Men of passive tempers look somewhat lightly over the offences of Britain, and, still hoping for the best, are apt to call out, Come we shall be friends again for all this. But examine the passions and feelings of mankind. Bring the doctrine of reconciliation to the touchstone of nature, and then tell me, whether you can hereafter love, honor, and faithfully serve the power that hath carried fire and sword into your land? . . .

It is repugnant to reason, to the universal order of things, to all examples from the former ages, to suppose, that this continent can longer remain subject to any external power. The most sanguine in Britain does not think so. The utmost stretch of human wisdom cannot, at this time, compass a plan short of separation, which can promise the continent even a year's security. Reconciliation is a fallacious dream. Nature hath deserted the connection, and Art cannot supply her place. For, as Milton wisely expresses, "never can true reconcilement grow where wounds of deadly hate have pierced so deep. . . ."

To say, they will never attempt it again is idle and visionary, we thought so at the repeal of the stamp act, yet a year or two undeceived us; as well we may suppose that nations, which have been once defeated, will never renew the quarrel.

As to government matters, it is not in the powers of Britain to do this continent justice: The business of it will soon be too weighty, and intricate, to be managed with any tolerable degree of convenience, by a power, so distant from us, and so very ignorant of us; for if they cannot conquer us, they cannot govern us. . . .

I am not induced by motives of pride, party, or resentment to espouse the doctrine of separation and independence; I am clearly, positively, and conscientiously persuaded that it is the true interest of this continent to be so; that every thing short of that is mere patchwork, that it can afford no lasting felicity,—that it is leaving the sword to our children, and shrinking back at a time, when, a little more, a little farther, would have rendered this continent the glory of the earth. . . .

If there is any true cause of fear respecting independence it is because no plan is yet laid down. Men do not see their way out; wherefore, as an opening into that business I offer the following hints; . . .

Let the assemblies be annual, with a President only. The representation more equal. Their business wholly domestic, and subject to the authority of a continental congress.

Let each colony be divided into six, eight, or ten, convenient districts, each district to send a proper number of delegates to congress, so that each colony send at least thirty. The whole number in congress will be at least three hundred ninety. Each congress to sit . . . and to choose a president by the following method. When the delegates are met, let a colony be taken from the whole thirteen colonies by lot, after which let the whole congress choose (by ballot) a president from out of the delegates of that province. In the next Congress, let a colony be taken by lot from twelve only, omitting that colony from which the president was taken in the former congress, and so proceeding on till the whole thirteen shall have had their proper rotation. And in order that nothing may pass into a law but what is satisfactorily just, not less than three fifths of the congress to be called a majority. He that will promote discord, under a government so equally formed as this, would join Lucifer in his revolt.

But as there is a peculiar delicacy, from whom, or in what manner, this business must first arise, and as it seems most agreeable and consistent, that it should come from some intermediate body between the governed and the governors, that is between the Congress and the people, let a Continental Conference be held, in the following manner, and for the following purpose:

A committee of twenty-six members of Congress, viz., two for each colony. Two members for each house of assembly, or provincial convention; and five representatives of the people at large, to be chosen in the capital city or town of each province, for, and in behalf of the whole province, by as many qualified voters as shall think proper to attend from all parts of the province for that purpose; or, if more convenient, the representatives may be chosen in two or three of the most populous parts thereof. In this conference, thus assembled, will be united, the two grand principles of business, knowledge and power. The members of Congress, Assemblies, or Conventions, by having had experience in national concerns, will be able and useful counselors, and the whole, being empowered by the people will have a truly legal authority.

The conferring members being met, let their business be to frame a Continental Charter, or Charter of the United Colonies; (answering to what is called the Magna Charta of England) fixing the number and manner of choosing members of Congress, members of Assembly, with their date of sitting, and drawing the line of business and jurisdiction between them: always remembering, that our strength is continental, not provincial: Securing freedom and property to all men, and above all things the free exercise of religion, according to the dictates of conscience; with such other matter as is necessary for a charter to contain. Immediately after which, the said conference to dissolve, and the bodies which shall be chosen conformable to the said charter, to be the legislators and governors of this continent for the time being: Whose peace and happiness, may God preserve, Amen. . . .

A government of our own is our natural right: And when a man seriously reflects on the precariousness of human affairs, he will become convinced, that it is infinitely wiser and safer, to form a constitution of our own in a cool deliberate manner, while we have it in our power, than to trust such an interesting event to time and chance. If we omit it now, some may hereafter arise, who laying hold of popular disquietudes, may collect together the desperate and the discontented, and by assuming to themselves the powers of government, may sweep away the liberties of the continent like a deluge. Should the government of America return again into the hands of Britain, the tottering situation of things, will be a temptation for some desperate adventurer to try his fortune; and in such a case, what relief can Britain give? Ere she could hear the news the fatal business might be done, and ourselves suffering like the wretched Britons under the oppression of the Conqueror. Ye that oppose independence now, ye know not what ye do; ye are opening a door to eternal tyranny, by keeping vacant the seat of government. . . .

O ye that love mankind! Ye that dare oppose, not only the tyranny, but the tyrant, stand forth! Every spot of the old world is overrun with oppression. Freedom hath been hunted round the globe. Asia, and Africa, have long expelled her. Europe regards her like a stranger, and England hath given her warning to depart. O! receive the fugitive, and prepare in time an asylum for mankind.

*Source*: Thomas Paine, *Common Sense* (New York: Prometheus Books, 1995), 21–42.

---

## DOCUMENT 5: The Virginia Declaration of Rights (1776)

On June 12, 1776, the Virginia Constitutional Convention adopted the Virginia Declaration of Rights, authored by George Mason. It was, and remains, one of the seminal documents of the times: Thomas Jefferson was profoundly influenced by it and drew upon it for the Declaration of Independence; portions were widely copied by other colonies; and it was a basis for the Bill of Rights.

\* \* \*

I   That all men are by nature equally free and independent, and have certain inherent rights, of which, when they enter into a state of society, they cannot, by any compact, deprive or divest their posterity; namely, the enjoyment of life and liberty, with the means of acquiring and possessing property, and pursuing and obtaining happiness and safety.

II   That all power is vested in, and consequently derived from, the people; that magistrates are their trustees and servants, and at all times amenable to them.

III   That government is, or ought to be, instituted for the common benefit, protection, and security of the people, nation or community; of all the various modes and forms of government that is best, which is capable of producing the greatest degree of happiness and safety and is most effectually secured against the danger of maladministration; and that, whenever any government shall be found inadequate or contrary to these purposes, a majority of the community hath an indubitable, unalienable, and indefeasible right to reform, alter or abolish it, in such manner as shall be judged most conducive to the public weal.

IV   That no man, or set of men, are entitled to exclusive or separate emoluments or privileges from the community, but in consideration of public services; which, not being descendible, neither ought the offices of magistrate, legislator, or judge be hereditary.

V   That the legislative and executive powers of the state should be separate and distinct from the judicative; and, that the members of the two first may be restrained from oppression by feeling and participating the burthens of the people, they should, at fixed periods, be reduced to a private station, return into that body from which they were originally taken, and the vacancies be supplied by frequent, certain, and regular elections in which all, or any part of the former members, to be again eligible, or ineligible, as the laws shall direct.

VI   That elections of members to serve as representatives of the people in assembly ought to be free; and that all men, having sufficient evidence of permanent common interest with, and attachment to, the community have the right of suffrage and cannot be taxed or deprived of their property for public uses without their own consent or that of their representatives so elected, nor bound by any law to which they have not, in like manner, assented, for the public good.

VII   That all power of suspending laws, or the execution of laws, by any authority without consent of the representatives of the people is injurious to their rights and ought not to be exercised.

VIII   That in all capital or criminal prosecutions a man hath a right to demand the cause and nature of his accusation, to be confronted with the accusers and witnesses, to call for evidence in his favor, and to a speedy trial by an impartial jury of his vicinage, without whose unanimous consent he cannot be found guilty, nor can he be compelled to give evidence against himself; that no man be deprived of his liberty except by the law of the land or the judgement of his peers.

IX That excessive bail ought not to be required, nor excessive fines imposed; nor cruel and unusual punishments inflicted.

X That general warrants, whereby any officer or messenger may be commanded to search suspected places without evidence of a fact committed, or to seize any person or persons not named, or whose offense is not particularly described and supported by evidence, are grievous and oppressive and ought not to be granted.

XI That in controversies respecting property and in suits between man and man, the ancient trial by jury is preferable to any other and ought to be held sacred.

XII That the freedom of the press is one of the greatest bulwarks of liberty and can never be restrained but by despotic governments.

XIII That a well regulated militia, composed of the body of the people, trained to arms, is the proper, natural, and safe defense of a free state; that standing armies, in time of peace, should be avoided as dangerous to liberty; and that, in all cases, the military should be under strict subordination to, and be governed by, the civil power.

XIV That the people have a right to uniform government; and therefore, that no government separate from, or independent of, the government of Virginia, ought to be erected or established within the limits thereof.

XV That no free government, or the blessings of liberty, can be preserved to any people but by a firm adherence to justice, moderation, temperance, frugality, and virtue and by frequent recurrence to fundamental principles.

XVI That religion, or the duty which we owe to our Creator and the manner of discharging it, can be directed by reason and conviction, not by force or violence; and therefore, all men are equally entitled to the free exercise of religion, according to the dictates of conscience; and that it is the mutual duty of all to practice Christian forbearance, love, and charity towards each other.

*Source*: Virginia Declaration of Rights, written by George Mason and adopted by the Virginia Constitutional Convention, June 12, 1776. *The Annals of America, Volume 2, 1755–1783*, Helen Hemmingway Benton, Publisher (Chicago, IL: Encyclopedia Brittanica, Inc., 1968), 432–433.

## DOCUMENT 6: The Northwest Ordinance (1787)

While political debates raged in the original American colonies, settlers, trappers, speculators, and others increasingly moved westward into the lands west of the Alleghenies. This vast territory, which would eventually become Ohio, Indiana, Illinois, Michigan, and Wisconsin, came under the control of the Congress of the Confederation when Virginia and other states turned their various holdings over to the newly formed central government.

Pressure soon arose for a consistent policy approach to the territories in order to ease commerce and define the rights of those living and doing business there. In response, the Continental Congress passed several "ordinances," the most important of which by far was the Northwest Ordinance. Drawing heavily upon Thomas Jefferson's *Report of Government for Western Lands*, it provided for interim governing procedures, the eventual formation of states, the encouragement of education, inheritance rights, and the protection of civil liberties. The ordinance also prohibited slavery within the territory and provided that "the utmost good faith" should be shown to the Indians, whose property was to be safe from exploitation.

\* \* \*

Be it ordained by the United States in Congress assembled, That the said territory, for the purposes of temporary government, be one district, subject, however, to be divided into two districts, as future circumstances may, in the opinion of Congress, make it expedient. . . .

Art. 1. No person, demeaning himself in a peaceable and orderly manner, shall ever be molested on account of his mode of worship or religious sentiments, in the said territory.

Art. 2. The inhabitants of the said territory shall always be entitled to the benefits of the writ of habeas corpus, and of the trial by jury; of a proportionate representation of the people in the legislature; and of judicial proceedings according to the course of the common law. All persons shall be bailable, unless for capital offenses, where the proof shall be evident or the presumption great. All fines shall be moderate; and no cruel or unusual punishments shall be inflicted. No man shall be deprived of his liberty or property, but by the judgment of his peers or the law of the land; and, should the public exigencies make it necessary, for the common preservation, to take any person's property, or to demand his particular services, full compensation shall be made for the same. And, in the just preservation of rights and property, it is understood and declared, that no law ought ever to be made, or have force in the said territory, that shall, in any manner whatever, interfere with or affect private contracts or engagements, bona fide, and without fraud, previously formed.

Art. 3. Religion, morality, and knowledge, being necessary to good government and the happiness of mankind, schools and the means of education shall forever be encouraged. The utmost good faith shall always be observed towards the Indians; their lands and property shall never be taken from them without their consent; and, in their property, rights, and liberty, they shall never be invaded or disturbed, unless in just and lawful wars authorized by Congress; but laws founded in justice and humanity, shall from time to time be made for preventing wrongs being done to them, and for preserving peace and friendship with them.

Art. 4. The said territory, and the States which may be formed therein, shall forever remain a part of this Confederacy of the United States of America, subject to the Articles of Confederation, and to such alterations therein as shall be constitutionally made; and to all the acts and ordinances of the United States in Congress assembled, conformable thereto. The inhabitants and settlers in the said territory shall be subject to pay a part of the federal debts contracted or to be contracted, and a proportional part of the expenses of government, to be apportioned on them by Congress according to the same common rule and measure by which apportionments thereof shall be made on the other States; and the taxes for paying their proportion shall be laid and levied by the authority and direction of the legislatures of the district or districts, or new States, as in the original States, within the time agreed upon by the United States in Congress assembled. The legislatures of those districts or new States, shall never interfere with the primary disposal of the soil by the United States in Congress assembled, nor with any regulations Congress may find necessary for securing the title in such soil to the bona fide purchasers. No tax shall be imposed on lands the property of the United States; and, in no case, shall nonresident proprietors be taxed higher than residents. The navigable waters leading into the Mississippi and St. Lawrence, and the carrying places between the same, shall be common highways and forever free, as well to the inhabitants of the said territory as to the citizens of the United States, and those of any other States that may be admitted into the confederacy, without any tax, impost, or duty therefor.

Art. 5. There shall be formed in the said territory, not less than three nor more than five States; and the boundaries of the States, as soon as Virginia shall alter her act of cession, and consent to the same, shall become fixed and established as follows, to wit: The western State in the said territory, shall be bounded by the Mississippi, the Ohio, and Wabash Rivers; a direct line drawn from the Wabash and Post Vincents [Fort Vincennes] due north to the territorial line between the United States and Canada; and, by the said territorial line, to the Lake of the Woods and Mississippi. The middle State shall be bounded by the said direct line, the Wabash from Post Vincents to the Ohio, by the Ohio, by the direct line, drawn due north from the mouth of the Great Miami, to the said territorial line, and by the said territorial line. The eastern State shall be bounded by the last mentioned direct line, the Ohio, Pennsylvania, and the said territorial line: Provided, however, and it is further understood and declared, that the boundaries of these three States shall be subject so far to be altered, that, if Congress shall hereafter find it expedient, they shall have authority to form one or two States in that part of the said territory which lies north of an east and west line drawn through the southerly bend or extreme of Lake Michigan. And, whenever any of the said States shall have sixty thousand free inhabitants therein, such State shall be admitted, by its delegates, into the Congress of the United States, on an equal footing with the original States in all respects whatever, and shall be at liberty to form a permanent constitution and State government: Provided, the constitution and government so to be formed, shall be republican, and in conformity to the principles contained in these articles; and, so far as it can be consistent with the general interest of the confederacy, such admission shall be allowed at an earlier period, and when there may be a less number of free inhabitants in the State than sixty thousand.

Art. 6. There shall be neither slavery nor involuntary servitude in the said territory, otherwise than in the punishment of crimes whereof the party shall have been duly convicted: Provided, always, That any person escaping into the same, from whom labor or service is lawfully claimed in any one of the original States, such fugitive may be lawfully reclaimed and conveyed to the person claiming his or her labor or service as aforesaid.

Be it ordained by the authority aforesaid, That the resolutions of the 23rd of April, 1784, relative to the subject of this ordinance, be, and the same are hereby repealed and declared null and void.

*Source*: B. P. Poore, *The Federal and State Constitutions, Colonial Charters, and Other Organic Laws of the United States*, 2d ed. (Washington, DC: Government Printing Office, 1877), 429–432.

---

## DOCUMENT 7: First Amendment, United States Constitution (1791)

The First Amendment to the Constitution has just 45 words, but they are among the most important in the American lexicon. Many scholars believe that the First Amendment was the *first* amendment because it is the groundwork for all our other liberties. Read as an organic whole, it protects nothing less than the integrity and autonomy of the individual conscience. The First Amendment prohibits government from interfering with the individual's right to receive and disseminate ideas and information, and to form and hold opinions or beliefs based upon that free exchange.

The First Amendment reflects the founders' faith in the "marketplace of ideas" and their belief that freedom ultimately depends upon the vigilance of an informed and educated citizenry.

\* \* \*

Congress shall make no law respecting an establishment of religion, or prohibiting the free exercise thereof; or abridging the freedom of speech, or of the press, or the right of the people peaceably to assemble, and to petition the Government for a redress of grievances.

*Source*: United States Constitution, Amendment One.

## DOCUMENT 8: The Alien and Sedition Acts (1798)

The ink was barely dry on the First Amendment and the remainder of the Bill of Rights in 1798 when Congress passed four laws, known collectively as the Alien and Sedition Acts. These measures were a response to the threat of war with France, and they occasioned acrimonious debate; some historians attribute Thomas Jefferson's election as president in 1800 to widespread public opposition to the acts. The Sedition Act gave the government wide powers to put down "treasonable" activities. Twenty-five men were arrested under the authority of the Sedition Act, mostly editors of Republican newspapers. Ten of them were convicted, and their newspapers were forced to close.

\* \* \*

### A. THE ALIEN ACT

Section 1. *Be it enacted by the Senate and House of Representatives of the United States of America, in Congress assembled,* that it shall be lawful for the President of the United States at any time during the continuance of this act to order all such aliens as he shall judge dangerous to the peace and safety of the United States, or shall have reasonable grounds to suspect are concerned in any treasonable or secret machinations against the government thereof, to deport out of the territory of the United States within such time as shall be expressed in such order, which order shall be served on such alien by delivering him a copy thereof or leaving the same at his usual abode, and returned to the office of the secretary of state by the marshal or other person to whom the same shall be directed. And in case any alien so ordered to depart shall be found at large within the United States after the time limited in such order for his departure, and not having obtained a license from the President to reside therein, or having obtained such license shall not have conformed thereto, be imprisoned for a term not exceeding three years, and shall never after be admitted to become a citizen of the United States.

*Provided always, and be it further enacted*, that if any alien so ordered to depart shall prove to the satisfaction of the President, by evidence to be taken before such person or persons as the President shall direct, who are for that purpose hereby authorized to administer oaths, that no injury or danger to the United States will arise from suffering such alien to reside therein, the President may grant a license to such alien to remain within the United States for such time as he shall judge proper, and at such place as he may designate. And the President may also require of such alien to enter into a bond to the United States, in such penal sum as he may direct, with one or more sufficient sureties to the satisfaction of the person authorized by the President to take the same, conditioned for the good behavior of such alien during his residence in the United States, and not violating his license, which license the President may revoke whenever he shall think proper.

Section 2. *And be it further enacted*, that it shall be lawful for the President of the United States, whenever he may deem it necessary for the public safety, to order to be removed out of the territory thereof any alien who may or shall be in prison in pursuance of this act; and to cause to be arrested and sent out of the United States such of those aliens as shall have been ordered to depart therefrom and shall not have obtained a license as aforesaid, in all cases where, in the opinion of the President, the public safety requires a speedy removal. And if any alien so removed or sent out of the United States by the President shall voluntarily return thereto, unless by permission of the President of the United States, such alien on conviction thereof shall be imprisoned so long as, in the opinion of the President, the public safety may require.

Section 3. *And be it further enacted*, that every master or commander of any ship or vessel which shall come into any port of the United States after the first day of July next shall immediately, on his arrival, make report in writing to the collector or other chief officer of the customs of such port of all aliens, if any, on board his vessel, specifying their names, age, the place of nativity, the country from which they shall have come, the nation to which they belong and owe allegiance, their occupation, and a description of their persons, as far as he shall be informed thereof; and, on failure, every such master and commander shall forfeit and pay $300, for the payment whereof on default of such master or commander such vessel shall also be held and may, by such collector or other officer of the customs, be detained. And it shall be the duty of such collector or other officer of the customs forthwith to transmit to the office of the Department of State true copies of all such returns.

Section 4. *And be it further enacted*, that the Circuit and District courts of the United States shall respectively have cognizance of all crimes and offenses against this act. And all marshals and other officers of the United States are required to execute all precepts and orders of the President of the United States issued in pursuance or by virtue of this act.

Section 5. *And be it further enacted*, that it shall be lawful for any alien who may be ordered to be removed from the United States, by virtue of this act, to take with him such part of his goods, chattels, or other property as he may find convenient; and all property left in the United States by any alien who may be removed, as aforesaid, shall be and remain subject to his order and disposal, in the same manner as if this act had not been passed.

Section 6. *And be it further enacted*, that this act shall continue and be in force for and during the term of two years from the passing thereof.

## B. THE SEDITION ACT

Section 1. *Be it enacted by the Senate and House of Representatives of the United States of America, in Congress assembled*, that if any persons shall unlawfully combine or conspire together with intent to oppose any measure or measures of the government of the United States which are or shall be directed by proper authority, or to impede the operation of any law of the United States, or to intimidate or prevent any person holding a place or office in or under the government of the United States from undertaking, performing, or executing his trust or duty; and if any person or persons, with intent as aforesaid, shall counsel, advise, or attempt to procure any insurrection, riot, unlawful assembly, or combination, whether such conspiracy, threatening, counsel, advice, or attempt shall have the proposed effect or not, he or they shall be deemed guilty of a high misdemeanor, and on conviction before any court of the United States having jurisdiction thereof shall be punished by a fine not exceeding $5,000 and by imprisonment during a term not less than six months nor exceeding five years; and further, at the discretion of the court, may be held to find sureties for his good behavior in such sum and for such time as the said court may direct.

Section 2. *And be it further enacted*, that if any person shall write, print, utter, or publish, or shall cause or procure to be written, printed, uttered, or published, or shall knowingly and willingly assist or aid in writing, printing, uttering, or publishing any false, scandalous, and malicious writing or writings against the government of the United States, or either house of the Congress of the United States, or the President of the United

States with intent to defame the said government, or either house of the said Congress, or the said President, or to bring them, or either of them, into contempt or disrepute; or to excite against them, or either or any of them, the hatred of the good people of the United States, or to stir up sedition within the United States, or to excite any unlawful combinations therein, for opposing or resisting any law of the United States, or any act of the President of the United States, done in pursuance of any such law, or of the powers in him vested by the Constitution of the United States, or to resist, oppose, or defeat any such law or act, or to aid, encourage or abet any hostile designs of any foreign nation against the United States, their people, or government, then such person being thereof convicted before any court of the United States having jurisdiction thereof shall be punished by a fine not exceeding $2,000 and by imprisonment not exceeding two years.

Section 3. *And be it further enacted and declared*, that if any person shall be prosecuted under this act, for the writing or publishing any libel aforesaid, it shall be lawful for the defendant, upon the trial of the cause, to give evidence in his defense, the truth of the matter contained in the publication charged as a libel. And the jury who shall try the cause shall have a right to determine the law and the fact, under the direction of the court, as in other cases.

Section 4. *And be it further enacted*, that this act shall continue and be in force until the third day of March, 1801, and no longer; *provided*, that the expiration of the act shall not prevent or defeat a prosecution and punishment of any offense against the law during the time it shall be in force.

*Source*: Statute 596 (1798).

---

## DOCUMENT 9: The Kentucky and Virginia Resolutions (1798)

Thomas Jefferson and James Madison were understandably outraged by passage of the Alien and Sedition Acts. As the principal architects of the new nation's Constitution and Bill of Rights, they believed the acts to be unconstitutional and responded to their passage by drafting resolutions for consideration by the legislatures of Kentucky and Virginia. Jefferson kept his authorship a secret. Both states passed the resolutions, Kentucky on November 16, 1798, and Virginia on December 24 of the same year.

While the resolutions differed somewhat in language, both asserted the right of state governments to determine the validity of federal law. In this view, the federal government is the creature of the states and can exercise only those powers expressly delegated to it by the states. Since no power over free speech had been delegated, no such power could be constitutionally exercised.

\* \* \*

## A. THE KENTUCKY RESOLUTIONS[1]

### November, 1798

1. *Resolved*, That the several States composing the United States of America, are not united on the principle of unlimited submission to their general government; but that, by a compact under the style and title of a Constitution for the United States, and of amendments thereto, they constituted a general government for special purposes—delegated to that government certain definite powers, reserving, each State to itself, the residuary mass of right to their own self-government; and that whensoever the general government assumes undelegated powers, its acts are unauthoritative, void, and of no force: that to this compact each State acceded as a State, and is an integral party, its co-States forming, as to itself, the other party: that the government created by this compact was not made the exclusive or final judge of the extent of the powers delegated to itself; since that would have made its discretion, and not the Constitution, the measure of its powers; but that, as in all other cases of compact among powers having no common judge, each party has an equal right to judge for itself, as well of infractions as of the mode and measure of redress.

2. *Resolved*, That the Constitution of the United States, having delegated to Congress a power to punish treason, counterfeiting the securities and current coin of the United States, piracies, and felonies committed on the high seas, and offences against the law of nations, and no other crimes whatsoever; and it being true as a general principle, and one of the amendments to the Constitution having also declared, that "the powers not delegated to the United States by the Constitution, nor prohibited by it to the States, are reserved to the States respectively, or to the people," therefore the act of Congress, passed on the 14th day of July, 1798, and intituled "An Act in addition to the act intituled An Act for the punishment of certain crimes against the United States," as also the act passed by them on the — day of June, 1798, intituled "An Act to punish frauds committed on the bank of the United States," (and all their

---

[1]Jefferson kept his authorship of these resolutions—a protest against the Alien and Sedition Acts—a secret. The resolutions were adopted by the Kentucky legislature on November 10, 1798.

other acts which assume to create, define, or punish crimes, other than those so enumerated in the Constitution,) are altogether void, and of no force; and that the power to create, define, and punish such other crimes is reserved, and, of right, appertains solely and exclusively to the respective States, each within its own territory.

3. *Resolved*, That it is true as a general principle, and is also expressly declared by one of the amendments to the Constitution, that "the powers not delegated to the United States by the Constitution, nor prohibited by it to the States, are reserved to the States respectively, or to the people"; and that no power over the freedom of religion, freedom of speech, or freedom of the press being delegated to the United States by the Constitution, nor prohibited by it to the States, all lawful powers respecting the same did of right remain, and were reserved to the States or the people: that thus was manifested their determination to retain to themselves the right of judging how far the licentiousness of speech and of the press may be abridged without lessening their useful freedom, and how far those abuses which cannot be separated from their use should be tolerated, rather than the use be destroyed. And thus also they guarded against all abridgment by the United States of the freedom of religious opinions and exercises, and retained to themselves the right of protecting the same, as this State, by a law passed on the general demand of its citizens, had already protected them from all human restraint or interference. And that in addition to this general principle and express declaration, another and more special provision has been made by one of the amendments to the Constitution, which expressly declares, that "Congress shall make no law respecting an establishment of religion, or prohibiting the free exercise thereof, or abridging the freedom of speech or of the press": thereby guarding in the same sentence, and under the same words, the freedom of religion, of speech, and of the press: insomuch, that whatever violated either, throws down the sanctuary which covers the others, and that libels, falsehood, and defamation, equally with heresy and false religion, are withheld from the cognizance of federal tribunals. That, therefore, the act of Congress of the United States, passed on the 14th day of July, 1798, intituled "An Act in addition to the act intituled An Act for the punishment of certain crimes against the United States," which does abridge the freedom of the press, is not law, but is altogether void, and of no force.

4. *Resolved*, That alien friends are under the jurisdiction and protection of the laws of the State wherein they are: that no power over them has been delegated to the United States, nor prohibited to the individual States, distinct from their power over citizens. And it being true as a general principle and one of the amendments to the Constitution having also declared, that "the powers not delegated to the United States by the Constitution, nor prohibited by it to the States, are reserved to the States

respectively, or to the people," the act of the Congress of the United States, passed on the — day of July, 1798, intituled "An Act concerning aliens," which assumes powers over alien friends, not delegated by the Constitution, is not law, but is altogether void, and of no force.

5. *Resolved*, That in addition to the general principle, as well as the express declaration, that powers not delegated are reserved, another and more special provision, inserted in the Constitution from abundant caution, has declared that "the migration or importation of such persons as any of the States now existing shall think proper to admit, shall not be prohibited by the Congress prior to the year 1808": that this commonwealth does admit the migration of alien friends, described as the subject of the said act concerning aliens: that a provision against prohibiting their migration, is a provision against all acts equivalent thereto, or it would be nugatory: that to remove them when migrated, is equivalent to a prohibition of their migration, and is, therefore, contrary to the said provision of the Constitution, and void.

6. *Resolved*, That the imprisonment of a person under the protection of the laws of this commonwealth, on his failure to obey the simple *order* of the President to depart out of the United States, as is undertaken by said act intituled "An Act concerning aliens," is contrary to the Constitution, one amendment to which has provided that "no person shall be deprived of liberty without due progress of law"; and that another having provided that in all criminal prosecutions the accused shall enjoy the right to public trial by an impartial jury, to be informed of the nature and cause of the accusation, to be confronted with the witnesses against him, to have compulsory process for obtaining witnesses in his favor, and to have the assistance of counsel for his defence," the same act, undertaking to authorize the President to remove a person out of the United States, who is under the protection of the law, on his own suspicion, without accusation, without jury, without public trial, without confrontation of the witnesses against him, without hearing witnesses in his favor, without defence, without counsel, is contrary to the provision also of the Constitution, is therefore not law, but utterly void, and of no force: that transferring the power of judging any person, who is under the protection of the laws, from the courts to the President of the United States, as is undertaken by the same act concerning aliens, is against the article of the Constitution which provides that "the judicial power of the United States shall be vested in courts, the judges of which shall hold their offices during good behavior"; and that the said act is void for that reason also. And it is further to be noted, that this transfer of judiciary power is to that magistrate of the general government who already possesses all the Executive, and a negative on all Legislative powers.

7. *Resolved*, That the construction applied by the General Government (as is evidenced by sundry of their proceedings) to those parts of the

Constitution of the United States which delegate to Congress a power "to lay and collect taxes, duties, imports, and excises, to pay the debts, and provide for the common defense and general welfare of the United States," and "to make all laws which shall be necessary and proper for carrying into execution the powers vested by the Constitution in the government of the United States, or in any department or officer thereof," goes to the destruction of all limits prescribed to their power by the Constitution: that words meant by the instrument to be subsidiary only to the execution of limited powers, ought not to be so construed as themselves to give unlimited powers, nor a part to be so taken as to destroy the whole residue of that instrument: that the proceedings of the General Government under color of these articles, will be a fit and necessary subject of revisal and correction, at a time of greater tranquillity, while those specified in the preceding resolutions call for immediate redress.

8th. *Resolved*, That a committee of conference and correspondence be appointed, who shall have in charge to communicate the preceding resolutions to the Legislatures of the several States; to assure them that this commonwealth continues in the same esteem of their friendship and union which it has manifested from that moment at which a common danger first suggested a common union: that it considers union, for specified national purposes, and particularly to those specified in their late federal compact, to be friendly to the peace, happiness and prosperity of all the States: that faithful to that compact, according to the plain intent and meaning in which it was understood and acceded to by the several parties, it is sincerely anxious for its preservation: that it does also believe, that to take from the States all the powers of self-government and transfer them to a general and consolidated government, without regard to the special delegations and reservations solemnly agreed to in that compact, is not for the peace, happiness or prosperity of these States; and that therefore this commonwealth is determined, as it doubts not its co-States are, to submit to undelegated, and consequently unlimited powers in no man, or body of men on earth: that in cases of an abuse of the delegated powers, the members of the general government, being chosen by the people, a change by the people would be the constitutional remedy; but, where powers are assumed which have not been delegated, a nullification of the act is the rightful remedy: that every State has a natural right in cases not within the compact, (*casus non fœderis*), to nullify of their own authority all assumptions of power by others within their limits: that without this right, they would be under the dominion, absolutely and unlimited, of whosoever might exercise this right of judgment for them: that nevertheless, this commonwealth, from motives of regard and respect for its co-States, has wished to communicate with them on the subject: that with them alone it is proper to communicate, they alone being parties to the compact, and solely authorized to judge in the last resort of the powers exercised under it, Congress being not a party, but merely the creature of the compact, and subject as to its assumptions of power to the final judgment of those by whom, and for whose use itself and its powers were all created and modified: that if the acts before specified should stand, these conclusions would flow from them; that the general government may place any act they think proper on the list of crimes, and punish it themselves whether enumerated or not enumerated by the constitution as cognizable by them: that they may transfer its cognizance to the President, or any other person, who may himself be the accuser, counsel, judge and jury, whose *suspicions* may be the evidence, his *order* the sentence, his *officer* the executioner, and breast the sole record of the transaction: that a very numerous and valuable description of the inhabitants of these States being, by this precedent, reduced, outlaws, to the absolute dominion of one man, and the barrier of the Constitution thus swept away from us all, no rampart now remains against the passions and the powers of a majority in Congress to protect from a like exportation, or other more grievous punishment, the minority of the same body, the legislatures, judges, governors, and counsellors of the States, nor their other peaceable inhabitants, who may venture to reclaim the constitutional rights and liberties of the States and people, or who for other causes, good or bad, may be obnoxious to the views, or marked by the suspicions of the President, or be thought dangerous to his or their election, or other interests, public or personal: that the friendless alien has indeed been selected as the safest subject of a first experiment; but the citizen will soon follow, or rather, has already followed, for already has a sedition act marked him as its prey: that these and successive acts of the same character, unless arrested at the threshold, necessarily drive these States into revolution and blood, and will furnish new calumnies against republican government, and new pretexts for those who wish it to be believed that man cannot be governed but by a rod of iron: that it would be a dangerous delusion were a confidence in the men of our choice to silence our fears for the safety of our rights: that confidence is everywhere the parent of despotism—free government is founded in jealousy, and not in confidence; it is jealousy and not confidence which prescribes limited constitutions, to bind down those whom we are obliged to trust with power: that our Constitution has accordingly fixed the limits to which, and no further, our confidence may go; and let the honest advocate of confidence read the Alien and Sedition acts, and say if the Constitution has not been wise in fixing limits to the government it created, and whether we should be wise in destroying those limits. Let him say what the government is, if it be not a tyranny, which the men of our choice have conferred on our President, and the President of our choice has assented to, and accepted over the friendly strangers to whom the mild spirit of our country and its laws have pledged hospitality and protection: that the men of our choice have more respected the bare *suspicions* of the President, than the solid right of innocence, the claims of justification, the sacred force of truth, and the forms and substance of law and justice. In questions of power, then, let no more be heard of confidence in man, but bind him down from mischief by the chains of the Constitution. That this commonwealth does therefore call on its co-States for an expression of their sentiments on the acts concerning aliens, and for the punishment of certain crimes herein before specified, plainly declaring whether these acts are or are not authorized by the federal compact. And it doubts not that their sense will be so announced as to prove their attachment unaltered to limited government, whether general or particular. And that the rights and liberties of their co-States will be exposed to no dangers by remaining embarked in a common bottom with their own. That they will concur with this commonwealth in considering the said acts as so palpably against the Constitution as to amount to an undisguised declaration that that compact is not meant to be the measure of the powers of the General Government, but that it will proceed in the exercise over these States, of all powers whatsoever: that they will view this as seizing the rights of the States, and consolidating them in the hands of the General Government, with a power assumed to bind the States (not merely as the cases made federal, *casus fœderis* but), in all cases whatsoever, by laws made, not with their consent, but by others against their consent: that this would be to surrender the form of government we have chosen, and live under one deriving its powers from its own will, and not from our authority; and that the co-States, recurring to their natural right in cases not made federal, will concur in declaring these acts void, and of no force, and will each take measures of its own for providing that neither these acts, nor any others of the General Government not plainly and intentionally authorized by the Constitution, shall be exercised within their respective territories.

9th. *Resolved*, That the said committee be authorized to communicate by writing or personal conferences, at any times or places whatever, with any person or persons who may be appointed by any one or more co-States to correspond or confer with them; and that they lay their proceedings before the next session of Assembly.

*Source*: The Kentucky Resolutions, reprinted in Saul K. Padover, ed., *The Complete Jefferson* (New York: Duell, Sloan & Pearce, 1943), 128–134.

## B. THE VIRGINIA RESOLUTIONS

*Resolved*, that the General Assembly of Virginia does unequivocally express a firm resolution to maintain and defend the Constitution of the

United States, and the constitution of this state against every aggression, either foreign or domestic; and that they will support the government of the United States in all measures warranted by the former.

That this Assembly most solemnly declares a warm attachment to the union of the states, to maintain which it pledges its powers; and that, for this end, it is their duty to watch over and oppose every infraction of those principles which constitute the only basis of that union, because a faithful observance of them can alone secure its existence and the public happiness.

That this Assembly does explicitly and peremptorily declare that it views the powers of the federal government as resulting from the compact to which the states are parties, as limited by the plain sense and intention of the instrument constituting that compact, as no further valid than they are authorized by the grants enumerated in that compact; and that, in case of a deliberate, palpable, and dangerous exercise of other powers, not granted by the said compact, the states who are parties thereto have the right, and are in duty bound to interpose for arresting the progress of the evil and for maintaining, within their respective limits the authorities, rights, and liberties appertaining to them.

That the General Assembly does also express its deep regret that a spirit has, in sundry instances, been manifested by the federal government to enlarge its powers by forced constructions of the constitutional charter which defines them; and that indications have appeared of a design to expound certain general phrases (which, having been copied from the very limited grant of powers in the former Articles of Confederation, were the less liable to be misconstrued) so as to destroy the meaning and effect of the particular enumeration which necessarily explains and limits the general phrases, and so as to consolidate the states, by degrees, into one sovereignty, the obvious tendency and inevitable result of which would be to transform the present republican system of the United States into an absolute or at best, a mixed monarchy.

*That the General Assembly does particularly protest against the palpable and alarming infractions of the Constitution in the two late cases of the Alien and Sedition Acts, passed at the last session of Congress: the first of which exercises a power nowhere delegated to the federal government, and which by uniting legislative and judicial powers to those of executive, subverts the general principles of free government, as well as the particular organization and positive provisions of the federal Constitution and the other of which acts exercises in like manner, a power not delegated by the Constitution, but, on the contrary, expressly and positively forbidden by one of the amendments thereto, a power which more than any other, ought to produce universal alarm, because it is leveled against the right of freely examining public characters and measures, and of free communication among the people thereon, which has ever been justly deemed the only effectual guardian of every other right.*

That this state having, by its Convention which ratified the federal Constitution, expressly declared that, among other essential rights, "the liberty of conscience and the press cannot be canceled, abridged, restrained, or modified, by any authority of the United States," and from its extreme anxiety to guard these rights from every possible attack of sophistry and ambition, having, with other states, recommended an amendment for that purpose, which amendment was, in due time, annexed to the Constitution, it would mark a reproachful inconsistency and criminal degeneracy if an indifference were now shown to the most palpable violation of one of the rights thus declared and secured, and to the establishment of a precedent which may be fatal to the other.

That the good people of this commonwealth, having ever felt, and continuing to feel, the most sincere affection for their brethren of the other states; the truest anxiety for establishing and perpetuating the union of all; and the most scrupulous fidelity to that Constitution, which is the pledge of mutual friendship and the instrument of mutual happiness; the General Assembly does solemnly appeal to the like dispositions in the other states, in confidence that they will concur with this commonwealth in declaring, as it does hereby declare, that the acts aforesaid are unconstitutional; and that the necessary and proper measures will be taken *by each* for cooperating with this state, in maintaining unimpaired the authorities, rights, and liberties, reserved to the states respectively, or to the people.

*Source: The Annals of America, Volume 4, 1797–1820,* William Benton, Publisher (Chicago, IL: Encyclopedia Brittanica, Inc. 1968), 66–67.

## DOCUMENT 10: "Of the Liberty of Thought and Discussion" (John Stuart Mill, 1859)

John Stuart Mill was one of the towering intellects of his time, and his influence on western thought has been profound. He was the eldest son of James Mill, a Scottish philosopher, who subjected his son to a rigorous and unconventional education beginning at the tender age of three. By ten, John was reading Plato and Demosthenes; by twenty, he was an acknowledged leader of the Utilitarian school of philosophy, had formed a debating society, and had begun publishing a literary magazine. The rigors of his upbringing, however, caused him to suffer a breakdown while still in his twenties, and to re-examine many of the positions he had formed under the influence of his father. *On Liberty* is arguably the greatest of Mill's works, and one portion of it in particular, "Of the Liberty of Thought and Discussion," created a philosophical base upon which much First Amendment jurisprudence would eventually rest.

* * *

In order more fully to illustrate the mischief of denying a hearing to opinions because we, in our own judgment, have condemned them, it will be desirable to fix down the discussion to a concrete case; and I choose, by preference, the cases which are least favourable to me—in which the argument against freedom of opinion, both on the score of truth and on that of utility, is considered the strongest. Let the opinions impugned be the belief in a God and in a future state, or any of the commonly received doctrines of morality. To fight the battle on such ground, gives a great advantage to an unfair antagonist; since he will be sure to say (and many who have no desire to be unfair will say it internally), Are these the doctrines which you do not deem sufficiently certain to be taken under the protection of law? Is the belief in a God one of the opinions, to feel sure of which, you hold to be assuming infallibility? But I must be permitted to observe, that it is not the feeling sure of a doctrine (be it what it may) which I call an assumption of infallibility. It is the undertaking to decide that question *for others*, without allowing them to hear what can be said on the contrary side. And I denounce and reprobate this pretension not the less, if put forth on the side of my most solemn convictions. However positive any one's persuasion may be, not only of the falsity, but of the pernicious consequences—not only of the pernicious consequences, but (to adopt expressions which I altogether condemn) the immorality and impiety of an opinion; yet if, in pursuance of that private judgment, though backed by the public judgment of his country or his cotemporaries [*sic*], he prevents the opinion from being heard in its defence, he assumes infallibility. And so far from the assumption being less objectionable or less dangerous because the opinion is called immoral or impious, this is the case of all others in which it is most fatal. These are exactly the occasions on which the men of one generation commit those dreadful mistakes, which excite the astonishment and horror of posterity. It is among such that we find the instances memorable in history, when the arm of the law has been employed to root out the best men and the noblest doctrines; with deplorable success as to the men, though some of the doctrines have survived to be (as if in mockery) invoked, in defence of similar conduct towards those who dissent from *them*, or from their received interpretation.

Mankind can hardly be too often reminded, that there was once a man named Socrates, between whom and the legal authorities and public opinion of his time, there took place a memorable collision. Born in an age and country abounding in individual greatness, this man has been handed down to us by those who best knew both him and the age, as the most virtuous man in it; while *we* know him as the head and prototype of all subsequent teachers of virtue, the source equally of the lofty inspiration of Plato and the judicious utilitarianism of Aristotle, 'I maëstri di color che sanno,' the two headsprings of ethical as of all other philosophy. This acknowledged master of all the eminent thinkers who have since lived—whose fame, still growing after more than two thousand years, all but outweighs the whole remainder of the names which make his native city illustrious—was put to death by his countrymen, after a judicial conviction, for impiety and immorality. Impiety, in denying the gods recognized by the State; indeed his accuser asserted . . . that he believed in no gods at all. Immorality, in being, by his doctrines and instruction, a "corruptor of youth." Of these charges the tribunal, there is every ground for believing, honestly found him guilty, and condemned the man who probably of all then born had deserved best of mankind, to be put to death as a criminal.

To pass from this to the only other instance of judicial iniquity, the mention of which, after the condemnation of Socrates, would not be an anticlimax: the event which took place on Calvary rather more than eighteen hundred years ago. The man who left on the memory of those who witnessed his life and conversation, such an impression of his moral grandeur, that eighteen subsequent centuries have done homage to him as the Almighty in person, was ignominiously put to death, as what? As a blasphemer. Men did not merely mistake their benefactor, they mistook him for the exact contrary of what he was, and treated him as that prodigy of impiety, which they themselves are now held to be, for their treatment of him. The feelings with which mankind now regard these lamentable transactions, especially the later of the two, render them extremely unjust in their judgment of the unhappy actors. These were, to all appearance, not bad men—not worse than men commonly are, but rather the contrary; men who possessed in a full, or somewhat more than a full measure, the religious, moral, and patriotic feelings of their time and people: the very kind of men who, in all times, our own included, have every chance of passing through life blameless and respected. The high-priest who rent his garments when the words were pronounced, which, according to all the ideas of his country, constituted the blackest guilt, was in all probability quite as sincere in his horror and indignation, as the generality of respectable and pious men now are in the religious and moral sentiments they profess; and most of those who now shudder at his conduct, if they had lived in this time, and been born Jews, would have acted precisely as he did. Orthodox Christians who are tempted to think that those who stoned to death the first martyrs must have been worse men than they themselves are, ought to remember that one of those persecutors was Saint Paul.

*Source*: John Stuart Mill, *Essential Works of John Stuart Mill*, edited by Max Lerner (New York: Bantam Books, 1961), 268–304.

# Part III

# 1900–1950: A Half-Century of Paternalism

In the first half of the twentieth century, the ringing affirmations of liberty that had accompanied the founding of the new country encountered the inevitable pressures for conformity to majority opinion in matters religious, political, and sexual.

In Tennessee, a young teacher would be tried, essentially, for blasphemy—teaching the theory of evolution in the public schools. Moralists like Anthony Comstock, whose name would come to stand for prudery, agitated for laws censoring books, magazines, and the new medium of film. As the century approached the halfway mark, fear of the communist menace and subversive activities led to unprecedented restrictions on political expression. The experiment with free speech seemed likely to end in a flurry of self-righteous legislation.

There were, fortunately, countervailing forces. In the 1920s, the American Civil Liberties Union was formed; it would earn a reputation as "liberty's lawyer" in cases where constitutional free speech guarantees had been ignored. The Supreme Court would issue opinions reminding citizens of the extent and meaning of the free speech provisions of the First Amendment. And citizens would participate vigorously in the debate over suppression of ideas that lawmakers considered "too dangerous" for public consumption.

## DOCUMENT 11: Fourteenth Amendment, United States Constitution (1868)

The Fourteenth Amendment was ratified in 1868 and added the concept of "equal protection of the laws" to our constitutional vocabulary. The Amendment was important for a number of reasons, but its greatest significance was the change it effected in the relationship of state and federal governments. Before the Fourteenth Amendment, the Bill of Rights restrained only the *federal* government. State and local governments could—and did—infringe religious liberties, freedom of speech, freedom of the press, and other rights protected by the Bill of Rights.

Beginning with the 1925 case *Gitlow v. New York*, the Supreme Court engaged in "selective incorporation" of the Bill of Rights, by which it meant using the Fourteenth Amendment to apply the protections of the Bill of Rights to the states. In *Gitlow*, the Court held that the free speech and press guarantees of the First Amendment are "fundamental rights and liberties," protected against state infringement by the due process provisions of the Fourteenth Amendment.

While proponents of state's rights have disagreed with the Court's use of the Fourteenth Amendment to limit state action, most scholars find clear evidence that its sponsors intended to make the Bill of Rights binding on the states. Justice Hugo Black, in a dissenting opinion in *Adamson v. California*, concluded (along with fellow justices William O. Douglas, Frank Murphy, and Wiley Rutledge) that application of the Bill of Rights to the states was one of the Amendment's "chief objects," and as evidence he appended to his opinion a thirty-three-page summary of the congressional debates leading to ratification. Many newspapers and magazines that covered the ratification of the Amendment reported a similar understanding of its meaning.

\* \* \*

SECTION 1. All persons born or naturalized in the United States and subject to the jurisdiction thereof, are citizens of the United States and of the State wherein they reside. No State shall make or enforce any law which shall abridge the privileges or immunities of citizens of the United States; or shall any State deprive any person of life, liberty, or property, without due process of law; nor deny to any person within its jurisdiction the equal protection of the laws.

SECTION 2. Representatives shall be apportioned among the several States according to their respective numbers, counting the whole number of persons in each State, excluding Indians not taxed. But when the right to vote at any election for the choice of electors for President and Vice President of the United States, Representatives in Congress, the Executive and Judicial officers of a State, or the members of the Legislature thereof, is denied to any of the male inhabitants of such State, being twenty-one years of age, and citizens of the United States, or in any way abridged, except for participation in rebellion, or other crime, the basis of representation therein shall be reduced in the proportion which the number of such male citizens shall bear to the whole number of male citizens twenty-one years of age in such State.

SECTION 3. No person shall be a Senator or Representative in Congress, or elector of President and Vice President, or hold any office, civil or military, under the United States, or under any State, who, having previously taken an oath, as a member of Congress, or as an officer of the United States, or as a member of any State legislature, or as an executive or judicial officer of any State, to support the Constitution of the United States, shall have engaged in insurrection or rebellion against the same, or given aid or comfort to the enemies thereof. But Congress may by a vote of two-thirds of each House, remove such disability.

SECTION 4. The validity of the public debt of the United States, authorized by law, including debts incurred for payment of pensions and bounties for services in suppressing insurrection or rebellion, shall not be questioned. But neither the United States nor any State shall assume or pay any debt or obligation incurred in aid of insurrection or rebellion against the United States, or any claim for the loss or emancipation of any slave; but all such debts, obligations and claims shall be held illegal and void.

SECTION 5. The Congress shall have power to enforce, by appropriate legislation, the provisions of this article.

*Source*: United States Constitution, Amendment Fourteen.

---

## DOCUMENT 12: "The Regulation of Films" (*Nation*, 1915)

It did not take long for the ringing declarations about liberty to encounter the realities of the political process. While Mill and other libertarian theorists recognized that government action based upon popular opinion could be just as illegitimate as action taken in the face of voter sentiment, those whose power derived from the popular franchise frequently saw things differently.

The first half of the twentieth century saw the emergence of tensions that persist today: between majority "morality" and individual rights; between legislatures and the courts; and between defenders of individual liberty and those who would use government to define the limits of acceptable expression. During this period, the free-speech principles enshrined in the First Amendment were applied to new methods of communication: the motion picture, radio, and television all became genuine mass media, and new modes of transportation increased book, magazine, and newspaper circulation. As the population spread westward, regional differences added to the volatile mix of opinion. Aggrieved citizens demanded that government "do something" about speech they deemed improper, and the increased presence of books and other media virtually ensured that increasing numbers of people would be aggrieved.

One of the first films to arouse public passions was *The Birth of a Nation*, which was widely decried as racist and ahistorical. The following article from the *Nation* reflected the opinions of many who called for censorship and justified that position by the increased harm made possible by the new medium of motion pictures.

* * *

Wherever it goes, the "Birth of a Nation" film arouses widespread indignation. In Boston the excitement has been at white heat, because of a series of hearings before Mayor, Governor, and a committee of the Legislature. A judge has been found with authority and courage enough to cut out the most objectionable scene. The press has been full of arguments for and against the film and the proposed legislation. Many clergymen have preached about the play; and ex-President Elliot, speaking in a Cambridge church, was one of those who protested against its falsification of history. Never before have the colored people of Boston been so united and determined, or appeared to better advantage, and their white friends have rallied in great force to their aid. Gov. Walsh, ex-Congressman McCall, and Lieut. Gov. Cushing have spoken out emphatically against permitting the play to continue, though the Mayor sided with the producers—as the Mayor of New York has failed to recognize in his utterances the gravity of the situation, or to rise to the emergency, being content with the promise of certain slight exclusions, which appear to be of little or no value. The play continues to do the devilish work of misrepresentation and of arousing race hatred.

That Mayor Mitchel has had little legal authority to deal with the play is admitted, though there are differences of opinion as to just what powers were available. But this alleged lack of authority is to be remedied by an ordinance now before the Board of Aldermen to empower the Commissioner of Licenses to revoke, suspend, or annul any moving-picture license "for cause after a trial." The ordinance further reads:

Proof shall be taken before the Commissioner of Licenses upon notice of not less than two (2) days to the proprietor, manager, or person in charge of said place, to show cause why such license should not be revoked, annulled, or suspended. The Commissioner of Licenses shall hear the proofs and allegations in each case, and determine the same, and any place the license for which shall have been revoked, annulled, or suspended shall not thereafter be licensed again to the same licensee within one year, under the provisions of said sections. On any examination before a Commissioner of Licenses, pursuant to a notice to show cause as aforesaid, the accused party may be a witness in his own behalf.

This plainly constitutes the Commissioner of Licenses a censor of all moving-picture plays, precisely as the Mayor of every town in Massachusetts, except Boston, now has similar powers. That the plan has its defects is obvious, for a Commissioner of Licenses with bad judgment might work a considerable amount of harm.

But this risk is inevitable with any censorship, and no bill has as yet been suggested to the Massachusetts Legislature—which is bent on passing some measure before it adjourns—that is free from defects of one kind or another, save the proposal to put Boston on an equal footing with the other cities of Massachusetts. The truth is that this new means for public amusement and education has brought with it grave perils which we are only just beginning to realize, for side by side with its educational possibilities are the dangers of unrestricted propaganda. As the Rev. Dr. Crothers has pointed out, we have lulled ourselves into a sense of security by repeating to ourselves that the "past at least is secure." But along comes this play, which is not only designed to make large sums for its promoters, but is admittedly a deliberate propaganda to degrade and injure ten millions of citizens, besides misrepresenting some of the noblest figures in our past, Stevens, Sumner, and Lincoln, and perverting history, if only by the one-sidedness of its portrayal. . . .

Yet so excellent a newspaper as the Boston *Advertiser* feels that the proposed censorship may be a most dangerous infringement of our freedom of speech and of expression, on a par with the efforts to suppress Garrison and Phillips in anti-slavery days. The Boston *Transcript* and *Herald* appear to believe that if one bill proposed should become a law any citizens who indulged in a fight over a play could stop it, and that any play with a lesson to teach or one which undertook to dwell on the weaknesses of a group of our citizens might easily be driven off the stage. The plan of an official censor for whom the Mayor is responsible, with such a trial as is provided in the pending Aldermanic ordinance in New York, seems for the moment the best way out.

*Source*: "The Regulation of Films," *Nation* 100 (May 6, 1915): 486–487.

---

## DOCUMENT 13: "Birth Control and Public Morals: An Interview with Anthony Comstock" (Mary Alden Hopkins, 1915)

The term "Comstockery" was coined as a result of the efforts of one man, Anthony Comstock, to protect the nation's morals. As the leading figure in the Society for the Suppression of Vice, Comstock was responsible for the passage of federal laws closing the ports and mails to material he deemed "vile," including information on contraception, and for the arrest and conviction of hundreds of people who transgressed his and the society's notions of morality. While the following interview from the May 22, 1915, issue of *Harper's Weekly* may make Comstock sound like a caricature to many contemporary readers, he represented the views of many and was a major force in his time.

\* \* \*

"Have read your article. Self control and obedience to Nature's laws, you seem to overlook. Let men and women live a life above the level of the beasts. I see nothing in either of your articles along these lines. Existing laws are an imperative necessity in order to prevent the downfall of youths of both sexes," wrote Mr. Anthony Comstock, secretary of the New York Society for the Suppression of Vice, replying to my request for an interview on the subject of Birth Control.

During the interview which he kindly allowed me, he reiterated his belief in the absolute necessity of drastic laws.

"To repeal the present laws would be a crime against society," he said, "and especially a crime against young women."

Although the name Anthony Comstock is known all over the country and over most of the civilized world, comparatively few people know for exactly what Mr. Comstock stands and what he has accomplished. It has been the policy of those who oppose his work to speak flippantly of it and to minimize its results. The Society for the Suppression of Vice was formed to support Mr. Comstock, from the beginning he has been its driving force, and it is giving him only the credit which is due him to say that the tremendous accomplishments of the society in its fight against vicious publications for the last forty years have been in reality the accomplishments of Mr. Comstock.

Up to 1914, Mr. Comstock had caused to be arraigned in state and federal courts 3697 persons, of whom 2740 were either convicted or pleaded guilty. On these were imposed fines to the extent of $237,134.30 and imprisonment to the length of 565 years, 11 months, and 20 days.

To this remarkable record of activity can be added since that date 176 arrests and 141 convictions.

The story of how Mr. Comstock began his unusual profession is as interesting as the story of any of the famous captains of industry. He has, if one may borrow a stage term, "created" his unique position.

"My attention was first drawn to the publication of vile books fortythree years ago when I was a clerk here in New York City," said Mr. Comstock.

"There was in existence at that time a kind of circulating library where my fellow clerks went, made a deposit, and received the vilest of literature, and after reading it, received back the deposit or took other books. I saw young men being debauched by this pernicious influence.

"On March 2nd, 1872, I brought about the arrest of seven persons dealing in obscene books, pictures, and articles. I found that there were 169 books, some of which had been in circulation since before I was born and which were publicly advertised and sold in connection with articles for producing abortion, prevention of conception, articles to aid seductions, and for indiscreet and immoral use. I had four publishers dealing in these arrested and the plates for 167 of those books destroyed. The other two books dropped out of sight. I have not seen a copy of one of them for forty years."

From this time on Mr. Comstock devoted his attention to this work, although it was, as he once said, like standing at the mouth of a sewer. Several times men whom he has arrested, have later tried to kill him.

There were no laws covering this ostracized business at that time. In March, 1873, Mr. Comstock secured the passage of stringent federal laws closing the mails and the ports to this atrocious business. Two days afterwards, upon the request of certain Senators, Mr. Comstock was appointed Special Agent of the Post Office Department to enforce these laws. He now holds the position of Post Office Inspector. The federal law as it at present stands is as follows:

**United States Criminal Code, Section 211. (Act of March 4th, 1909, Chapter 321, Section 211, United States Statutes at Large, vol. 35, part 1, page 1088 et seq.)**

Every obscene, lewd, or lascivious and every filthy book, pamphlet, picture, paper, letter, writing, print, or other publication of an indecent character, and every article or thing designated, adapted or intended for preventing conception or procuring abortion, or for any indecent or immoral use; and every article, instrument, substance, drug, medicine, or thing which is advertised or described in a manner calculated to lead another to use or apply it for preventing conception or producing abortion, or for any indecent or immoral purpose; and every written or printed card, circular, book, pamphlet, advertisement or notice of any kind giving information, directly, or indirectly, where or how or by what means any of the hereinbefore mentioned matters, articles or things may be obtained or made, or where or by whom any act or operation of any kind for the procuring or producing of abortion will be done or performed, or how or by what means conception may be prevented or abortion produced, whether sealed or unsealed; and every letter, packet, or package or other mail matter containing any filthy, vile, or indecent thing, device or substance; and every paper, writing, advertisement or representation that any article, instrument, substance, drug, medicine or thing may, or can be used or applied for preventing conception or producing abortion, or for any indecent or immoral purpose; and every description calculated to induce or incite a person to so use or apply any such article, instrument, substance, drug, medicine, or thing, is hereby declared to be non-mailable matter, and shall not be conveyed in the mails or delivered from any post office or by any letter carrier. Whosoever shall knowingly deposit or cause to be deposited for mailing or delivery, anything declared by this section to be non-mailable, or shall knowingly take, or cause the same to be taken, from the mails for the purpose of circulating or disposing thereof, or of aiding in the circulation or disposition of the same, shall be fined not more than $5,000, or imprisoned not more than five years, or both.

Any one who has the patience to read through this carefully drawn law will see that it covers—well, everything. The detailed accuracy with which it is constructed partly explains Mr. Comstock's almost uniform success in securing convictions. One possible loophole suggested itself to me.

"Does it not," I asked, "allow the judge considerable leeway in deciding whether or not a book or a picture, is immoral?"

"No," replied Mr. Comstock, "the highest courts in Great Britain and the United States, have laid down the test in all such matters. What he has to decide is *whether or not it might arouse in young and inexperienced minds, lewd or libidinous thoughts.*"

In these words lies the motive of Mr. Comstock's work—the protection of children under twenty-one. If at times his ban seems to some to be too sweepingly applied it is because his faith looks forward to a time when there shall be in all the world not one object to awaken sensuous thoughts in the minds of young people. He expressed this sense of the terrible danger in which young people stand and his society's duty toward them in his fortieth annual report:

... we first of all return thanks to Almighty God, the giver of every good and perfect gift, for the opportunities of service for Him in defense of the morals of the more than forty-two million youths and children twenty-one years of age, or under, in the United States of America. His blessings upon our efforts during the past year call for profound thanksgiving to Almighty God and for grateful and loyal service in the future.

This Society in a peculiar manner is permitted to stand at a vital and strategic point where the foes to moral purity seek to concentrate their most deadly forces against the integrity of the rising generation. We have been assigned by the Great Commander to constantly face some of the most insidious and deadly forces for evil that Satan is persistently aligning against the integrity of the children of the present age.

And in a letter read at the fortieth anniversary he expresses himself thus:

There are three points of special importance to be emphasized:

1. Every child is a character-builder.
2. In the heart of every child there is a chamber of imagery, memory's storehouse, the commissary department in which is received, stored up and held in reserve every good or evil influence for future requisition.
3. "Be not deceived, God is not mocked. For whatsoever a man soweth that he shall also reap." "Keep thy heart with all diligence, for out of it are the issues of life."

The three great crime-breeders of today are intemperance, gambling, and evil reading. The devil is sowing his seed for his future harvest. There is nothing so much to be dreaded as that which perverts the imagination, sears the conscience, hardens the heart, and damns the soul.

If you allow the devil to decorate the Chamber of Imagery in your heart with licentious and sensual things, you will find that he has practically thrown a noose around your neck and will forever after exert himself to draw you away from the "Lamb of God which taketh away sins of the world." You have practically put rope on memory's bell and placed the other end of the rope in the devil's hands, and, though you may will out your mind, the memory of some vile story or picture that you may have looked upon, be assured that even in your most solitary moments the devil will ring memory's bell and call up the hateful thing to turn your thoughts away from God and undermine all aspirations for holy things.

Let me emphasize one fact, supported by my nearly forty-two years of public life in fighting this particular foe. My experience leads me to the conviction that once these matters enter through the eye and ear into the chamber of imagery in the heart of the child, nothing but the grace of God can ever erase or blot it out.

Finally, brethren, "let us not be weary in well doing, for in due season we shall reap if we faint not." Raise over each of your heads the banner of the Lord Jesus Christ. Look to Him as your Commander and Leader.

I was somewhat confused at first that Mr. Comstock should class contraceptives with pornographic objects which debauch children's fancies, for I knew that the European scientists who advocate their use have no desire at all to debauch children. When I asked Mr. Comstock about this, he replied—with scant patience of "theorizers" who do not know human nature:

"If you open the door to anything, the filth will all pour in and the degradation of youth will follow."

The federal law, which we have quoted, covers only matter sent by post. This would leave large unguarded fields were it not for the state laws. The year following the passage of the federal law, Mr. Comstock obtained the passage of drastic laws in several states, and later in all states. The New York state law reads as follows:

### Section 1142 of the Penal Law:

A person who sells, lends, gives away, or in any manner exhibits or offers to sell, lend or give away, or has in his possession with intent to sell, lend or give away, or advertises, or offers for sale, loan or distribution, any instrument or article, or any recipe, drug or medicine for the prevention of conception or for causing unlawful abortion, or purporting to be for the prevention of conception, or for causing unlawful abortion, or advertises, or holds out representations that it can be so used or applied or any such description as will be calculated to lead another to so use or apply any such article, recipe, drug, medicine or instrument, or who writes or prints, or causes to be written or printed, a card, circular, pamphlet, advertisement or notice of any kind, or gives information orally, stating when, where, how, of whom, or by what means such an instrument, article, recipe, drug or medicine can be purchased or obtained, or who manufactures any such instrument, article, recipe, drug or medicine, is guilty of a misdemeanor, and shall be liable to the same penalties as provided in section eleven hundred and forty-one of this chapter.

This punishment is a sentence of not less than ten days nor more than one year's imprisonment or a fine not less than fifty dollars or both fine and imprisonment for each offense.

"Do not these laws handicap physicians?" I asked, remembering that this criticism is sometimes made.

"They do not," replied Mr. Comstock emphatically. "No reputable physician has ever been prosecuted under these laws. Have you ever known of one?" I had not, and he continued, "Only infamous doctors who advertise or send their foul matter by mail. A reputable doctor may tell his patient in his office what is necessary, and a druggist may sell on a doctor's written prescription drugs which he would not be allowed to sell otherwise."

This criticism of the laws interfering with doctors is so continuously made that I asked again:

"Do the laws never thwart the doctor's work; in cases, for instance, where pregnancy would endanger a woman's life?"

Mr. Comstock replied with the strongest emphasis:

"A doctor is allowed to bring on an abortion in cases where a woman's life is in danger. And is there anything in these laws that forbids a doctor's telling a woman that pregnancy must not occur for a certain length of time or at all? Can they not use self-control? Or must they sink to the level of the beasts?"

"But," I protested, repeating an argument often brought forward, although I felt as if my persistence was somewhat placing me in the ranks of those who desire evil rather than good, "If the parents lack that self-control, the punishment falls upon the child."

"It does not," replied Mr. Comstock. "The punishment falls upon the parents. When a man and woman marry they are responsible for their children. You can't reform a family in any of these superficial ways. You have to go deep down into their minds and souls. The prevention of conception would work the greatest demoralization. God has set certain natural barriers. If you turn loose the passions and break down the fear you bring worse disaster than the war. It would debase sacred things, break down the health of women and disseminate a greater curse than the plagues and diseases of Europe."

*Source*: Mary Alden Hopkins, "Birth Control and Public Morals: An Interview with Anthony Comstock," *Harper's Weekly 60* (May 22, 1915): 489–490.

---

## DOCUMENT 14: The Espionage Act of 1917

During wartime, national security concerns often collide with the free-speech guarantees of the First Amendment. In 1917, at the height of the First World War, Congress passed the Espionage Act, which, among other provisions, condemned "disloyal, scurrilous and abusive language" directed at the government.

\* \* \*

SECTION 3. Whoever, when the United States is at war, shall willfully make or convey false reports or false statements with intent to interfere with the operation or success of the military or naval forces of the United States, or to promote the success of its enemies, or shall willfully make or convey false reports, or false statements, . . . or incite insubordination, disloyalty, mutiny, or refusal of duty, in the military or naval forces of the United States, or shall willfully obstruct . . . the recruiting or enlistment service of the United States, or . . . shall willfully utter, print, write, or publish any disloyal, profane, scurrilous, or abusive language about the form of government of the United States, or the Constitution of the United States, or the military or naval forces of the United States . . . or shall willfully display the flag of any foreign enemy, or shall willfully . . . urge, incite, or advocate any curtailment of production . . . or advocate, teach, defend, or suggest the doing of any of the acts or things in this section enumerated and whoever shall by word or act support or favor the cause of any country with which the United States is at war or by word or act oppose the cause of the United States therein, shall be punished by a fine of not more than $10,000 or imprisonment for not more than twenty years, or both.

*Source*: Section 3, Espionage Act of June 15, 1917, United States Statutes at Large, (Washington, DC: Government Printing Office, 1917), C. 30, 33, 40 Stat. 217, 219.

## DOCUMENT 15: *Schenck v. United States; Baer v. United States* (1919)

In 1919, three separate challenges to the Espionage Act were heard by the United States Supreme Court and rejected. The first of the three decisions to be handed down, *Schenck v. United States*, was issued on March 3, 1919, and was authored by Justice Oliver Wendell Holmes; it contains his famous observation that the Constitution does not protect someone who falsely shouts "fire" in a crowded theater. Schenck was an antiwar activist; his case was consolodated with *Baer v. United States*, which involved similar facts and raised the same legal issues.

\* \* \*

MR. JUSTICE HOLMES delivered the opinion of the court.

This is an indictment in three counts. The first charges a conspiracy to violate the Espionage Act ... causing and attempting to cause insubordination, in the military and naval forces of the United States, and to obstruct the recruiting and enlistment service of the United States, when the United States was at war with the German Empire, to-wit, that the defendants wilfully conspired to have printed and circulated to men who had been called and accepted for military service under the Act of May 18, 1917, a document set forth and alleged to be calculated to cause such insubordination and obstruction. The count alleges overt acts in pursuance of the conspiracy, ending in the distribution of the document set forth. The second count alleges a conspiracy to commit an offence against the United States, to-wit, to use the mails for the transmission of matter declared to be non-mailable by Title XII, § 2 of the Act of June 15, 1917, to-wit, the above mentioned document, with an averment of the same overt acts. The third count charges an unlawful use of the mails for the transmission of the same matter and otherwise as above. The defendants were found guilty on all the counts. They set up the First Amendment to the Constitution forbidding Congress to make any law abridging the freedom of speech, or of the press, and bringing the case here on that ground have argued some other points also of which we must dispose. ...

The document in question upon its first printed side recited the first section of the Thirteenth Amendment, said that the idea embodied in it was violated by the Conscription Act and that a conscript is little better than a convict. In impassioned language it intimated that conscription was despotism in its worst form and a monstrous wrong against humanity in the interest of Wall Street's chosen few. It said "Do not submit to intimidation," but in form at least confined itself to peaceful measures such as a petition for the repeal of the act. The other and later printed side of the sheet was headed "Assert Your Rights." It stated reasons for alleging that any one violated the Constitution when he refused to recognize "your right to assert your opposition to the draft," and went on "If you do not assert and support your rights, you are helping to deny or disparage rights which it is the solemn duty of all citizens and residents of the United States to retain." It described the arguments on the other side as coming from cunning politicians and a mercenary capitalist press, and even silent consent to the conscription law as helping to support an infamous conspiracy. It denied the power to send our citizens away to foreign shores to shoot up the people of other lands, and added that words could not express the condemnation such cold-blooded ruthlessness deserves, winding up "You must do your share to maintain, support and uphold the rights of the people of this country." Of course the documents would not have been sent unless it had been intended to have some effect, and we do not see what effect it could be expected to have upon persons subject to the draft except to influence them to obstruct the carrying of it out. The defendants do not deny that the jury might find against them on this point.

But it is said, suppose that that was the tendency of this circular, it is protected by the First Amendment to the Constitution. Two of the strongest expressions are said to be quoted respectively from well-known public men. It well may be that the prohibition of laws abridging the freedom of speech is not confined to previous restraints, although to prevent them may have been the main purpose. . . . We admit that in many places and in ordinary times the defendants in saying all that was said in the circular would have been within their constitutional rights. But the character of every act depends upon the circumstances in which it is done. . . . The most stringent protection of free speech would not protect a man in falsely shouting fire in a theatre and causing a panic. It does not even protect a man from an injunction against uttering words that may have all the effect of force. . . . The question in every case is whether the words used are used in such circumstances and are of such a nature as to create a clear and present danger that they will bring about the substantive evils that Congress has a right to prevent. It is a question of proximity and degree. When a nation is at war many things that might be said in time of peace are such a hindrance to its effort that their utterance will not be endured so long as men fight and that no Court could regard them as protected by any constitutional right. It seems to be admitted that if an actual obstruction of the recruiting service were proved, liability for words that produced that effect might be enforced. The statute of 1917 in § 4 punishes conspiracies to obstruct as well as actual obstruction. If the act, (speaking, or circulating a paper,) its tendency and the intent with which it is done are the same, we perceive no ground for saying that success alone warrants making the act a crime.

*Source:* 249 U.S. 47 (1919).

---

## DOCUMENT 16: *Debs v. United States* (1919)

The second decision, also authored by Holmes and issued the following week, was *Debs v. United States*. Eugene Debs was a socialist and antiwar activist. A black man, he had spoken out passionately against the mistreatment of African Americans, and his polemics had attracted considerable attention within the intellectual community.

\* \* \*

MR. JUSTICE HOLMES delivered the opinion of the court.

This is an indictment under the Espionage Act of June 15, 1917. . . . It . . . alleges that on or about June 16, 1918, at Canton, Ohio, the defendant caused and incited and attempted to cause and incite insubordination, disloyalty, mutiny and refusal of duty in the military and naval forces of the United States and with intent so to do delivered, to an assembly of people, a public speech, set forth. The fourth count alleges that he obstructed and attempted to obstruct the recruiting and enlistment service of the United States and to that end and with that intent delivered the same speech. . . . There was a demurrer to the indictment on the ground that the statute is unconstitutional as interfering with free speech, contrary to the First Amendment, and to the several counts as insufficiently stating the supposed offense. . . . The defendant was found guilty and was sentenced to ten years' imprisonment on each of the two counts, the punishment to run concurrently on both.

The main theme of the speech was socialism, its growth, and a prophecy of its ultimate success. With that we have nothing to do, but if a part of the manifest intent of the more general utterances was to encourage those present to obstruct the recruiting service and if in passages such encouragement was directly given, the immunity of the general theme may not be enough to protect the speech. The speaker began by saying that he had just returned from a visit to the workhouse in the neighborhood where three of their most loyal comrades were paying the penalty for their devotion to the working class—these being Wagenknecht, Baker and Ruthenberg, who had been convicted of aiding and abetting another in failing to register for the draft. . . .

After considerable discourse that it is unnecessary to follow, he took up the case of Kate Richards O'Hare, convicted of obstructing the enlistment service, praised her for her loyalty to socialism and otherwise, and said that she was convicted on false testimony, under a ruling that would seem incredible to him if he had not had some experience with a Federal Court. We mention this passage simply for its connection with evidence put in at the trial. The defendant spoke of other cases, and then, after dealing with Russia, said that the master class has always declared the war and the subject class has always fought the battles—that the subject class has had nothing to gain and all to lose, including their lives; that the working class, who furnish the corpses, have never yet had a voice in declaring war and have never yet had a voice in declaring peace. . . .

The defendant addressed the jury himself, and while contending that his speech did not warrant the charges said "I have been accused of obstructing the war. I admit it. Gentlemen, I abhor war. I would oppose the war if I stood alone." The statement was not necessary to warrant the jury in finding that one purpose of the speech, whether incidental or not does not matter, was to oppose not only war in general but this war, and that the opposition was so expressed that its natural and intended effect would be to obstruct recruiting. If that was intended and if, in all the circumstances, that would be its probable effect, it would not be protected by reason of its being part of a general program and expressions of a general and conscientious belief. . . .

There was introduced also an "Anti-war Proclamation and Program" adopted at St. Louis in April, 1917, coupled with testimony that about an hour before his speech the defendant had stated that he approved of that platform in spirit and in substance. The defendant referred to it in his address to the jury, seemingly with satisfaction and willingness that it should be considered in evidence. . . . This document contained the usual suggestion that capitalism was the cause of the war and that our entrance into it "was instigated by the predatory capitalists in the United States." It alleged that the war of the United States against Germany could not "be justified even on the plea that it is a war in defense of American rights or American 'honor.' " It said "We brand the declaration of war by our Government as a crime against the people of the United States and against the nations of the world. In all modern history there has been no war more unjustifiable than the war in which we are about to engage." Its first recommendation was, "continuous, active, and public opposition to the war, through demonstrations, mass petitions, and all other means within our power." Evidence that the defendant accepted this view and this declaration of his duties at the time that he made his

speech is evidence that if in that speech he used words tending to obstruct the recruiting service he meant that they should have that effect. . . .

Without going into further particulars we are of opinion that the verdict . . . for obstructing and attempting to obstruct the recruiting service
of the United States, must be sustained.

*Source:* 249 U.S. 211 (1919).

---

## DOCUMENT 17: *Abrams v. United States* (1919)

Later that year, on November 10, Justice John Clarke delivered the
Supreme Court's opinion in *Abrams v. United States*. Surprisingly, in
view of his authorship of *Schenck* and *Debs*, Holmes filed an eloquent
dissent, in which Justice Louis Brandeis joined. It is in this dissenting
opinion that we get a glimpse of Holmes's discomfort with the direction
his own precedents were taking the Court, and see the beginning of
his development into a champion of the First Amendment.

\* \* \*

MR. JUSTICE CLARKE delivered the opinion of the court.
    . . . The five plaintiffs in error, hereinafter designated the defendants,
were convicted of conspiring to violate provisions of the Espionage
Act. . . .

It will not do to say, as is now argued, that the only intent of these
defendants was to prevent injury to the Russian cause. Men must be
held to have intended, and to be accountable for, the effects which their
acts were likely to produce. Even if their primary purpose and intent
was to aid the cause of the Russian Revolution, the plan of action which
they adopted necessarily involved, before it could be realized, defeat of
the war program of the United States, for the obvious effect of this appeal, if it should become effective, as they hoped it might, would be to
persuade persons of character such as those whom they regarded themselves as addressing, not to aid government loans and not to work in
ammunition factories, where their work would produce "bullets, bayo-
nets, cannon" and other munitions of war, the use of which would cause
the "murder" of Germans and Russians. . . .

That the interpretation we have put upon these articles, circulated in
the greatest port of our land, from which great numbers of soldiers were
at the time taking ship daily, and in which great quantities of war supplies of every kind were at the time being manufactured for transpor-

tation overseas, is not only the fair interpretation of them, but that it is the meaning which their authors consciously intended should be conveyed by them to others is further shown by the additional writings found in the meeting place of the defendant group and on the person of one of them. . . .

. . . the language of these circulars was obviously intended to provoke and to encourage resistance to the United States in the war, as the third count runs, and, the defendants, in terms, plainly urged and advocated a resort to a general strike of workers in ammunition factories for the purpose of curtailing the production of ordnance and munitions necessary and essential to the prosecution of the war as is charged in the fourth count. Thus it is clear not only that some evidence but that much persuasive evidence was before the jury tending to prove that the defendants were guilty as charged in both the third and fourth counts of the indictment and under the long established rule of law hereinbefore stated the judgment of the District Court must be

*Affirmed.*

MR. JUSTICE HOLMES dissenting. . . .

I never have seen any reason to doubt that the questions of law that alone were before this Court in the cases of *Schenck, Frohwerk* and *Debs*, 249 U.S. 47, 204, 211, were rightly decided. I do not doubt for a moment that by the same reasoning that would justify punishing persuasion to murder, the United States constitutionally may punish speech that produces or is intended to produce a clear and imminent danger that it will bring about forthwith certain substantive evils that the United States constitutionally may seek to prevent. The power undoubtedly is greater in time of war than in time of peace because war opens dangers that do not exist at other times.

But as against dangers peculiar to war, as against others, the principle of the right to free speech is always the same. It is only the present danger of immediate evil or an intent to bring it about that warrants Congress in setting a limit to the expression of opinion where private rights are not concerned. Congress certainly cannot forbid all effort to change the mind of the country. Now nobody can suppose that the surreptitious publishing of a silly leaflet by an unknown man, without more, would present any immediate danger that its opinions would hinder the success of the government arms or have any appreciable tendency to do so. Publishing those opinions for the very purpose of obstructing, however, might indicate a greater danger and at any rate would have the quality of an attempt. So I assume that the second leaflet if published for the purposes alleged in the fourth count might be punishable. But it seems pretty clear to me that nothing less than that would bring these papers within the scope of this law. . . .

In this case sentences of twenty years imprisonment have been imposed for the publishing of two leaflets that I believe the defendants had as much right to publish as the Government has to publish the Constitution of the United States now vainly invoked by them. . . .

I wholly disagree with the argument of the Government that the First Amendment left the common law as to seditious libel in force. History seems to me against the notion. I had conceived that the United States through many years had shown its repentance for the Sedition Act of 1798, by repaying fines that it imposed. Only the emergency that makes it immediately dangerous to leave the correction of evil counsels to time warrants making any exception to the sweeping command, "Congress shall make no law . . . abridging the freedom of speech." Of course I am speaking only of expressions of opinion and exhortations, which were all that were uttered here, but I regret that I cannot put into more impressive words my belief that in their conviction upon this indictment the defendants were deprived of their rights under the Constitution of the United States.

MR. JUSTICE BRANDEIS concurs with the foregoing opinion.

*Source*: 250 U.S. 616 (1919).

---

## DOCUMENT 18: "What Is Left of Free Speech" (Gerard C. Henderson, 1919)

The three cases sparked considerable discussion in the press, as demonstrated by the article that follows. On December 10, 1919, shortly after the Supreme Court handed down the *Abrams* opinion, the *New Republic* published an article by Gerard C. Henderson, "What Is Left of Free Speech." Had these three cases remained good law, we might be asking a similar question today.

\* \* \*

On November 10th, the Supreme Court sustained the conviction of three Russian anarchists and a Russian Socialist, supporters of the Soviet regime, for publishing two circulars attacking the President for his Russian policy, and advocating a general strike to prevent intervention in Russia. Three of them had been sentenced to prison for twenty years, and one, a woman, for fifteen years.

In this decision more important issues were at stake than the liberty and, perhaps, the life of four misguided and fanatical aliens. "I regret," said Mr. Justice Holmes in his dissenting opinion, "that I cannot put into more impressive words my belief that in their conviction upon this indictment the defendants were deprived of their rights under the Constitution of the United States." The injustice which they suffered may be corrected by executive clemency when saner times have arrived, but the constitutional precedent which the Supreme Court has set cannot be so easily wiped out. It is important to examine critically the limits and implications of the majority opinion of the court, and to inquire how seriously it has encroached upon those traditions of liberty of opinion, of speech and publication which Americans in the past have cherished so dearly.

The inquiry is not a simple one. Free speech, as a principle to be applied in the courts, is not an absolute, self-defining concept, to be accepted or rejected without qualification. The First Amendment, "Congress shall make no law . . . abridging the freedom of speech, or of the press," expresses no more than a warm emotional bias toward the free expression of opinion, which should infect the minds of Congress and of the Courts when they approach the task of defining the permissible limits of speech and publication. It does not contain the precise measurements and angles of the complicated juristic plan which maps out the boundaries at which freedom of speech ends and crime begins.

It is easy to catalogue cases which are clearly within or clearly without the limits of free speech. A man shouts "fire" in a crowded theatre, or he tells a mob to lynch a prisoner in the county jail, or exhorts a company of soldiers to disobey their officers. Of course the law can reach him, despite the First Amendment. Another man writes a letter to his morning paper, pointing out that the fire-escapes in the theatre are defective, and the theatre a tinderbox, or he makes a speech attacking the state officials for failing to bring the criminal to speedy justice, or, perhaps, he publicly advocates abolishing the salute as a military institution. It is just as clear that the Constitution protects him, though the indirect effect may be to make the next evening's theatre crowd panicky, to spread the lynching fever among the mob, or to promote disaffection among the soldiers. But the lines which mark off these two groups of illustrations are still far apart.

In mapping out the large debatable area between the two lines, a juristic principle has been developed which somewhat narrows the field of uncertainty. To be punishable under the Constitution, spoken or written words must fulfill two requirements: they must accomplish or come near to accomplishing some result which the law may legitimately guard against, and there must have been an intent, on the part of the man who uttered or published them, to accomplish the result. Into the refinements which have been made as to the relation between these two requirements, the purposes of this article do not make it necessary to enter. It is said, for instance, that if the intent is fixed upon some object which it is of superlative importance to prevent, such as the success of the nation's enemies in war, speech which only remotely tends toward such a result is punishable; and conversely if the speech itself has a direct and immediate tendency to effect some result which the state can prohibit, the intent may be dispensed with. An avowed enemy propagandist during war, for instance, could be punished even if his propaganda was absurd and ineffectual. One who published sailing dates of troop transports could be punished even if his intent was innocent. Excepting extreme cases of this character, however, it is generally true that unless both requirements are present, the nearness to the dangerous result, and the intent to bring it about, the language is protected under the Constitution.

This general principle, however, leaves two important questions open, and it is around these questions that recent legal controversy as to freedom of speech and press has revolved.

One is a question of degree: how near must the spoken or written words come to producing the dangerous result, before they became punishable? The other is a question of interpretation. What does the word "intend" mean? Does it imply that the words were motivated by a desire to bring about the prohibited result? Such, perhaps, would be the layman's interpretation of the phrase. Or is it enough that the words are spoken or written for other and permissible purposes, but under conditions which made it likely that the prohibited result would come as a necessary by-product? Upon these two questions liberal and reactionary opinion has divided. Those who have felt more strongly the impulse toward liberty of speech and press, which inspired the First Amendment, have contended that only speech or writing which comes dangerously near to accomplishing the prohibited result can be punished. Those who have feared more acutely the subversive effects of unorthodox opinion have urged the suppression of words which could have only a remote tendency toward producing the evil. Those, again, who have championed the principle that the social good which comes from free expression of honest opinion overrides the incidental harm which may come as a by-product, have maintained that only a specific and purposeful intent to bring about the prohibited result will render spoken or written words punishable. Those who were dominated by fear for the safety of established institutions have been satisfied with the wholly technical and somewhat fictitious "intent" comprised in a knowledge that the prohibited result may perhaps be promoted.

This bare summary of the legal form which the free speech controversy has assumed, is necessary if we are to understand what was decided by the Supreme Court in the Abrams case; for the two issues which I have defined were directly involved and directly decided by the court.

The defendants were tried under an indictment containing four counts.

The first charged the violation of the clause in the Espionage law condemning "disloyal, scurrilous and abusive language about the form of government of the United States," and the second violation of the clause forbidding language "intended to bring the form of government of the United States into contempt, scorn, contumely and disrepute." The Supreme Court did not expressly sustain the conviction under these two counts. It rejected without argument the contention of the lawyers for the defense that "the acts charged against the defendants," (presumably including the acts charged in the first and second counts) were protected by the First Amendment, asserting that the claim was "definitely negatived" in the Schenk and Baer cases and the Frohwerk case, decided last March. In neither of these cases, however, were the clauses in question involved. The Schenk and Baer cases and the Frohwerk case involved conspiracies to oppose the draft, and were brought under the Espionage act of 1917, before the clauses involved in counts one and two of the Abrams indictment had been added to the law. The Debs case (which the court did not cite) was brought under the law as amended in 1918, but the only counts before the court were based on obstruction to recruiting, and causing insubordination among troops. The conclusion seems warranted that the constitutionality of the clauses covering abusive language and language bringing the government into "contempt, scorn," etc., is still an open question.

But there are suggestions in the Abrams case which not only imply that the clauses are constitutional, but give them a very wide construction. The court quotes abusive language published by the defendants, attacking the President (in language so intemperate that it might have been taken from the New York Tribune's attacks on President Lincoln during the Civil War) and referring to the United States as a capitalistic nation. . . . Later the court says that "A technical distinction may, perhaps, be taken between disloyal and abusive language applied to the *form* of our government or language of like character and intended to produce like results directed against the President and Congress." The court did not pass upon this "technical" question, since the decision was ultimately rested upon the third and fourth counts, but the language clearly implies that if the abusive and ill-mannered epithets had been directed against the form of our government, instead of against its personnel, they could constitutionally have been punished.

It is difficult to find any sensible theory of freedom of utterance which would justify this intimation. The government can by law protect itself against violent overthrow or forcible aggression. It can prevent speech which comes dangerously near to bringing about a forcible attack on the government. It cannot prevent speech which can at most awaken in the listeners a feeling of contempt and scorn for the government. The only way government can lawfully protect its own reputation is to govern honorably and wisely. The court quotes some general language, such as "Workers of the World, Awake! Rise! Put down your enemy and mine," and concludes that "This is clearly an appeal to the 'workers' of this country to arise and put down by force the Government of the United States, which they characterize as their 'hypocritical,' 'cowardly,' and 'capitalistic' enemy." In a vague and remote sense, the desire forcibly to overthrow the government may have been present in the mind of the writer of this language. But to hold that general appeals of this sort, circulated in New York City by four unknown Russians, could come within measurable distance of success in provoking forcible attacks on the American form of government is literally fantastic. The suggestion that such language could be punishable ranges the Supreme Court on the extreme right of the reactionary view as to the necessary proximity between the spoken or written word and the prohibited result. And to sustain the clauses in the Espionage law literally, we would have to go back to the infamous common law of sedition, to get rid of which was one of the objects of the American revolution and the main purpose of the First amendment.

The third count in the Abrams case charged language intended to provoke resistance to the United States in the war, and the fourth, language urging curtailment of production of munitions with intent to hinder the United States in the prosecution of the war. The evidence was clear that the purpose of the defendants—the desire which motivated their action—was to prevent military intervention in Russia. Both of the pamphlets so stated, and one of them expressly attacked German militarism. There was not the remotest evidence of pro-Germanism. The court found, however, that the "obvious effect" of the appeal, "if it should become effective," would be to hamper the war against Germany, and the "men must be held to have intended . . . the effects which their acts are likely to produce." Here also the court takes the reactionary side in the free speech controversy, by interpreting "intent" not in the usual sense, of purpose, or expectation and desire, but in the technical and unusual sense of knowledge that the consequences may follow. Indeed the court's language leaves it doubtful whether even knowledge is necessary. Perhaps it is enough that the consequences "are likely," even if the defendants had no thought of them!

On the two principle [sic] issues in the modern legal controversy over free speech, the Supreme Court has, therefore, definitely cast its weight on the reactionary side, on the side which fears the free interchange of opinion, and relies on force rather than reason to preserve the authority of the state and the stability of our institutions.

It is, perhaps, too early to gauge the ultimate effect of the Abrams decision on the course of American jurisprudence. Two immediate effects can be clearly discerned. The court has succeeded in making out of four unbalanced and incoherent Russians four martyrs in the cause of true Americanism. And it has shifted to Congress the task of preserving the spirit of the First Amendment as a living force in American law. Even if the immediate wrongs are righted, even if the President pardons the four Russians and Congress changes the statute, the Court has rendered a decision which must stand for years as a sinister landmark in the history of freedom of speech in America.

*Source*: Gerard C. Henderson, "What Is Left of Free Speech," *New Republic 21* (December 10, 1919): 50–52.

## DOCUMENT 19: "Guardian of Liberty: American Civil Liberties Union" (c. 1920)

By 1920, the government had assumed responsibility for—and authority over—many aspects of American life. The language of the First Amendment must have seemed a cruel joke to antiwar demonstrators who were in jail merely for holding "seditious" opinions opposing war. The guarantees of the Fourteenth Amendment must have seemed equally hollow to African Americans experiencing racial segregation and acts of violence, and to women, who had few legal rights.

It was in this environment that a young man named Roger Baldwin and a group of his friends founded the American Civil Liberties Union (ACLU) in 1920. The mission of the new organization was to restrain government, to prevent it from infringing the liberties secured to citizens by the Bill of Rights. The small organization would grow to be a primary guarantor of individual liberty; fully 80 percent of major Supreme Court cases since 1920 have been brought by or have otherwise involved the ACLU.

It is difficult to overestimate the ACLU's impact as America's first public interest law firm. It has "leveled the playing field" by providing free legal services to those with grievances against the government. Because government so often acts with the approval of the majority (as John Stuart Mill foresaw), the ACLU has represented clients who would have found it difficult or impossible to obtain representation, even if money were not an obstacle.

\* \* \*

The American system of government is built on two basic, counterbalancing principles: 1) that the majority of the people, through democratically elected representatives, governs the country and 2) that the power of even a democratic majority must be limited to insure individual rights. In every era of American history, the government has tried to expand its authority at the expense of individual rights. The American Civil Liberties Union exists to make sure that doesn't happen, and to fight back when it does.

The mission of the ACLU is to assure that the Bill of Rights—amendments to the Constitution that guard against unwarranted governmental control—are preserved for each new generation. To understand the ACLU's purpose, it is important to distinguish between the Constitution and the Bill of Rights. The Constitution itself, whose bicentennial we celebrated in 1987, authorizes the government to act. The Bill of Rights limits that authority.

**First Amendment rights**: These include freedom of speech, association and assembly, freedom of the press, and freedom of religion, including the strict separation between church and state.

**Equal protection of the law**: The right to equal treatment regardless of race, sex, religion, national origin, sexual orientation, age, physical handicap, or other such classification. These rights apply to the voting booth, the classroom, the workplace and the courts.

**Due process of law**: The right to be treated fairly when facing criminal charges or other serious accusations that can result in such penalties as loss of employment, exclusion from school, denial of housing, or cut-off of benefits.

**The right to privacy**: The right to a guaranteed zone of personal privacy and autonomy which cannot be penetrated by the government or by other institutions, like employers, with substantial influence over an individual's rights.

**Expanding those protections**: Although some segments of our population have traditionally been denied these rights, the ACLU works to extend protection to racial minorities, homosexuals, mental patients, prisoners, soldiers, children in the custody of the state, the handicapped, and Native Americans.

When Roger Baldwin founded the ACLU in 1920, civil liberties were in a sorry state. Citizens were sitting in jail for holding antiwar views. U.S. Attorney General Palmer was conducting raids upon aliens suspected of holding unorthodox opinions. Racial segregation was the law of the land and violence against blacks was routine. Sex discrimination was firmly institutionalized; it wasn't until 1920 that women even got the vote. Constitutional rights for homosexuals, the poor, prisoners, mental patients, and other special groups were literally unthinkable. And, perhaps most significantly, the Supreme Court had yet to uphold a single free speech claim under the First Amendment.

*"We must remember that a right lost to one is lost to all. The ACLU remembers and it acts. The cause it serves so well is an imperative of freedom."—William Reece Smith, Jr., former president, American Bar Association.*

Source: ACLU Briefing Paper, "Guardian of Liberty: American Civil Liberties Union," 1992.

---

## DOCUMENT 20: The Scopes Trial (1925)

One famous case in which the ACLU was involved was the trial of a young Tennessee science teacher named John Scopes, who was charged with violating a Tennessee law forbidding the teaching of evolution.

Today, we tend to think of the Scopes trial in the context of the First Amendment's Establishment Clause, because the law required public school teachers to teach a religious dogma rather than generally accepted scientific principles. In fact, the case demonstrates the impossibility of separating the First Amendment guarantees of free speech and of conscience; John Scopes was being forced by the Tennessee legislature not only to pay lip service to a dogma he did not accept, but he was being prosecuted for his speech in the classroom, for teaching what he believed to be accurate and consistent with his professional responsibilities.

The ACLU sent famed trial lawyer Clarence Darrow to represent Scopes, while the equally famous William Jennings Bryan, a former three-time presidential candidate and foe of the theory of evolution, represented the State. Although Scopes was convicted, the case is largely remembered as an example of what can happen to freedom of speech when those in power are willing to use the law to suppress those who do not share their beliefs.

The following exchange between Darrow and Bryan is one of the most famous in American jurisprudence. Bryan died suddenly a few days afterward; many observers felt that his humiliation on the stand was the real cause of his death.

\* \* \*

### Darrow's Examination of Bryan

Hays—The defense desires to call Mr. Bryan as a witness, and, of course, the only question here is whether Mr. Scopes taught what these children said he taught, we recognize what Mr. Bryan says as a witness would not be very valuable. We think there are other questions involved, and we should want to take Mr. Bryan's testimony for the purpose of our record, even if your honor thinks it is not admissible in general, so we wish to call him now.

The Court—Do you think you have a right to his testimony or evidence like you did these others?

McKenzie—I don't think it is necessary to call him, calling a lawyer who represents a client.

The Court—If you ask him about any confidential matter, I will protect him, of course.

Darrow—On scientific matters, Col. Bryan can speak for himself.

Bryan—If your honor please, I insist that Mr. Darrow can be put on the stand, and Mr. Malone and Mr. Hays.

The Court—Call anybody you desire. Ask them any questions you wish.

Bryan—Then, we will call all three of them.

Darrow—Not at once?

Bryan—Where do you want me to sit?

The Court—Mr. Bryan, you are not objecting to going on the stand?

Bryan—Not at all.

The Court—Do you want Mr. Bryan sworn?

Darrow—No.

Bryan—I can make affirmation; I can say "So help me God, I will tell the truth."

Darrow—No, I take it you will tell the truth, Mr. Bryan.

EXAMINATION OF W. J. BRYAN BY CLARENCE DARROW, OF COUNSEL FOR
THE DEFENSE:

Q—You have given considerable study to the Bible, haven't you, Mr. Bryan?

A—Yes, sir, I have tried to.

Q—Then you have made a general study of it?

A—Yes, I have; I have studied the Bible for about fifty years, or sometime more than that, but, of course, I have studied it more as I have become older than when I was but a boy.

Q—You claim that everything in the Bible should be literally interpreted?

A—I believe everything in the Bible should be accepted as it is given there: some of the Bible is given illustratively. For instance: "Ye are the salt of the earth." I would not insist that man was actually salt, or that he had flesh of salt, but it is used in the sense of salt as saving God's people.

Q—But when you read that Jonah swallowed the whale—or that the whale swallowed Jonah—excuse me please—how do you literally interpret that?

A—When I read that a big fish swallowed Jonah—it does not say whale.

Q—Doesn't it? Are you sure?

A—That is my recollection of it. A big fish, and I believe it, and I believe in a God who can make a whale and can make a man and make both what He pleases.

Q—Mr. Bryan, doesn't the New Testament say whale?

A—I am not sure. My impression is that it says fish; but it does not make so much difference; I merely called your attention to where it says fish—it does not say whale.

Q—But in the New Testament it says whale, doesn't it?

A—That may be true; I cannot remember in my own mind what I read about it.

Q—Now, you say, the big fish swallowed Jonah, and he there remained how long—three days—and then he spewed him upon the land. You believe that the big fish was made to swallow Jonah?

A—I am not prepared to say that; the Bible merely says it was done.

Q—You don't know whether it was the ordinary run of fish, or made for that purpose?

A—You may guess; you evolutionists guess.

Q—But when we do guess, we have a sense to guess right.

A—But do not do it often.

Q—You are not prepared to say whether that fish was made especially to swallow a man or not?

A—The Bible doesn't say, so I am not prepared to say.

Q—You don't know whether that was fixed up specifically for the purpose.

A—No, the Bible doesn't say.

Q—But do you believe He made them—that He made such a fish and that it was big enough to swallow Jonah?

A—Yes, sir. Let me add: One miracle is just as easy to believe as another.

Q—It is for me.

A—It is for me.

Q—Just as hard?

A—It is hard to believe for you, but easy for me. A miracle is a thing performed beyond what man can perform. When you get within the realm of miracles; and it is just as easy to believe the miracle of Jonah as any other miracle in the Bible.

Q—Perfectly easy to believe that Jonah swallowed the whale?

A—If the Bible said so; the Bible doesn't make as extreme statements as evolutionists do.

\* \* \*

Q—The Bible says Joshua commanded the sun to stand still for the purpose of lengthening the day, doesn't it, and you believe it?

A—I do.

Q—Do you believe at that time the entire sun went around the earth?

A—No, I believe that the earth goes around the sun.

Q—Do you believe that the men who wrote it thought that the day could be lengthened or that the sun could be stopped?

A—I don't know what they thought.

Q—You don't know?

A—I think they wrote the fact without expressing their own thoughts.

Q—Have you an opinion as to whether or not the men who wrote that thought—

Gen. Stewart—I want to object, your honor; it has gone beyond the pale of any issue that could possibly be injected into this lawsuit, except by imagination. I do not think the defendant has a right to conduct the examination any further and I ask your honor to exclude it.

The Witness—It seems to me it would be too exacting to confine the defense to the facts; if they are not allowed to get away from the facts, what have they to deal with?

The Court—Mr. Bryan is willing to be examined. Go ahead.

* * *

Mr. Darrow—I read that years ago. Can you answer my question directly? If the day was lengthened by stopping either the earth or the sun, it must have been the earth?

A—Well, I should say so.

* * *

Q—Now, Mr. Bryan, have you ever pondered what would have happened to the earth if it had stood still?

A—No.

Q—You have not?

A—No; the God I believe in could have taken care of that, Mr. Darrow.

Q—I see. Have you ever pondered what would naturally happen to the earth if it stood still suddenly?

A—No.

Q—Don't you know it would have been converted into molten mass of matter?

A—You testify to that when you get on the stand, I will give you a chance.

Q—Don't you believe it?

A—I would want to hear expert testimony on that.

Q—You have never investigated that subject?

A—I don't think I have ever had the question asked.

Q—Or ever thought of it?

A—I have been too busy on things that I thought were of more importance than that.

Q—You believe the story of the flood to be a literal interpretation?

A—Yes, sir.

Q—When was that Flood?

A—I would not attempt to fix the date. The date is fixed, as suggested this morning.

Q—About 4004 B.C.?

A—That has been the estimate of a man that is accepted today. I would not say it is accurate.

Q—That estimate is printed in the Bible?

A—Everybody knows, at least, I think most of the people know, that was the estimate given.

Q—But what do you think that the Bible, itself says? Don't you know how it was arrived at?

A—I never made a calculation.

Q—A calculation from what?

A—I could not say.

Q—From the generations of man?

A—I would not want to say that.

Q—What do you think?

A—I do not think about things I don't think about.

Q—Do you think about things you do think about?

A—Well, sometimes.

(Laughter in the court yard.)

Policeman—Let us have order.

* * *

Stewart—Your honor, he is perfectly able to take care of this, but we are attaining no evidence. This is not competent evidence.

Witness—These gentlemen have not had much chance—they did not come here to try this case. They came here to try revealed religion. I am here to defend it and they can ask me any question they please.

The Court—All right.

(Applause from the court yard.)

Darrow—Great applause from the bleachers.

Witness—From those whom you call "yokels."

Darrow—I have never called them yokels.

Witness—That is the ignorance of Tennessee, the bigotry.

Darrow—You mean who are applauding you?

Witness—Those are the people whom you insult.

Darrow—You insult every man of science and learning in the world because he does not believe in your fool religion.

The Court—I will not stand for that.

Darrow—For what he is doing?

The Court—I am talking to both of you.

* * *

Q—Wait until you get to me. Do you know anything about how many people there were in Egypt 3,500 years ago, or how many people there were in China 5,000 years ago?

A—No.

Q—Have you ever tried to find out?

A—No, sir. You are the first man I ever heard of who has been interested in it. (Laughter.)

Q—Mr. Bryan, am I the first man you ever heard of who had been interested in the age of human societies and primitive man?

A—You are the first man I ever heard speak of the number of people at those different periods.

Q—Where have you lived all your life?

A—Not near you. (Laughter and applause.)

Q—Nor near anybody of learning?

A—Oh, don't assume you know it all.

Q—Do you know there are thousands of books in our libraries on all those subjects I have been asking you about?

A—I couldn't say, but I will take your word for it.

Q—Did you ever read a book on primitive man? Like Tyler's Primitive Culture, or Boaz, or any of the great authorities?

A—I don't think I ever read the ones you mentioned.

Q—Have you ever read any?

A—Well I have read a little from time to time. But I didn't pursue it, because I didn't know I was to be called as a witness.

Q—You have never in all your life made any attempt to find out about the other peoples of the earth—how old their civilizations are—how long they had existed on the earth, have you?

A—No, sir, I have been so well satisfied with the Christian religion that I have spent no time trying to find arguments against it.

* * *

Q—Have you any idea how old the earth is?

A—No.

Q—The Book you have introduced in evidence tells you, doesn't it?

A—I don't think it does, Mr. Darrow.

Q—Let's see whether it does; is this the one?

A—That is the one, I think.

Q—It says B.C. 4004?

A—That is Bishop Usher's calculation.

Q—That is printed in the Bible you introduced?

A—Yes, sir.

* * *

Q—Would you say that the earth was only 4,000 years old?

A—Oh, no; I think it is much older than that.

Q—How much?

A—I couldn't say.

Q—Do you say whether the Bible itself says it is older than that?

A—I don't think the Bible says itself whether it is older or not.

Q—Do you think the earth was made in six days?

A—Not six days of twenty-four hours.

Q—Doesn't it say so?

A—No, sir.

* * *

The Court—Are you about through, Mr. Darrow?

Darrow—I want to ask a few more questions about the creation.

The Court—I know. We are going to adjourn when Mr. Bryan comes off the stand for the day. Be very brief, Mr. Darrow. Of course, I believe I will make myself clearer. Of course, it is incompetent testimony before the jury. The only reason I am allowing this to go in at all is that they may have it in the appellate court as showing what the affidavit would be.

Bryan—The reason I am answering is not for the benefit of the superior court. It is to keep these gentlemen from saying I was afraid to meet them and let them question me, and I want the Christian world to know that any atheist, agnostic, unbeliever, can question me anytime as to my belief in God, and I will answer him.

Darrow—I want to take an exception to this conduct of this witness. He may be very popular down here in the hills. I do not need to have his explanation for his answer.

* * *

Bryan—Your honor, they have not asked a question legally and the only reason they have asked any question is for the purpose, as the question about Jonah was asked, for a chance to give this agnostic an opportunity to criticize a believer in the word of God; and I answered the question in order to shut his mouth so that he cannot go out and tell his atheistic friends that I would not answer his questions. That is the only reason, no more reason in the world.

Malone—Your honor on this very subject, I would like to say that I would have asked Mr. Bryan—and I consider myself as good a Christian as he is—every question that Mr. Darrow has asked him for the purpose of bringing out whether or not there is to be taken in this court a literal interpretation of the Bible, or whether, obviously, as these questions indicate, if a general and literal construction cannot be put upon the parts of the Bible which have been covered by Mr. Darrow's questions. I hope for the last time no further attempt will be made by counsel on the other side of the case, or Mr. Bryan, to say the defense is concerned at all with Mr. Darrow's particular religious views or lack of religious views. We are here as lawyers with the same right to our views. I have the same right to mine as a Christian as Mr. Bryan has to his, and we do not intend to have this case charged by Mr. Darrow's agnosticism or Mr. Bryan's brand of Christianity. (A great applause.)

The Court—I will pass on each question as asked, if it is objected to.

Mr. Darrow:

Q—Mr. Bryan, do you believe that the first woman was Eve?

A—Yes.

Q—Do you believe she was literally made out of Adam's rib?

A—I do.

Q—Did you ever discover where Cain got his wife?

A—No, sir; I leave the agnostics to hunt for her.

Q—You have never found out?

A—I have never tried to find.

Q—You have never tried to find?

A—No.

Q—The Bible says he got one, doesn't it? Were there other people on the earth at that time?

A—I cannot say.

Q—You cannot say. Did that ever enter your consideration?

A—Never bothered me.

Q—There were no others recorded, but Cain got a wife.

A—That is what the Bible says.

Q—Where she came from you do not know. All right. Does the statement, "The morning and the evening were the first day," and "The morning and the evening were the second day," mean anything to you?

A—I do not think it necessarily means a twenty-four-hour day.

Q—You do not?

A—No.

Q—What do you consider it to be?

A—I have not attempted to explain it. If you will take the second chapter—let me have the book. (Examining Bible.) The fourth verse of the second chapter says: "These are the generations of the heavens and of the earth, when they were created in the day that the Lord God made the earth and the heavens," the word "day" there in the very next chapter is used to describe a period. I do not see that there is any necessity for construing the words, "the evening and the morning," as meaning necessarily a twenty-four-hour day, "in the day when the Lord made the heaven and the earth."

Q—Then, when the Bible said, for instance, "and God called the firmament heaven. And the evening and the morning were the second day," that does not necessarily mean twenty-four hours?

A—I do not think it necessarily does.

Q—Do you think it does or does not?

A—I know a great many think so.

Q—What do you think?

A—I do not think it does.

Q—You think those were not literal days?

A—I do not think they were twenty-four-hour days.

Q—What do you think about it?

A—That is my opinion—I do not know that my opinion is better on that subject than those who think it does.

Q—You do not think that?

A—No. But I think it would be just as easy for the kind of God we believe in to make the earth in six days as in six years or in 6,000,000 years or in 600,000,000 years. I do not think it important whether we believe one or the other.

Q—Do you think those were literal days?

A—My impression is they were periods, but I would not attempt to argue as against anybody who wanted to believe in literal days.

* * *

Q—I will read it to you from the Bible: "And the Lord God said unto the serpent, because thou hast done this, thou art cursed above all cattle, and above every beast of the field; upon thy belly shalt thou go and dust shalt thou eat all the days of thy life." Do you think that is why the serpent is compelled to crawl upon its belly?

A—I believe that.

Q—Have you any idea how the snake went before that time?

A—No, sir.

Q—Do you know whether he walked on his tail or not?

A—No, sir. I have no way to know. (Laughter in audience).

Q—Now, you refer to the cloud that was put in heaven after the flood, the rainbow. Do you believe in that?

A—Read it.

Q—All right, Mr. Bryan, I will read it for you.

Bryan—Your Honor, I think I can shorten this testimony. The only purpose Mr. Darrow has is to slur at the Bible, but I will answer his question. I will answer it all at once, and I have no objection in the world, I want the world to know that this man, who does not believe in a God, is trying to use a court in Tennessee—

Darrow—I object to that.

Bryan—(Continuing) to slur at it, and while it will require time, I am willing to take it.

Darrow—I object to your statement. I am exempting you on your fool ideas that no intelligent Christian on earth believes.

The Court—Court is adjourned until 9 o'clock tomorrow morning.

*Source:* John Scopes, *The World's Most Famous Court Trial: State of Tennessee v. John T. Scopes* (New York: Da Capo Press, 1971), 284–304.

## DOCUMENT 21: *Gitlow v. People of New York* (1925)

*Gitlow v. People of New York*, decided in 1925, is one of the most famous cases in First Amendment jurisprudence. Benjamin Gitlow was convicted under a statute proscribing "criminal anarchy," essentially for publishing an inflammatory pamphlet. Once again, the constitutional challenge was mounted on the basis of the Fourteenth Amendment, this time the due-process provisions of that amendment, and once again, the Supreme Court found freedom of speech and the press to be "among the personal rights and liberties protected by the due process clause of the Fourteenth Amendment from impairment by the States." While the Court proceeded to uphold the validity of the statute under which Gitlow had been charged, the majority reiterated the right of all Americans to the protection of the First Amendment's free-speech provisions. It was once again Justice Holmes, with whom Justice Brandeis concurred, who would have applied the principle of the facts of the case before the Court.

\* \* \*

MR. JUSTICE HOLMES, dissenting.

MR. JUSTICE BRANDEIS and I are of opinion that this judgment should be reversed. . . . If what I think the correct test is applied, it is manifest that there was no present danger of an attempt to overthrow the government by force on the part of the admittedly small minority who shared the defendant's views. It is said that this manifesto was more than a theory, that it was an incitement. Every idea is an incitement. It offers itself for belief and if believed it is acted on unless some other belief outweighs it or some failure of energy stifles the movement at its birth. The only difference between the expression of an opinion and an incitement in the narrower sense is the speaker's enthusiasm for the result. Eloquence may set fire to reason. But whatever may be thought of the redundant discourse before us it had no chance of starting a present conflagration. If in the long run the beliefs expressed in proletarian dictatorship are destined to be accepted by the dominant forces of the community, the only meaning of free speech is that they should be given their chance and have their way.

If the publication of this document had been laid as an attempt to induce an uprising against government at once and not at some indefinite time in the future it would have presented a different question. The object would have been one with which the law might deal, subject to the doubt whether there was any danger that the publication could produce any result, or in other words, whether it was not futile and too remote from possible consequences. But the indictment alleges the publication and nothing more.

*Source*: 268 U.S. 652 (1925).

---

## DOCUMENT 22: "Freedom of Speech and Its Limitations" (Roger Hoar, 1927)

It would be a mistake to suppose that all or even most censorship in the United States was in reaction to the perceived political threat emanating from Russia. Bluestockings were constantly busy "protecting" public morality, and the well-known phrase "banned in Boston" reflected genuine elements of the history of that city. But Boston was hardly unique. As the next two documents demonstrate, government officials and other pundits of the times frequently departed from the lofty sentiments of the founders and the philosophers who had inspired the drafting of the First Amendment's free-speech provisions. In 1927, in response to actions taken by Boston to ban Sinclair Lewis's *Elmer Gantry*, Theodore Dreiser's *An American Tragedy*, and several other books of serious literary merit, the *New York Times Magazine* ran an article detailing similar actions against Walt Whitman's *Leaves of Grass*.

That same year, in an article from *American Mercury*, Roger Sherman Hoar suggested a tongue-in-cheek basis upon which the Supreme Court might uphold the Tennessee law banning the teaching of evolution, which was the subject of the Scopes appeal then under way.

\* \* \*

The Corpus Juris, a leading law encyclopedia, says: "Freedom of speech and freedom of the press are the corner-stones of Anglo-Saxon democratic institutions," citing as its authority a decision by the Supreme Court of Wisconsin, that citadel of popular rights. But an inspection of the source itself reveals the fact that the court merely said:

Freedom of speech and freedom of the press have always been *supposed to be* the very corner-stones of Anglo-Saxon democratic institutions.

But the supposition is so firmly established in the popular (and even in the legal) mind that, although the constitution of Massachusetts (in company with those of only three other States of the Union) contains no guaranty of freedom of speech, yet Massachusetts (being "the cradle of liberty") has always nursed more isms per square mentality than any other State. In fact, the Supreme Judicial Court of that Commonwealth has so far forgotten itself and its constitution as to decide one of the leading cases on freedom of speech on the assumption that the State constitution actually contains such a guaranty.

Any fundamental principle of constitutional law is apt, sooner or later, to run counter to some other fundamental principle. When Greek meets Greek, then comes the tug of war. When an irresistible force meets an immovable body, something has got to give. Freedom of speech, being guaranteed by the Federal Constitution and by the Bill of Rights of every State except Delaware, Massachusetts, New Hampshire and North Carolina, is an irresistible force. Let us see if there is not some immovable body which it occasionally meets.

To lead up to the discovery of such an immovable body, permit me to digress for a moment, and give a bit of the history of this alleged fundamental right of free speech. Everyone knows, of course, that free speech has received of late some pretty hard knocks at the hands of the police power, the law of libel and slander, the regulation of the United States mails, the various censorships, etc.; but, on the other hand, it has always served as a convenient excuse for the upsetting of obnoxious statutes by the courts. Thus, when various American legislatures enacted laws requiring that employers must give discharged employees written statements as to the reasons for their discharge—which laws, of course, were of the sort that nice little courts *must* declare unconstitutional—the courts were hard put for grounds, until by a stroke of genius it occurred to some corporation lawyer to allege that such laws constituted an abridgment of the right of free speech. The courts promptly fell in line with this idea. Thus the Supreme Court of Kansas said:

It would seem that the liberty to remain silent is a correlative of the freedom of speech. If one *must* speak, he cannot be said freely to speak.

And the Supreme Court of Texas said:

The liberty to write or speak includes the corresponding right to be silent, also to decline to write . . . To say that one can be compelled at the instance of another party to do what he has the constitutional liberty to do or not is a contradiction that is not susceptible of reconciliation.

The reasoning employed in these decisions can be further extended. If freedom *not* to speak is a necessary correlative of freedom *to* speak, then it would seem clear that another correlative is the right not to *listen* to another's free speech if one does not want to be annoyed by it. To the right of freedom *of* speech, in other words, there should be added the right of freedom *from* speech. This new right is based upon the fundamental principle of the right of privacy, which may be traced through Anglo-Saxon jurisprudence clear back to the Roman law.

The individual surrenders to society many rights and privileges which he would be free to exercise in a state of nature in exchange for the benefits which he receives as a member of society. But he is not presumed to surrender *all* those rights; and the public has no more license, without his consent, to invade the domain of such rights as it is necessarily to be presumed he has reserved, than he has to violate the valid regulations of the organized government under which he lives. The right of privacy has its foundation in the instincts of nature. Each individual as instinctively resents any encroachment upon his private rights as he does the withdrawal of the rights which are of a public nature. The right of privacy in matters purely private is therefore derived from natural law.

Although neither Blackstone nor any other of the commentators have expressly referred to this right of privacy, yet the illustrations given by them as to what would be a violation of the absolute rights of individuals tacitly assume its existence. This tacit recognition is even more conclusive than an express mention would be. When the law guarantees to all individuals the right to "life, liberty and the pursuit of happiness," these inalienable rights comprise something more than the mere privilege of breathing and existing. An individual has a right to enjoy life in any way that may be most agreeable and pleasant to him, provided that in such enjoyment he does not invade the rights of his neighbor.

The *injuries* of the Roman law embraced all of those wrongs which are a direct invasion of the rights of the person and the rights of property. But it included more. An outrage was committed, not only by striking with the fists or with a club or lash, but also by merely shouting until a crowd gathered around the victim; and it was considered a legal wrong merely to follow a woman or a young boy or girl. And, in unequivocal terms, the law declared that these illustrations were not exhaustive, but that an injury or legal wrong might be committed "by numberless other acts."

The fact that merely to attract public attention to another was punishable shows that the ancient law fully recognized the fundamental right of an individual to be let alone. This was carried over into the Common Law of England and America, and appears from time to time in various places, conspicuous examples being: the abatement of private nuisances resulting from noises which interfere with one's enjoyment of one's home, even though the noises may arise from the carrying-on of a lawful occupation; the conception that "every man's house is his castle"; and the suppression of eavesdroppers and common scolds. Instances might be multiplied where the Common Law has both tacitly and expressly recognized the right of an individual to repose and privacy.

The right of the people to be secure in their persons, houses, papers and effects, against unreasonable searches and seizures, which is so fully protected both in the Federal Constitution and in the constitutions of most of the States, is not a right *created* by those instruments, but rather is an ancient preexisting right, merely recognized and perpetuated by them. It is a part of the more general right of privacy, the right to be let alone.

In my book on "Constitutional Conventions" I pointed out that the rights, conceded or guaranteed by the various constitutions, are really based upon a higher sanction, and I liken these constitutions to the man who was trying to show his authority over his dog by ordering him to sit up and beg. The dog refused to obey. Finally the man, still determined to show his authority, cried out: "Well, then, lie down! I *will* be minded!" Thus it is seen that there is a fundamental right of privacy, the right to be let alone, various parts of which right have been expressly embodied in our constitutions, and which has been recognized in its entirety by the Civil Law of Rome and by the Common Law of England and America. This right has been recognized in conflict with the right of freedom of the press, and has frequently come off the victor, as in cases involving the unauthorized publication of personal photographs. The cases in which the freedom of the press have been held superior to the right of privacy may be explained on the ground that, in those cases, the individual concerned has waived his or her right of privacy by becoming a public character.

What will happen when the right to be let alone runs counter to the right of freedom of speech? The two rights have already clashed in the long line of legal decisions rendered on peaceful picketing in labor disputes. The basic conflict in such decisions is between the right of the strikers, on the one hand, to express their sentiments freely, and the right of the workers, on the other hand, to be relieved from annoyance. Although this true nature of the conflict has not always been expressly recognized by the courts, which have often based their opinions on such collateral matters as property rights and freedom of contract, the fact remains that the decision has always gone to the strikers or to the employers according to the extent of the annoyance which the free (often very free) speech of the pickets was causing to the employees on their way to and from work. And the best judicial minds have recognized this conflict between the right of freedom of speech and the right of freedom *from* speech.

Thus Chief Justice Taft has said:

We are a social people and the accosting by one another in an inoffensive way and an offer by one to communicate and discuss information with a view to influencing the other's actions are not regarded as aggression or a violation of that other's rights. If, however, the offer is declined, as it may rightfully be, then persistence, importunity, following and dogging become unjustifiable annoyance and obstruction, which is likely to savor of intimidation. From all this the person sought to be influenced has a right to be free.

And that clear-thinker, Vice Chancellor Pitney of New Jersey, who later became a Justice of the Supreme Court, has said:

No person has a right to impose upon another his arguments or persuasions against the will of that other person to listen.

Although those two decisions were rendered in labor disputes, the fact should not be lost sight of that the language used and the principles involved are equally applicable to any and every sort of conflict between the two fundamental, but opposed, rights: the right of freedom of speech, and the right to be let alone.

Therefore one may prophesy that eventually freedom *from* speech will be accorded full recognition in the text-books on Constitutional Law.

And it is not beyond the realm of possibility that, when the Supreme Court of the United States finally passes on the monkey trial at Dayton, the learned Justices may sustain the anti-evolution law on the ground that the simple mountaineers of Tennessee have a fundamental constitutional right to protect their children from having to listen to the free speech of the evolutionists.

In conclusion, I wish to assert the following principle: that freedom of speech connotes a willing listener, and that the right of freedom of speech ceases to exist if the listener is unwilling to listen.

*Source*: Roger Hoar, "Freedom of Speech and Its Limitations," *American Mercury* 10 (February 1927): 202–204.

---

## DOCUMENT 23: "Dirty Hands: A Federal Customs Officer Looks at Art" (Perry Hobbs, 1930)

During the 1920s and 1930s, censorship efforts were often focused upon Customs, where a concerted effort was made to prevent the importation of "dirty books" from Europe. As a consequence, many books widely considered to be great works of fiction were not allowed to be imported into the United States.

Wherever there is censorship there is, of course, a censor whose job it is to decide for others what they might safely read. The following article by Perry Hobbs purports to be an interview with such an individual; Hobbs uses the interview to demonstrate the essential arbitrary nature of the judgments made and the belief structures that motivate some individuals to "protect" others from materials they find personally troubling.

* * *

He was a small man, not running much over five feet five, but I was physically very much aware of him. He gave off a confusion of qualities which would have put a dog in ecstasies but which can only puzzle a man. His hair was of that slick black kind—combed like a boy's on the side and a little ragged at the extremities—that strongly suggests baldness underneath. Forehead and chin were vertically cleft along the line of a rather flat nose and contrasted with a wide, tight, succulently red mouth. A floppy black windsor tie dragged on his chest. He wore no coat. A vest buttoned once at the bottom enclosed a yellow and green plaid shirt and supported a mildly straining belly. The pants were dark, wrinkled at the crotch and baggy at the knees. I did not much notice his hands at the time, but I recall that they were muscular ad very hairy, and that the left one incongruously exposed a large signet ring. Altogether, I could not keep my eyes off him.

Nor could I have done so in any wise while I remembered his office. He was, this small man, censor of printed matter for an eastern port. As I had had the most excellent reasons to know during my years in the book business, his authority was practically supreme, his opinions irreversible, and his taste above impeachment. It was this authority which had brought me to his office. He was representing, for me, the benevolent side of bureaucracy, for he had agreed to return a certain book to England instead of confiscating it. I was representing my old employer, who was too busy that morning to come in himself. I had brought with me, by the censor's instructions, string, paper, corrugated cardboard, and an addressed label: these the government does not furnish those it favors.

Our initial contact was pleasant. He had the book on his desk, all ready for me, and very agreeably got me some sealing wax and glue. While I was doing up the bundle and burning my fingers on the melting wax, I reflected on the innocuous character of the book in question. It was a volume in a series called "The Art of Eastern Love." The series was mostly composed of translation and paraphrase of various Indian texts, and circulated, I knew, freely enough in England. I wondered if perhaps it had not been banned largely on account of its inflammatory title; so I asked him what he found wrong with it. He was eager to talk.

"It's too blasé," he said: and for the rest of the time I was there I had nothing to do but prompt him occasionally. He had the great merit of believing, in his own way, in the dignity of his job and in his own qualifications thereof. "It's too blasé," he repeated, "It's not as bad as some; it's not nearly so bad as a good many. I thought it was dull, myself. But it treats a sacred subject in a blasé way, and nothing like that can get by me. You ought to see the stuff that comes in here. You ought to have the opportunity to see the vile, filthy stuff that comes in here. There's no doubt about it, it's filthy. I read it all and I know. But," he said, drawing himself up a little and raising his voice, "none of it gets by me. The kind of books you fellows get, I mean the ones you don't get, are sweet and virtuous beside the ones I'm thinking of. You can't imagine the vile stuff they try and get in."

I said I thought I could imagine very well, and asked him if he had ever felt that so much contact with filth had not perhaps injured him a little. Had he ever felt the beginning of corruption? He looked at me sharply, then spoke softly. "Listen," he said. "I'm speaking in my official capacity. As a human being I get a big kick out of some of those books. I get a thrill. I'm not any different from the next man." He paused, with a reminiscent illumination on his face, "I been here at this job six years now, I used to hit the high spots. I suppose I've read more dirty books than any man in New England, and I could make the biggest collection of erotica in this country if I wanted to. Why, in the last two years I've seized 272 different titles—thousands of volumes—and I've read them all."

Then, with a genuinely persuasive pathos, he went on. "If everybody was like you and me everything would be all right; that is, it would if we could keep things to ourselves. But you know how it is. You'd do it yourself. I do it myself. As a human being I get a pretty big thrill out of this stuff. I read a dirty book and if it's any good I get a kick. But what do I do? Do I keep it to myself? No. I pick out the juicy spots and tell my friends about them. I hand it around and circulate it. It's only natural. You'd do the same. The same with a dirty picture. If it's got its good points, it's real hot, you want to show it off. Of course, you do. Everybody does. I do it myself. And that's just where the trouble comes in. You know and I know that sort of thing can't go on. That sort of stuff gets into the hands of young boys and girls—and what happens? They're too innocent and too immature to handle it the way you and I do, so their minds get polluted. Why sometimes . . ." He paused: his eyes beaded and glistened. "Why, sometimes it's the contact of innocence with this filthy stuff that sinks a boy into foul habits for a lifetime. Naturally the government steps in here; and that's my job. I don't let anything get by me if I can help it. I act in my official capacity and there's an end to it. But I just wanted you to know I'm a human being.

"Of course," he went on—and somehow the more he talked the more rasping his voice seemed—"there's books and books. I don't see anything wrong, personally, with a book like Balzac's 'Droll Stories.' Those are what you might call snappy stories, that's all. I don't mind them, and mostly I let them get by, especially if they're going to a reputable house. There's some editions that are illustrated, though, and the pictures are too hot. They make a raw book out of it. That makes a difference, and I have to call a halt there. And Straponola, there's nothing wrong with that. 'Droll Stories' and Straponola, those are just snappy stories, and that's all—that is, the best of them. I wish they were all like that."

The gesture was not mightily convincing and had a small air of oratory. I said he must have some difficulty in deciding whether or not to confiscate a particular book. He answered with surprising confidence.

"Oh, no. As a matter of fact, I find it easier all the time. It's much easier now than it used to be. You see, well," he said, and then, with that pleased look people wear when proposing conundrums, he asked if I were married, and after my negative he went on: "Well, I am, and that makes a big difference. You'd be surprised. I've been married quite a while now, and the work gets easier all the time. You'll find out what I mean, you'll be able to decide things like this much better. Why, before

I was married, sometimes I'd go easy on the stuff. But marriage makes a big difference. You learn what things are and what they aren't."

I missed the point and inquired if he might not be more explicit. How exactly did his domestic economy affect his judgments of books? How exactly would he decide upon a book in any given instance? It would seem to me, I said, very difficult to devise a system which would apply to more than one book—books being so very different among themselves and serving such contradictory purposes. In any event I admired his courage.

He took me up quickly, gleefully, with that assurance which substitutes in public life for spontaneity as well as for the more intellectual virtues. "It's easy," said he, "and takes no courage. I just figure out whether I can read the book aloud in mixed company. If I can, it gets by: if I can't it don't, and that's all. You don't need to go any further."

I could not help imagining this small, energetic man in the middle of a great mixed circle of spinster aunts and avuncular beards—all on squeaky wooden benches—reading aloud from, say, the "Ulysses" of James Joyce. So satisfying was this image that I very nearly kept the peace: but I did offer a trifling suggestion on the ground that some books were what was called literature.

"Literature!" he said, and in his mouth it was an expletive of magnificent proportions, an exhaustive, bursting flatulence. "Literature! Don't speak to me about literature. Or classics." I have not heard a word sound more thoroughly obscene than this simple, if controversial, word "classics." He went on: "Yes, I know. People come in here and they call up and they write letters and try and tell me a thing is literature. I know the argument." He put on a finicky tone. " 'You can't suppress this book because it is part of our classic heritage . . . ' That's tripe. Why, I've had people come in here and tell me that Aristophanes' 'Lysistrata' is a classic. It's a treatise on pederasty. Pederasty." He spat the word at me.

I said I thought the play was a little more than that. "No," he said shortly, "that's all it is: pederasty. But I've had worse books than that called classics. Books you never even heard of. Do you know what a classic is? No. Well, I'll tell you. And it's straight. A classic is a dirty book somebody is trying to get by me.

"And as for literature. I'm a student of literature myself. I enjoy good literature, and when I was younger I took a course in comparative literature myself. So you see, I know what I'm talking about. And if somebody don't like what I say, why they can take it to the Secretary of the Treasury, and maybe, by the time they get through, they'll learn better."

At this point, I reminded him that a few months previously "Candide" had been refused entry, and that later the ban had been raised. Indignant innocence—or was it hurt pride?—raised a husky voice.

"Some swell banker friend of Mellon's put up a howl. That's why that's that. But it don't happen often. There's very few times I get over-ruled, very few times. I can count them. But about 'Candide,' I'll tell you. For years we've been letting that book get by. There were so many dif-ferent editions, all sizes and kinds, some illustrated and some plain, that we figured the book must be all right. Then one of us happened to read it. It's a filthy book, and I think the ruling ought to have been upheld. And it would have been if that banker fellow hadn't got into it."

As light-heartedly as I could, I mentioned to him the vote taken in the Senate at the instance of the Senator from New Mexico, and suggested that if the action were sustained he might shortly be out of a job, as the censorship of books on the ground of obscenity would then be altogether removed from the tariff.

He was very confident on this matter. "It won't go through. If the Senate doesn't reverse itself, the House will take care of it. The Senate just wasn't thinking what it was about. If that got through everything would be upset and we wouldn't know where we were at. I said so myself to my own Senator. On Armistice Day after his speech, I went up to him and I said, 'Bill, did you know what you were voting for when you voted to amend that book section in the tariff?' He looked at me kind of funny. Then he smiled and said no, he guessed he didn't. 'Well,' I said, 'I'll tell you. You voted to overturn the whole machinery of gov-ernment. You voted to change the whole procedure of the courts.' I don't think he'll vote the same the next time it comes up."

There was one question I had been very much wanting to ask him, but had been afraid of the answer the oracle might give. He seemed in such a pleasant mood after the story about Senator Bill that I thought I might risk it, at least in a declarative form. So I described my experience over a term of five years in the book business with the demand for such books as his office had refused entry. Bankers, lawyers, scholars, men both socially and professionally reputable, I said, almost exclusively made up the list of customers. Much better men, I said, than either he or I, as I was sure he would admit. Should not their taste and knowledge, their position and reputation, be given some consideration in matters of this kind? Why should we except their judgment on this point alone?

He was ready for me. My verbosity had but let him gather breath. "That's just where you find the dirtiest minds, in the men higher up. I know. When I was younger, I used to hit the high spots. I used to go all round. I've seen all kinds of people. And I never saw a workingman, anyone who worked for a living, who was a pervert. It was all the other kind, men higher up, wealthy men: bankers and lawyers. You work for a living and you'll be all right. I know. I tell you I've seen them all. The wealthy class is full of perverts. Look at me," he said, shoving his hands in my face. "Did you ever see a pervert with dirty hands? Did you?"

I looked quickly down and made sure mine were gloved; else I had been suspect. Again he said it, with a ferocious intonation. "Did you ever see a pervert with dirty hands?"

Though we could not agree on this point, we parted amicably. As I walked up the street I looked into the windows and wondered. And I also wondered whether it was because Utah is so far from any customs office that Senator Smoot is enabled to speak so righteously of censorship in the tariff.

*Source*: Perry Hobbs, "Dirty Hands: A Federal Customs Official Looks at Art," *New Republic* 62 (April 1930): 188–190.

---

## DOCUMENT 24: *Lovell v. City of Griffin* (1938)

Many legal scholars believe that the Fourteenth Amendment was intended to make the entire Bill of Rights binding on state and local government; however, the Supreme Court did not take that approach. Instead, it engaged in an incremental process, called incorporation, during which it defined so-called "fundamental" liberties and made those binding on the states through the language of the Fourteenth Amendment.

A year after Justice Benjamin Cardozo addressed the issue of incorporation of the First Amendment, the Supreme Court heard a Georgia free-speech case that offered an ideal vehicle for elaborating on that theme. In *Lovell* a unanimous Court (Cardozo, however, did not participate) declared the law in terms that are familiar to us today: freedom of speech and freedom of the press are fundamental liberties; the Fourteenth Amendment guarantees those liberties against state as well as federal infringement; a city ordinance forbidding distribution of literature without first gaining the permission of the city manager is void; the rules protecting freedom of the press are not limited to newspapers, but extend to pamphlets and leaflets.

\* \* \*

MR. CHIEF JUSTICE HUGHES delivered the opinion of the Court. . . .

The ordinance in question is as follows:

"Section 1. That the practice of distributing, either by hand or otherwise, circulars, handbooks, advertising, or literature of any kind, whether said articles are being delivered free, or whether same are being sold, within the limits of the City of Griffin, without first obtaining written permission from the City Manager of the City of Griffin, such practice shall be deemed a nuisance, and punishable as an offense against the City of Griffin. . . ."

The violation, which is not denied, consisted of the distribution without the required permission of a pamphlet and magazine in the nature of religious tracts, setting forth the gospel of the "Kingdom of Jehovah." Appellant did not apply for a permit, as she regarded herself as sent "by Jehovah to do His work" and that such an application would have been "an act of disobedience to His commandment." . . .

Freedom of speech and freedom of the press, which are protected by the First Amendment from infringement by Congress, are among the fundamental personal rights and liberties which are protected by the Fourteenth Amendment from invasion by state action. . . . It is also well settled that municipal ordinances adopted under state authority constitute state action and are within the prohibition of the amendment. . . .

The ordinance in its broad sweep prohibits the distribution of "circulars, handbooks, advertising, or literature of any kind." It manifestly applies to pamphlets, magazines and periodicals. The evidence against appellant was that she distributed a certain pamphlet and a magazine called the "Golden Age." Whether in actual administration the ordinance is applied, as apparently it could be, to newspapers does not appear. The City Manager testified that "every one applies to me for a license to distribute literature in this City. None of these people (including defendant) secured a permit from me to distribute literature in the City of Griffin." The ordinance is not limited to "literature" that is obscene or offensive to public morals or that advocates unlawful conduct. There is no suggestion that the pamphlet and magazine distributed in the instant case were of that character. The ordinance embraces "literature" in the widest sense. . . .

We think that the ordinance is invalid on its face. Whatever the motive which induced its adoption, its character is such that it strikes at the very foundation of the freedom of the press by subjecting it to license and censorship. The struggle for the freedom of the press was primarily directed against the power of the licensor. It was against that power that John Milton directed his assault by his "Appeal for the Liberty of Unlicensed Printing." And the liberty of the press became initially a right to publish *"without* a license what formerly could be published only *with* one."* While this freedom from previous restraint upon publication cannot be regarded as exhausting the guaranty of liberty, the prevention of that restraint was a leading purpose in the adoption of the constitutional provision. . . . Legislation of the type of the ordinance in question would restore the system of license and censorship in its baldest form.

The liberty of the press is not confined to newspapers and periodicals. It necessarily embraces pamphlets and leaflets. . . .

The ordinance cannot be saved because it relates to distribution and not to publication. "Liberty of circulating is as essential to that freedom as liberty of publishing; indeed, without the circulation, the publication would be of little value." . . .

As the ordinance is void on its face, it was not necessary for appellant to seek a permit under it. She was entitled to contest its validity in answer to the charge against her. . . .

The judgment is reversed and the cause is remanded for further proceedings not inconsistent with this opinion.

*Source*: 303 U.S. 444 (1938). Notes omitted.

---

## DOCUMENT 25: "Facts of Life" (*Time*, 1938)

While the *Lovell* case began to hint at a more vigorous concern for freedom of expression, official censorship continued to operate. On April 11, 1938—barely two weeks after the *Lovell* decision was handed down—*Life* magazine published pictures from an educational motion picture called *The Birth of a Baby*, and a firestorm erupted. The following article from *Time*, published on April 18, 1938, details public reaction to the publication and the various attempts to censor it.

\* \* \*

By a squeamish generation-before-last, "the facts of life" were considered shameful. That the process of which every human is a product is still considered so by countless people is not only a shameful but a dangerous state of affairs to U.S. doctors and health officers. Nevertheless, the old taboos die hard. Last week produced an interesting anomaly in the record of modern public health education: a four-page spread of text and pictures of how babies are born. Although it had been approved by the U.S. Post Office, it was banned by local law officers in the Commonwealth of Pennsylvania and some 60 other communities. No copies were permitted to cross the Canadian border. The birth pictures appeared in the April 11 issue of 17-month-old LIFE.

LIFE's pictures were taken from an educational motion picture called *The Birth of a Baby*. Produced twelve months ago by the American Committee on Maternal Welfare, Inc. and sponsored by 16 medical and social service societies, favorably previewed by a majority of 12,000 doctors and clubwomen, the picture showed a woman's life through pregnancy and childbirth (TIME, April 4). Climax of the film's 72 minutes was the actual birth of a baby. Medical groups from the American Medical Association down endorsed the film and its serious purpose: the reduction of sickness and death among mothers and offspring. Last week *The Birth of a Baby* was drawing crowds in Minnesota, but the problem of getting the picture past squeamish local censors had delayed its showing in many States, notably New York. At the suggestion of the film's producers, LIFE reproduced 35 pictures from the cinema. The magazine notified its 650,000 subscribers in advance, so that they could decide whether or not to let their children see them, printed the pictures in center pages so that they could be easily removed by family censors. The magazine's print order, 2,040,000, was held to the previous week's level.

Pittsfield, Mass. was the first to cry havoc. Police authorities in Boston and many other New England city jumped into line. New Orleans, one of the three cities west of the Mississippi which banned LIFE, used an 1884 statute to pull the magazine off the newsstands. In Tucson, only far-Western city to object, the publisher of the Arizona *Star* sold 25 copies of LIFE over his own counter in defiance of the police. The Memphis *Press-Scimitar* contrasted the local ban on LIFE with open sale at the same time of *Sex Guide, The Nudist* and *Tattle Tales*. Though William Jay Schieffelin, vice president of the New York Society for the Suppression of Vice, thought "LIFE rendered a public service by picturing in a decent way the facts about the birth of a baby which every child should know," New York State's Knights of Columbus complained to New York City's five county district attorneys. Result was that District Attorney Samuel L. Foley of The Bronx arrested four news dealers for selling indecent literature. LIFE prepared to defend them, as it did dealers in Boston.

Meantime, preponderantly to LIFE's defense sprang an articulate sector of the medical and social service professions. When the police chief of New Haven, Conn. confiscated copies and arrested a dealer, the testimony of two Yale medical professors and a Congregational minister persuaded a judge to dismiss the case. Said the minister, the Rev. Dr. Oscar Maurer: "The failure of parents to acquaint their offspring with the facts of life justifies public agencies doing so."

*Source*: "Facts of Life," *Time* 31, no. 16 (April 18, 1938): 57–58.

---

## DOCUMENT 26: *Schneider v. State (Town of Irvington)* (1939)

In 1939, the Supreme Court handed down an opinion invalidating four municipal ordinances which had restricted, but not outlawed, the distribution of leaflets in the public streets. The communities involved had each claimed a concern for littering and obstruction of traffic, rather than the messages being transmitted by the leaflets themselves. In striking down the ordinances, the Court engaged in the further development of rules that would become increasingly important in First Amendment free-speech analysis.

\* \* \*

MR. JUSTICE ROBERTS delivered the opinion of the Court.

Four cases are here, each of which presents the question whether regulations embodied in a municipal ordinance abridge the freedom of speech and of the press secured against state invasion by the Fourteenth Amendment of the Constitution. . . .

Although a municipality may enact regulations in the interest of the public safety, health, welfare or convenience, these may not abridge the individual liberties secured by the Constitution to those who wish to speak, write, print or circulate information or opinion.

Municipal authorities, as trustees for the public, have the duty to keep their communities' streets open and available for movement of people and property, the primary purpose to which the streets are dedicated. So long as legislation to this end does not abridge the constitutional liberty of one rightfully upon the street to impart information through speech or the distribution of literature, it may lawfully regulate the conduct of those using the streets. For example, a person could not exercise this liberty by taking his stand in the middle of a crowded street, contrary to traffic regulations, and maintain his position to the stoppage of all traffic; a group of distributors could not insist upon a constitutional right to form a cordon across the street and to allow no pedestrian to pass who did not accept a tendered leaflet; nor does the guarantee of freedom of speech or of the press deprive a municipality of power to enact regulations against throwing literature broadcast in the streets. Prohibition of such conduct would not abridge the constitutional liberty since such activity bears no necessary relationship to the freedom to speak, write, print or distribute information or opinion.

This court has characterized the freedom of speech and that of the press as fundamental personal rights and liberties. The phrase is not an empty one and was not lightly used. It reflects the belief of the framers of the Constitution that exercise of the rights lies at the foundation of free government by free men. It stresses, as do many opinions of this court, the importance of preventing the restriction of enjoyment of these liberties. . . .

The Los Angeles, the Milwaukee, and the Worcester ordinances under review do not purport to license distribution but all of them absolutely prohibit it in the streets and, one of them, in other public places as well. . . .

Conceding that fraudulent appeals may be made in the name of charity and religion, we hold a municipality cannot, for this reason, require all who wish to disseminate ideas to present them first to police authorities for their consideration and approval, with a discretion in the police to say some ideas may, while others may not, be carried to the homes of citizens; some persons may, while others may not, disseminate information from house to house. Frauds may be denounced as offenses and punished by law. Trespasses may similarly be forbidden. If it is said that these means are less efficient and convenient than bestowal of power on police authorities to decide what information may be disseminated from house to house, and who may impart the information, the answer is that considerations of this sort do not empower a municipality to abridge freedom of speech and press.

We are not to be taken as holding that commercial soliciting and canvassing may not be subjected to such regulation as the ordinance requires. Nor do we hold that the town may not fix reasonable hours when canvassing may be done by persons having such objects as the petitioner. Doubtless there are other features of such activities which may be regulated in the public interest without prior licensing or other invasion of constitutional liberty. We do hold, however, that the ordinance in question, as applied to the petitioner's conduct, is void, and she cannot be punished for acting without a permit.

The judgment in each case is reversed and the causes are remanded for further proceedings not inconsistent with this opinion.

*Reversed.*

*Source*: 308 U.S. 147 (1939).

---

## DOCUMENT 27: *Cantwell v. Connecticut* (1940)

With its decision in *Cantwell v. Connecticut* in 1940, the Supreme Court began to flesh out the doctrines that have become essential to our modern understanding of the First Amendment. The case involved distribution of literature on the streets by Jehovah's Witnesses. At times, the distribution was accompanied by solicitation of funds. Connecticut charged Jesse Cantwell with violating a statute that required a license to solicit. Because he had played a record containing anti-Catholic sentiments in a predominantly Catholic neighborhood, he was also charged with breach of the peace.

The Court reasoned that the license requirement amounted to a prior restraint of religious activity analogous to prior restraint of speech. With respect to the charge of breach of the peace, it expressed concern about the overbreadth of laws that allow the executive and judicial branches of government too wide a discretion in their application.

\* \* \*

MR. JUSTICE ROBERTS delivered the opinion of the Court.

... On the day of their arrest the appellants were engaged in going singly from house to house on Cassius Street in New Haven. They were individually equipped with a bag containing books and pamphlets on religious subjects, a portable phonograph and a set of records, each of which, when played, introduced, and was a description of, one of the books. Each appellant asked the person who responded to his call for permission to play one of the records. If permission was granted he asked the person to buy the book described and, upon refusal, he solicited such contribution towards the publication of the pamphlets as the listener was willing to make. If a contribution was received a pamphlet was delivered upon condition that it would be read.

Cassius Street is in a thickly populated neighborhood, where about ninety per cent of the residents are Roman Catholics. A phonograph record, describing a book entitled "Enemies," included an attack on the Catholic religion. None of the persons interviewed were members of Jehovah's Witnesses.

The statute under which the appellants were charged provides:

"No person shall solicit money, services, subscriptions or any valuable thing for any alleged religious, charitable or philanthropic cause, from other than a member of the organization for whose benefit such person is soliciting or within the county in which such person or organization is located unless such cause shall have been approved by the secretary of the public welfare council. Upon application of any person in behalf of such cause, the secretary shall determine whether such cause is a religious one or is a bona fide object of charity or philanthropy and conforms to reasonable standards of efficiency and integrity, and, if he shall so find, shall approve the same and issue to the authority in charge a certificate to that effect. Such certificate may be revoked at any time. Any person violating any provision of this section shall be fined not more than one hundred dollars or imprisoned not more than thirty days or both." ...

... We hold that the statute, as construed and applied to the appellants, deprives them of their liberty without due process of law in contravention of the Fourteenth Amendment. The fundamental concept of liberty embodied in that Amendment embraces the liberties guaranteed by the First Amendment. ... The constitutional inhibition of legislation on the subject of religion has a double aspect. On the one hand, it forestalls compulsion by law of the acceptance of any creed or the practice of any form of worship. Freedom of conscience and freedom to adhere to such religious organization or form of worship as the individual may choose cannot be restricted by law. On the other hand, it safeguards the free exercise of the chosen form of religion. Thus the Amendment embraces two concepts,—freedom to believe and freedom to act. The first is absolute but, in the nature of things, the second cannot be. Conduct remains subject to regulation for the protection of society. The freedom to act must have appropriate definition to preserve the enforcement of that protection. In every case the power to regulate must be so exercised as not, in attaining a permissible end, unduly to infringe the protected freedom. No one would contest the proposition that a State may not, by statute, wholly deny the right to preach or to disseminate religious views. Plainly such a previous and absolute restraint would violate the terms of the guarantee. It is equally clear that a State may by general and non-discriminatory legislation regulate the times, the places, and the manner of soliciting upon its streets, and of holding meetings thereon; and may in other respects safeguard the peace, good order and comfort of the community, without unconstitutionally invading the liberties protected by the Fourteenth Amendment. The appellants are right in their insistence that the Act in question is not such a regulation. If a certificate is procured, solicitation is permitted without restraint but, in the absence of a certificate, solicitation is altogether prohibited.

The appellants urge that to require them to obtain a certificate as a condition of soliciting support for their views amounts to a prior restraint on the exercise of their religion within the meaning of the Constitution. The State insists that the Act, as construed by the Supreme Court of Connecticut, imposes no previous restraint upon the dissemination of religious views or teaching but merely safeguards against the perpetration of frauds under the cloak of religion. Conceding that this is so, the question remains whether the method adopted by Connecticut to that end transgresses the liberty safeguarded by the Constitution.

The general regulation, in the public interest, of solicitation, which does not involve any religious test and does not unreasonably obstruct or delay the collection of funds, is not open to any constitutional objection, even though the collection be for a religious purpose. Such regulation would not constitute a prohibited previous restraint on the free exercise of religion or interpose an inadmissible obstacle to its exercise.

It will be noted, however, that the Act requires an application to the secretary of the public welfare council of the State; that he is empowered to determine whether the cause is a religious one, and that the issue of a certificate depends upon his affirmative action. If he finds that the cause is not that of religion, to solicit for it becomes a crime. He is not to issue a certificate as a matter of course. His decision to issue or refuse it involves appraisal of facts, the exercise of judgment, and the formation of an opinion. He is authorized to withhold his approval if he determines that the cause is not a religious one. Such a censorship of religion as the means of determining its right to survive is a denial of liberty protected by the First Amendment and included in the liberty which is within the protection of the Fourteenth. . . .

The offense known as breach of the peace embraces a great variety of conduct destroying or menacing public order and tranquility. It includes not only violent acts but acts and words likely to produce violence in others. No one would have the hardihood to suggest that the principle of freedom of speech sanctions incitement to riot or that religious liberty connotes the privilege to exhort others to physical attack upon those belonging to another sect. When clear and present danger of riot, disorder, interference with traffic upon the public streets, or other immediate threat to public safety, peace, or order, appears, the power of the State to prevent or punish is obvious. Equally obvious is it that a State may not unduly suppress free communication of views, religious or other, under the guise of conserving desirable conditions. Here we have a situation analogous to a conviction under a statute sweeping in a great variety of conduct under a general and indefinite characterization, and leaving to the executive and judicial branches too wide a discretion in its application.

Having these considerations in mind, we note that Jesse Cantwell, on April 26, 1938, was upon a public street, where he had a right to be, and where he had a right peacefully to impart his views to others. . . .

We find in the instant case no assault or threatening of bodily harm, no truculent bearing, no intentional discourtesy, no personal abuse. On the contrary, we find only an effort to persuade a willing listener to buy a book or to contribute money in the interest of what Cantwell, however misguided others may think him, conceived to be true religion.

In the realm of religious faith, and in that of political belief, sharp differences arise. In both fields the tenets of one man may seem the rankest error to his neighbor. To persuade others to his own point of view, the pleader, as we know, at times, resorts to exaggeration, to vilification of men who have been, or are, prominent in church or state, and even to false statement. But the people of this nation have ordained in the light of history, that, in spite of the probability of excesses and abuses, these liberties are, in the long view, essential to enlightened opinion and right conduct on the part of the citizens of a democracy.

*Source*: 310 U.S. 296 (1940).

---

## DOCUMENT 28: *Chaplinsky v. New Hampshire* (1942)

In *Chaplinsky*, the Supreme Court delivered its famous "fighting words" decision, an extension of the "clear and present danger" doctrine, upholding Chaplinsky's conviction for breach of the peace. The result in the case seems inconsistent with much of the language in *Cantwell*, issued a mere two years earlier.

The issue of whether any particular expression conveys an idea continues to be hotly debated today. Antipornography crusaders justify the suppression of material they deem obscene on the grounds that such materials do not convey ideas and are thus not entitled to First Amendment protection. Civil libertarians respond that it is precisely because an offensive idea is being transmitted that suppression is desired, and that it subverts the First Amendment to allow government to decide whether an utterance qualifies as an idea.

\* \* \*

MR. JUSTICE MURPHY delivered the opinion of the Court.

Appellant, a member of the sect known as Jehovah's Witnesses, was convicted . . . for violation of . . . the Public Laws of New Hampshire. . . .

The complaint charged that appellant, "with force and arms, in a certain public place in said city of Rochester, to wit, on the public sidewalk on the easterly side of Wakefield Street, near unto the entrance of the City Hall, did unlawfully repeat, the words following, addressed to the complainant, that is to say, 'You are a God damned racketeer' and 'a damned Fascist and the whole government of Rochester are Fascists or agents of Fascists,' the same being offensive, derisive and annoying words and names." . . .

. . . appellant raised the questions that the [New Hampshire] statute [prohibiting offensive, divisive, or annoying words] was invalid under the Fourteenth Amendment of the Constitution of the United States, in that it placed an unreasonable restraint on freedom of speech, freedom of the press, and freedom of worship, and because it was vague and indefinite. These contentions were overruled and the case comes here on appeal. . . .

Allowing the broadest scope to the language and purpose of the Fourteenth Amendment, it is well understood that the right of free speech is not absolute at all times and under all circumstances. There are certain well-defined and narrowly limited classes of speech, the prevention and punishment of which have never been thought to raise any Constitutional problem. These include the lewd and obscene, the profane, the libelous, and the insulting or "fighting" words—those which by their very utterance inflict injury or tend to incite an immediate breach of the peace. It has been well observed that such utterances are no essential part of any exposition of ideas, and are of such slight social value as a step to truth that any benefit that may be derived from them is clearly outweighed by the social interest in order and morality. "Resort to epithets or personal abuse is not in any proper sense communication of information or opinion safeguarded by the Constitution, and its punishment as a criminal act would raise no question under that instrument." . . .

We are unable to say that the limited scope of the statute as thus construed contravenes the Constitutional right of free expression. It is a statute narrowly drawn and limited to define and punish specific conduct lying within the domain of state power, the use in a public place of words likely to cause a breach of the peace. . . . This conclusion necessarily disposes of appellant's contention that the statute is so vague and indefinite as to render a conviction thereunder a violation of due process. A statute punishing verbal acts, carefully drawn so as not unduly to impair liberty of expression, is not too vague for a criminal law.

*Source*: 315 U.S. 568 (1942).

---

## DOCUMENT 29: *West Virginia State Board of Education v. Barnette* (1943)

In 1943, the Supreme Court handed down a watershed decision in *West Virginia State Board of Education v. Barnette*. The issue was deceptively simple: could a state require the children of Jehovah's Witnesses to salute the flag, in violation of their religious beliefs, as a condition of public school attendance? The Court had affirmed the practice just three years before, in *Minersville School District v. Gobitis*. In the midst of the Second World War, expressions of patriotism were taken very seriously; across the nation, Jehovah's Witnesses and their children were physically and verbally abused for their refusal to salute the flag. Some were seriously hurt. Meanwhile, in the wake of the *Gobitis* decision, school boards around the country had adopted rules punishing and expelling children who refused to salute the flag.

Indeed, the *Barnette* case presents a fundamental dilemma that continues to bedevil the American system. If the Bill of Rights is intended as a libertarian "brake" on the power of the majority, how far can the courts go in invalidating the will of the citizenry, expressed at the ballot box in a democratic system? What is the balance to be achieved between the will of the people and the rights that are guaranteed to individuals? *Barnette* goes to the heart of the tension inherent in the American system.

\* \* \*

MR. JUSTICE JACKSON delivered the opinion of the Court. . . .

Appellees, citizens of the United States and of West Virginia, brought suit in the United States District Court for themselves and others similarly situated asking its injunction to restrain enforcement of these laws and regulations against Jehovah's Witnesses. The Witnesses are an unincorporated body teaching that the obligation imposed by law of God is superior to that of laws enacted by temporal government. Their religious beliefs include a literal version of Exodus, Chapter 20, verses 4 and 5, which says: "Thou shalt not make unto thee any graven image, or any likeness of anything that is in heaven above, or that is in the earth beneath, or that is in the water under the earth; thou shalt not bow down thyself to them nor serve them." They consider that the flag is an "image" within this command. For this reason they refuse to salute it. . . .

The freedom asserted by these appellees does not bring them into collision with rights asserted by any other individual. It is such conflicts which most frequently require intervention of the State to determine where the rights of one end and those of another begin. But the refusal of these persons to participate in the ceremony does not interfere with or deny rights of others to do so. Nor is there any question in this case that their behavior is peaceable and orderly. The sole conflict is between authority and rights of the individual. The State asserts power to condition access to public education on making a prescribed sign and profession and at the same time to coerce attendance by punishing both parent and child. The latter stand on a right of self-determination in matters that touch individual opinion and personal attitude. . . .

. . . It is now a commonplace that censorship or suppression of expression of opinion is tolerated by our Constitution only when the expression presents a clear and present danger of action of a kind the State is empowered to prevent and punish. It would seem that involuntary affirmation could be commanded only on even more immediate and urgent grounds than silence. But here the power of compulsion is invoked without any allegation that remaining passive during a flag salute ritual creates a clear and present danger that would justify an effort even to muffle expression. To sustain the compulsory flag salute we are required to say that a Bill of Rights which guards the individual's right to speak his own mind, left it open to public authorities to compel him to utter what is not in his mind. . . .

. . . The question which underlies the flag salute controversy is whether such a ceremony so touching matters of opinion and political attitude may be imposed upon the individual by official authority under powers committed to any political organization under our Constitution. . . .

The Fourteenth Amendment, as now applied to the States, protects the citizen against the State itself and all of its creatures—Boards of Education not excepted. These have, of course, important, delicate, and highly discretionary functions, but none that they may not perform within the limits of the Bill of Rights. That they are educating the young for citizenship is reason for scrupulous protection of Constitutional freedoms of the individual, if we are not to strangle the free mind at its source and teach youth to discount important principles of our government as mere platitudes. . . .

The very purpose of a Bill of Rights was to withdraw certain subjects from the vicissitudes of political controversy, to place them beyond the reach of majorities and officials and to establish them as legal principles to be applied by the courts. . . .

National unity as an end which officials may foster by persuasion and example is not in question. The problem is whether under our Constitution compulsion as here employed is a permissible means for its achievement. . . .

The case is made difficult not because the principles of its decision are obscure but because the flag involved is our own. Nevertheless, we apply the limitations of the Constitution with no fear that freedom to be intellectually and spiritually diverse or even contrary will disintegrate the social organization. To believe that patriotism will not flourish if patriotic ceremonies are voluntary and spontaneous instead of a compulsory routine is to make an unflattering estimate of the appeal of our institutions to free minds. We can have intellectual individualism and the rich cultural diversities that we owe to exceptional minds only at the price of occasional eccentricity and abnormal attitudes. When they are so harmless to others or to the State as those we deal with here, the price is not too great. But freedom to differ is not limited to things that do not matter much. That would be a mere shadow of freedom. The test of its substance is the right to differ as to things that touch the heart of the existing order.

If there is any fixed star in our constitutional constellation, it is that no official, high or petty, can prescribe what shall be orthodox in politics, nationalism, religion, or other matters of opinion or force citizens to confess by word or act their faith therein. If there are any circumstances which permit an exception, they do not now occur to us.

We think the action of the local authorities in compelling the flag salute and pledge transcends constitutional limitations on their power and invades the sphere of intellect and spirit which it is the purpose of the First Amendment to our Constitution to reserve from all official control.

The decision of this Court in *Minersville School District v. Gobitis* and the holdings of those few *per curiam* decisions which preceded and foreshadowed it are overruled, and the judgment enjoining enforcement of the West Virginia Regulation is

*Affirmed.*

*  *  *

Mr. Justice Black and Mr. Justice Douglas, concurring: . . .

Words uttered under coercion are proof of loyalty to nothing but self-interest. Love of country must spring from willing hearts and free minds, inspired by a fair administration of wise laws enacted by the people's elected representatives within the bounds of express constitutional prohibitions. These laws must, to be consistent with the First Amendment, permit the widest toleration of conflicting viewpoints consistent with a society of free men.

*Source*: 319 U.S. 624 (1943).

# DOCUMENT 30: "The Easy Chair" (Bernard DeVoto, 1944)

In 1944, Bernard DeVoto, a well-known writer, agreed to help the Massachusetts Civil Liberties Union (the Massachusetts affiliate of the American Civil Liberties Union) mount a challenge to a statute prohibiting the purchase or sale of "obscene" books. DeVoto arranged to purchase *Strange Fruit*, a book by one Lillian Smith, from a shopowner who had also volunteered to violate the law in the interest of testing its constitutionality. The following article was written by DeVoto for *Harper's Magazine*, where it appeared in July 1944. If the piece sounds contemporary, it is because these same arguments and counterarguments are still being made, although usually with respect to library video policies, rap-music lyrics, and the Internet rather than books.

*  *  *

In the May Easy Chair I described the illegal suppression in Boston of Miss Lillian Smith's novel, *Strange Fruit*. . . .

It was decided to force the responsible public officials to accept responsibility for the suppression of *Strange Fruit*. A Cambridge bookseller proved willing to sell a copy of the novel for the purpose of making a test case. The Civil Liberties Union asked me to buy a copy from him. When our arrangements had been made, we asked the publishers of the book to co-operate with us and they agreed to. I take care to say this flatly, for some of our opponents have repeatedly alleged in print that the test case was made on the publishers' initiative and for the primary purpose of advertising the book. That allegation is entirely untrue. . . .

In the presence of the Cambridge police, then, I bought a copy of the novel from the bookseller. The police confiscated it, charged me with buying an obscene book with intent to lend or circulate it, and charged the bookseller with possessing an obscene book with intent to sell, and with selling it. In the lower court I was found not guilty and the bookseller was found guilty on both counts. . . .

. . . the stature [in question] stimulates meditation. It covers every kind of printed matter, picture, image, phonograph record, "or other thing" which is obscene, indecent, or impure, or manifestly tends to corrupt the morals of youth. The statute makes it a crime to import, print, publish, sell, or distribute any such item. It makes it a crime to introduce such an item into a school or into a family. Finally, it makes it a crime to receive or to possess such an item for the purpose of exhibiting it or loaning it, or with intent to introduce it into a family.

I count myself an ordinary and ordinarily decent citizen. I have a library of several thousand volumes. By the interpretation adopted by the police, by the criteria of the Boston booksellers' committee and the local society which undertakes to improve Boston morals, many hundreds of those volumes come under the statute. I bought them with intent to introduce them into a home, my own. I have lent many of them. I have received many from publishers without paying for them, and the publishers introduced them into my home. Unless a high court construes the statute otherwise, then, I have committed, not once but many hundreds of times, a crime punishable by a fine of two thousand dollars and a sentence of two and one-half years in jail. Every official and every trustee of a public library in Massachusetts has frequently committed the same crime. Many thousands of citizens of Massachusetts commit that crime every day. . . .

I think it is futile to try, for purposes of literary censorship, to define impurity, indecency, and a manifest tendency to corrupt the morals of youth. And I think it is extremely dangerous to forbid the ownership of any books whatsoever and almost as dangerous to try to limit their circulation. To establish a reliable public policy I am willing to compromise with those who think otherwise—I am willing to state a point beyond which I will not urge the individual's rights if my adversaries will secure him so far. But I do so in a profound conviction that if there be any evil in circulating literature, any measure to limit it is a far greater danger than the one it undertakes to prevent.

Our opponents try to define erotic stimulation in such a way that they can, so they believe, limit it short of action. There is no satisfactory index to such a definition and I can imagine no limitation that would not seriously infringe basic rights. Certainly literature can be an erotic stimulant, though certainly also it must always be one of the weakest. But it is absurd to limit literature while other, stronger stimulants go free—

and it is quite impossible to determine what they may be. Everyone knows from his own experience—and psychology would inform him if he did not—that the world is full of sexual stimulants, that casual and accidental association may endow anything at all with erotic significance and so with the power of stimulation. Everyone lives his daily life in an environment which at any moment may thrust sex into his consciousness—from the song of birds to the melody of a waltz, from a department store window to the way a woman walks down a sidewalk, from a glimpse of a landscape to a memory of one's youth. The idea that the world can be wiped free of such suggestions is not only abhorrent, it is obviously preposterous. Moreover, I do not understand the ground on which anyone who may chance to want casual stimulation, from literature or otherwise, can be denied it.

In fact, we must go well beyond that. The Bible, Shakespeare, and many other literary classics contain impure, obscene, or sexually stimulating passages but no one would forbid their circulation—they are not obscene books, they do not manifestly tend to corrupt the morals of youth. The same must be said of all seriously written fiction, poetry, and drama. But I doubt if society can, either intelligently or expediently, draw the line I draw when I say "seriously written."

Take a celebrated eighteenth-century novel, *The Memoirs of a Prostitute*. It is graceful, charming, and amusing—and it is pornographic in fact and in intent. But I can see no grounds in law or statecraft on which John Doe, the ordinary decent citizen, can be forbidden to own it or to lend it privately to his friends. If John Doe must not be constrained, on what ground can we deny the same freedom to Richard Roe, who is perhaps by no means ordinarily decent? In short, how and wherefore can we prohibit even vulgar, disgusting and deliberately exciting pornography to either Doe or Roe so long as he remains orderly in possessing it and uses it in socially inoffensive ways? I happen to dislike blatant pornography, but neither dislike nor a difference of taste sanctions me to forbid it to others. Taste, fastidiousness, and moral judgment are one thing, but the legal enforcement of them on others is something else. I do not see how such discriminations can be given the sanction of law without curtailing a basic civil right. The right to own and read pornography appears to me unquestionable.

Justice Holmes reminded us that the freedom constitutionally guaranteed the press extends to ideas which, perhaps, we may hate and abhor. It is the hateful, the abhorrent idea whose freedom must be most vigorously defended, since there will be serious pressure against no other ideas. This principle is nowhere more urgent than in literature which deals with the perilous and paradoxical matter of sex, since not only our most profound beliefs are involved but also inflammatory prejudices and violent unconscious drives. The right to treat sex decently must by all means be secured, and most protests against censorship, including our current one, are intended to secure that right. But there would appear to be another right as well, a right to write and read pornography in socially peaceful ways. Whether there is or not, I can see no way of giving indecency a legal definition without opening the door to evils far worse than indecency.

Those who hold otherwise think of literature as an incitement to action. We must forbid people to read a given book, they believe, because if they read it they will forthwith seek sexual intercourse, perhaps committing seduction or rape in their haste. One of my current opponents holds that we must not modify the Massachusetts statute because "every time there is a sex murder we find the murderer's room full of sex pulp magazines." The more common argument is that though adults cannot be driven wild by a printed page we must not let them have a given book because some adolescent might get hold of it. But we must take care of the potential sex murderer as we take care of other psychopaths. We do not forbid the sale of liquor because dipsomaniacs use it, of matches because pyromaniacs use them, or of automobiles because nymphomaniacs use them. We put no limitation on their socially acceptable use, and refuse to regard them as incitements to crime on the ground that the young or the morally crippled have access to them. We protect society from the psychopath, we do not force it to conform to his disease. And, even if elements of society are dangerous to adolescents, we cannot rearrange it for their protection. After the ordinary measures of public safety have been taken, the ordinary activity of adults must proceed without reference to the young.

It is obviously true that an adolescent may encounter a book in a private home or a public library or a bookstore. But that risk, and the supposed risk that it may excite him, cannot be obviated without curtailing the essential liberties of everyone. A clear and present danger, I am willing to agree, might be a peddler trying to sell blatant pornography to high-school students in the back rooms of corner stores. I am willing to forbid the *surreptitious* sale of such literature to adolescents. I am willing to make it illegal, on behalf of adolescents—and on behalf of the inevitable father who touches off most censorship in the fear, the usually belated fear, that his daughter may find something in a book that is altogether new to her.

But I require something of that father in return. He must help me to make sure that the police, once they have been empowered to do so much, do not do more. He must defend the rights of adults to read whatever they may choose to read. He must defend them, especially, in their right to read books whose treatment of sex he himself hates and abhors. He must bind himself to do so in the contract which binds me to protect his daughter from pornography. But let him do so for a weightier reason as well: that, if he does not, then he and all the rest of us will be put in peril. . . .

Between protecting your daughter from the chance of encountering *The Memoirs of a Prostitute* and forbidding you to read *Venus and Adonis* or the nineteenth chapter of Genesis there is only a single step, across an almost impalpable line. But short as that step is, the next one is still shorter. Once taken, it will forbid you to read whatever offends the caprice or endangers the interest of those who make the prohibition— Marx, the catechism, the Declaration of Independence, Mr. Roosevelt's speeches, or the editorial page of a newspaper which any gang of revolutionaries, bigots, ward politicians, or mere fools may happen to hate, fear, or dislike. That knife is at your throat and you put it there when you consented to the first step. You consented to the political infringement of an intellectual liberty, and there are always forces interested in extending that infringement. When you voluntarily agreed to the first step, you agreed to let a breach be made in the common, fundamental defense. That breach is an open invitation to whoever may profit by widening it.

*Source*: Bernard DeVoto, "The Easy Chair: The Strange Fruit Case," *Harper's Magazine* 189 (July 1944), 148–151.

# Part IV

# The 1950s: McCarthyism, Racism, and Censorship

It has become fashionable with the passage of time to look back on the 1950s as an idyllic era, a time when every neat, suburban home had a tidy front yard, and the intact family's dad barbecued on the patio while mom baked cookies in the kitchen and Junior and Sally romped with Spot the dog. The doors did not need to be locked, and everyone went to church on Sunday. While that reality undoubtedly existed for some, there were far less pleasant realities for people unfortunate enough to belong to despised political, racial, or religious minorities.

The 1950s were characterized by the excesses of Senator Joseph McCarthy, whose name has become shorthand for the witch-hunts of the House Un-American Activities Committee and the responses to those activities: the infamous Hollywood blacklist, which destroyed the careers of hundreds of talented people who were suspected of Communist sympathies; the copious files on Americans from every walk of life maintained by J. Edgar Hoover, director of the Federal Bureau of Investigation who cited national security concerns but frequently used information uncovered by the FBI to exert political muscle; the sensationalized treason trials of Alger Hiss (indicted in 1948, but convicted in 1950) and Julius and Ethel Rosenberg; and the passage of legislation intended to protect America from Communist infiltration by severely restricting what individual Americans could read and with whom they might safely associate.

It is easy to criticize the government's overreaction today, when the Soviet Union no longer exists and historical evidence of any significant domestic threat to the United States is scant. But the Soviet threat was very real in the 1950s, and the outcome of the Cold War was by no means certain. We must examine the actions taken with a due regard for the information then available. Even the American Civil Liberties Union, that paragon of free-speech protection, went through an anti-Communist stage in the 1950s, expelling suspected Communists from its board.

Adding to the social turmoil created by the Cold War was the beginning of the civil rights movement. Whites and blacks alike were coming to recognize that political organization was essential if the treatment of African Americans was to be improved. The country would not pass civil rights legislation until 1964; the years leading up to that achievement were characterized by the growth of organizations like the National Association for the Advancement of Colored People (NAACP) that were dedicated to obtaining equal treatment under the law for black citizens. These associations were viewed with great alarm, not just by states (predominantly but not exclusively southern) where segregation was strongest, but by those who viewed all disaffected groups as breeding grounds for Communist infiltration. The seeds of the tumultuous 1960s were all taking root beneath the seemingly serene surface of the 1950s.

---

## DOCUMENT 31: The Internal Security Act of 1950 (The McCarran Act)

---

The decade began with the passage by Congress, over President Truman's veto, of the Internal Security Act of 1950, also known as the McCarran Act. The measure restricted immigration (forbidding entry to communists, "totalitarians" and their sympathizers) and made it easier to deport resident aliens who were suspected of complicity with the feared "communist menace." The measure was initially sponsored by then Representative Richard Nixon and Representative Karl Mundt. In the Senate, it owed its passage to the sponsorship of Patrick McCarran, who headed the Senate Judiciary Committee.

* * *

NECESSITY FOR LEGISLATION

SEC. 2. As a result of evidence adduced before various committees of the Senate and House of Representatives, the Congress hereby finds that—

(1) There exists a world Communist movement which, in its origins,

its development, and its present practice, is a world-wide revolutionary movement whose purpose it is, by treachery, deceit, infiltration into other groups (governmental and otherwise), espionage, sabotage, terrorism, and any other means deemed necessary, to establish a Communist totalitarian dictatorship in the countries throughout the world through the medium of a world-wide Communist organization.

(2) The establishment of a totalitarian dictatorship in any country results in the suppression of all opposition to the party in power, the subordination of the rights of individuals to the state, the denial of fundamental rights and liberties which are characteristic of a representative form of government, such as freedom of speech, of the press, of assembly, and of religious worship, and results in the maintenance of control over the people through fear, terrorism, and brutality.

(3) The system of government known as a totalitarian dictatorship is characterized by the existence of a single political party, organized on a dictatorial basis, and by substantial identity between such party and its policies and the government and governmental policies of the country in which it exists.

(4) The direction and control of the world Communist movement is vested in and exercised by the Communist dictatorship of a foreign country.

(5) The Communist dictatorship of such foreign country, in exercising such direction and control and in furthering the purposes of the world Communist movement, establishes or causes the establishment of, and utilizes, in various countries, action organizations which are not free and independent organizations, but are sections of a world-wide Communist organization and are controlled, directed, and subject to the discipline of the Communist dictatorship of such foreign country.

(6) The Communist action organizations so established and utilized in various countries, acting under such control, direction, and discipline, endeavor to carry out the objectives of the world Communist movement by bringing about the overthrow of existing governments by any available means, including force if necessary, and setting up Communist totalitarian dictatorships which will be subservient to the most powerful existing Communist totalitarian dictatorship. Although such organizations usually designate themselves as political parties, they are in fact constituent elements of the world-wide Communist movement and promote the objectives of such movement by conspiratorial and coercive tactics, instead of through the democratic processes of a free elective system or through the freedom-preserving means employed by a political party which operates as an agency by which people govern themselves.

(7) In carrying on the activities referred to in paragraph (6), such

Communist organizations in various countries are organized on a secret, conspiratorial basis and operate to a substantial extent through organizations, commonly known as "Communist fronts", which in most instances are created and maintained, or used, in such manner as to conceal the facts as to their true character and purposes and their membership. One result of this method of operation is that such affiliated organizations are able to obtain financial and other support from persons who would not extend such support if they knew the true purposes of, and the actual nature of the control and influence exerted upon, such "Communist fronts".

(8) Due to the nature and scope of the world Communist movement, with the existence of affiliated constituent elements working toward common objectives in various countries of the world, travel of Communist members, representatives, and agents from country to country facilitates communication and is a prerequisite for the carrying on of activities to further the purposes of the Communist movement.

(9) In the United States those individuals who knowingly and willfully participate in the world Communist movement, when they so participate, in effect repudiate their allegiance to the United States, and in effect transfer their allegiance to the foreign country in which is vested the direction and control of the world Communist movement.

(10) In pursuance of communism's stated objectives, the most powerful existing Communist dictatorship has, by the methods referred to above, already caused the establishment in numerous foreign countries of Communist totalitarian dictatorships, and threatens to establish similar dictatorships in still other countries.

(11) The agents of communism have devised clever and ruthless espionage and sabotage tactics which are carried out in many instances in form or manner successfully evasive of existing law.

(12) The Communist network in the United States is inspired and controlled in large part by foreign agents who are sent into the United States ostensibly as attachés of foreign legations, affiliates of international organizations, members of trading commissions, and in similar capacities, but who use their diplomatic or semidiplomatic status as a shield behind which to engage in activities prejudicial to the public security.

(13) There are, under our present immigration laws, numerous aliens who have been found to be deportable, many of whom are in the subversive, criminal, or immoral classes who are free to roam the country at will without supervision or control.

(14) One device for infiltration by Communists is by procuring naturalization for disloyal aliens who use their citizenship as a badge for admission into the fabric of our society.

(15) The Communist movement in the United States is an organi-

zation numbering thousands of adherents, rigidly and ruthlessly disciplined. Awaiting and seeking to advance a moment when the United States may be so far extended by foreign engagements, so far divided in counsel, or so far in industrial or financial straits, that overthrow of the Government of the United States by force and violence may seem possible of achievement, it seeks converts far and wide by an extensive system of schooling and indoctrination. Such preparations by Communist organizations in other countries have aided in supplanting existing governments. The Communist organization in the United States, pursuing its stated objectives, the recent successes of Communist methods in other countries, and the nature and control of the world Communist movement itself, present a clear and present danger to the security of the United States and to the existence of free American institutions, and make it necessary that Congress, in order to provide for the common defense, to preserve the sovereignty of the United States as an independent nation, and to guarantee to each State a republican form of government, enact appropriate legislation recognizing the existence of such world-wide conspiracy and designed to prevent it from accomplishing its purpose in the United States.

DEFINITIONS

Sec. 3. For the purposes of this title—

(1) The term "person" means an individual or an organization.

(2) The term "organization" means an organization, corporation, company, partnership, association, trust, foundation, or fund; and includes a group of persons, whether or not incorporated, permanently or temporarily associated together for joint action on any subject or subjects.

(3) The term "Communist-action organization" means—

(a) any organization in the United States (other than a diplomatic representative or mission of a foreign government accredited as such by the Department of State) which (i) is substantially directed, dominated, or controlled by the foreign government or foreign organization controlling the world Communist movement referred to in section 2 of this title, and (ii) operates primarily to advance the objectives of such world Communist movement as referred to in section 2 of this title; and

(b) any section, branch, fraction, or cell of any organization defined in subparagraph (a) of this paragraph which has not complied with the registration requirements of this title.

(4) The term "Communist-front organization" means any organization in the United States (other than a Communist-action organization as defined in paragraph (3) of this section) which (A) is substantially directed, dominated, or controlled by a Communist-action organization, and (B)

is primarily operated for the purpose of giving aid and support to a Communist-action organization, a Communist foreign government or the world Communist movement referred to in section 2 of this title.

(5) The term "Communist organization" means a Communist-action organization or a Communist-front organization.

(6) The term "to contribute funds or services" includes the rendering of any personal service and the making of any gift, subscription, loan, advance, or deposit, of money or of anything of value, and also the making of any contract, promise, or agreement to contribute funds or services, whether or not legally enforcible.

(7) The term "facility" means any plant, factory or other manufacturing, producing or service establishment, airport, airport facility, vessel, pier, water-front facility, mine, railroad, public utility, laboratory, station, or other establishment or facility, or any part, division, or department of any of the foregoing. The term "defense facility" means any facility designated and proclaimed by the Secretary of Defense pursuant to section 5 (b) of this title and included on the list published and currently in effect under such subsection, and which is in compliance with the provisions of such subsection respecting the posting of notice of such designation.

(8) The term "publication" means any circular, newspaper, periodical, pamphlet, book, letter, post card, leaflet, or other publication.

(9) The term "United States", when used in a geographical sense, includes the several States, Territories, and possessions of the United States, the District of Columbia, and the Canal Zone.

(10) The term "interstate or foreign commerce" means trade, traffic, commerce, transportation, or communication (A) between any State, Territory, or possession of the United States (including the Canal Zone), or the District of Columbia, and any place outside thereof, or (B) within any Territory or possession of the United States (including the Canal Zone), or within the District of Columbia.

(11) The term "Board" means the Subversive Activities Control Board created by section 12 of this title.

(12) The term "final order of the Board" means an order issued by the Board under section 13 of this title, which has become final as provided in section 14 of this title.

(13) The term "advocates" includes advises, recommends, furthers by overt act, and admits belief in; and the giving, loaning, or promising of support or of money or anything of value to be used for advocating any doctrine shall be deemed to constitute the advocating of such doctrine.

(14) The term "world communism" means a revolutionary movement, the purpose of which is to establish eventually a Communist totalitarian dictatorship in any or all the countries of the world through the medium of an internationally coordinated Communist movement.

(15) The terms "totalitarian dictatorship" and "totalitarianism" mean and refer to systems of government not representative in fact, characterized by (A) the existence of a single political party, organized on a dictatorial basis, with so close an identity between such party and its policies and the governmental policies of the country in which it exists, that the party and the government constitute an indistinguishable unit, and (B) the forcible suppression of opposition to such party.

(16) The term "doctrine" includes, but is not limited to, policies, practices, purposes, aims, or procedures.

(17) The giving, loaning, or promising of support or of money or any other thing of value for any purpose to any organization shall be conclusively presumed to constitute affiliation therewith; but nothing in this paragraph shall be construed as an exclusive definition of affiliation.

(18) "Advocating the economic, international, and governmental doctrines of world communism" means advocating the establishment of a totalitarian Communist dictatorship in any or all of the countries of the world through the medium of an internationally coordinated Communist movement.

(19) "Advocating the economic and governmental doctrines of any other form of totalitarianism" means advocating the establishment of totalitarianism (other than world communism) and includes, but is not limited to, advocating the economic and governmental doctrines of fascism and nazism.

### CERTAIN PROHIBITED ACTS

SEC. 4. (a) It shall be unlawful for any person knowingly to combine, conspire, or agree with any other person to perform any act which would substantially contribute to the establishment within the United States of a totalitarian dictatorship, as defined in paragraph (15) of section 3 of this title, the direction and control of which is to be vested in, or exercised by or under the domination or control of, any foreign government, foreign organization, or foreign individual: *Provided, however,* That this subsection shall not apply to the proposal of a constitutional amendment.

(b) It shall be unlawful for any officer or employee of the United States or of any department or agency thereof, or of any corporation the stock of which is owned in whole or in major part by the United States or any department or agency thereof, to communicate in any manner or by any means, to any other person whom such officer or employee knows or has reason to believe to be an agent or representative of any foreign government or an officer or member of any Communist organization as defined in paragraph (5) of section 3 of this title, any information of a kind which shall have been classified by the President (or by the head of any such department, agency, or corporation with the approval of the President) as affecting the security of the United States, knowing or having reason to know that such information has been so classified, unless such officer or employees shall have been specifically authorized by the President, or by the head of the department, agency, or corporation by which this officer or employee is employed, to make such disclosure of such information.

(c) It shall be unlawful for any agent or representative of any foreign government, or any officer or member of any Communist organization as defined in paragraph (5) of section 3 of this title, knowingly to obtain or receive, or attempt to obtain or receive, directly or indirectly, from any officer or employee of the United States or of any department or agency thereof or of any corporation the stock of which is owned in whole or in major part by the United States or any department or agency thereof, any information of a kind which shall have been classified by the President (or by the head of any such department, agency, or corporation with the approval of the President) as affecting the security of the United States, unless special authorization for such communication shall first have been obtained from the head of the department, agency, or corporation having custody of or control over such information.

(d) Any person who violates any provision of this section shall, upon conviction thereof, be punished by a fine of not more than $10,000, or imprisonment for not more than ten years, or by both such fine and such imprisonment, and shall, moreover, be thereafter ineligible to hold any office, or place of honor, profit, or trust created by the Constitution or laws of the United States.

(e) Any person may be prosecuted, tried, and punished for any violation of this section at any time within ten years after the commission of such offense, notwithstanding the provisions of any other statute of limitations: *Provided,* That if at the time of the commission of the offense such person is an officer or employee of the United States or of any department or agency thereof, or of any corporation the stock of which is owned in whole or in major part by the United States or any department or agency thereof, such person may be prosecuted, tried, and punished for any violation of this section at any time within ten years after such person has ceased to be employed as such officer or employee.

(f) Neither the holding of office nor membership in any Communist organization by any person shall constitute per se a violation of subsection (a) or subsection (c) of this section or of any other criminal statute. The fact of the registration of any person under section 7 or section 8 of this title as an officer or member of any Communist organization shall not be received in evidence against such person in any prosecution for any alleged violation of subsection (a) or subsection (c) of this section or for any alleged violation of any other criminal statute.

EMPLOYMENT OF MEMBERS OF COMMUNIST ORGANIZATIONS

SEC. 5. (a) When a Communist organization, as defined in paragraph (5) of section 3 of this title, is registered or there is in effect a final order of the Board requiring such organization to register, it shall be unlawful—

(1) For any member of such organization, with knowledge or notice that such organization is so registered or that such order has become final—

(A) in seeking, accepting, or holding any nonelective office or employment under the United States, to conceal or fail to disclose the fact that he is a member of such organization; or

(B) to hold any nonelective office or employment under the United States; or

(C) in seeking, accepting, or holding employment in any defense facility, to conceal or fail to disclose the fact that he is a member of such organization; or

(D) if such organization is a Communist-action organization, to engage in any employment in any defense facility.

(2) For any officer or employee of the United States or of any defense facility, with knowledge or notice that such organization is so registered or that such order has become final—

(A) to contribute funds or services to such organization; or

(B) to advise, counsel or urge any person, with knowledge or notice that such person is a member of such organization, to perform, or to omit to perform, any act if such act or omission would constitute a violation of any provision of subparagraph (1) of this subsection.

(b) The Secretary of Defense is authorized and directed to designate and proclaim, and from time to time revise, a list of facilities, as defined in paragraph (7) of section 3 of this title, with respect to the operation of which he finds and determines that the security of the United States requires the application of the provisions of subsection (a) of this section. The Secretary shall cause such list as designated and proclaimed, or any revision thereof, to be promptly published in the Federal Register, and shall promptly notify the management of any facility so listed; whereupon such management shall immediately post conspicuously, and thereafter while so listed keep posted, notice of such designation in such form and in such place or places as to give reasonable notice thereof to all employees of, and to all applicants for employment in, such facility.

(c) As used in this section, the term "member" shall not include any individual whose name has not been made public because of the prohibition contained in section 9 (b) of this title.

DENIAL OF PASSPORTS TO MEMBERS OF COMMUNIST ORGANIZATIONS

SEC. 6. (a) When a Communist organization as defined in paragraph (5) of section 3 of this title is registered, or there is in effect a final order of the Board requiring such organization to register, it shall be unlawful for any member of such organization, with knowledge or notice that such organization is so registered or that such order has become final—

    (1) to make application for a passport, or the renewal of a passport, to be issued or renewed by or under the authority of the United States; or

    (2) to use or attempt to use any such passport.

(b) When an organization is registered, or there is in effect a final order of the Board requiring an organization to register, as a Communist-action organization, it shall be unlawful for any officer or employee of the United States to issue a passport to, or renew the passport of, any individual knowing or having reason to believe that such individual is a member of such organization.

(c) As used in this section, the term "member" shall not include any individual whose name has not been made public because of the prohibition contained in section 9 (b) of this title.

REGISTRATION AND ANNUAL REPORTS OF COMMUNIST ORGANIZATIONS

SEC. 7. (a) Each Communist-action organization (including any organization required, by a final order of the Board, to register as a Communist-action organization) shall, within the time specified in subsection (c) of this section, register with the Attorney General, on a form prescribed by him by regulations, as a Communist-action organization.

(b) Each Communist-front organization (including any organization required, by a final order of the Board, to register as a Communist-front organization) shall, within the time specified in subsection (c) of this section, register with the Attorney General, on a form prescribed by him by regulations, as a Communist-front organization.

(c) The registration required by subsection (a) or (b) shall be made—

    (1) in the case of an organization which is a Communist-action organization or a Communist-front organization on the date of the enactment of this title, within thirty days after such date;

    (2) in the case of an organization becoming a Communist-action organization or a Communist-front organization after the date of the enactment of this title, within thirty days after such organization becomes a Communist-action organization or a Communist-front organization, as the case may be; and

    (3) in the case of an organization which by a final order of the Board is required to register, within thirty days after such order becomes final.

(d) The registration made under subsection (a) or (b) shall be accompanied by a registration statement, to be prepared and filed in such manner and form as the Attorney General shall by regulations prescribe, containing the following information:

(1) The name of the organization and the address of its principal office.

(2) The name and last-known address of each individual who is at the time of filing of such registration statement, and of each individual who was at any time during the period of twelve full calendar months next preceding the filing of such statement, an officer of the organization, with the designation or title of the office so held, and with a brief statement of the duties and functions of such individual as such officer.

(3) An accounting, in such form and detail as the Attorney General shall by regulations prescribe, of all moneys received and expended (including the sources from which received and the purposes for which expended) by the organization during the period of twelve full calendar months next preceding the filing of such statement.

(4) In the case of a Communist-action organization, the name and last-known address of each individual who was a member of the organization at any time during the period of twelve full calendar months preceding the filing of such statement.

(5) In the case of any officer or member whose name is required to be shown in such statement, and who uses or has used or who is or has been known by more than one name, each name which such officer or member uses or has used or by which he is known or has been known.

(e) It shall be the duty of each organization registered under this section to file with the Attorney General on or before February 1 of the year following the year in which it registers, and on or before February 1 of each succeeding year, an annual report, prepared and filed in such manner and form as the Attorney General shall by regulations prescribe, containing the same information which by subsection (d) is required to be included in a registration statement, except that the information required with respect to the twelve-month period referred to in paragraph (2), (3), or (4) of such subsection shall, in such annual report, be given with respect to the calendar year preceding the February 1 on or before which such annual report must be filed.

(f) (1) It shall be the duty of each organization registered under this section to keep, in such manner and form as the Attorney General shall by regulations prescribe, accurate records and accounts of moneys received and expended (including the sources from which received and purposes for which expended) by such organization.

(2) it shall be the duty of each Communist-action organization registered under this section to keep, in such manner and form as the Attorney General shall by regulations prescribe, accurate records of the names

and addresses of the members of such organization and of persons who actively participate in the activities of such organization.

(g) It shall be the duty of the Attorney General to send to each individual listed in any registration statement or annual report, filed under this section, as an officer or member of the organization in respect of which such registration statement or annual report was filed, a notification in writing that such individual is so listed; and such notification shall be sent at the earliest practicable time after the filing of such registration statement or annual report. Upon written request of any individual so notified who denies that he holds any office or membership (as the case may be) in such organization, the Attorney General shall forthwith initiate and conclude at the earliest practicable time an appropriate investigation to determine the truth or falsity of such denial, and, if the Attorney General shall be satisfied that such denial is correct, he shall thereupon strike from such registration statement or annual report the name of such individual. If the Attorney General shall decline or fail to strike the name of such individual from such registration statement or annual report within five months after receipt of such written request, such individual may file with the Board a petition for relief pursuant to section 13 (b) of this title.

(h) In the case of failure on the part of any organization to register or to file any registration statement or annual report as required by this section, it shall be the duty of the executive officer (or individual performing the ordinary and usual duties of an executive officer) and of the secretary (or individual performing the ordinary and usual duties of a secretary) of such organization, and of such officer or officers of such organization as the Attorney General shall by regulations prescribe, to register for such organization, to file such registration statement, or to file such annual report, as the case may be.

REGISTRATION OF MEMBERS OF COMMUNIST-ACTION ORGANIZATIONS

SEC. 8. (a) Any individual who is or becomes a member of any organization concerning which (1) there is in effect a final order of the Board requiring such organization to register under section 7 (a) of this title as a Communist-action organization, (2) more than thirty days have elapsed since such order has become final, and (3) such organization is not registered under section 7 of this title as a Communist-action organization, shall within sixty days after said order has become final, or within thirty days after becoming a member of such organization, whichever is later, register with the Attorney General as a member of such organization.

(b) Each individual who is or becomes a member of any organization which he knows to be registered as a Communist-action organization under section 7 (a) of this title, but to have failed to include his name upon the list of members thereof filed with the Attorney General, pursuant to the provisions of subsections (d) and (e) of section 7 of this title, shall, within sixty days after he shall have obtained such knowledge, register with the Attorney General as a member of such organization.

(c) The registration made by any individual under subsection (a) or (b) of this section shall be accompanied by a registration statement to be prepared and filed in such manner and form, and containing such information, as the Attorney General shall by regulations prescribe.

*Source*: Internal Security Act of September 22, 1950 (64 Statutes-at-Large 987).

## DOCUMENT 32: Veto of the Internal Security Act of 1950

It was an act of political courage to veto the measure, but President Harry Truman did just that. In his veto message, sent to the House of Representatives on September 22, 1950, he cited practical difficulties with the act and decried the probable infringement of important First Amendment rights. The House overrode the veto on September 22, 1950, and the Senate overrode it on September 23.

\* \* \*

The basic error of these sections is that they move in the direction of suppressing opinion and belief. This would be a very dangerous course to take, not because we have any sympathy for Communist opinions, but because any governmental stifling of the free expression of opinion is a long step toward totalitarianism. . . .

We can and we will prevent espionage, sabotage, or other actions endangering our national security. But we would betray our finest traditions if we attempted, as this bill would attempt, to curb the simple expression of opinion. This we should never do, no matter how distasteful the opinion may be to the vast majority of our people. The course proposed by this bill would delight the Communists, for it would make a mockery of the Bill of Rights and of our claims to stand for freedom in the world.

And what kind of effect would these provisions have on the normal expression of political views? Obviously, if this law were on the statute books, the part of prudence would be to avoid saying anything that might be construed by someone as not deviating sufficiently from the current Communist propaganda line. And since no one could be sure in advance what views were safe to express, the inevitable tendency would be to express no views on controversial subjects.

The result could only be to reduce the vigor and strength of our political life—an outcome that the Communists would happily welcome, but that free men should abhor. . . .

This is a time when we must marshall all our resources and all the moral strength of our free system in self-defense against the threat of Communist aggression. We will fail in this, and we will destroy all that we seek to preserve, if we sacrifice the liberties of our citizens in a misguided attempt to achieve national security.

*Source: Public Papers of the Presidents of the United States, 1950, Harry S Truman* (Washington, DC: Government Printing Office, 1965), 649–653.

## DOCUMENT 33: The Smith Act (1940)

The clash of fears and constitutional philosophies that characterized the Cold War was displayed prominently in the multitude of opinions handed down in *Dennis v. United States* (1951). This case had been brought under the Smith Act of 1940. Section 2 of the act made it a crime to "print, publish, edit, issue, circulate, sell, distribute or publicly display any written or printed matter advocating, advising or teaching" the violent overthrow of the government; Section 3 proscribed the organization of "any society, group, or assembly of persons" to engage in such advocacy.

\* \* \*

[CHAPTER 439]

### AN ACT

To prohibit certain subversive activities; to amend certain provisions of law with respect to the admission and deportation of aliens; to require the fingerprinting and registration of aliens; and for other purposes.

*Be it enacted by the Senate and House of Representatives of the United States of America in Congress assembled,*

### TITLE I

SECTION 1. (a) It shall be unlawful for any person, with intent to interfere with, impair, or influence the loyalty, morale, or discipline of the military or naval forces of the United States—

(1) to advise, counsel, urge, or in any manner cause insubordination,

disloyalty, mutiny, or refusal of duty by any member of the military or naval forces of the United States; or

(2) to distribute any written or printed matter which advises, counsels, or urges insubordination, disloyalty, mutiny, or refusal of duty by any member of the military or naval forces of the United States.

(b) For the purposes of this section, the term "military or naval forces of the United States" includes the Army of the United States, as defined in section 1 of the National Defense Act of June 3, 1916, as amended (48 Stat. 153; U.S.C., title 10, sec. 2), the Navy Marine Corps, Coast Guard, Naval Reserve, and Marine Corps Reserve of the United States; and, when any merchant vessel is commissioned in the Navy or is in the service of the Army or the Navy, includes the master, officers, and crew of such vessel.

SEC. 2. (a) It shall be unlawful for any person—

(1) to knowingly or willfully advocate, abet, advise, or teach the duty, necessity, desirability, or propriety of overthrowing or destroying any government in the United States by force or violence, or by the assassination of any officer of any such government;

(2) with the intent to cause the overthrow or destruction of any government in the United States, to print, publish, edit, issue, circulate, sell, distribute, or publicly display any written or printed matter advocating, advising, or teaching the duty, necessity, desirability, or propriety of overthrowing or destroying any government in the United States by force or violence;

(3) to organize or help to organize any society, group, or assembly of persons who teach, advocate, or encourage the overthrow or destruction of any government in the United States by force or violence; or to be or become a member of, or affiliate with, any such society, group, or assembly of persons, knowing the purposes thereof.

(b) For the purpose of this section, the term "government in the United States" means the Government of the United States, the government of any State, Territory, or possession of the United States, the government of the District of Columbia, or the government of any political subdivision of any of them.

SEC. 3. It shall be unlawful for any person to attempt to commit, or to conspire to commit, any of the acts prohibited by the provisions of this title.

SEC. 4. Any written or printed matter of the character described in section 1 or section 2 of this Act, which is intended for use in violation of this Act, may be taken from any house or other place in which it may be found, or from any person in whose possession it may be, under a search warrant issued pursuant to the provisions of title XI of the Act entitled "An Act to punish acts of interference with the foreign relations, the neutrality and the foreign commerce of the United States, to punish espionage, and better to enforce the criminal laws of the United States, and for other purposes", approved June 15, 1917 (40 Stat. 228; U.S.C., title 18, ch. 18).

SEC. 5. (a) Any person who violates any of the provisions of this title shall, upon conviction thereof, be fined not more than $10,000 or imprisoned for not more than ten years, or both.

(b) No person convicted of violating any of the provisions of this title shall, during the five years next following his conviction, be eligible for employment by the United States, or by any department or agency thereof (including any corporation the stock of which is wholly owned by the United States).

## TITLE II

SEC. 20. Section 19 of the Immigration Act of February 5, 1917 (39 Stat. 889; U.S.C., title 8, sec. 155), as amended, is amended by inserting, after "SEC. 19.", the letter "(a)", and by adding at the end of such section the following new subsections:

"(b) Any alien of any of the classes specified in this subsection, in addition to aliens who are deportable under other provisions of law, shall, upon warrant of the Attorney General, be taken into custody and deported:

"(1) Any alien who, at any time within five years after entry, shall have, knowingly and for gain, encouraged induced, assisted, abetted, or aided any other alien to enter or to try to enter the United States in violation of law.

"(2) Any alien who, at any time after entry, shall have on more than one occasion, knowingly and for gain, encouraged, induced, assisted, abetted, or aided any other alien or aliens to enter or to try to enter the United States in violation of law.

"(3) Any alien who, at any time after entry, shall have been convicted of possessing or carrying in violation of any law any weapon which shoots or is designed to shoot automatically or semi-automatically more than one shot without manual reloading, by a single function of the trigger, or a weapon commonly called a sawed-off shotgun.

"(4) Any alien who, at any time within five years after entry, shall have been convicted of violating the provisions of title I of the Alien Registration Act, 1940.

"(5) Any alien who, at any time after entry, shall have been convicted more than once of violating the provisions of title I of the Alien Registration Act, 1940.

No alien who is deportable under the provisions of paragraph (3), (4), or (5) of this subsection shall be deported until the termination of his imprisonment or the entry of an order releasing him on probation or parole.

"(c) In the case of any alien (other than one to whom subsection (d) is applicable) who is deportable under any law of the United States and who has proved good moral character for the preceding five years, the Attorney General may (1) permit such alien to depart the United States to any country of his choice at his own expense, in lieu of deportation, or (2) suspend deportation of such alien if not racially inadmissible or ineligible to naturalization in the United States if he finds that such deportation would result in serious economic detriment to a citizen or legally resident alien who is the spouse, parent, or minor child of such deportable alien. If the deportation of any alien is suspended under the provisions of this subsection for more than six months, all of the facts and pertinent provisions of law in the case shall be reported to the Congress within ten days after the beginning of its next regular session, with the reasons for such suspension. The Clerk of the House shall have such report printed as a public document. If during that session the two Houses pass a concurrent resolution stating in substance that the Congress does not favor the suspension of such deportation, the Attorney General shall thereupon deport such alien in the manner provided by law. If during that session the two Houses do not pass such a resolution, the Attorney General shall cancel deportation proceedings upon the termination of such session, except that such proceedings shall not be canceled in the case of any alien who was not legally admitted for permanent residence at the time of his last entry into the United States, unless such alien pays to the Commissioner of Immigration and Naturalization a fee of $18 (which fee shall be deposited in the Treasury of the United States as miscellaneous receipts). Upon the cancelation of such proceedings in any case in which such fee has been paid, the Commissioner shall record the alien's admission for permanent residence as of the date of his last entry into the United States and the Secretary of State shall, if the alien was a quota immigrant at the time of entry and was not charged to the appropriate quota, reduce by one the immigration quota of the country of the alien's nationality as defined in section 12 of the Act of May 26, 1924 (U.S.C., title 8, sec. 212), for the fiscal year then current or next following.

"(d) The provisions of subsection (c) shall not be applicable in the case of any alien who is deportable under (1) the Act of October 16, 1918 (40 Stat. 1008; U.S.C., title 8, sec. 137), entitled 'An Act to exclude and expel from the United States aliens who are members of the anarchist and similar classes', as amended; (2) the Act of May 26, 1922, entitled 'An Act to amend the Act entitled "An Act to prohibit the importation and use of opium for other than medicinal purposes", approved February 9, 1909, as amended' (42 Stat. 596; U.S.C., title 21, sec. 175); (3) the Act of February 18, 1931, entitled 'An Act to provide for the deportation of aliens convicted and sentenced for violation of any law regulating traffic in narcotics', as amended (46 Stat. 1171; U.S.C., title 8, sec. 156a); (4) any of the provisions of so much of subsection (a) of this section as relates to criminals, prostitutes, procurers, or other immoral persons, the mentally and physically deficient, anarchists, and similar classes; or (5) subsection (b) of this section."

SEC. 21. The Act entitled "An Act to provide for the deportation of aliens convicted and sentenced for violation of any law regulating traffic in narcotics", approved February 18, 1931, is amended—

(1) By striking out the words "and sentenced";

(2) By inserting after the words "any statute of the United States" the following: "or of any State, Territory, possession, or of the District of Columbia"; and

(3) By inserting after the word "heroin" a comma and the word "marihuana".

SEC. 22. No alien shall be deportable by reason to the amendments made by section 20 or 21 on account of any act committed prior to the date of enactment of this Act.

SEC. 23. (a) The first paragraph of section 1 of the Act entitled "An Act to exclude and expel from the United States aliens who are members of the anarchistic and similar classes", approved October 16, 1918, as amended, is amended to read as follows:

"That any alien who, at any time, shall be or shall have been a member of any one of the following classes shall be excluded from admission into the United States:".

(b) Section 2 of such Act of October 16, 1918, as amended, is amended to read as follows:

"SEC. 2. Any alien who was at the time of entering the United States, or has been at any time thereafter, a member of any one of the classes of aliens enumerated in section 1 of this Act, shall, upon the warrant of the Attorney General, be taken into custody and deported in the manner provided in the Immigration Act of February 5, 1917. The provisions of this section shall be applicable to the classes of aliens mentioned in this Act, irrespective of the time of their entry into the United States."

## TITLE III

SEC. 30. No visa shall hereafter be issued to any alien seeking to enter the United States unless said alien has been registered and fingerprinted in duplicate. One copy of the registration and fingerprint record shall be retained by the consul. The second copy shall be attached to the alien's visa and shall be taken up by the examining immigrant inspector at the port of arrival of the alien in the United States and forwarded to the Department of Justice, at Washington, District of Columbia.

Any alien seeking to enter the United States who does not present a visa (except in emergency cases defined by the Secretary of State), a reentry permit, or a border-crossing identification card shall be excluded from admission to the United States.

Sec. 31. (a) It shall be the duty of every alien now or hereafter in the United States, who (1) is fourteen years of age or older, (2) has not been registered and fingerprinted under section 30, and (3) remains in the United States for thirty days or longer, to apply for registration and to be fingerprinted before the expiration of such thirty days.

(b) It shall be the duty of every parent or legal guardian of any alien now or hereafter in the United States, who (1) is less than fourteen years of age, (2) has not been registered under section 30, and (3) remains in the United States for thirty days or longer, to apply for the registration of such alien before the expiration of such thirty days. Whenever any alien attains his fourteenth birthday in the United States he shall, within thirty days thereafter, apply in person for registration and to be fingerprinted.

Sec. 32. Notwithstanding the provisions of sections 30 and 31—

(a) The application for the registration and fingerprinting, or for the registration, of any alien who is in the United States on the effective date of such sections may be made at any time within four months after such date.

(b) No foreign government official, or member of his family, shall be required to be registered or fingerprinted under this title.

(c) The Commissioner is authorized to prescribe, with the approval of the Attorney General, special regulations for the registration and finger-printing of (1) alien seamen, (2) holders of borders crossing identification cards, (3) aliens confined in institutions within the United States, (4) aliens under order of deportation, and (5) aliens of any other class not lawfully admitted to the United States for permanent residence.

Sec. 33. (a) All applications for registration and fingerprinting under section 31 shall be made at post offices or such other places as may be designated by the Commissioner.

(b) It shall be the duty of every postmaster, with such assistance as shall be provided by the Commissioner, to register and fingerprint any applicant for registration and fingerprinting under such section, and for such purposes to designate appropriate space in the local post office for such registration and fingerprinting. Every postmaster shall forward promptly to the Department of Justice, at Washington, District of Columbia, the registration and fingerprint record of every alien registered and fingerprinted by him. The Commissioner may designate such other places for registration and fingerprinting as may be necessary for carrying out the provisions of this Act, and provide for registration and fingerprinting of aliens at such places by officers or employees of the Immigration and Naturalization Service designated by the Commissioner. The duties imposed upon any postmaster under this Act shall also be performed by any employees at the post office of such postmaster who are designated by the postmaster for such purpose.

SEC. 34. (a) The Commissioner is authorized and directed to prepare forms for the registration and fingerprinting of aliens under this title. Such forms shall contain inquiries with respect to (1) the date and place of entry of the alien into the United States; (2) activities in which he has been and intends to be engaged; (3) the length of time he expects to remain in the United States; (4) the criminal record, if any, of such alien; and (5) such additional matters as may be prescribed by the Commissioner, with the approval of the Attorney General.

(b) All registration and fingerprint records made under the provisions of this title shall be secret and confidential, and shall be made available only to such persons or agencies as may be designated by the Commissioner, with the approval of the Attorney General.

(c) Every person required to apply for the registration of himself or another under this title shall submit under oath the information required for such registration. Any person authorized to register aliens under this title shall be authorized to administer oaths for such purpose.

SEC. 35. Any alien required to be registered under this title who is a resident of the United States shall notify the Commissioner in writing of each change of residence and new address within five days from the date of such change. Any other alien required to be registered under this title shall notify the Commissioner in writing of his address at the expiration of each three months' period of residence in the United States. In the case of an alien for whom a parent or legal guardian is required to apply for registration, the notices required by this section shall be given by such parent or legal guardian.

SEC. 36. (a) Any alien required to apply for registration and to be fingerprinted who willfully fails or refuses to make such application or to be fingerprinted, and any parent or legal guardian required to apply for the registration of any alien who willfully fails or refuses to file application for the registration of such alien shall, upon conviction thereof be fined not to exceed $1,000 or be imprisoned not more than six months, or both.

(b) Any alien, or any parent or legal guardian of any alien, who fails to give written notice to the Commissioner of change of address as required by section 35 of this Act shall, upon conviction thereof, be fined not to exceed $100, or be imprisoned not more than thirty days, or both.

(c) Any alien or any parent or legal guardian of any alien, who files an application for registration containing statements known by him to be false, or who procures or attempts to procure registration of himself or another person through fraud, shall, upon conviction thereof, be fined not to exceed $1,000, or be imprisoned not more than six months, or both; and any alien so convicted within five years after entry into the United States shall, upon the warrant of the Attorney General, be taken into custody and be deported in the manner provided in sections 19 and 20 of the Immigration Act of February 5, 1917, as amended.

Sec. 37. (a) The Commissioner, with the approval of the Attorney General, is authorized and empowered to make and prescribe, and from time to time to change and amend, such rules and regulations not in conflict with this Act as he may deem necessary and proper in aid of the administration and enforcement of this title (including provisions for the identification of aliens registered under this title); except that all such rules and regulations, insofar as they relate to the performance of functions by consular officers or officers or employees in the Postal Service, shall be prescribed by the Secretary of State and the Postmaster General, respectively, upon recommendation of the Attorney General. The powers conferred upon the Attorney General by this Act and all other powers of the Attorney General relating to the administration of the Immigration and Naturalization Service may be exercised by the Attorney General through such officers of the Department of Justice, including officers of the Immigration and Naturalization Service, attorneys, special attorneys, and special assistants to the Attorney General, as he may designate specifically for such purposes.

(b) The Commissioner is authorized to make such expenditures, to employ such additional temporary and permanent employees, and to rent such quarters outside the District of Columbia as may be necessary for carrying out the provisions of this title.

Sec. 38. (a) For the purposes of this title—

(1) the term "United States", when used in a geographical sense, means the States, the Territories of Alaska and Hawaii, the District of Columbia, Puerto Rico, and the Virgin Islands;

(2) the term "Commissioner" means the Commissioner of Immigration and Naturalization.

(b) The provisions of this title shall take effect upon the date of enactment of this Act; except that sections 30 and 31 shall take effect sixty days after the date of its enactment.

Sec. 39. The President is authorized to provide, by Executive order, for the registration and fingerprinting, in a manner as nearly similar to that provided in this title as he deems practicable, of aliens in the Panama Canal Zone.

### TITLE IV

Sec. 40. If any provision of this Act, or the application thereof to any person or circumstance, is held invalid, the remainder of the Act and the application of such provision to other persons or circumstances, shall not be affected thereby.

Sec. 41. This Act may be cited as the "Alien Registration Act, 1940".
Approved, June 28, 1940.

*Source*: Smith Act of June 28, 1940, 54 Stat. 670 (see present 18 U.S.C. 2385).

## DOCUMENT 34: *Dennis v. United States* (1951)

Officers of the Communist party of the United States were charged under the Smith Act in 1948 and were duly convicted. The conviction was upheld at the appellate-court level by Judge Learned Hand. Chief Justice Fred M. Vinson borrowed heavily from Judge Hand's decision in his majority opinion affirming the appellate-court decision. Justice Hugo Black's dissent made the case for the First Amendment in terms that resonate with us today. Justice William D. Douglas's dissent, more focused on procedural issues, warned against the fallacy that ideas that are abhorrent are necessarily powerful.

\* \* \*

MR. CHIEF JUSTICE VINSON announced the judgment of the Court and an opinion in which MR. JUSTICE REED, MR. JUSTICE BURTON and MR. JUSTICE MINTON join. . . .

The indictment charged the petitioners with wilfully and knowingly conspiring (1) to organize as the Communist Party of the United States of America a society, group and assembly of persons who teach and advocate the overthrow and destruction of the Government of the United States by force and violence, and (2) knowingly and wilfully to advocate and teach the duty and necessity of overthrowing and destroying the Government of the United States by force and violence. The indictment further alleged that § 2 of the Smith Act proscribes these acts and that any conspiracy to take such action is a violation of § 3 of the Act. . . .

In this case we are squarely presented with the application of the "clear and present danger" test, and must decide what that phrase imports. We first note that many of the cases in which this Court has reversed convictions by use of this or similar tests have been based on the fact that the interest which the State was attempting to protect was itself too insubstantial to warrant restriction of speech. . . . Overthrow of the Government by force and violence is certainly a substantial enough interest for the Government to limit speech. Indeed, this is the ultimate value of any society, for if a society cannot protect its very structure from armed internal attack, it must follow that no subordinate value can be protected. If, then, this interest may be protected, the literal problem which is presented is what has been meant by the use of the phrase "clear and present danger" of the utterances bringing about the evil within the power of Congress to punish. . . .

Chief Judge Learned Hand, writing for the majority below, interpreted the phrase as follows: "In each case [courts] must ask whether the gravity of the 'evil,' discounted by its improbability, justifies such invasion of free speech as is necessary to avoid the danger." . . . We adopt this statement of the rule. As articulated by Chief Judge Hand, it is as succinct and inclusive as any other we might devise at this time. It takes into consideration those factors which we deem relevant, and relates their significances. More we cannot expect from words. . . .

We hold that § § 2 (a) (1), 2 (a) (3) and 3 of the Smith Act do not inherently, or as construed or applied in the instant case, violate the First Amendment and other provisions of the Bill of Rights, or the First and Fifth Amendments because of indefiniteness. Petitioners intended to overthrow the Government of the United States as speedily as the circumstances would permit. Their conspiracy to organize the Communist Party and to teach and advocate the overthrow of the Government of the United States by force and violence created a "clear and present danger" of an attempt to overthrow the Government by force and violence. They were properly and constitutionally convicted for violation of the Smith Act. The judgments of conviction are

*Affirmed.*

\* \* \*

MR. JUSTICE BLACK, dissenting. . . .

So long as this Court exercises the power of judicial review of legislation, I cannot agree that the First Amendment permits us to sustain laws suppressing freedom of speech and press on the basis of Congress' or our own notions of mere "reasonableness." Such a doctrine waters down the First Amendment so that it amounts to little more than an admonition to Congress. The Amendment as so construed is not likely to protect any but those "safe" or orthodox views which rarely need its protection. . . .

Public opinion being what it now is, few will protest the conviction of these Communist petitioners. There is hope, however, that in calmer times, when present pressures, passions and fears subside, this or some later Court will restore the First Amendment liberties to the high preferred place where they belong in a free society.

MR. JUSTICE DOUGLAS, dissenting.

If this were a case where those who claimed protection under the First Amendment were teaching the techniques of sabotage, the assassination of the President, the filching of documents from public files, the planting of bombs, the art of street warfare, and the like, I would have no doubts. The freedom to speak is not absolute; the teaching of methods of terror and other seditious conduct should be beyond the pale along with obscenity and immorality. This case was argued as if those were the facts.

The argument imported much seditious conduct into the record. That is easy and it has popular appeal, for the activities of Communists in plotting and scheming against the free world are common knowledge. But the fact is that no such evidence was introduced at the trial. There is a statute which makes a seditious conspiracy unlawful. Petitioners, however, were not charged with a "conspiracy to overthrow" the Government. They were charged with a conspiracy to form a party and groups and assemblies of people who teach and advocate the overthrow of our Government by force or violence and with a conspiracy to advocate and teach its overthrow by force and violence. It may well be that indoctrination in the techniques of terror to destroy the Government would be indictable under either statute. But the teaching which is condemned here is of a different character. . . .

The First Amendment provides that "Congress shall make no law . . . abridging the freedom of speech." The Constitution provides no exception. This does not mean, however, that the Nation need hold its hand until it is in such weakened condition that there is no time to protect itself from incitement to revolution. Seditious conduct can always be punished. But the command of the First Amendment is so clear that we should not allow Congress to call a halt to free speech except in the extreme case of peril from the speech itself. The First Amendment makes confidence in the common sense of our people and in their maturity of judgment the great postulate of our democracy. Its philosophy is that violence is rarely, if ever, stopped by denying civil liberties to those advocating resort to force. The First Amendment reflects the philosophy of Jefferson "that it is time enough for the rightful purposes of civil government, for its officers to interfere when principles break out into overt acts against peace and good order." The political censor has no place in our public debates. Unless and until extreme and necessitous circumstances are shown, our aim should be to keep speech unfettered and to allow the processes of law to be invoked only when the provocateurs among us move from speech to action.

*Source*: 341 U.S. 494 (1951).

---

## DOCUMENT 35: *Beauharnais v. Illinois* (1952)

In 1952, the justices of the Supreme Court included Hugo Black, Felix Frankfurter, and William O. Douglas, all powerful intellects and even more powerful personalities. Frankfurter was an exponent of a very limited role for the federal judiciary; his deference to the legislative branch of government led him to uphold legislative actions that he clearly thought unwise. Black and Douglas, on the other hand, were passionate defenders of individual liberty and a more activist role for the judiciary. In *Beauharnais v. Illinois*, these differences were cast in sharp relief.

The case involved a conviction under an Illinois statute that criminalized group libel. Beauharnais was a member of a white supremacy group, the White Circle League. He had produced and distributed a leaflet decrying "mongrelization" and demanding legislative action to "halt the encroachment . . . by the negro." At issue was the constitutionally of the statute. The Supreme Court, by a 5–4 majority, upheld the law. The opposing views reflected in the following pages are echoed by legal scholars, judges, and pundits today: what should be the role of the Supreme Court, and how shall we define and protect the liberties enumerated in the Bill of Rights?

\* \* \*

MR. JUSTICE FRANKFURTER delivered the opinion of the Court. . . .

Libelous utterances not being within the area of constitutionally protected speech, it is unnecessary, either for us or for the State courts, to consider the issues behind the phrase "clear and present danger." Certainly no one would contend that obscene speech, for example, may be punished only upon a showing of such circumstances. Libel, as we have seen, is in the same class.

We find no warrant in the Constitution for denying to Illinois the power to pass the law here under attack. But it bears repeating—although it should not—that our finding that the law is not constitutionally objectionable carries no implication of approval of the wisdom of the legislation or of its efficacy. These questions may raise doubts in our minds as well as in others. It is not for us, however, to make the legislative judgment. We are not at liberty to erect those doubts into fundamental law.

*Affirmed.*

MR. JUSTICE BLACK, with whom MR. JUSTICE DOUGLAS concurs, dissenting.

This case is here because Illinois inflicted criminal punishment on Beauharnais for causing the distribution of leaflets in the city of Chicago. The conviction rests on the leaflet's contents, not on the time, manner or place of distribution. Beauharnais is head of an organization that opposes amalgamation and favors segregation of white and colored people. After discussion, an assembly of his group decided to petition the mayor and council of Chicago to pass laws for segregation. Volunteer members of the group agreed to stand on street corners, solicit signers to petitions addressed to the city authorities, and distribute leaflets giving information about the group, its beliefs and its plans. In carrying out this program a solicitor handed out a leaflet which was the basis of this prosecution. . . .

. . . Freedom of petition, assembly, speech and press could be greatly abridged by a practice of meticulously scrutinizing every editorial, speech, sermon or other printed matter to extract two or three naughty words on which to hang charges of "group libel." The *Chaplinsky* case makes no such broad inroads on First Amendment freedoms. Nothing Mr. Justice Murphy wrote for the Court in that case or in any other case justifies any such inference. . . .

This Act sets up a system of state censorship which is at war with the kind of free government envisioned by those who forced adoption of our Bill of Rights. . . .

We are told that freedom of petition and discussion are in no danger "while this Court sits." This case raises considerable doubt. Since those who peacefully petition for changes in the law are not to be protected "while this Court sits," who is? I do not agree that the Constitution leaves freedom of petition, assembly, speech, press or worship at the mercy of a case-by-case, day-by-day majority of this Court. I had supposed that our people could rely for their freedom on the Constitution's commands, rather than on the grace of this Court on an individual case basis. To say that a legislative body can, with this Court's approval, make it a crime to petition for and publicly discuss proposed legislation seems as farfetched to me as it would be to say that a valid law could be enacted to punish a candidate for President for telling the people his views. I think the First Amendment, with the Fourteenth, "absolutely" forbids such laws without any "ifs" or "buts" or "whereases." Whatever the danger, if any, in such public discussions, it is a danger the Founders deemed outweighed by the danger incident to the stifling of thought and speech. The Court does not act on this view of the Founders. It calculates what it deems to be the danger of public discussion, holds the scales are tipped on the side of state suppression, and upholds state censorship. This method of decision offers little protection to First Amendment liberties "while this Court sits."

If there be minority groups who hail this holding as their victory, they might consider the possible relevancy of this ancient remark:

"Another such victory and I am undone. . . ."

MR. JUSTICE DOUGLAS, dissenting.

. . . Debate and argument even in the courtroom are not always calm and dispassionate. Emotions sway speakers and audiences alike. Intemperate speech is a distinctive characteristic of man. Hotheads blow off and release destructive energy in the process. They shout and rave, exaggerating weaknesses, magnifying error, viewing with alarm. So it had been from the beginning; and so it will be throughout time. The Framers of the Constitution knew human nature as well as we do. They too had lived in dangerous days; they too knew the suffocating influence of orthodoxy and standardized thought. They weighed the compulsions for restrained speech and thought against the abuses of liberty. They chose liberty. That should be our choice today no matter how distasteful to us the pamphlet of Beauharnais may be. It is true that this is only one decision which may later be distinguished or confined to narrow limits. But it represents a philosophy at war with the First Amendment—a constitutional interpretation which puts free speech under the legislative thumb. It reflects an influence moving ever deeper into our society. It is notice to the legislatures that they have the power to control unpopular blocs. It is a warning to every minority that when the Constitution guarantees free speech it does not mean what it says.

*Source*: 343 U.S. 250 (1952).

---

## DOCUMENT 36: "The Legion and the Library" (Loren P. Beth, 1952)

While the courts were finding reasons to allow government suppression of distasteful ideas, it is important to understand that efforts to control the flow of information had a great deal of support from the general public. "The Legion and the Library" appeared in the *New Republic* in July 1952. In it, Loren P. Beth discusses the efforts of an American Legion post in Peoria, Illinois, to pressure the local library to remove certain films that the Legion deemed subversive. With minor changes, the article could be rerun today; since the mid-1990s the targets have been videos and Internet access.

\* \* \*

Peoria, Ill., a city of 110,000 on the banks of the placid Illinois River, has gained a reputation as a center of vice and crime—a reputation which residents are likely to resent. To them it is a friendly place with many fine residential areas, a superb park system, and a bustling, prosperous business and industrial base, a center of Midwest conservatism, so ingrown that no Democrat has been sent to Congress from Peoria, since it was touched by the progressive surge of the Wilson years.

Peoria is also a very active center of American Legion activities, one of which is the subject of this article. A local Legion chapter, Peoria Post Number Two, maintains an extremely active "Americanism" committee, which occupies its time ferreting out "subversive" tendencies in much the same fashion as its counterpart in the House of Representatives. It concerns itself, of course, with the textbooks used in the local schools; but it has gone beyond this common Legion activity to attack the public library's movie-procurement policy, as well as to oppose the proposed United Nations Covenant of Human Rights. So outspoken is this Midwestern Dies committee that local residents are somewhat reluctant, if not actually afraid, to oppose it publicly.

During the summer of 1950, the Americanism committee turned its suspicious eye on several movies which were being made available to the general public on a loan basis by the Peoria Public Library. This library, like most of its big-city sisters, has in recent years gone beyond the traditional conception of a library as a place for books, and lends not only books but also records and films. The particular movies under scrutiny by the Legion were three: *Brotherhood of Man, Boundary Lines* and *Peoples of the USSR*. The first was, as the title implies, a plea for interracial understanding; the second, an examination in cartoon form of the way in which boundary lines may become barriers to understanding among peoples; and the third, a documentary showing the different national and racial groups composing the population of the Soviet Union. All were made during or shortly after the war. In the Legion's opinion, each picture contained Communist propaganda. Therefore, said these Americanists, they should not pollute the minds of other Americans who were not subtle enough to distinguish the propaganda. (This writer has not yet figured out what it is about a Legionnaire that makes him more qualified to find propaganda than anyone else, but this point apparently has not occurred to the Americanism Committee.) In any case, the controversy dragged on into the winter months and even now cannot be considered settled, with the major bone of contention being the question of whether or not the films actually do contain Communist propaganda. The assumption by almost everyone has been that if they *do* contain propaganda, they must not be handled by Peoria's Library.

Should the films be withdrawn, if they do contain propaganda? This poses an important question of library policy, for if propaganda movies can be proscribed, logical extension could easily lead to equal proscription of books. Thus the whole policy of a library would become involved in the metaphysical and impossible task of screening every book, magazine or movie to see whether or not it contains Communist propaganda.

We also have here in an obvious if covert form the vital question, what *is* Communist propaganda? In *Brotherhood of Man*, the only thing this reviewer could find that sounded Communistic was the advocacy of racial brotherhood; but racial brotherhood, as an ideal, was proposed quite some time before the Communist Party was born. Obviously, the thought process which leads to the pillaging of an idea just because Communists espouse it can be carried to extreme lengths. Marx, after all, was in favor of public schools. It would be difficult, if not impossible, if movies were to be culled for subversive propaganda, for the censor to avoid using his own personal conceptions of good and bad as a guide.

Under attack from the Legion, the librarian sounded off strongly in favor of the freedom of the library to choose its own films. The librarian, however, was caught in a rather weak tactical position. He made, first, the tactical mistake of denying that propaganda existed in the films, implying to some critics that if so, they should be withdrawn from circulation. This the Legion set out to prove. It found that one of the films was produced by a Hollywood writer already investigated by a Congressional committee. This discovery added to the hue and cry, and convinced many people without further argument that all three movies should be purged.

Second, the librarian works as a hired employee of the library board, which under Illinois law is appointed by the mayor, and is apparently quite responsive to loud noises coming from politically influential quarters like the American Legion. Both board and librarian, therefore, felt unable to take a strong line. The outcome of the preliminary skirmishes was the withdrawal of the films from "general" circulation. Special rules were set up under which only groups legitimately "studying propaganda" would be permitted to view them. For practical purposes, this conceded all that the Legion had asked; but there was still concern that the same selection policies would prevail in the future.

The battle over the three movies, however, was not yet over. The second round came in connection with a fourth film, the United Nations' production, *Of Human Rights*, which advocates the universal adoption of a Bill of Rights. Certain groups in the United States are opposing any such charter, claiming that it will infringe on American sovereignty. The Chicago *Tribune's* former representative in the U.S. Senate, C. Wayland Brooks, has taken up this cause, abetted by the ubiquitous Peoria Legion Post Number Two. One may, of course, legitimately oppose a Universal Covenant of Human Rights. It is to be hoped that one has an equal right to favor it. The critical point here is that the Legion again demanded the withdrawal of this frankly propagandistic film on the grounds that it showed violations of human rights in this country but not in Russia.

At about this time another local pressure group entered the picture, this time on the opposite side. Many Peoria ministers had viewed the campaign against the first three movies with misgivings. Several had spoken in favor of the films on grounds that they were not propagandistic; a few had opposed any censorship regardless of the propaganda issue: one (in East Peoria) had even dared to show the films to his congregation so that it could decide for itself. The clerics were also concerned over the fact that the librarian might lose his job because of the tempest. Eventually, the Peoria Ministerial Association passed, by a large majority, a resolution firmly opposing any sort of censorship and strongly backing the librarian.

Such pressure from the liberal side encouraged the library board; it was further emboldened by the fact that the attack on the UN movie was not nearly as successful in arousing the public as the earlier campaign had been. Consequently, the board rescinded its partial ban on the first films, and all four are now in general circulation. However, every new movie the library purchases which, in the opinion of the librarian, is "controversial," is to be previewed before a group of leading citizens representing local civic organizations. Then the movie will be released, with the written comments of the reviewers attached to the film can. Administratively, this may prove to be a difficult business; but it has a more serious objection, which is that, like the Communist Party, the American Legion is vigilant, intolerant and energetic in applying pressure against all who challenge its views.

These qualities stand out in the latest episode in the Legion's textbook campaign. Shortly after a local forum program last winter, during which a *Tribune* reporter denounced a high-school civics text (Magruder's *American Government*) as subversive, the Legion suddenly awoke to the fact that this same text was in use in the Peoria high schools! The Americanism committee at once moved on the school board. Within a few weeks, and in spite of a favorable report on the book by a specially created teachers' committee, the school board officially retired Magruder from use. (This even though a new edition had changed most of the "subversive" passages!)

Here the matter stands at present. The library uneasily awaits further battles, as no doubt do the schools. The attack has not yet reached the hilltop campus of Bradley University, but there is little doubt that it will; the university draws heavily from Peoria both for its 2,500 students and for its present and future financial support, and is thus peculiarly susceptible to pressures.

The deeper implications of the library campaign, however, are not restricted to Peoria. They involve basic questions of policy for public libraries the country over. Should they refrain from buying "controversial" films in order to avoid the same troubles that have beset the Peoria institution? Most librarians will be very reluctant to shoulder personally the responsibility for defending the educational and informational tasks which are basic to the existence of the public library system. The result may well be that libraries will feel free to show only those movies which favor nothing; because espousal of any cause may offend some group.

Even were one to accept the idea of some sort of censorship for library films, however, one would still be faced with the important considerations of who will be the censor and under what restrictions. What the

Legion committee ostensibly desires is a new librarian who will apply its concepts of Americanism. But even if such a librarian could be found, it is questionable whether librarians serving the entire community should be hired and fired, or forced to cater to, the behests of a small group of self-styled patriots.

A final striking aspect of the Legion campaign was the attitude of the local press. Peoria has two daily papers, the morning *Star* and the evening *Journal*. Both are managed by the same business interests. Although they frequently differ in policy, both are critical of the Democratic administration and of the present city government. Both papers have supported the Legion all down the line. They seem to have adopted the viewpoint that the Legion, since by definition it is a patriotic organization, must always be right, and that therefore it should be supported editorially, with the result that the populace of Peoria is hardly aware that there are two sides to the question. The only dissenting voices heard in Peoria on this issue have been those of outsiders and, to a lesser degree, of some of the political scientists on the University faculty.

Too many men will share the Legion's prejudices in the mistaken belief that they are acting as conservatives should. They are in fact storing up trouble for themselves in years in which conservatism may hold the place of unpopularity that suspected radicalism holds today. As Justice Holmes saw so clearly, freedom for the thought that we hate is more important to democracy than freedom for the thoughts we like. Can the zealots of Peoria Post Number Two and their backers learn only when it is too late that suppression invites explosion; and that nothing is more desirable than forbidden fruit?

*Source*: Loren P. Beth, "The Legion and the Library," *New Republic* 127 (July 14, 1952): 11–13.

---

## DOCUMENT 37: "The Freedom to Read" (1953)

In 1953, the Westchester Conference of the American Library Association and the American Book Publishers Council issued a response to these and similar efforts. Entitled "The Freedom to Read," the document remains an important statement of principles of the American Library Association and the Association of American Publishers, successor to the Book Publishers Council.

\* \* \*

The freedom to read is essential to our democracy. It is continuously under attack. Private groups and public authorities in various parts of the country are working to remove books from sale, to censor textbooks, to label "controversial" books, to distribute lists of "objectionable" books or authors, and to purge libraries. Those actions apparently rise from a view that our national tradition of free expression is no longer valid; that censorship and suppression are needed to avoid the subversion of politics and the corruption of morals. We, as citizens devoted to the use of books and as librarians and publishers responsible for disseminating them, wish to assert the public interest in the preservation of the freedom to read.

We are deeply concerned about these attempts at suppression. Most such attempts rest on a denial of the fundamental premise of democracy: that the ordinary citizen, by exercising his critical judgment, will accept the good and reject the bad. The censors, public and private, assume that they should determine what is good and what is bad for their fellow-citizens.

We trust Americans to recognize propaganda, and to reject it. We do not believe they need the help of censors to assist them in this task. We do not believe they are prepared to sacrifice their heritage of a free press in order to be "protected" against what others think may be bad for them. We believe they still favor free enterprise in ideas and expression.

We are aware, of course, that books are not alone in being subjected to efforts of suppression. We are aware that these efforts are related to a larger pattern of pressures being brought against education, the press, films, radio and television. The problem is not only one of actual censorship. The shadow of fear cast by these pressures leads, we suspect, to an even larger voluntary curtailment of expression by those who seek to avoid controversy.

Such pressure toward conformity is perhaps natural to a time of uneasy change and pervading fear. Especially when so many of our apprehensions are directed against an ideology, the expression of a dissident idea becomes a thing feared in itself, and we tend to move against it as against a hostile deed, with suppression.

And yet suppression is never more dangerous than in such a time of social tension. Freedom has given the United States the elasticity to endure strain. Freedom keeps open the path of novel and creative solutions, and enables change to come by choice. Every silencing of a heresy, every enforcement of an orthodoxy, diminishes the toughness and resilience of our society and leaves it the less able to deal with stress.

Now as always in our history, books are among our greatest instruments of freedom. They are almost the only means for making generally available ideas or manners of expression that can initially command only a small audience. They are the natural medium for the new idea and the untried voice from which come the original contributions to social growth. They are essential to the extended discussion which serious thought requires, and to the accumulation of knowledge and ideas into organized collections.

We believe that free communication is essential to the preservation of a free society and a creative culture. We believe that these pressures towards conformity present the danger of limiting the range and variety of inquiry and expression on which our democracy and our culture depend. We believe that every American community must jealously guard the freedom to publish and to circulate, in order to preserve its own freedom to read. We believe that publishers and librarians have a profound responsibility to give validity to that freedom to read by making it possible for the readers to choose freely from a variety of offerings.

The freedom to read is guaranteed by the Constitution. Those with faith in free men will stand firm on these constitutional guarantees of essential rights and will exercise the responsibilities that accompany these rights.

We therefore affirm these propositions:

1. It is in the public interest for publishers and librarians to make available the widest diversity of views and expressions, including those which are unorthodox or unpopular with the majority.

   Creative thought is by definition new, and what is new is different. The bearer of every new thought is a rebel until his idea is refined and tested. Totalitarian systems attempt to maintain themselves in power by the ruthless suppression of any concept which challenges the established orthodoxy. The power of a democratic system to adapt to change is vastly strengthened by the freedom of its citizens to choose widely from among conflicting opinions offered freely to them. To stifle every nonconformist idea at birth would mark the end of the democratic process. Furthermore, only through the constant activity of weighing and selecting can the democratic mind attain the strength demanded by times like these. We need to know not only what we believe but why we believe it.

2. Publishers, librarians and booksellers do not need to endorse every idea or presentation contained in the books they make available. It would conflict with the public interest for them to establish their own political, moral or aesthetic views as a standard for determining what books would be published or circulated.

   Publishers and librarians serve the education process by helping to make available knowledge and ideas required for the growth of the mind and the increase of learning. They do not foster education by imposing as mentors the patterns of their own thought.

   The people should have the freedom to read and consider a broader range of ideas than those that may be held by a single librarian or publisher or government or church. It is wrong that what one man can read should be confined to what another thinks proper.

3. It is contrary to the public interest for publishers or librarians to determine the acceptability of a book on the basis of the personal history or political affiliations of the author.

A book should be judged as a book. No art or literature can flourish if it is to be measured by the political views of private lives of its creators. No society of free men can flourish which draws up lists of writers to whom it will not listen, whatever they may have to say.

4. There is no place in our society for efforts to coerce the tastes of others, to confine adults to the reading matter deemed suitable for adolescents, or to inhibit the efforts of writers to achieve artistic expression.

To some, much of modern literature is shocking. But is not much of life itself shocking? We cut off literature at the source if we prevent serious artists from dealing with the stuff of life. Parents and teachers have a responsibility to prepare the young to meet the diversity of experiences in life to which they will be exposed, as they have a responsibility to help them learn to think critically for themselves. These are affirmative responsibilities, not to be discharged simply by preventing them from reading works for which they are not yet prepared. In these matters taste differs, and taste cannot be legislated; nor can machinery be devised which will suit the demands of one group without limiting the freedom of others.

5. It is not in the public interest to force a reader to accept with any book the prejudgment of a label characterizing the book or author as subversive or dangerous.

The idea of labeling presupposes the existence of individuals or groups with wisdom to determine by authority what is good or bad for the citizens. It presupposes that each individual must be directed in making up his mind about the ideas he examines. But Americans do not need others to do their thinking for them.

6. It is the responsibility of publishers and librarians, as guardians of the people's freedom to read, to contest encroachments upon that freedom by individuals or groups seeking to impose their own standards or tastes upon the community at large.

It is inevitable in the give and take of the democratic process that the political, the moral, or the aesthetic concepts of an individual or group will occasionally collide with those of another individual or group. In a free society each individual is free to determine for himself what he wishes to read, and each group is free to determine what it will recommend to its freely associated members. But no group has the right to take the law into its own hands, and to impose its own concept of politics or morality upon other members of a democratic society. Freedom is no freedom if it is accorded only to the accepted and the inoffensive.

7. It is the responsibility of publishers and librarians to give full meaning to the freedom to read by providing books that enrich the quality and diversity of thought and expression. By the exercise of this affirmative responsibility, bookmen can demonstrate that the answer to a bad book is a good one, the answer to a bad idea is a good idea.

The freedom to read is of little consequence when expended on the trivial; it is frustrated when the reader cannot obtain matter for his purpose. What is needed is not only the absence of restraint, but the positive provision of opportunity for the people to read the best that has been thought and said. Books are the major channel by which the intellectual inheritance is handed down, and the principal means of its testing and growth. The defense of their freedom and integrity, and the enlargement of their service to society, requires of all bookmen the utmost of their faculties, and deserves of all citizens the fullest of their support.

We state these propositions neither lightly nor as easy generalizations. We here stake out a lofty claim for the value of books. We do so because we believe that they are good, possessed of enormous variety and usefulness, worthy of cherishing and keeping free. We realize that the application of these propositions may mean the dissemination of ideas and manners of expression that are repugnant to many people. We do not state these propositions in the comfortable belief that what people read is unimportant. We believe rather that what people read is deeply important; that ideas can be dangerous, but that the suppression of ideas is fatal to a democratic society. Freedom itself is a dangerous way of life, but it is ours.

*Source*: American Library Association, "The Freedom to Read," June 25, 1953, revised January 28, 1972. Reprinted by permission of the American Library Association.

---

## DOCUMENT 38: *Roth v. United States* (1957)

Few First Amendment issues have proved as intractable as obscenity. Even youngsters today can articulate the test, first enunciated in *Roth v. United States* in 1957, that in order to be found to be obscene, material must be "utterly without redeeming social importance." It does not take a great deal of reflection to realize how subjective a standard this can be; one person's definition of mildly racy is another person's example of moral rot.

The Supreme Court in *Roth* began by holding that obscenity is not protected by the First Amendment; that ruling necessitated a definition of obscenity. Justice Brennan, writing for the majority, began that task with the obvious: sex and obscenity are not synonymous. The test, he said, must be "whether to the average person, applying contemporary community standards, the dominant theme of the material taken as a whole appeals to prurient interest." The problems inherent in this definition are illuminated by the opinions, concurring and dissenting alike, filed by Chief Justice Earl Warren, Justice John Marshall Harlan, and Justices William O. Douglas and Hugo Black.

\* \* \*

MR. JUSTICE BRENNAN delivered the opinion of the Court. . . .

The dispositive question is whether obscenity is utterance within the area of protected speech and press. Although this is the first time the question has been squarely presented to this Court, either under the First Amendment or under the Fourteenth Amendment, expressions found in numerous opinions indicate that this Court has always assumed that obscenity is not protected by the freedoms of speech and press. . . .

The guaranties of freedom of expression in effect in 10 of the 14 States which by 1792 had ratified the Constitution, gave no absolute protection for every utterance. Thirteen of the 14 States provided for the prosecution of libel, and all of those States made either blasphemy or profanity, or both, statutory crimes. As early as 1712, Massachusetts made it criminal to publish "any filthy, obscene, or profane song, pamphlet, libel or mock sermon" in imitation or mimicking of religious services. . . .

In light of this history, it is apparent that the unconditional phrasing of the First Amendment was not intended to protect every utterance. . . .

The protection given speech and press was fashioned to assure unfettered interchange of ideas for the bringing about of political and social changes desired by the people. . . .

All ideas having even the slightest redeeming social importance—unorthodox ideas, controversial ideas, even ideas hateful to the prevailing climate of opinion—have the full protection of the guaranties, unless excludable because they encroach upon the limited area of more important interests. But implicit in the history of the First Amendment is the rejection of obscenity as utterly without redeeming social importance. This rejection for that reason is mirrored in the universal judgment that obscenity should be restrained, reflected in the international agreement of over 50 nations, in the obscenity laws of all of the 48 States, and in the 20 obscenity laws enacted by the Congress from 1842 to 1956. This is the same judgment expressed by this Court in *Chaplinsky* v. *New Hampshire* . . . :

". . . There are certain well-defined and narrowly limited classes of speech, the prevention and punishment of which have never been thought to raise any Constitutional problem. *These include the lewd and obscene. . . .*" . . .

We hold that obscenity is not within the area of constitutionally protected speech or press. . . .

However, sex and obscenity are not synonymous. Obscene material is material which deals with sex in a manner appealing to prurient interest. The portrayal of sex, *e.g.*, in art, literature and scientific works, is not itself sufficient reason to deny material the constitutional protection of freedom of speech and press. Sex, a great and mysterious motive force in human life, has indisputably been a subject of absorbing interest to mankind through the ages; it is one of the vital problems of human interest and public concern. . . .

. . . It is therefore vital that the standards for judging obscenity safeguard the protection of freedom of speech and press for material which does not treat sex in a manner appealing to prurient interest.

The early leading standard of obscenity allowed material to be judged merely by the effect of an isolated excerpt upon particularly susceptible persons. . . . Some American courts adopted this standard but later decisions have rejected it and substituted this test: whether to the average person, applying contemporary community standards, the dominant theme of the material taken as a whole appeals to prurient interest. The *Hicklin* test, judging obscenity by the effect of isolated passages upon the most susceptible persons, might well encompass material legitimately treating with sex, and so it must be rejected as unconstitutionally restrictive of the freedoms of speech and press. On the other hand, the substituted standard provides safeguards adequate to withstand the charge of constitutional infirmity. . . .

MR. JUSTICE HARLAN, . . . dissenting. . . .

I regret not to be able to join the Court's opinion. I cannot do so because I find lurking beneath its disarming generalizations a number of problems which not only leave me with serious misgivings as to the future effect of today's decisions, but which also, in my view, call for different results in these two cases. . . .

. . . Many juries might find that Joyce's "Ulysses" or Bocaccio's [*sic*] "Decameron" was obscene, and yet the conviction of a defendant for selling either book would raise, for me, the gravest constitutional problems, for no such verdict could convince me, without more, that these books are "utterly without redeeming social importance." In short, I do not understand how the Court can resolve the constitutional problems now before it without making its own independent judgment upon the character of the material upon which these convictions were based. I am very much afraid that the broad manner in which the Court has decided these cases will tend to obscure the peculiar responsibilities resting on state and federal courts in this field and encourage them to rely on easy labeling and jury verdicts as a substitute for facing up to the tough individual problems of constitutional judgment involved in every obscenity case. . . .

MR. JUSTICE DOUGLAS, with whom MR. JUSTICE BLACK concurs, dissenting.

When we sustain these convictions, we make the legality of a publication turn on the purity of thought which a book or tract instills in the mind of the reader. I do not think we can approve that standard and be faithful to the command of the First Amendment, which by its terms is a restraint on Congress and which by the Fourteenth is a restraint on the States. . . .

The standard of what offends "the common conscience of the community" conflicts, in my judgment, with the command of the First Amendment that "Congress shall make no law . . . abridging the freedom of speech, or of the press." Certainly that standard would not be an acceptable one if religion, economics, politics or philosophy were involved. How does it become a constitutional standard when literature treating with sex is concerned?

Any test that turns on what is offensive to the community's standards is too loose, too capricious, too destructive of freedom of expression to be squared with the First Amendment. Under that test, juries can censor, suppress, and punish what they don't like, provided the matter relates to "sexual impurity" or has a tendency "to excite lustful thoughts." This is community censorship in one of its worst forms. It creates a regime where in the battle between the literati and the Philistines, the Philistines are certain to win. If experience in this field teaches anything, it is that "censorship of obscenity has almost always been both irrational and indiscriminate." . . .

I would give the broad sweep of the First Amendment full support. I have the same confidence in the ability of our people to reject noxious literature as I have in their capacity to sort out the true from the false in theology, economics, politics, or any other field.

*Source*: 354 U.S. 476 (1957).

---

## DOCUMENT 39: *National Association for the Advancement of Colored People v. Alabama ex rel. Patterson, Attorney General* (1958)

By the latter part of the 1950s, the seeds had been sown for what would become, in the 1960s, the civil rights movement. In the American South, resistance to these trends was intense; ingrained attitudes and institutionalized segregation frequently made activism on behalf of black citizens dangerous. Even the simple act of joining an activist organization could have serious consequences.

In 1958, the Supreme Court reviewed actions by the attorney general and the courts of Alabama against the National Association for the Advancement of Colored People (NAACP). The state had taken the position that the organization was an out-of-state business required to register under Alabama's business laws and had demanded copious amounts of information, including the NAACP's membership lists. The organization complied with the other requests, but refused to turn over its membership information, citing associational freedoms secured by the First and Fourteenth Amendments. Alabama courts then found the NAACP in contempt and fined it $100,000—an enormous amount in 1958, and one likely to ruin a struggling civil rights organization. The Supreme Court reversed the contempt citation. While the Court's action was largely applauded by editorial writers and commentators, the case was frequently cited by Southern office-holders and political candidates as evidence that the balance of power between state and federal governments was shifting too far in favor of the latter, eroding states' rights and perogatives.

One of the attorneys on the brief for the NAACP was a young lawyer who would provide long and distinguished service to the Supreme Court in later life: a passionate advocate for equality named Thurgood Marshall.

\* \* \*

MR. JUSTICE HARLAN delivered the opinion of the Court.

We review from the standpoint of its validity under the Federal Constitution a judgment of civil contempt entered against petitioner, the National Association for the Advancement of Colored People, in the courts of Alabama. The question presented is whether Alabama, consistently with the Due Process Clause of the Fourteenth Amendment, can compel petitioner to reveal to the State's Attorney General the names and addresses of all its Alabama members and agents, without regard to their positions or functions in the Association. The judgment of contempt was based upon petitioner's refusal to comply fully with a court order requiring in part the production of membership lists. Petitioner's claim is that the order, in the circumstances shown by this record, violated rights assured to petitioner and its members under the Constitution. . . .

Petitioner . . . contended that its activities did not subject it to the qualification requirements of the statute and that in any event what the State sought to accomplish by its suit would violate rights to freedom of speech and assembly guaranteed under the Fourteenth Amendment to the Constitution of the United States. . . .

Effective advocacy of both public and private points of view, particularly controversial ones, is undeniably enhanced by group association, as this Court has more than once recognized by remarking upon the close nexus between the freedoms of speech and assembly. . . . It is beyond debate that freedom to engage in association for the advancement of beliefs and ideas is an inseparable aspect of the "liberty" assured by the Due Process Clause of the Fourteenth Amendment, which embraces freedom of speech. . . . Of course, it is immaterial whether the beliefs sought to be advanced by association pertain to political, economic, religious or cultural matters, and state action which may have the effect of curtailing the freedom to associate is subject to the closest scrutiny. . . .

It is important to bear in mind that petitioner asserts no right to absolute immunity from state investigation, and no right to disregard Alabama's laws. As shown by its substantial compliance with the production order, petitioner does not deny Alabama's right to obtain from it such information as the State desires concerning the purposes of the Association and its activities within the State. Petitioner has not objected to divulging the identity of its members who are employed by or hold official positions with it. It has urged the rights solely of its ordinary rank-and-file members. This is therefore not analogous to a case involving the interest of a State in protecting its citizens in their dealings with paid solicitors or agents of foreign corporations by requiring identification. . . .

We hold that the immunity from state scrutiny of membership lists which the Association claims on behalf of its members is here so related to the right of the members to pursue their lawful private interests privately and to associate freely with others in so doing as to come within the protection of the Fourteenth Amendment. And we conclude that Alabama has fallen short of showing a controlling justification for the deterrent effect on the free enjoyment of the right to associate which disclosure of membership lists is likely to have. Accordingly, the judgment of civil contempt and the $100,000 fine which resulted from petitioner's refusal to comply with the production order in this respect must fall.

*Source*: 357 U.S. 449 (1958).

## DOCUMENT 40: "Freedom of Association Upheld by High Court" (*Christian Century*, 1958)

Some First Amendment issues are straightforward: can the government suppress a book or film? Can it prevent a demonstration? Others are less clear-cut. States certainly have the right to regulate the conduct of business within their borders, and all states require corporations to register and provide basic information about their structure and officers.

The State of Alabama argued that it had the right to require disclosure of an organization's membership list, even when that disclosure might endanger members, as it undoubtedly would have done in the case of the NAACP in the 1950s.

Despite the attempt to characterize the issue as one of "states rights" rather than First Amendment associational freedom, the following commentary from *Christian Century* following the Supreme Court's rejection of Alabama's argument was typical of media reaction. The press saw Alabama's law as a pretext for infringing the rights of citizens, rather than a legitimate attempt to regulate business.

\* \* \*

By denying to Alabama the right to compel the National Association for the Advancement of Colored People to divulge its lists of members in that state, the Supreme Court has once more proved a bulwark of American liberty. In a unanimous opinion the court closed its 1957–58 term by upholding as a "fundamental freedom" the citizen's "freedom to engage in association for the advancement of beliefs and ideas." The N.A.A.C.P. had submitted all the other data demanded by the state, including the names of its officers and directors. But it successfully contended that submission to the state of the names of its members would expose them to persecution on account of their beliefs. Justice John Marshall Harlan, who delivered the court's ruling, said: "This court has recognized the vital relationship between freedom to associate and privacy in one's associations. . . . Inviolability of privacy in group association may in many circumstances be indispensable to preservation of freedom of association, particularly where a group espouses dissident beliefs." He noted that the organization had proved that in the past revelation of the identity of its members had exposed them to "economic reprisal, loss of employment, threat of physical coercion and other manifestations of public hostility." The decision has the effect of endorsing the purposes of the N.A.A.C.P. as consistent with legality, for the court pointed out that in some instances the public interest demands disclosure of membership of an organization. In its steady insistence before the courts that all citizens be accorded the full rights of citizenship, the N.A.A.C.P. renders a service of importance to every American. That this function is accepted by Negroes is indicated by the statement in the latest bulletin of the Montgomery Improvement Association, which conducted a successful and peaceful struggle for integration on the buses of that Alabama city: "Although . . . at present no direct relationship is sustained, every segment of the struggle accepts in loyalty and in principle the N.A.A.C.P. headquarters as the headquarters of our struggle for justice, human dignity and the realization of the Christian and democratic ideals." This issue of the M.I.A. bulletin says that there are "50,000 qualified Negro voters" in Alabama, and that the organization has paid out over $2,500 in costs of defending Negroes in various court cases. It also reports that "the re-pairing and rebuilding of the [three] bombed churches [in Montgomery] is nearing completion." The M.I.A., whose address is 530 South Union St., Montgomery 4, Ala., raised $28,000 for this cause. After two years and six months, it continues to hold mass meetings where the people "sing and pray and get their spirits lifted and get fresh directions." The Rev. Martin Luther King, Jr. is its president.

*Source*: "Freedom of Association Upheld by High Court," *Christian Century*, July 16, 1958, 821–822.

# Part V

---

# 1960–1998: Smut, Cyberspace, and Political Correctness

The 1960s ushered in an era of social upheaval. Minorities, notably African Americans, asserted their right to equality before the law. Women, freed from the imperatives of biology by advances in birth control, entered the work force in increasing numbers. Technology changed the dimensions of life everywhere; the ubiquitous television screen, a novelty through the early part of the 1950s, brought information instantly and insistently into living rooms both urban and remote.

Television also brought the realities of the Vietnam War into the nation's living rooms, forcing Americans to confront that conflict and the political issues surrounding it with an immediacy previous conflicts had never equaled. The 1960s were characterized by political activism—antiwar activities, the civil rights movement—and by hippies who simply wanted to "turn on and drop out," to use the phrase of the time. A United States president resigned in disgrace in 1974, and the journalists who documented the behavior that brought him down increasingly insisted upon the constitutional prerogatives due the press (which we now call the media). While the turmoil of these years had substantially subsided by the late 1970s, it is not an exaggeration to say that the political, social, and legal landscapes we occupy today were shaped in important ways by that decade.

During this time, Americans began to experience the constant acceleration of the rate of technological progress that has profoundly affected all of our lives. If birth control freed women to work, it also was a major factor in the so-called sexual revolution. Cyberspace and the creation of the Internet have changed the world irrevocably and in ways we are only dimly coming to understand. Medical science has given citizens longer and healthier lives—and decisions our grandparents never had to make. Faster communication and travel have created a global economy and are speeding us toward a truly global community. Changing patterns of immigration have made America diverse in ways that were unthinkable a mere generation ago; the tensions that have accompanied that diversity have led to attempts to pass "hate-speech" laws and bring "politically correct" speech and behavior to college campuses.

Massive social changes do not occur without provoking reactions from those who fear the consequences of change or simply find themselves in a world greatly at odds with their desires and beliefs. During the industrial revolution, the Luddites took hammers and clubs to the newfangled machinery that had displaced English weavers. America in the decades between 1960 and the millennium has seen similar phenomena. Every social change has occasioned shrill criticisms and dire warnings from various groups: those who believe that libraries should carry only books, eschewing "newfangled" means of communication like videos, those who proclaim the dangers of the Internet (often from their very own World Wide Web sites), preachers who oppose civil rights for gays and lesbians on biblical grounds, or those who respond to free-trade initiatives with predictions of a takeover by the United Nations.

In such an environment, how do courts give meaning and effect to the principles of the First Amendment? What would James Madison have to say about porn on the Internet? How would Thomas Paine have reacted to the *New York Times* printing the Pentagon Papers? How would any of the Founding Fathers have reacted to *Playboy*? Is the First Amendment still a relevant and serviceable statement of philosophy in this brave new world?

## DOCUMENT 41: "The Playboy Philosophy" (Hugh Hefner, 1963)

*Playboy Magazine* was the creation of Hugh Hefner, who scandalized America not only with centerfolds featuring naked women, but with glossy advertisements and articles celebrating a seemingly hedonistic approach to life. The magazine also carried articles of substance by authors who were—or would become—famous.

In December 1962, Hefner attempted to respond to criticism of the magazine and to define what it stood for by publishing "The Playboy

Philosophy." There would be an additional twenty-four installments totaling 150,000 words and not concluding until May 1966. Several installments were roundtable discussions with clergy.

"The Playboy Philosophy" was Hefner's attempt to spell out his guiding principles and editorial credo. The effort did more, however; it helped define what became known as "the new morality." The essential element of that morality was an insistence upon individual autonomy, on the right of individuals to make their personal moral choices free of government interference. "The Playboy Philosophy" may have been originally intended merely as a defense of naked women and sexual pleasure, but it became a defining document for a generation, framing public debate on issues ranging from liberty to libertinism.

* * *

The Playboy Philosophy is predicated on our belief in the importance of the individual and his rights as a member of a free society. That's our most basic premise—the starting point from which everything else in which we believe evolves. We hold that man's personal self-interest is natural and good, and that it can be channeled, through reason, to the benefit of the individual and his society; the belief that morality should be based upon reason; the conviction that society should exist as man's servant, not as his master; the idea that the purpose in man's life should be found in the full living of life and the individual pursuit of happiness.

We would point out the utter lack of justification in the state's making unlawful certain private acts performed by two consenting adults. Organized religion may preach against them if they wish—and there may well be some logic in their doing so, since extreme sexual permissiveness is not without its negative aspects—but there can be no possible justification for religion's using the state to coercively control the sexual conduct of the members of a free society. . . .

Church-state legislation has made common criminals of us all. Dr. Alfred Kinsey has estimated that if the sex laws of the United States were conscientiously enforced, 90 percent of the adult population would be in prison. . . .

We cannot accept the argument that it is some flaw in the nature of man, some weakness, or devil in the flesh, that produces our sexual yearnings and behavior; we reject as totally without foundation the premise of the prude, who would have us believe that man would be healthier and happier if he were somehow able to curb these natural desires. . . .

All sexual intercourse outside of church-state-sanctioned bonds of matrimony is prohibited under the statutes on fornication and adultery; all nonprocreative sexual activity, between the same and opposite sexes, both inside and outside of marriage, and including any undue familiarity with household pets, is prohibited under the statutes on sodomy.

Our state laws on sodomy are derived directly from the religious doctrine that the only natural purpose of sex is procreation; it follows, therefore, that non-procreative sex is a "crime against nature." . . .

So intimately is sex interrelated with the rest of human experience that it is impossible to conceive of a society existing, as we know it, without benefit of the primal sex urge. Most certainly, if such a society did exist, it would be a very cold, totalitarian and barbarous one. The existence of two sexes, and their attraction for each other, must be considered the major civilizing influence in our world. As much as religion has done for the development and growth of society, sex has done more.

Since one of the things *Playboy* is especially concerned about is the depersonalizing influence of our entire society, and considerable editorial attention is given to the problem of establishing individual identity, through sex and as many other avenues of expression as may be available in a more permissive society, it is wrong to suggest that we favor depersonalized sex.

We certainly think that personal sex is preferable to impersonal sex, because it includes the greatest emotional rewards; but we can see no logical justification for opposing the later [*sic*], unless it is irresponsible, exploitive, coercive or in some way hurts one of the individuals involved. . . .

Even if all of the religious leaders of the nation were of a single mind on the subject, it is clear that in this free democracy, they would have no right to force a universal code of sexual conduct upon the rest of society. Our religious leaders, of every faith, can loudly proclaim their moral views to one and all, and attempt to persuade us as to the correctness of their beliefs—they have this right and, indeed, it is expected of them. They have no right, however, to attempt in any way to force their beliefs upon others through coercion. And most especially, they have no right to use the power of the Government to implement such coercion.

Since no such common agreement exists among the clergy of modern America, it is all the more incredible—if no more monstrous—to consider the extent to which religious dogma and superstition have, all democratic ideals and constitutional guarantees to the contrary, found their way into our civil law. And nowhere is this unholy alliance between church and state more obvious than in matters of sex. In our most personal behavior, no citizen of the United States is truly free. . . .

The Supreme Court's definition of obscenity makes reference to "contemporary community standards." Thus, the obscenity of yesterday is not necessarily the obscenity of today, and the obscenity of today need not be the obscenity of tomorrow. Contemporary community standards never remain static but offer ever-changing criteria for judgment. It is the subjective nature of obscenity that [disturbed] great men like Supreme Court Justice Hugo Black, who [felt] that the freedoms guaranteed by our Constitution should be absolutes—a solid, unshakable foundation upon which our democracy is built. . . .

Progress necessarily requires the exchange of outdated ideas for new and better ones. By keeping open all lines of communication in our culture, every new idea—no matter how seemingly perverse, improper or peculiar—has its opportunity to be considered, to be challenged, and ultimately to be accepted or rejected by society as a whole or by some small part of it. This is the important advantage that a free society has over a totalitarian one, for in the free exchange of ideas, the best will ultimately win out. A dictatorship, with its pre-established dogma, is chained to the past; a free society may draw from the past, the present and the future.

*Source*: Hugh Hefner, "The Playboy Philosophy," 1963. www.playboy.com/faq/faq/PBFAQ/philosophy.

---

## DOCUMENT 42: "An Infinite Number of Monkeys" (*Christian Century*, 1963)

As might be imagined, public reception to "The Playboy Philosophy" was not generally positive. While much of the reaction to Hugh Hefner's argument was angry or scandalized, perhaps the bulk of the criticism was simply dismissive. A good example is the following opinion piece "An Infinite Number of Monkeys" that appeared in *Christian Century*.

* * *

Mathematicians contend that if you place a monkey in front of a typewriter and give him an infinite amount of paper and time, sooner or later he will accidentally type in the correct order the words that make up Shakespeare's *Hamlet*. A comic we know has a time-saving suggestion: get an infinite number of monkeys to do the job instantaneously. Now we find that an infinite number of monkeys do exist and that they are employed as researchers by Hugh M. Hefner, editor of *Playboy* magazine. Bustling about the *Playboy* library, they pirate hundreds of erudite quotations to be used out-of-context fashion in the apparently interminable articles—ten so far—in the magazine's series called "The Playboy

Philosophy." The price of the magazine has risen since the series began and may have to go higher if those researching monkeys keep busy.

We are glad to know that the midwest's tradition of amateur philosophizing has not gone out of style. In the 19th century the fad was Platonism; now it is Epicureanism—of a sort. Close upon the September issue's "Playboy Forum" in which numbers of M.D.s and M.P.s and D.D.s and Ph.D.s offer favorable comments on the oracle's endlessly proliferating "philosophy," chapter ten in the soup serial begins. Editor Hefner in this installment discusses "the Sexual Revolution currently taking place in society" and proposes to develop a "new morality." Last month he gave a "brief history of sexual suppression since early Christendom through the Middle Ages"; in the current issue he considers the Renaissance, the Reformation and—of course—Puritanism and Victorianism.

What other popular magazine offers sober discussions of imminent cataclysm, eschatology, sacerdotal celibacy, the *Malleus Maleficarum*, incubus and succubus, total depravity, authoritarian dogma, theocratic society, predestination? Where else can you in a few pages find strung together Augustine, Origen, Chrysostom, St. Paul, Tertullian, Gregory the Great, Innocent VIII, Martin Luther, John Calvin, John Wesley, John Knox, Aquinas, Oliver Cromwell, Paul IV, Jeremy Collins and John Styles—all of whom, says Hefner, were antisexual? And where else can you learn that "150 of those who disagreed with [Calvin] were put to death in Geneva"?

We must admit that we are rather impressed by Hefner's "Look, Ma! No hands!" approach to church history; he can string together more references in an article than Toynbee can in a volume. Roland Bainton, Ernst Troeltsch, Seward Hiltner, Ernst Renan, Lord Acton, David Mace, Moses, and William Graham Cole are among those from whom he wrests supportive quotes. Sad to say, Christians have often given reason for critics such as Hefner to find fault. But are they to be blamed for as much as he blames them for? Hefner decries American morality as "an amalgamation of the superstitious paganism and masochistic asceticism of early Christianity [and] the prohibitively strict, severe, joyless, authoritarian, unresponsive, book-banning, pleasure-baiting dogma of Calvinist Protestantism, Puritanism and Victorianism." It is this morality, Hefner claims, which causes today's unhappy marriages, frequent divorces, sex perversions, etc.

We hope the monkeys soon tire and that Hefner, a man of not inconsiderable talents, will think of better ways to employ those talents. We have certain misgivings whether he will actually be able to produce the "new, more realistic, rational, human and humane sexual morality" which he promises in an installment which remains, no doubt, an infinite distance ahead.

*Source*: "An Infinite Number of Monkeys: Researchers for Playboy Philosophy Series," *Christian Century*, August 28, 1963, 1063.

## DOCUMENT 43: *Freedman v. Maryland* (1965)

As recently as 1965, when the Supreme Court handed down its decision in *Freedman v. Maryland*, four states—Maryland, New York, Virginia, and Kansas—had active movie-censorship laws. Those statutes required the prior submission of films to a censorship board and prohibited their showing until the censor had "passed" on them. While the majority in *Freedman* held the Maryland law unconstitutional, the opinion did not go so far as to apply full First Amendment protection to films. Justice William O. Douglas, concurring on behalf of himself and Justice Hugo Black, urged such a step.

\* \* \*

MR. JUSTICE DOUGLAS, whom MR. JUSTICE BLACK joins, concurring.

On several occasions I have indicated my view that movies are entitled to the same degree and kind of protection under the First Amendment as other forms of expression. . . . For the reasons there stated, I do not believe any form of censorship—no matter how speedy or prolonged it may be—is permissible. As I see it, a pictorial presentation occupies as preferred a position as any other form of expression. If censors are banned from the publishing business, from the pulpit, from the public platform—as they are—they should be banned from the theatre. I would not admit the censor even for the limited role accorded him in *Kingsley Books, Inc.* v. *Brown*. . . . I adhere to my dissent in that case. . . . Any authority to obtain a temporary injunction gives the State "the paralyzing power of a censor." . . . The regime of *Kingsley Books* "substitutes punishment by contempt for punishment by jury trial." . . . I would put an end to all forms and types of censorship and give full literal meaning to the command of the First Amendment.

*Source*: 380 U.S. 51 (1965).

## DOCUMENT 44: *United States v. O'Brien* (1968)

Sexual morals were not the only standards that were changing rapidly in the late 1960s. Increasing numbers of young men were doing what their fathers would have found unthinkable: they were resisting the draft, rebelling not only against their country's call to arms but against the notion that their country had the right to issue such a call. One of the methods protesters used to express that rebellion was the public burning of their draft cards.

The First Amendment protects the expression of ideas. It does not prevent government from outlawing actions. In *United States v. O'Brien*, the Supreme Court upheld the constitutionality of a law making it a crime to forge, alter, knowingly destroy, or knowingly mutilate a draft card.

\* \* \*

MR. CHIEF JUSTICE WARREN delivered the opinion of the Court.

On the morning of March 31, 1966, David Paul O'Brien and three companions burned their Selective Service registration certificates on the steps of the South Boston Courthouse. A sizable crowd, including several agents of the Federal Bureau of Investigation, witnessed the event. . . . After he was advised of his right to counsel and to silence, O'Brien stated to FBI agents that he had burned his registration certificate because of his beliefs, knowing that he was violating federal law. He produced the charred remains of the certificate, which, with his consent, were photographed.

For this act, O'Brien was indicted, tried, convicted, and sentenced in the United States District Court for the District of Massachusetts. He did not contest the fact that he had burned the certificate. He stated in argument to the jury that he burned the certificate publicly to influence others to adopt his antiwar beliefs, as he put it, "so that other people would reevaluate their positions with Selective Service, with the armed forces, and reevaluate their place in the culture of today, to hopefully consider my position." . . .

. . . A law prohibiting destruction of Selective Service certificates no more abridges free speech on its face than a motor vehicle law prohibiting the destruction of drivers' licenses, or a tax law prohibiting the destruction of books and records.

O'Brien nonetheless argues that the 1965 Amendment is unconstitutional in its application to him, and is unconstitutional as enacted because what he calls the "purpose" of Congress was "to suppress freedom of speech." We consider these arguments separately. . . .

. . . we find that because of the Government's substantial interest in assuring the continuing availability of issued Selective Service certificates, because amended § 462 (b) is an appropriately narrow means of protecting this interest and condemns only the independent noncommunicative impact of conduct within its reach, and because the noncommunicative impact of O'Brien's act of burning his registration certificate frustrated the Government's interest, a sufficient governmental interest has been shown to justify O'Brien's conviction. . . .

It is a familiar principle of constitutional law that this Court will not strike down an otherwise constitutional statute on the basis of an alleged illicit legislative motive. As the Court long ago stated:

"The decisions of this court from the beginning lend no support whatever to the assumption that the judiciary may restrain the exercise of lawful power on the assumption that a wrongful purpose or motive has caused the power to be exerted."

*Source*: 391 U.S. 367 (1968).

---

## DOCUMENT 45: *Brandenburg v. Ohio* (1969)

It is a commonplace of First Amendment law that even noxious ideas must be given constitutional deference—that the government cannot suppress speech merely because the speaker or his or her ideas are detestable. As prior cases in this volume have demonstrated, such an approach to free speech was anything but commonplace on the Supreme Court until relatively recent times.

In *Brandenburg v. Ohio*, the Court used the conviction of a Ku Klux Klan member under Ohio's criminal syndicalism statute as a vehicle to finally overrule *Whitney v. California*, and to expressly rule that mere advocacy of violence or other hateful or subversive ideas, unaccompanied by any illegal act, was protected speech.

\* \* \*

MR. JUSTICE DOUGLAS, concurring. . . .

The Court quite properly overrules *Whitney v. California*, . . . which involved advocacy of ideas which the majority of the Court deemed unsound and dangerous.

Mr. Justice Holmes . . . moved closer to the First Amendment ideal when he said in dissent in *Gitlow v. New York* . . . :

"Every idea is an incitement. It offers itself for belief and if believed it is acted on unless some other belief outweighs it or some failure of energy stifles the movement at its birth. The only difference between the expression of an opinion and an incitement in the narrower sense is the speaker's enthusiasm for the result. Eloquence may set fire to reason. But whatever may be thought of the redundant discourse before us it had no chance of starting a present conflagration. If in the long run the beliefs expressed in proletarian dictatorship are destined to be accepted by the dominant forces of the community, the only meaning of free speech is that they should be given their chance and have their way." . . .

One's beliefs have long been thought to be sanctuaries which government could not invade. *Barenblatt* is one example of the ease with which that sanctuary can be violated. The lines drawn by the Court between the criminal act of being an "active" Communist and the innocent act of being a nominal or inactive Communist mark the difference only between deep and abiding belief and casual or uncertain belief. But I think that all matters of belief are beyond the reach of subpoenas or the probings of investigators. That is why the invasions of privacy made by investigating committees were notoriously unconstitutional. That is the deep-seated fault in the infamous loyalty-security hearings which, since 1947 when President Truman launched them, have processed 20,000,000 men and women. Those hearings were primarily concerned with one's thoughts, ideas, beliefs, and convictions. They were the most blatant violations of the First Amendment we have ever known.

The line between what is permissible and not subject to control and what may be made impermissible and subject to regulation is the line between ideas and overt acts. . . .

. . . [S]peech is, I think, immune from prosecution. Certainly there is no constitutional line between advocacy of abstract ideas as in *Yates* and advocacy of political action as in *Scales*. The quality of advocacy turns on the depth of the conviction; and government has no power to invade that sanctuary of belief and conscience.

*Source:* 395 U.S. 444 (1969).

---

## DOCUMENT 46: *Street v. New York* (1969)

On the afternoon of June 6, 1966, Sydney Street was listening to the radio in his Brooklyn apartment when he heard that civil rights crusader James Meredith had been shot by a sniper in Mississippi. He took a neatly folded American flag, which he kept and had formerly displayed on holidays, to a nearby intersection, where he lit a match and burned it. A small crowd gathered. A police officer who witnessed the incident testified that Street, an African American, admitted ownership of the flag and justified burning it by saying, "If they let that happen to Meredith we don't need an American flag." He was convicted of malicious mischief. In reversing the conviction, the Supreme Court avoided the issue it would later address in *Texas v. Johnson* (see Document 59): whether the act of flag burning is constitutionally protected as a form of political expression. Instead, the Court found that since the conviction "could" have been based upon the content of Street's speech, it could not be sustained.

* * *

MR. JUSTICE HARLAN delivered the opinion of the Court. . . .

We next consider whether it is our duty to reverse if we find, as we do in Parts III and IV, *infra*, that Street's words could have been an independent cause of his conviction and that a conviction for uttering such words would violate the Constitution.

That such is our duty is made apparent by a number of decisions of this Court. In the leading case of *Stromberg* v. *California*, . . . the appellant was convicted by a jury under a California statute making it an offense publicly to display a red flag for any one of three purposes. Finding that it would be unconstitutional to punish one who displayed for the first-named reason, this Court rejected the state court's reasoning that the appellant's conviction could nevertheless be sustained because the other two statutory reasons were severable and constitutional. This Court said:

"The verdict against the appellant was a general one. It did not specify the ground upon which it rested. . . . [I]t is impossible to say under which clause of the statute the conviction was obtained. If any one of these clauses . . . was invalid, it cannot be determined upon this record that the appellant was not convicted under that clause. . . . It follows that . . . the conviction cannot be upheld." . . .

It is true that in the present case the general verdict was rendered by a judge, not a jury. However, if the ground of the judge's decision cannot be ascertained from the record, then the danger of unconstitutional conviction is not significantly less than in the cases just discussed. . . . Nor would it be appropriate to remand the case to the trial judge for a *post hoc* explanation of the grounds of his decision. . . . Hence, we conclude that the case is governed by the rule of *Stromberg*, and that appellant's conviction must be set aside if we find that it could have been based solely upon his words and that a conviction resting on such a basis would be unconstitutional—a matter to which we shall turn in a moment.

Moreover, even assuming that the record precludes the inference that appellant's conviction might have been based *solely* on his words, we are still bound to reverse if the conviction could have been based upon *both* his words and his act. . . .

We take the rationale of *Thomas* to be that when a single-count indictment or information charges the commission of a crime by virtue of the defendant's having done both a constitutionally protected act and one

which may be unprotected, and a guilty verdict ensues without eluci-
dation, there is an unacceptable danger that the trier of fact will have
regarded the two acts as "intertwined" and have rested the conviction
on both together. . . . There is no comparable hazard when the indictment
or information is in several counts and the conviction is explicitly declared to rest on findings of guilt on certain of those counts, for in such
instances there is positive evidence that the trier of fact considered each
count on its own merits and separately from the others.

*Source*: 394 U.S. 576 (1969).

---

**DOCUMENT 47:** *Tinker v. Des Moines Independent Community
School District* **(1969)**

---

*Tinker v. Des Moines Independent Community School District* is one
of a relative handful of cases dealing with the free-speech rights of
students in a public school. At the height of public debate over the
merits of the Vietnam War, three public school students in Des Moines,
Iowa, wore black armbands to class. The armbands were intended as
a protest against the war and American policy in Southeast Asia. Other
than the armbands, the students were quiet and passive; there was no
disruption of school order and discipline. They were given a choice:
remove the armbands or be suspended from school. The Supreme
Court found that students did not "shed their constitutional rights at the
schoolhouse gate," and that the suspensions were improper.

* * *

MR. JUSTICE FORTAS delivered the opinion of the Court. . . .

In December 1965, a group of adults and students in Des Moines held
a meeting at the Eckhardt home. The group determined to publicize their
objections to the hostilities in Vietnam and their support for a truce by
wearing black armbands during the holiday season and by fasting on
December 16 and New Year's Eve. Petitioners and their parents had previously engaged in similar activities, and they decided to participate in
the program.

The principals of the Des Moines schools became aware of the plan to
wear armbands. On December 14, 1965, they met and adopted a policy
that any student wearing an armband to school would be asked to remove it, and if he refused he would be suspended until he returned
without the armband. Petitioners were aware of the regulation that the
school authorities adopted.

On December 16, Mary Beth and Christopher wore black armbands to their schools. John Tinker wore his armband the next day. They were all sent home and suspended from school until they would come back without their armbands. They did not return to school until after the planned period for wearing armbands had expired—that is, until after New Year's Day. . . .

The District Court recognized that the wearing of an armband for the purpose of expressing certain views is the type of symbolic act that is within the Free Speech Clause of the First Amendment. . . . As we shall discuss, the wearing of armbands in the circumstances of this case was entirely divorced from actually or potentially disruptive conduct by those participating in it. It was closely akin to "pure speech" which, we have repeatedly held, is entitled to comprehensive protection under the First Amendment. . . .

First Amendment rights, applied in light of the special characteristics of the school environment, are available to teachers and students. It can hardly be argued that either students or teachers shed their constitutional rights to freedom of speech or expression at the schoolhouse gate. This has been the unmistakable holding of this Court for almost 50 years. . . . [T]his Court, in opinions by Mr. Justice McReynolds, held that the Due Process Clause of the Fourteenth Amendment prevents States from forbidding the teaching of a foreign language to young students. Statutes to this effect, the Court held, unconstitutionally interfere with the liberty of teacher, student, and parent. . . .

. . . On the other hand, the Court has repeatedly emphasized the need for affirming the comprehensive authority of the States and of school officials, consistent with fundamental constitutional safeguards, to prescribe and control conduct in the schools. . . . Our problem lies in the area where students in the exercise of First Amendment rights collide with the rules of the school authorities. . . .

The school officials banned and sought to punish petitioners for a silent, passive expression of opinion, unaccompanied by any disorder or disturbance on the part of petitioners. There is here no evidence whatever of petitioners' interference, actual or nascent, with the schools' work or of collision with the rights of other students to be secure and to be let alone. Accordingly, this case does not concern speech or action that intrudes upon the work of the schools or the rights of other students. . . .

The District Court concluded that the action of the school authorities was reasonable because it was based upon their fear of a disturbance from the wearing of the armbands. But, in our system, undifferentiated fear or apprehension of disturbance is not enough to overcome the right to freedom of expression. Any departure from absolute regimentation may cause trouble. Any variation from the majority's opinion may inspire fear. Any word spoken, in class, in the lunchroom, or on the campus, that deviates from the views of another person may start an argument or cause a disturbance. But our Constitution says we must take this risk, . . . and our history says that it is this sort of hazardous freedom—this kind of openness—that is the basis of our national strength and of the independence and vigor of Americans who grow up and live in this relatively permissive, often disputatious, society. . . .

It is also relevant that the school authorities did not purport to prohibit the wearing of all symbols of political or controversial significance. The record shows that students in some of the schools wore buttons relating to national political campaigns, and some even wore the Iron Cross, traditionally a symbol of Nazism. The order prohibiting the wearing of armbands did not extend to these. Instead, a particular symbol—black armbands worn to exhibit opposition to this Nation's involvement in Vietnam—was singled out for prohibition. Clearly, the prohibition of expression of one particular opinion, at least without evidence that it is necessary to avoid material and substantial interference with schoolwork or discipline, is not constitutionally permissible. . . .

Under our Constitution, free speech is not a right that is given only to be so circumscribed that it exists in principle but not in fact. Freedom of expression would not truly exist if the right could be exercised only in an area that a benevolent government has provided as a safe haven for crackpots. The Constitution says that Congress (and the States) may not abridge the right to free speech. This provision means what it says. We properly read it to permit reasonable regulation of speech-connected activities in carefully restricted circumstances. But we do not confine the permissible exercise of First Amendment rights to a telephone booth or the four corners of a pamphlet, or to supervised and ordained discussion in a school classroom. . . .

*Reversed and remanded.*

*Source:* 393 U.S. 503 (1969).

---

## DOCUMENT 48: *Miller v. California* (1973)

On June 21, 1973, the Supreme Court handed down two related opinions, *Miller v. California* and *Paris Adult Theatre I v. Slaton*. Once again, the issue was the power of government to proscribe obscenity, and once again, the justices were unable even to agree upon the definition of obscenity. As Justice Brennan noted in his lengthy and scholarly dissent in *Paris Adult Theatre I*, "one cannot say with certainty that material is obscene until at least five members of this Court, applying inevitably obscure standards, have pronounced it so."

The cases presented distinct issues. In *Miller*, advertisements for sexually explicit materials had been mailed to persons who had not requested them and who were offended by them; in *Paris Adult Theatre I*, pornographic films had been shown in an "adults only" theater, which had posted warnings of their contents and demanded proof that ticket buyers were at least twenty-one years old. Writing for the Court in *Miller*, Chief Justice Warren Burger revisited the definition of obscenity, refining the famous three-pronged test (works that, taken as a whole, appeal to the prurient interest; that portray sexual conduct in a patently offensive manner; and that, taken as a whole, do not have serious literary, artistic, political, or scientific value) and reiterating the Court's position that obscene materials do not enjoy First Amendment protection. In *Paris Adult Theatre I*, he again upheld the state's right to prosecute, finding it constitutionally irrelevant that the materials were seen only by consenting adults.

* * *

MR. CHIEF JUSTICE BURGER delivered the opinion of the Court.

This is one of a group of "obscenity-pornography" cases being reviewed by the Court in a re-examination of [the] standards which must be used to identify obscene material that a State may regulate. . . .

Appellant conducted a mass mailing campaign to advertise the sale of illustrated books, euphemistically called "adult" material. . . . Appellant's conviction was specifically based on his conduct in causing five unsolicited advertising brochures to be sent through the mail. . . . The brochures . . . primarily . . . consist of pictures and drawings very explicitly depicting men and women in groups of two or more engaging in a variety of sexual activities, with genitals often prominently displayed.

I

This case involves the application of a State's criminal obscenity statute to a situation in which sexually explicit materials have been thrust by aggressive sales action upon unwilling recipients. . . .

II

. . . obscene material is unprotected by the First Amendment. . . . [However,] State statutes designed to regulate obscene materials must be carefully limited. . . . As a result, we now confine the permissible scope of such regulation to work which depict or describe sexual conduct. That conduct must be specifically defined by the applicable state law, as written or authoritatively construed. . . .

The basic guidelines for the trier of fact must be: (a) whether "the average person, applying contemporary community standards" would find that the work, taken as a whole, appeals to the prurient interest . . . ; (b) whether the work depicts or describes, in a patently offensive way, sexual conduct specifically defined by the applicable state law; and (c) whether the work, taken as a whole, lacks serious literary, artistic, political, or scientific value. We do not adopt as a constitutional standard the *"utterly without redeeming social value"* test of *Memoirs v. Massachusetts*. . . .

We emphasize that it is not our function to propose regulatory schemes for the States. . . . It is possible, however, to give a few plain examples of what a state could define for regulation under part (b) of the standard announced in this opinion, *supra*:

(a) Patently offensive representations or descriptions of ultimate sexual acts, normal or perverted, actual or simulated.

(b) Patently offensive representations or descriptions of masturbation, excretory functions, and lewd exhibition of the genitals.

Sex and nudity may not be exploited without limit by films or pictures exhibited or sold in places of public accommodation any more than live sex and nudity can be exhibited or sold without limit in such public places. At a minimum, prurient, patently offensive depiction or description of sexual conduct must have serious literary, artistic, political, or scientific value to merit First Amendment protection. . . . In resolving the inevitably sensitive questions of fact and law, we must continue to rely on the jury system, accompanied by the safeguards that judges, rules of evidence, presumption of innocence, and other protective features provide, as we do with . . . other offenses against society and its individual members.

Mr. JUSTICE BRENNAN . . . now maintains that no formulation of this Court, the Congress, or the States can adequately distinguish obscene material unprotected by the First Amendment from protected expression. . . . Under the holdings announced today, no one will be subject to prosecution for the sale or exposure of obscene materials unless these materials depict or describe patently offensive "hard core" sexual conduct specifically defined by the regulating state law, as written or construed. We are satisfied that these specific prerequisites will provide fair notice to a dealer in such materials that his public and commercial activities may bring prosecution. . . .

Mr. JUSTICE BRENNAN also emphasizes "institutional stress" in justification of his change of view. . . . It is certainly true that the absence, since *Roth*, of a single majority view of this Court as to proper standards for testing obscenity has placed a strain on both state and federal courts. But today, for the first time since *Roth* was decided in 1957, a majority of this Court has agreed on concrete guidelines to isolate "hard core" pornography from expression protected by the First Amendment. Now we may abandon the casual practice of *Redrup v. New York* . . . and attempt to provide positive guidance to federal and state courts alike.

This may not be an easy road, free from difficulty. But no amount of "fatigue" should lead us to adopt a convenient "institutional" rationale—an absolutist, "anything goes" view of the First Amendment—because it will lighten our burdens. . . .

## III

Under a National Constitution, fundamental First Amendment limitations on the powers of the States do not vary from community to community, but this does not mean that there are, or should or can be, fixed, uniform national standards of precisely what appeals to the "prurient interest" or is "patently offensive." These are essentially questions of fact, and our Nation is simply too big and too diverse for this Court to reasonably expect that such standards could be articulated for all 50 States in a single formulation, even assuming the prerequisite consensus exists. . . .

It is neither realistic nor constitutionally sound to read the First Amendment as requiring that the people of Maine or Mississippi accept public depiction of conduct found tolerable in Las Vegas, or New York City. . . . People in different States vary in their tastes and attitudes, and this diversity is not to be strangled by the absolutism of imposed uniformity. . . . We hold that the requirement that the jury evaluate the materials with reference to "contemporary standards of the State of California" . . . is constitutionally adequate.

## IV

The dissenting Justices sound the alarm of repression. But, in our view, to equate the free and robust exchange of ideas and political debate with commercial exploitation of obscene material demeans the grand conception of the First Amendment. . . . The First Amendment protects works which, taken as a whole, have serious literary, artistic, political, or scientific value, regardless of whether the government or a majority of the people approve of the ideas these works represent. . . . But the public portrayal of hard-core sexual conduct for its own sake, and for the ensuing commercial gain, is a different matter.

There is no evidence, empirical or historical, that the stern 19th century American censorship of public distribution and display of material relating to sex . . . in any way limited or affected expression of serious literary, artistic, political, or scientific ideas. . . .

In sum, we (a) reaffirm the *Roth* holding that obscene material is not protected by the First Amendment; (b) hold that such material can be regulated by the States, subject to the specific safeguards enunciated above, without a showing that the material is "*utterly* without redeeming social value"; and (c) hold that obscenity is to be determined by applying "contemporary community standards." ...

*Vacated and remanded.*

MR. JUSTICE DOUGLAS, dissenting. ...

... The idea that the First Amendment permits punishment for ideas that are "offensive" to the particular judge or jury sitting in judgment is astounding. No greater leveler of speech or literature has ever been designed. ...

... I do not think we, the judges, were ever given the constitutional power to make definitions of obscenity. If it is to be defined, let the people debate and decide by a constitutional amendment what they want to ban as obscene. ... Whatever the choice, the courts will have some guidelines. Now we have none except our own predilections.

MR. JUSTICE BRENNAN, with whom MR. JUSTICE STEWART and MR. JUSTICE MARSHALL join, dissenting.

In my dissent in *Paris Adult Theatre I* v. *Slaton*, ... I noted that I had no occasion to consider the extent of state power to regulate the distribution of sexually oriented material ... to unconsenting adults. ... I need not now decide [that question.] For it is clear that under my dissent in *Paris Adult Theatre I*, the statute under which the prosecution was brought is unconstitutionally overbroad, and therefore invalid on its face.

*Source:* 413 U.S. 15 (1973).

---

## DOCUMENT 49: *Paris Adult Theatre I v. Slaton, District Attorney* (1973)

MR. JUSTICE BRENNAN, with whom MR. JUSTICE STEWART and MR. JUSTICE MARSHALL join, dissenting.

This case requires the Court to confront once again the vexing problem of reconciling state efforts to suppress sexually oriented expression with the protections of the First Amendment, as applied to the States through the Fourteenth Amendment. ...

... The decision of the Georgia Supreme Court rested squarely on its conclusion that the State could constitutionally suppress these films even if they were displayed only to persons over the age of 21 who were aware of the nature of their contents and who had consented to viewing them. For the reasons set forth in this opinion, I am convinced of the invalidity of that conclusion of law, and I would therefore vacate the judgment of the Georgia Supreme Court. I have no occasion to consider the extent of state power to regulate the distribution of sexually oriented materials to juveniles or to unconsenting adults. Nor am I required, for the purposes of this review, to consider whether or not these petitioners had, in fact, taken precautions to avoid exposure of films to minors or unconsenting adults. . . .

As a result of our failure to define standards with predictable application to any given piece of material, there is no probability of regularity in obscenity decisions by state and lower federal courts. That is not to say that these courts have performed badly in this area or paid insufficient attention to the principles we have established. The problem is, rather, that one cannot say with certainty that material is obscene until at least five members of this Court, applying inevitably obscure standards, have pronounced it so. The number of obscenity cases on our docket gives ample testimony to the burden that has been placed upon this Court. . . .

Our experience since *Roth* requires us not only to abandon the effort to pick out obscene materials on a case-by-case basis, but also to reconsider a fundamental postulate of *Roth*: that there exists a definable class of sexually oriented expression that may be totally suppressed by the Federal and State Governments. Assuming that such a class of expression does in fact exist, I am forced to conclude that the concept of "obscenity" cannot be defined with sufficient specificity and clarity to provide fair notice to persons who create and distribute sexually oriented materials, to prevent substantial erosion of protected speech as a byproduct of the attempt to suppress unprotected speech, and to avoid very costly institutional harms. Given these inevitable side effects of state efforts to suppress what is assumed to be *unprotected* speech, we must scrutinize with care the state interest that is asserted to justify the suppression. For in the absence of some very substantial interest in suppressing such speech, we can hardly condone the ill effects that seem to flow inevitably from the effort. . . .

If, as the Court today assumes, "a state legislature may . . . act on the . . . assumption that commerce in obscene books, or public exhibitions focused on obscene conduct, have a tendency to exert a corrupting and debasing impact leading to antisocial behavior," . . . then it is hard to see how state-ordered regimentation of our minds can ever be forestalled. For if a State, in an effort to maintain or create a particular moral tone, may prescribe what its citizens cannot read or cannot see, then it would seem to follow that in pursuit of that same objective a State could decree that its citizens must read certain books or must view certain films. . . . However laudable its goal—and that is obviously a question on which reasonable minds may differ—the State cannot proceed by means that violate the Constitution. . . .

. . . Even a legitimate, sharply focused state concern for the morality of the community cannot, in other words, justify an assault on the protections of the First Amendment. . . . Where the state interest in regulation of morality is vague and ill defined, interference with the guarantees of the First Amendment is even more difficult to justify.

In short, while I cannot say that the interests of the State—apart from the question of juveniles and unconsenting adults—are trivial or nonexistent, I am compelled to conclude that these interests cannot justify the substantial damage to constitutional rights and to this Nation's judicial machinery that inevitably results from state efforts to bar the distribution even of unprotected material to consenting adults. . . . I would hold, therefore, that at least in the absence of distribution to juveniles or obtrusive exposure to unconsenting adults, the First and Fourteenth Amendments prohibit the State and Federal Governments from attempting wholly to suppress sexually oriented materials on the basis of their allegedly "obscene" contents. Nothing in this approach precludes those governments from taking action to serve what may be strong and legitimate interests through regulation of the manner of distribution of sexually oriented material.

*Source*: 413 U.S. 49 (1973).

## DOCUMENT 50: *Jenkins v. Georgia* (1974)

While the *Miller* and *Paris Adult Theatre I* cases were wending their way through the appeals process, another case arising in Georgia graphically demonstrated the essentially arbitrary nature of obscenity law. As if to underscore the accuracy of Justice Brennan's observations in his *Paris Adult Theatre I* dissent, a Georgia jury convicted a theater operator on an obscenity charge for showing the commercial film *Carnal Knowledge*. Appeal of that conviction came to the Supreme Court on the heels of *Miller* and *Paris Adult Theatre I*, forcing the Court to reinterpret its own rule so as to avoid a ridiculous result.

The jury in the small Georgia town had decided that the film appealed to prurient interests and was patently offensive under relevant community standards. This was a movie that had been widely shown and critically acclaimed; Ann-Margret had been nominated for an Academy Award for her portrayal of one of the leads. *Carnal Knowledge* had been shown without incident in twenty-nine other Georgia towns and had been booked by forty to fifty more.

Justice William Rehnquist, writing for the majority, stated that the "new rule" enunciated in *Miller* required reversal; more telling, however, was his statement that "our own viewing of the film satisfies us that 'Carnal Knowledge' could not be found under the *Miller* standards to depict sexual conduct in a patently offensive way." In other words, we know it when we see it—and we didn't see it.

\* \* \*

MR. JUSTICE REHNQUIST delivered the opinion of the Court. . . .

We agree with the Supreme Court of Georgia's implicit ruling that the Constitution does not require that juries be instructed in state obscenity cases to apply the standards of a hypothetical statewide community. *Miller* approved the use of such instructions; it did not mandate their use. What *Miller* makes clear is that state juries need not be instructed to apply "national standards." We also agree with the Supreme Court of Georgia's implicit approval of the trial court's instructions directing jurors to apply "community standards" without specifying what "community." *Miller* held that it was constitutionally permissible to permit juries to rely on the understanding of the community from which they came as to contemporary community standards, and the States have considerable latitude in framing statutes under this element of the *Miller* decision. A State may choose to define an obscenity offense in terms of "contemporary community standards" as defined in *Miller* without further specification, as was done here, or it may choose to define the standards in more precise geographic terms, as was done by California in *Miller*. . . .

There is little to be found in the record about the film "Carnal Knowledge" other than the film itself. However, appellant has supplied a variety of information and critical commentary, the authenticity of which appellee does not dispute. The film appeared on many "Ten Best" lists for 1971, the year in which it was released. Many but not all of the reviews were favorable. We believe that the following passage from a review which appeared in the Saturday Review is a reasonably accurate description of the film:

"[It is basically a story] of two young college men, roommates and lifelong friends forever preoccupied with their sex lives. Both are first met as virgins. Nicholson is the more knowledgeable and attractive of the two; speaking colloquially, he is a burgeoning bastard. Art Garfunkel is his friend, the nice but troubled guy straight out of those early Feiffer cartoons, but real. He falls in love with the lovely Susan (Candice Bergen) and unknowingly shares her with his college buddy. As the 'safer' one of the two, he is selected by Susan for marriage.

"The time changes. Both men are in their thirties, pursuing successful careers in New York. Nicholson has been running through an average of a dozen women a year but has never managed to meet the right one, the one with the full bosom, the good legs, the properly rounded bottom. More than that, each and every one is a threat to his malehood and peace of mind, until at last, in a bar, he finds

Ann-Margaret [*sic*], an aging bachelor girl with striking cleavage and, quite obviously, something of a past. 'Why don't we shack up?' she suggests. They do and a horrendous relationship ensues, complicated mainly by her paranoidal desire to marry. Meanwhile, what of Garfunkel? The sparks have gone out of his marriage, the sex has lost its savor, and Garfunkel tries once more. And later, even more foolishly, again." . . .

Even though questions of appeal to the "prurient interest" or of patent offensiveness are "essentially questions of fact," it would be a serious misreading of *Miller* to conclude that juries have unbridled discretion in determining what is "patently offensive." Not only did we there say that "the First Amendment values applicable to the States through the Fourteenth Amendment are adequately protected by the ultimate power of appellate courts to conduct an independent review of constitutional claims when necessary," but we made it plain that under that holding "no one will be subject to prosecution for the sale or exposure of obscene materials unless these materials depict or describe patently offensive 'hard core' sexual conduct. . . ." . . .

Our own viewing of the film satisfies us that "Carnal Knowledge" could not be found under the *Miller* standards to depict sexual conduct in a patently offensive way.

*Source*: 418 U.S. 153 (1974).

---

## DOCUMENT 51: Federal Election Campaign Act of 1971

In 1971, Congress enacted sweeping legislation intended to "clean up" political campaigns. The Federal Election Campaign Act limited political contributions to federal candidates to $1,000 for individuals and $5,000 for political committees; it limited expenditures by individuals, groups, or candidates themselves; and it required detailed disclosure and record keeping by all political parties.

* * *

(b) *Contributions by persons and committees.*

(1) Except as otherwise provided by paragraph (2) and (3), no person shall make contributions to any candidate with respect to any election for Federal office which, in the aggregate, exceed $1,000.

(2) No political committee (other than a principal campaign committee) shall make contributions to any candidate with respect to any election for Federal office which, in the aggregate, exceed $5,000. Contributions by the national

committee of a political party serving as the principal campaign committee of a candidate for the office of President of the United States shall not exceed the limitation imposed by the preceding sentence with respect to any other candidate for Federal office. For purposes of this paragraph, the term "political committee" means an organization registered as a political committee under section 433, Title 2, United States Code, for a period of not less than 6 months which has received contributions from more than 50 persons and, except for any State political party organization, has made contributions to 5 or more candidates for Federal office.

(3) No individual shall make contributions aggregating more than $25,000 in any calendar year. For purposes of this paragraph, any contribution made in a year other than the calendar year in which the election is held with respect to which such contribution was made, is considered to be made during the calendar year in which such election is held.

(4) For purposes of this subsection—

(A) contributions to a named candidate made to any political committee authorized by such candidate, in writing, to accept contributions on his behalf shall be considered to be contributions made to such candidate, and

(B) contributions made to or for the benefit of any candidate nominated by a political party for election to the office of Vice President of the United States shall be considered to be contributions made to or for the benefit of the candidate of such party for election to the office of President of the United States.

(5) The limitations imposed by paragraphs (1) and (2) of this subsection shall apply separately with respect to each election, except that all elections held in any calendar year for the office of President of the United States (except a general election for such office) shall be considered to be one election.

(6) For purposes of the limitations imposed by this section, all contributions made by a person, either directly or indirectly, on behalf of a particular candidate, including contributions which are in any way earmarked or otherwise directed through an intermediary or conduit to such candidate, shall be treated as contributions from such person to such candidate. The intermediary or conduit shall report the original source and the intended recipient of such contribution to the Commission and to the intended recipient.

(c) *Limitations on expenditures.*

(1) No candidate shall make expenditures in excess of—

(A) $10,000,000 in the case of a candidate for nomination for election to the office of President of the United States, except that the aggregate of expenditures under this subparagraph in any one State shall not exceed twice the expenditure limitation applicable in such State to a candidate for nomination for election to the office of Senator, Delegate, or Resident Commissioner, as the case may be;

(B) $20,000,000, in the case of a candidate for election to the office of President of the United States;

(C) in the case of any campaign for nomination for election by a candidate for the office of Senator or by a candidate for the office of Representative from a State which is entitled to only one Representative, the greater of—

(i) 8 cents multiplied by the voting age population of the State (as certified under subsection (g));

(ii) $100,000;

(D) in the case of any campaign for election by a candidate for the office of Senator or by a candidate for the office of Representative from a State which is entitled to only one Representative, the greater of—

(i) 12 cents multiplied by the voting age population of the State (as certified under subsection (g)); or

(ii) $150,000.

*Source*: 18 U.S.C. §§ 608(b)(1), (3) (1970 ed. Supp. IV), set out in an appendix to *Buckley v. Valeo*, 424 U.S. 1 (1976).

---

## DOCUMENT 52: *Buckley v. Valeo, Secretary of the United States Senate* (1976)

In 1971, Congress passed Federal Election Campaign Act. It was amended in 1974. A challenge to its constitutionality was brought by Republican Senator James Buckley and former Democratic senator and Presidential candidate Eugene McCarthy (among others). They sued Francis Valeo, who was secretary of the Senate, as well as others (clerk of the House, etc.). Hence the case name: Buckley v. Valeo.

In 1976, in response to challenges to the legislation, the Supreme Court issued a 176-page opinion, *Buckley v. Valeo*. As daunting and technical as the opinion is in many respects, the heart of the controversy is starkly simple: is spending money speech? The Court held that it is, and invalidated the expenditure limits. At the same time, however, it upheld the contribution limits, setting up a dichotomy that has been widely criticized.

* * *

PER CURIAM. . . .

The Act's contribution and expenditure limitations operate in an area of the most fundamental First Amendment activities. Discussion of public issues and debate on the qualifications of candidates are integral to the operation of the system of government established by our Constitution. The First Amendment affords the broadest protection to such political expression in order "to assure [the] unfettered interchange of ideas for the bringing about of political and social changes desired by the people." . . . Although First Amendment protections are not confined to "the exposition of ideas," *Winters* v. *New York*, . . . "there is practically universal agreement that a major purpose of that Amendment was to protect the free discussion of governmental affairs, . . . of course includ[ing] discussions of candidates . . ." . . . This no more than reflects our "profound national commitment to the principle that debate on public issues should be uninhibited, robust, and wide-open." . . . In a republic where the people are sovereign, the ability of the citizenry to make informed choices among candidates for office is essential, for the identities of those who are elected will inevitably shape the course that we follow as a nation. . . .

The First Amendment protects political association as well as political expression. The constitutional right of association explicated in *NAACP* v. *Alabama* . . . stemmed from the Court's recognition that "[e]ffective advocacy of both public and private points of view, particularly controversial ones, is undeniably enhanced by group association." . . .

It is with these principles in mind that we consider the primary contentions of the parties with respect to the Act's limitations upon the giving and spending of money in political campaigns. Those conflicting contentions could not more sharply define the basic issues before us. Appellees contend that what the Act regulates is conduct, and that its effect on speech and association is incidental at most. Appellants respond that contributions and expenditures are at the very core of political speech, and that the Act's limitations thus constitute restraints on First Amendment liberty that are both gross and direct. . . .

A restriction on the amount of money a person or group can spend on political communication during a campaign necessarily reduces the quantity of expression by restricting the number of issues discussed, the depth of their exploration, and the size of the audience reached. This is because virtually every means of communicating ideas in today's mass society requires the expenditure of money. The distribution of the humblest handbill or leaflet entails printing, paper, and circulation costs. Speeches and rallies generally necessitate hiring a hall and publicizing the event. The electorate's increasing dependence on television, radio, and other mass media for news and information has made these expensive modes of communication indispensable instruments of effective political speech. . . .

By contrast with a limitation upon expenditures for political expression, a limitation upon the amount that any one person or group may contribute to a candidate or political committee entails only a marginal restriction upon the contributor's ability to engage in free communication. A contribution serves as a general expression of support for the candidate and his views, but does not communicate the underlying basis for the support. The quantity of communication by the contributor does not increase perceptibly with the size of his contribution, since the expression rests solely on the undifferentiated, symbolic act of contributing. At most, the size of the contribution provides a very rough index of the intensity of the contributor's support for the candidate. A limitation on the amount of money a person may give to a candidate or campaign organization thus involves little direct restraint on his political communication, for it permits the symbolic expression of support evidenced by a contribution but does not in any way infringe the contributor's freedom to discuss candidates and issues. While contributions may result in political expression if spent by a candidate or an association to present views to the voters, the transformation of contributions into political debate involves speech by someone other than the contributor.... 

The Act's contribution and expenditure limitations also impinge on protected associational freedoms. Making a contribution, like joining a political party, serves to affiliate a person with a candidate. In addition, it enables like-minded persons to pool their resources in furtherance of common political goals. The Act's contribution ceilings thus limit one important means of associating with a candidate or committee, but leave the contributor free to become a member of any political association and to assist personally in the association's efforts on behalf of candidates. And the Act's contribution limitations permit associations and candidates to aggregate large sums of money to promote effective advocacy. By contrast, the Act's $1,000 limitation on independent expenditures "relative to a clearly identified candidate" precludes most associations from effectively amplifying the voice of their adherents, the original basis for the recognition of First Amendment protection of the freedom of association.... The Act's constraints on the ability of independent associations and candidate campaign organizations to expend resources on political expression "is simultaneously an interference with the freedom of [their] adherents." ...

In sum, although the Act's contribution and expenditure limitations both implicate fundamental First Amendment interests, its expenditure ceilings impose significantly more severe restrictions on protected freedoms of political expression and association than do its limitations on financial contributions.

Source: 424 U.S. 1 (1976).

---

## DOCUMENT 53: *Virginia State Board of Pharmacy v. Virginia Citizens Consumer Council, Inc.* (1976)

Commentators have long questioned the distinction between commercial and noncommercial speech. In 1976 and again in 1977, the

Supreme Court revisited that distinction and acknowledged that commercial speech was not "wholly outside" the protection of the First and Fourteenth Amendments.

At issue in *Virginia State Board of Pharmacy* was a regulation of the State Pharmacy Board declaring "unprofessional" the advertisement of drug prices by registered pharmacists. Consumers challenged the regulation, arguing that the First Amendment protected their right to receive information that pharmacists would communicate through advertising and other promotional means. They also asserted that their right to access such information was not "commercial" in the same sense as the right of the pharmacists to disseminate the information, and that it should therefore be accorded greater protection than the Court had previously accorded to commercial speech. The Supreme Court, in a 7–1 opinion (Justice John Paul Stevens did not participate) held that government may not suppress the dissemination of concededly truthful information about entirely lawful activities.

\* \* \*

MR. JUSTICE BLACKMUN delivered the opinion of the Court. . . .

Once licensed, a pharmacist is subject to a civil monetary penalty, or to revocation or suspension of his license, if the Board finds that he "is not of good moral character," or has violated any of a number of stated professional standards (among them that he not be "negligent in the practice of pharmacy" or have engaged in "fraud or deceit upon the consumer . . . in connection with the practice of pharmacy"), or is guilty of "unprofessional conduct." . . . "Unprofessional conduct" is specifically defined in § 54–524.35, . . . the third numbered phrase of which relates to advertising of the price for any prescription drug, and is the subject of this litigation.

Inasmuch as only a licensed pharmacist may dispense prescription drugs in Virginia, . . . advertising or other affirmative dissemination of prescription drug price information is effectively forbidden in the State. Some pharmacies refuse even to quote prescription drug prices over the telephone. . . .

. . . The plaintiffs are an individual Virginia resident who suffers from diseases that require her to take prescription drugs on a daily basis, and two nonprofit organizations. Their claim is that the First Amendment entitles the user of prescription drugs to receive information that pharmacists wish to communicate to them through advertising and other promotional means, concerning the prices of such drugs. . . .

The appellants contend that the advertisement of prescription drug prices is outside the protection of the First Amendment because it is "commercial speech." There can be no question that in past decisions the

Court has given some indication that commercial speech is unprotected. In *Valentine* v. *Chrestensen*, . . . the Court upheld a New York statute that prohibited the distribution of any "handbill, circular . . . or other advertising matter whatsoever in or upon any street." The Court concluded that, although the First Amendment would forbid the banning of all communication by handbill in the public thoroughfares, it imposed "no such restraint on government as respects purely commercial advertising." . . . Further support for a "commercial speech" exception to the First Amendment may perhaps be found in *Breard* v. *Alexandria*, . . . where the Court upheld a conviction for violation of an ordinance prohibiting door-to-door solicitation of magazine subscriptions. The Court reasoned: "The selling . . . brings into the transaction a commercial feature," and it distinguished *Martin* v. *Struthers*, . . . where it had reversed a conviction for door-to-door distribution of leaflets publicizing a religious meeting, as a case involving "no element of the commercial." . . . Moreover, the Court several times has stressed that communications to which First Amendment protection was given were *not* "purely commercial." . . .

Here . . . the question whether there is a First Amendment exception for "commercial speech" is squarely before us. Our pharmacist does not wish to editorialize on any subject, cultural, philosophical, or political. He does not wish to report any particularly newsworthy fact, or to make generalized observations even about commercial matters. The "idea" he wishes to communicate is simply this: "I will sell you the X prescription drug at the Y price." Our question, then, is whether this communication is wholly outside the protection of the First Amendment. . . .

As to the particular consumer's interest in the free flow of commercial information, that interest may be as keen, if not keener by far, than his interest in the day's most urgent political debate. Appellees' case in this respect is a convincing one. Those whom the suppression of prescription drug price information hits the hardest are the poor, the sick, and particularly the aged. A disproportionate amount of their income tends to be spent on prescription drugs; yet they are the least able to learn, by shopping from pharmacist to pharmacist, where their scarce dollars are best spent. When drug prices vary as strikingly as they do, information as to who is charging what becomes more than a convenience. It could mean the alleviation of physical pain or the enjoyment of basic necessities. . . .

Moreover, there is another consideration that suggests that no line between publicly "interesting" or "important" commercial advertising and the opposite kind could ever be drawn. Advertising, however tasteless and excessive it sometimes may seem, is nonetheless dissemination of information as to who is producing and selling what product, for what reason, and at what price. So long as we preserve a predominantly free enterprise economy, the allocation of our resources in large measure will be made through numerous private economic decisions. It is a matter of public interest that those decisions, in the aggregate, be intelligent and well informed. To this end, the free flow of commercial information is indispensable.

*Source:* 425 U.S. 748 (1976).

---

## DOCUMENT 54: *Linmark Associates, Inc. v. Township of Willingboro* (1977)

In 1977, the Supreme Court used the precedent it had established in *Virginia State Board of Pharmacy* to strike down yet another restriction. A township ordinance in Willingboro, New Jersey had prohibited homeowners from posting "for sale" signs, in an effort to stem white flight. As blacks had moved into the neighborhoods, whites had feared that their property values would decrease and the township would become overwhelmingly black. Real-estate agents played upon these fears, and the resulting numbers of "for sale" signs further reinforced them.

Writing for a unanimous Court (Justice William Rehnquist, however, did not participate), Justice Thurgood Marshall acknowledged the public importance of encouraging integrated housing, but held that government could not effectuate that goal by infringing the First Amendment. He explicitly reiterated the language in *Virginia State Board of Pharmacy* extending a substantial amount of First Amendment protection to commercial speech.

\* \* \*

MR. JUSTICE MARSHALL delivered the opinion of the Court.

This case presents the question whether the First Amendment permits a municipality to prohibit the posting of "For Sale" or "Sold" signs when the municipality acts to stem what it perceives as the flight of white homeowners from a racially integrated community. . . .

. . . The Township Council here, like the Virginia Assembly in *Virginia Pharmacy Bd.*, acted to prevent its residents from obtaining certain information. That information, which pertains to sales activity in Willingboro, is of vital interest to Willingboro residents, since it may bear on one of the most important decisions they have a right to make: where to live and raise their families. The Council has sought to restrict the free flow of these data because it fears that otherwise homeowners will make decisions inimical to what the Council views as the homeowners' self-interest and the corporate interest of the township: they will choose to leave town. The Council's concern, then, was not with any commercial aspect of "For Sale" signs—with offerors communicating offers to offerees—but with the substance of the information communicated to Willingboro citizens. If dissemination of this information can be restricted, then every locality in the country can suppress any facts that reflect poorly on the locality, so long as a plausible claim can be made that disclosure would cause the recipients of the information to act "irrationally." ...

In invalidating this law, we by no means leave Willingboro defenseless in its effort to promote integrated housing. The township obviously remains free to continue "the process of education" it has already begun. It can give widespread publicity—through "Not for Sale" signs or other methods—to the number of whites remaining in Willingboro. And it surely can endeavor to create inducements to retain individuals who are considering selling their homes.

*Source*: 431 U.S. 85 (1977).

---

## DOCUMENT 55: *Board of Education, Island Trees Union Free School District No. 26 v. Pico, by his next friend Pico* (1982)

If the Supreme Court enjoyed a brief unanimity on the issue of commercial speech, that accord was short lived. In 1982, the Court was once again asked to determine the application of the First Amendment's free-speech provisions to a public school setting.

In a case that foreshadowed later actions by school boards elected to impose political and religious agendas, the Board of Education of the Island Trees Union Free School District in New York State ordered the removal of certain books from its school libraries. It characterized these books as "anti-American, anti-Christian, anti-Semitic, and just plain filthy," despite conclusions to the contrary reached by a committee of parents that the board itself had appointed. Students in the school district sued, asserting their First Amendment rights. (Pico was a student. Since minors cannot sue, their interests are represented by adults—typically parents. The legal term for this practice is "next friend.") The federal district court summarily ruled in favor of the school board; however, the court of appeals reversed, holding that the students were entitled to a trial on the merits of their claim that the board had removed books with which it disagreed, in contravention of the First Amendment. The Supreme Court affirmed, but not without evident discomfort.

* * *

The principal question presented is whether the First Amendment imposes limitations upon the exercise by a local school board of its discretion to remove library books from high school and junior high school libraries. . . .

In September 1975, petitioners Ahrens, Martin, and Hughes attended a conference sponsored by Parents of New York United (PONYU), a politically conservative organization of parents concerned about education legislation in the State of New York. At the conference these petitioners obtained lists of books described by Ahrens as "objectionable," . . . and by Martin as "improper fare for school students." . . . It was later determined that the High School library contained nine of the listed books, and that another listed book was in the Junior High School library. In February 1976, at a meeting with the Superintendent of Schools and the Principals of the High School and Junior High School, the Board gave an "unofficial direction" that the listed books be removed from the library shelves and delivered to the Board's offices, so that Board members could read them. When this directive was carried out, it became publicized, and the Board issued a press release justifying its action. It characterized the removed books as "anti-American, anti-Christian, anti-Sem[i]tic, and just plain filthy," and concluded that "[i]t is our duty, our moral obligation, to protect the children in our schools from this moral danger as surely as from physical and medical dangers." . . .

A short time later, the Board appointed a "Book Review Committee," consisting of four Island Trees parents and four members of the Island Trees schools staff, to read the listed books and to recommend to the Board whether the books should be retained, taking into account the books' "educational suitability," "good taste," "relevance," and "appropriateness to age and grade level." In July, the Committee made its final report to the Board, recommending that five of the listed books be retained and that two others be removed from the school libraries. . . .

. . . does the First Amendment impose any limitations upon the discretion of petitioners to remove library books from the Island Trees High School and Junior High School? . . . [I]f so, do the affidavits and other evidentiary materials before the District Court, construed most favorably to respondents, raise a genuine issue of fact whether petitioners might have exceeded those limitations? If we answer either of these questions in the negative, then we must reverse the judgment of the Court of Appeals and reinstate the District Court's summary judgment for petitioners. If we answer both questions in the affirmative, then we must affirm the judgment below. . . .

. . . just as access to ideas makes it possible for citizens generally to exercise their rights of free speech and press in a meaningful manner, such access prepares students for active and effective participation in the pluralistic, often contentious society in which they will soon be adult members. Of course all First Amendment rights accorded to students must be construed "in light of the special characteristics of the school environment." ... But the special characteristics of the school *library* make that environment especially appropriate for the recognition of the First Amendment rights of students. ...

... nothing in our decision today affects in any way the discretion of a local school board to choose books to *add* to the libraries of their schools. Because we are concerned in this case with the suppression of ideas, our holding today affects only the discretion to *remove* books. In brief, we hold that local school boards may not remove books from school library shelves simply because they dislike the ideas contained in those books and seek by their removal to "prescribe what shall be orthodox in politics, nationalism, religion, or other matters of opinion." ... Such purposes stand inescapably condemned by our precedents. ...

Standing alone, this evidence respecting the substantive motivations behind petitioners' removal decision would not be decisive. This would be a very different case if the record demonstrated that petitioners had employed established, regular, and facially unbiased procedures for the review of controversial materials. But the actual record in the case before us suggests the exact opposite. Petitioners' removal procedures were vigorously challenged below by respondents, and the evidence on this issue sheds further light on the issue of petitioners' motivations. Respondents alleged that in making their removal decision petitioners ignored "the advice of literary experts," the views of "librarians and teachers within the Island Trees School system," the advice of the Superintendent of Schools, and the guidance of publications that rate books for junior and senior high school students. ... Respondents also claimed that petitioners' decision was based solely on the fact that the books were named on the PONYU list received by petitioners Ahrens, Martin, and Hughes, and that petitioners "did not undertake an independent review of other books in the [school] libraries." ... Evidence before the District Court lends support to these claims. ...

... The evidence plainly does not foreclose the possibility that petitioners' decision to remove the books rested decisively upon disagreement with constitutionally protected ideas in those books, or upon a desire on petitioners' part to impose upon the students of the Island Trees High School and Junior High School a political orthodoxy to which petitioners and their constituents adhered. ...

*Affirmed.*

*Source*: 457 U.S. 853 (1982).

## DOCUMENT 56: *New York v. Ferber* (1982)

In *New York v. Ferber*, the conflict was between the First Amendment rights of those engaged in production of child pornography and the state's interest in protecting children. It was not much of a contest, as one might imagine. While there were several concurrences filed, there were no dissents. Justice Byron White delivered the majority opinion. He acknowledged that the statute in question did not limit its reach to materials that were legally obscene; rather, the statute criminalized distribution of any material depicting children engaged in sexual conduct. Nevertheless, after detailed discussion of the gravity of the harm to children so exploited, he concluded that the government could enact such restrictions on nonobscene materials without running afoul of the First Amendment.

\* \* \*

JUSTICE WHITE delivered the opinion of the Court. . . .

In recent years, the exploitive use of children in the production of pornography has become a serious national problem. The Federal Government and 47 States have sought to combat the problem with statutes specifically directed at the production of child pornography. At least half of such statutes do not require that the materials produced be legally obscene. Thirty-five States and the United States Congress have also passed legislation prohibiting the distribution of such materials; 20 States prohibit the distribution of material depicting children engaged in sexual conduct without requiring that the material be legally obscene. . . .

This case arose when Paul Ferber, the proprietor of a Manhattan bookstore specializing in sexually oriented products, sold two films to an undercover police officer. The films are devoted almost exclusively to depicting young boys masturbating. Ferber was indicted on two counts of violating . . . the two New York laws controlling dissemination of child pornography. After a jury trial, Ferber was acquitted of the two counts of promoting an obscene sexual performance, but found guilty of the two counts . . . which did not require proof that the films were obscene. Ferber's convictions were affirmed without opinion by the Appellate Division of the New York State Supreme Court. . . .

...We granted the State's petition for certiorari, 454 U.S. 1052 (1981), presenting the single question:

"To prevent the abuse of children who are made to engage in sexual conduct for commercial purposes, could the New York State Legislature, consistent with the First Amendment, prohibit the dissemination of material which shows children engaged in sexual conduct, regardless of whether such material is obscene?"...

...Like obscenity statutes, laws directed at the dissemination of child pornography run the risk of suppressing protected expression by allowing the hand of the censor to become unduly heavy. For the following reasons, however, we are persuaded that the States are entitled to greater leeway in the regulation of pornographic depictions of children.

*First.* It is evident beyond the need for elaboration that a State's interest in "safeguarding the physical and psychological well-being of a minor" is "compelling."...

*Second.* The distribution of photographs and films depicting sexual activity by juveniles is intrinsically related to the sexual abuse of children....

*Third.* The advertising and selling of child pornography provide an economic motive for and are thus an integral part of the production of such materials, an activity illegal throughout the Nation....

*Fourth.* The value of permitting live performances and photographic reproductions of children engaged in lewd sexual conduct is exceedingly modest, if not *de minimis.*...

...We note that the distribution of descriptions or other depictions of sexual conduct, not otherwise obscene, which do not involve live performance or photographic or other visual reproduction of live performances, retains First Amendment protection. As with obscenity laws, criminal responsibility may not be imposed without some element of scienter on the part of the defendant.

*Source:* 458 U.S. 747 (1982).

---

## DOCUMENT 57: Indianapolis Ordinance on Pornography (1984)

In 1984, Indianapolis, Indiana, passed an ordinance on pornography. The ordinance was part of a national attempt to define pornography as the "sexually explicit subordination of women," thus turning it into discrimination subject to regulation. The ordinance was supported by several fundamentalist Christian ministers. A certain irony to their support was duly noted in the news coverage of the proceedings: the alliance of the so-called radical feminists who had authored the ordinance with the religious right was unusual, to say the least.

* * *

### Section 16–3(q).

(q) Pornography shall mean the graphic sexually explicit subordination of women, whether in pictures or in words, that also includes one or more of the following:

(1) Women are presented as sexual objects who enjoy pain or humiliation; or

(2) Women are presented as sexual objects who experience sexual pleasure in being raped; or

(3) Women are presented as sexual objects tied up or cut up or mutilated or bruised or physically hurt, or as dismembered or truncated or fragmented or severed into body parts; or

(4) Women are presented being penetrated by objects or animals; or

(5) Women are presented in scenarios of degradation, injury, abusement, torture, shown as filthy or inferior, bleeding, bruised, or hurt in a context that makes these conditions sexual; and

(6) Women are presented as sexual objects for domination, conquest, violation, exploitation, possession, or use, or through postures, or positions of servility or submission or display.

The use of men, children, or transsexuals in the place of women in paragraphs (1) through (6) above shall also constitute pornography under this section.

* * *

### Section 16–3(g)(8).

(8) Defenses. Where the materials which are the subject matter of a complaint under paragraphs (4), (5), (6), or (7) of this subsection (g) are pornography, it shall not be a defense that the respondent did not know or intend that the materials were pornography or sex discrimination; provided, however, that in the cases under paragraph (g)(4) of Section 16–3, no damages or compensation for losses shall be recoverable unless the complainant proves that the respondent knew or had reason to know that the materials were pornography. Provided, further, that it shall be a defense to a complaint under paragraph (g)(4) of Section 16–3 that the materials complained of are those covered only by paragraphs (q)(6) of Section 16–3.

* * *

Section 16–17.

(a) A complaint charging that any person has engaged in or is engaging in a discriminatory practice prohibited by sections 16–14 and/or 16–15 may be filed with the office by any person claiming to be aggrieved by the practice, or by one or more members of the board or employees of the office who have reasonable cause to believe that a violation of sections 16–14 and 16–15 has occurred, in any of the following circumstances. . . .

(6) In the cases of trafficing [*sic*] in pornography, coercion into pornographic performances, and assault or physical attack due to pornography (as provided in Section 16–3(g)(7)) against the perpetrator(s), maker(s), seller(s), exhibitor(s), or distributor(s).

(7) In the case of forcing pornography on a person, against the perpetrator(s) and/or institution.

(b) In the case of trafficking in pornography, any woman may file a complaint as a woman acting against the subordination of women and any man, child, or transsexual may file a complaint but must prove injury in the same way that a woman is injured in order to obtain relief under this chapter.

(c) In the case of assault or physical attack due to pornography, compensation for losses or an award for damages shall not be assessed against (1) maker(s), for pornography made, (2) distributor(s), for pornography distributed, (3) seller(s), for pornography sold, or (4) exhibitor(s) for pornography exhibited, prior to the effective date of this act.

*Source*: 598 F. Supp. 1316, 1320.

---

## DOCUMENT 58: *American Booksellers Association, Inc. v. William H. Hudnut, III, Mayor, City of Indianapolis* (1985)

Immediately after the Indianapolis ordinance was signed into law, suit was filed on behalf of a large group of plaintiffs, including the American Booksellers Association, the Association for American Publishers, the Council for Periodical Distributors, and several others. In November 1984, Judge Sarah Evans Barker of the district court permanently enjoined enforcement of the ordinance, dismissing the proponents' argument that the measure targeted conduct rather than speech. The Seventh Circuit Court of Appeals affirmed her decision the following August, and it is its decision that follows, because on February 24, 1986, the Supreme Court unanimously issued a rare summary affirmance of the lower courts' rulings.

* * *

EASTERBROOK, Circuit Judge.

The Indianapolis ordinance does not refer to the prurient interest, to offensiveness, or to the standards of the community. It demands attention to particular depictions, not to the work judged as a whole. It is irrelevant under the ordinance whether the work has literary, artistic, political, or scientific value. The City and many amici point to these omissions as virtues. They maintain that pornography influences attitudes, and the statute is a way to alter the socialization of men and women rather than to vindicate community standards of offensiveness. And as one of the principal drafters of the ordinance has asserted, "if a woman is subjected, why should it matter that the work has other value?" Catharine A. MacKinnon, *Pornography, Civil Rights, and Speech.*

Civil rights groups and feminists have entered this case as amici on both sides. Those supporting the ordinance say that it will play an important role in reducing the tendency of men to view women as sexual objects, a tendency that leads to both unacceptable attitudes and discrimination in the workplace and violence away from it. Those opposing the ordinance point out that much radical feminist literature is explicit and depicts women in ways forbidden by the ordinance and that the ordinance would reopen old battles. It is unclear how Indianapolis would treat works from James Joyce's *Ulysses* to Homer's *Iliad*; both depict women as submissive objects for conquest and domination.

We do not try to balance the arguments for and against an ordinance such as this. The ordinance discriminates on the ground of the content of the speech. Speech treating women in the approved way—in sexual encounters "premised on equality"—is lawful no matter how sexually explicit. Speech treating women in the disapproved way—as submissive in matters sexual or as enjoying humiliation—is unlawful no matter how significant the literary, artistic, or political qualities of the work taken as a whole. The state may not ordain preferred viewpoints in this way. The Constitution forbids the state to declare one perspective right and silence opponents. . . .

Racial bigotry, anti-Semitism, violence on television, reporters' biases—these and many more influence the culture and shape our socialization. None is directly answerable by more speech, unless that speech too finds its place in the popular culture. Yet all is protected as speech, however insidious. Any other answer leaves the government in control of all of the institutions of culture, the great censor and director of which thoughts are good for us.

Sexual responses often are unthinking responses, and the association of sexual arousal with the subordination of women therefore may have a substantial effect. But almost all cultural stimuli provoke unconscious responses. Religious ceremonies condition their participants. Teachers convey messages by selecting what not to cover; the implicit message about what is off limits or unthinkable may be more powerful than the message for which they present rational argument. Television scripts contain unarticulated assumptions. People may be conditioned in subtle ways. If the fact that speech plays a role in a process of conditioning were enough to permit governmental regulation, that would be the end of freedom of speech. . . .

Much of Indianapolis's argument rests on the belief that when speech is "unanswerable," and the metaphor that there is a "marketplace of ideas" does not apply, the First Amendment does not apply either. The metaphor is honored; Milton's *Areopagitica* and John Stuart Mill's *On Liberty* defend freedom of speech on the ground that the truth will prevail, and many of the most important cases under the First Amendment recite this position. The Framers undoubtedly believed it. As a general matter it is true. But the Constitution does not make the dominance of truth a necessary condition of freedom of speech. To say that it does would be to confuse an outcome of free speech with a necessary condition for the application of the amendment.

A power to limit speech on the ground that truth has not yet prevailed and is not likely to prevail implies the power to declare truth. At some point the government must be able to say (as Indianapolis has said): "We know what the truth is, yet a free exchange of speech has not driven out falsity, so that we must now prohibit falsity." If the government may declare the truth, why wait for the failure of speech? Under the First Amendment, however, there is no such thing as a false idea, so the government may not restrict speech on the ground that in a free exchange truth is not yet dominant.

At any time, some speech is ahead in the game; the more numerous speakers prevail. Supporters of minority candidates may be forever "excluded" from the political process because their candidates never win, because few people believe their positions. This does not mean that freedom of speech has failed. . . .

We come, finally, to the argument that pornography is "low value" speech, that it is enough like obscenity that Indianapolis may prohibit it. . . .

At all events, "pornography" is not low value speech within the meaning of these cases. Indianapolis seeks to prohibit certain speech because it believes this speech influences social relations and politics on a grand scale, that it controls attitudes at home and in the legislature. This precludes a characterization of the speech as low value. True, pornography and obscenity have sex in common. But Indianapolis left out of its definition any reference to literary, artistic, political, or scientific value. The ordinance applies to graphic sexually explicit subordination in works great and small. The Court sometimes balances the value of speech against the costs of its restriction, but it does this by category of speech and not by the content of particular works. Indianapolis has created an approved point of view and so loses the support of these cases.

Any rationale we could imagine in support of this ordinance could not be limited to sex discrimination. Free speech has been on balance an ally of those seeking change. Governments that want stasis start by restricting speech. Culture is a powerful force of continuity; Indianapolis paints pornography as part of the culture of power. Change in any complex system ultimately depends on the ability of outsiders to challenge accepted views and the reigning institutions. Without a strong guarantee of freedom of speech, there is no effective right to challenge what is.

*Source*: United States Court of Appeals, Seventh Circuit 771 F. 2d 323 (1985).

---

## DOCUMENT 59: *Texas v. Johnson* (1989)

---

In 1989, the Supreme Court revisited the emotional issue of flag burning. In *Texas v. Johnson*, a divided Court ruled that flag burning was the expression of a political point of view and, as symbolic speech, could not be outlawed. The facts of the case were relatively simple: during the 1984 Republican convention in Dallas, Texas, a man named Gregory Lee Johnson participated in a political demonstration protesting the policies of the Reagan administration. The protest began with a march through Dallas streets and ended with Johnson burning the flag while protesters chanted. Johnson was subsequently convicted of desecration of a venerated object and sentenced to one year in prison. In a 5–4 decision, the Supreme Court affirmed the lower court's conclusion that the First Amendment protected Johnson.

\* \* \*

JUSTICE BRENNAN delivered the opinion of the Court.

After publicly burning an American flag as a means of political protest, Gregory Lee Johnson was convicted of desecrating a flag in violation of Texas law. This case presents the question whether his conviction is consistent with the First Amendment. We hold that it is not. . . .

Especially pertinent to this case are our decisions recognizing the communicative nature of conduct relating to flags. Attaching a peace sign to the flag . . . ; refusing to salute the flag . . . ; and displaying a red flag, . . .

we have held, all may find shelter under the First Amendment. . . . (treating flag "contemptuously" by wearing pants with small flag sewn into their seat is expressive conduct). That we have had little difficulty identifying an expressive element in conduct relating to flags should not be surprising. The very purpose of a national flag is to serve as a symbol of our country; it is, one might say, "the one visible manifestation of two hundred years of nationhood." . . . Thus, we have observed:

"[T]he flag salute is a form of utterance. Symbolism is a primitive but effective way of communicating ideas. The use of an emblem or flag to symbolize some system, idea, institution, or personality, is a short cut from mind to mind. Causes and nations, political parties, lodges and ecclesiastical groups seek to knit the loyalty of their followings to a flag or banner, a color or design." . . .

Pregnant with expressive content, the flag as readily signifies this Nation as does the combination of letters found in "America." . . .

The State of Texas conceded for purposes of its oral argument in this case that Johnson's conduct was expressive conduct. . . . Johnson burned an American flag as part—indeed, as the culmination—of a political demonstration that coincided with the convening of the Republican Party and its renomination of Ronald Reagan for President. The expressive, overtly political nature of this conduct was both intentional and overwhelmingly apparent. . . .

The State's position . . . amounts to a claim that an audience that takes serious offense at particular expression is necessarily likely to disturb the peace and that the expression may be prohibited on this basis. Our precedents do not countenance such a presumption. . . .

The State also asserts an interest in preserving the flag as a symbol of nationhood and national unity. . . . We are equally persuaded that this interest is related to expression in the case of Johnson's burning of the flag. The State, apparently, is concerned that such conduct will lead people to believe either that the flag does not stand for nationhood and national unity, but instead reflects other, less positive concepts, or that the concepts reflected in the flag do not in fact exist, that is, that we do not enjoy unity as a Nation. These concerns blossom only when a person's treatment of the flag communicates some message, and thus are related "to the suppression of free expression" within the meaning of *O'Brien*. We are thus outside of *O'Brien*'s test altogether. . . .

Texas' focus on the precise nature of Johnson's expression, moreover, misses the point of our prior decisions: their enduring lesson, that the government may not prohibit expression simply because it disagrees with its message, is not dependent on the particular mode in which one chooses to express an idea. If we were to hold that a State may forbid flag burning wherever it is likely to endanger the flag's symbolic role, but allow it wherever burning a flag promotes that role—as where, for example, a person ceremoniously burns a dirty flag—we would be saying that when it comes to impairing the flag's physical integrity, the flag itself may be used as a symbol—as a substitute for the written or spoken word or a "short cut from mind to mind"—only in one direction. We would be permitting a State to "prescribe what shall be orthodox" by saying that one may burn the flag to convey one's attitude toward it and its referents only if one does not endanger the flag's representation of nationhood and national unity. . . .

. . . To conclude that the government may permit designated symbols to be used to communicate only a limited set of messages would be to enter territory having no discernible or defensible boundaries. Could the government, on this theory, prohibit the burning of state flags? Of copies of the Presidential seal? Of the Constitution? In evaluating these choices under the First Amendment, how would we decide which symbols were sufficiently special to warrant this unique status? To do so, we would be forced to consult our own political preferences, and impose them on the citizenry, in the very way that the First Amendment forbids us to do. . . .

. . . We can imagine no more appropriate response to burning a flag than waving one's own, no better way to counter a flag burner's message than by saluting the flag that burns, no surer means of preserving the dignity even of the flag that burned than by—as one witness here did—according its remains a respectful burial. We do not consecrate the flag by punishing its desecration, for in doing so we dilute the freedom that this cherished emblem represents.

*Source:* 491 U.S. 397 (1989).

---

## DOCUMENT 60: St. Paul Bias-motivated Crime Ordinance (1990)

In 1990, the city of St. Paul, Minnesota, adopted a "Bias-motivated Crime Ordinance" that made it a crime to display a symbol that one knew or had reason to know "arouses anger, alarm or resentment in others on the basis of race, color, creed, religion or gender."

\* \* \*

Whoever places on public or private property a symbol, object, appellation, characterization or graffiti, including, but not limited to, a burning cross or Nazi swastika, which one knows or has reasonable grounds to know arouses anger, alarm or resentment in others on the basis of race, color, creed, religion or gender commits disorderly conduct and shall be guilty of a misdemeanor.

*Source*: St. Paul Bias-motivated Crime Ordinance, St. Paul, Minnesota, Legislative Code §292.02 (1990).

---

**DOCUMENT 61:** *Irving Rust v. Louis W. Sullivan, Secretary of Health and Human Services; New York v. Louis W. Sullivan, Secretary of Health and Human Services* **(1991)**

---

If the cases included in this volume demonstrate anything, it is the difficulty justices experience when they must apply principles in highly emotional contexts. From the Supreme Court's willingness to defer to national security concerns during wartime to the internal wrangling over flag burning, some of its least edifying opinions have involved issues of high visibility and public polarization. So it should not surprise us that the majority opinion in the 1991 case *Rust v. Sullivan* is, at best, disingenuous. The Court sidestepped the First Amendment issues raised by the regulation's challengers, and instead addressed the right of Congress to refuse to fund abortion services—a right no litigant had questioned.

While *Rust* was a free-speech case, it arose out of the divisive and contentious abortion issue. Congressional opponents of abortion included in the Public Health Service Act (1944) a provision that no federal funds going to family-planning agencies could be used "in programs where abortion is a method of family planning." In 1988, the secretary of health and human services issued regulations that went considerably farther; the regulations prohibited family-planning agencies that received federal funds from even discussing the option of abortion with patients. Title X projects could no longer engage in "counseling concerning, referrals for, and activities advocating" abortion. This rule would appear to be a clear violation of the First Amendment's free-speech guaranties.

\* \* \*

Chief Justice REHNQUIST delivered the opinion of the Court. . . .

. . . the regulations specify that a "Title X project may not provide counseling concerning the use of abortion as a method of family planning or provide referral for abortion as a method of family planning."
. . . Title X projects must refer every pregnant client "for appropriate prenatal and/or social services by furnishing a list of available providers

that promote the welfare of mother and unborn child." . . . The list may not be used indirectly to encourage or promote abortion, "such as by weighing the list of referrals in favor of health care providers which perform abortions, by including on the list of referral providers health care providers whose principal business is the provision of abortions, by excluding available providers who do not provide abortions, or by 'steering' clients to providers who offer abortion as a method of family planning." . . . The Title X project is expressly prohibited from referring a pregnant woman to an abortion provider, even upon specific request. One permissible response to such an inquiry is that "the project does not consider abortion an appropriate method of family planning and therefore does not counsel or refer for abortion." . . .

Petitioners contend that the regulations violate the First Amendment by impermissibly discriminating based on viewpoint because they prohibit "all discussion about abortion as a lawful option—including counseling, referral, and the provision of neutral and accurate information about ending a pregnancy—while compelling the clinic or counselor to provide information that promotes continuing a pregnancy to term." . . . They assert that the regulations violate the "free speech rights of private health care organizations that receive Title X funds, of their staff, and of their patients" by impermissibly imposing "viewpoint-discriminatory conditions on government subsidies" and thus "penaliz[e] speech funded with non–Title X monies." . . . Because "Title X continues to fund speech ancillary to pregnancy testing in a manner that is not evenhanded with respect to views and information about abortion, it invidiously discriminates on the basis of viewpoint." . . . petitioners also assert that while the Government may place certain conditions on the receipt of federal subsidies, it may not "discriminate invidiously in its subsidies in such a way as to 'ai[m] at the suppression of dangerous ideas.' " . . .

There is no question but that the statutory prohibition contained in § 1008 is constitutional. In *Maher v. Roe*, . . . we upheld a state welfare regulation under which Medicaid recipients received payments for services related to childbirth, but not for nontherapeutic abortions. The Court rejected the claim that this unequal subsidization worked a violation of the Constitution. We held that the government may "make a value judgment favoring childbirth over abortion, and . . . implement that judgment by the allocation of public funds." . . . Here the Government is exercising the authority it possesses . . . to subsidize family planning services which will lead to conception and childbirth, and declining to "promote or encourage abortion." The Government can, without violating the Constitution, selectively fund a program to encourage certain activities it believes to be in the public interest, without at the same time funding an alternative program which seeks to deal with the problem in another way. In so doing, the Government has not discriminated on the basis of viewpoint; it has merely chosen to fund one activity to the exclusion of the other. "[A] legislature's decision not to subsidize the exercise of a fundamental right does not infringe the right." . . . "A refusal to fund protected activity, without more, cannot be equated with the imposition of a 'penalty' on that activity." . . . "There is a basic difference between direct state interference with a protected activity and state encouragement of an alternative activity consonant with legislative policy." . . .

. . . our "unconstitutional conditions" cases involve situations in which the Government has placed a condition on the *recipient* of the subsidy rather than on a particular program or service, thus effectively prohibiting the recipient from engaging in the protected conduct outside the scope of the federally funded program. In *FCC v. League of Women Voters of Cal.*, we invalidated a federal law providing that noncommercial television and radio stations that receive federal grants may not "engage in editorializing." Under that law, a recipient of federal funds was "barred absolutely from all editorializing" because it "is not able to segregate its activities according to the source of its funding" and thus "has no way of limiting the use of its federal funds to all noneditorializing activities." The effect of the law was that "a noncommercial educational station that receives only 1% of its overall income from [federal] grants is barred absolutely from all editorializing" and "barred from using even wholly private funds to finance its editorial activity." . . . We expressly recognized, however, that were Congress to permit the recipient stations to "establish 'affiliate' organizations which could then use the station's facilities to editorialize with nonfederal funds, such a statutory mechanism would plainly be valid." . . . Such a scheme would permit the station "to make known its views on matters of public importance through its non-federally funded, editorializing affiliate without losing federal grants for its noneditorializing broadcast activities." . . .

The same principles apply to petitioners' claim that the regulations abridge the free speech rights of the grantee's staff. Individuals who are voluntarily employed for a Title X project must perform their duties in accordance with the regulation's restrictions on abortion counseling and referral. The employees remain free, however, to pursue abortion-related activities when they are not acting under the auspices of the Title X project. The regulations, which govern solely the scope of the Title X project's activities, do not in any way restrict the activities of those persons acting as private individuals. The employees' freedom of expression is limited during the time that they actually work for the project; but this limitation is a consequence of their decision to accept employment in a project, the scope of which is permissibly restricted by the funding authority.

[note in text]

Petitioners also contend that the regulations violate the First Amendment by penalizing speech funded with non–Title X monies. They argue that since Title

X requires that grant recipients contribute to the financing of Title X projects through the use of matching funds and grant-related income, the regulation's restrictions on abortion counseling and advocacy penalize privately funded speech.

We find this argument flawed for several reasons. First, Title X subsidies are just that, subsidies. The recipient is in no way compelled to operate a Title X project; to avoid the force of the regulations, it can simply decline the subsidy. . . . By accepting Title X funds, a recipient voluntarily consents to any restrictions placed on any matching funds or grant-related income. Potential grant recipients can choose between accepting Title X funds—subject to the Government's conditions that they provide matching funds and forgo abortion counseling and referral in the Title X project—or declining the subsidy and financing their own unsubsidized program. We have never held that the Government violates the First Amendment simply by offering that choice. Second, the Secretary's regulations apply only to Title X programs. A recipient is therefore able to "limi[t] the use of its federal funds to [Title X] activities." . . . It is in no way "barred from using even wholly private funds to finance" its pro-abortion activities outside the Title X program. . . . The regulations are limited to Title X funds; the recipient remains free to use private, non–Title X funds to finance abortion-related activities. . . .

. . . It could be argued by analogy that traditional relationships such as that between doctor and patient should enjoy protection under the First Amendment from Government regulation, even when subsidized by the Government. We need not resolve that question here, however, because the Title X program regulations do not significantly impinge upon the doctor-patient relationship. Nothing in them requires a doctor to represent as his own any opinion that he does not in fact hold. Nor is the doctor-patient relationship established by the Title X program sufficiently all encompassing so as to justify an expectation on the part of the patient of comprehensive medical advice. The program does not provide postconception medical care, and therefore a doctor's silence with regard to abortion cannot reasonably be thought to mislead a client into thinking that the doctor does not consider abortion an appropriate option for her. The doctor is always free to make clear that advice regarding abortion is simply beyond the scope of the program. In these circumstances, the general rule that the Government may choose not to subsidize speech applies with full force. . . .

The Secretary's regulations are a permissible construction of Title X and do not violate either the First or Fifth Amendments to the Constitution. Accordingly, the judgment of the Court of Appeals is

*Affirmed.*

Justice BLACKMUN, with whom Justice MARSHALL joins, with whom Justice STEVENS joins as to Parts II and III, and with whom Justice O'CONNOR joins as to Part I, dissenting.

Casting aside established principles of statutory construction and administrative jurisprudence, the majority in these cases today unnecessarily passes upon important questions of constitutional law. In so doing, the Court, for the first time, upholds viewpoint-based suppression of speech solely because it is imposed on those dependent upon the Government for economic support. Under essentially the same rationale, the majority upholds direct regulation of dialogue between a pregnant woman and her physician when that regulation has both the purpose and the effect of manipulating her decision as to the continuance of her pregnancy. I conclude that the Secretary's regulation of referral, advocacy, and counseling activities exceeds his statutory authority, and, also, that the regulations violate the First and Fifth Amendments of our Constitution. Accordingly, I dissent and would reverse the divided-vote judgment of the Court of Appeals.

*Source*: 111 S. Ct. 1759 (1991).

---

## DOCUMENT 62: *R. A. V. v. City of St. Paul, Minnesota* (1992)

In June of 1990, teenager R. A. V. burned a cross on the lawn of a home owned by a black family and was charged under the St. Paul ordinance, although, as the Supreme Court pointed out, there were a number of other ordinances that he had also violated. The question before the Court was the constitutionality of the "bias-motivated crime" legislation.

Both Justice Antonin Scalia, writing for the majority, and Justice Byron White, writing for three concurring justices, found the ordinance constitutionally defective. Scalia focused upon the content discrimination inherent in the law; White would have applied traditional overbreadth analysis. The ruling in *R. A. V.* sent a "political" message as well as a legal one: like the district court in *American Booksellers*, it served to remind such partisans that free speech, far from being the enemy, is a valuable ally in the fight for quality.

* * *

JUSTICE SCALIA delivered the opinion of the Court.

In the predawn hours of June 21, 1990, petitioner and several other teenagers allegedly assembled a crudely made cross by taping together broken chair legs. They then allegedly burned the cross inside the fenced yard of a black family that lived across the street from the house where petitioner was staying. Although this conduct could have been punished under any of a number of laws, one of the two provisions under which respondent city of St. Paul chose to charge petitioner (then a juvenile) was the St. Paul Bias-Motivated Crime Ordinance. . . .

. . . Assuming, *arguendo*, that all of the expression reached by the ordinance is proscribable under the "fighting words" doctrine, we nonetheless conclude that the ordinance is facially unconstitutional in that it prohibits otherwise permitted speech solely on the basis of the subjects the speech addresses. . . .

. . . The point of the First Amendment is that majority preferences must be expressed in some fashion other than silencing speech on the basis of its content. . . .

Let there be no mistake about our belief that burning a cross in someone's front yard is reprehensible. But St. Paul has sufficient means at its disposal to prevent such behavior without adding the First Amendment to the fire.

The judgment of the Minnesota Supreme Court is reversed, and the case is remanded for proceedings not inconsistent with this opinion.

*It is so ordered.*

*Source*: 505 U.S. 377 (1992).

---

## DOCUMENT 63: Wisconsin Statute on Hate Crimes (1989–1990)

It is an accepted axiom of First Amendment law that government cannot punish people for their thoughts and beliefs, no matter how odious. In our system, we punish wrongful actions, not wrongheaded beliefs.

In recent years, as America has begun to confront the extent of bias against racial and other minorities, there has been a move to enact "hate crimes" legislation that would impose additional penalties for crimes motivated by bigotry. Proponents of such legislation believe that a crime motivated by hatred of a particular group is more heinous than the same crime motivated by greed or individualized animosity, and should be punished more severely. First Amendment purists do not believe the constitution allows an increase in the punishment for a crime based upon the thought that prompted it.

While several states have enacted hate crimes legislation, Wisconsin's statute was the first to be considered by the United States Supreme Court, which unanimously upheld it. It should be noted that the Wisconsin statute was amended in 1992; however, the amendments were not at issue in that case, *Wisconsin v. Mitchell,* and are not included here.

* * *

(1) If a person does all of the following, the penalties for the underlying crime are increased as provided in sub. (2):

(a) Commits a crime under chs. 939 to 948.

(b) Intentionally selects the person against whom the crime under par. (a) is committed or selects the property which is damaged or otherwise affected by the crime under par. (a) because of the race, religion, color, disability, sexual orientation, national origin or ancestry of that person or the owner or occupant of that property.

(2) (a) If the crime committed under sub. (1) is ordinarily a misdemeanor other than a Class A misdemeanor, the revised maximum fine is $10,000 and the revised maximum period of imprisonment is one year in the county jail.

(b) If the crime committed under sub. (1) is ordinarily a Class A misdemeanor, the penalty increase under this section changes the status of the crime to a felony and the revised maximum fine is $10,000 and the revised maximum period of imprisonment is 2 years.

(c) If the crime committed under sub. (1) is a felony, the maximum fine prescribed by law for the crime may be increased by not more than $5,000 and the maximum period of imprisonment prescribed by law for the crime may be increased by not more than 5 years.

(3) This section provides for the enhancement of the penalties applicable for the underlying crime. The court shall direct that the trier of fact find a special verdict as to all of the issues specified in sub. (1).

(4) This section does not apply to any crime if proof of race, religion, color, disability, sexual orientation, national origin or ancestry is required for a conviction for that crime.

The statute was amended in 1992, but the amendments were not at issue in *Mitchell.*

*Source*: Wisconsin Statute §939.645 (1989–1990).

---

## DOCUMENT 64: *Wisconsin v. Mitchell* (1993)

---

Todd Mitchell was a black teenager who admittedly went looking for a white victim. He was charged and convicted under the Wisconsin Hate Crimes statue. As a result, he was sentenced to seven years, rather than the four years he would have received for committing exactly the same crime for a reason that didn't fall under the Wisconsin statute.

Mitchell appealed the imposition of the longer sentence, arguing that the extra three years were, in effect, punishment for an opinion and thus unconstitutional. The case was widely discussed. Opponents of Hate Crimes legislation pointed out that the criminal law has always punished intentional acts that harm others, no matter why those acts were committed, and expressed concern about this seeming departure from that practice. They also noted that the laws were intended to protect minorities, yet minorities like Todd Mitchell were being charged under them. The Wisconsin Supreme Court agreed with the opponents and struck down the law, but the United States Supreme Court reversed.

\* \* \*

CHIEF JUSTICE REHNQUIST delivered the opinion of the Court.

Respondent Todd Mitchell's sentence for aggravated battery was enhanced because he intentionally selected his victim on account of the victim's race. The question presented in this case is whether this penalty enhancement is prohibited by the First and Fourteenth Amendments. We hold that it is not. . . .

. . . The [Wisconsin] Supreme Court held that the statue "violates the First Amendment directly by punishing what the legislature has deemed to be offensive thought." . . . It rejected the State's contention "that the statute punishes only the 'conduct' of intentional selection of a victim." . . . According to the court, "[t]he statute punishes the 'because of' aspect of the defendant's selection, the *reason* the dependent selected the victim, the *motive* behind the selection." . . . And under *R. A. V.* v. *St. Paul*, . . . "the Wisconsin legislature cannot criminalize bigoted thought with which it disagrees." . . .

The Supreme Court also held that the penalty-enhancement statute was unconstitutionally overbroad. It reasoned that, in order to prove that a defendant intentionally selected his victim because of the victim's protected status, the State would often have to introduce evidence of the defendant's prior speech, such as racial epithets he may have uttered before the commission of the offense. This evidentiary use of protected speech, the court thought, would have a "chilling effect" on those who feared the possibility of prosecution for offenses subject to penalty enhancement. . . . Finally, the court distinguished antidiscrimination laws, which have long been held constitutional, on the ground that the Wisconsin statute punishes the "subjective mental process" of selecting a victim because of his protected status, whereas antidiscrimination laws prohibit "objective acts of discrimination." . . .

... We reverse. . . .

But the fact remains that under the Wisconsin statute the same criminal conduct may be more heavily punished if the victim is selected because of his race or other protected status than if no such motive obtained. Thus, although the statute punishes criminal conduct, it enhances the maximum penalty for conduct motivated by a discriminatory point of view more severely than the same conduct engaged in for some other reason or for no reason at all. Because the only reason for the enhancement is the dependent's discriminatory motive for selecting his victim, Mitchell argues (and the Wisconsin Supreme Court held) that the statute violates the First Amendment by punishing offenders' bigoted beliefs. . . .

Nothing in our decision last Term in *R. A. V.* compels a different result here. That case involved a First Amendment challenge to a municipal ordinance prohibiting the use of " 'fighting words' that insult, or provoke violence, 'on the basis of race, color, creed, religion or gender.' " . . . Because the ordinance only proscribed a class of "fighting words" deemed particularly offensive by the city—*i.e.*, those "that contain . . . messages of 'bias-motivated' hatred," . . . —we held that it violated the rule against content-based discrimination. . . . But whereas the ordinance struck down in *R. A. V.* was explicitly directed at expression (*i.e.*, "speech" or "messages"), . . . the statute in this case is aimed at conduct unprotected by the First Amendment.

Moreover, the Wisconsin statute singles out for enhancement bias-inspired conduct because this conduct is thought to inflict greater individual and societal harm. For example, according to the State and its *amici*, bias-motivated crimes are more likely to provoke retaliatory crimes, inflict distinct emotional harms on their victims, and incite community unrest. . . . The State's desire to redress these perceived harms provides an adequate explanation for its penalty-enhancement provision over and above mere disagreement with offenders' beliefs or biases. As Blackstone said long ago, "it is but reasonable that among crimes of different natures those should be most severely punished, which are the most destructive of the public safety and happiness." . . .

The First Amendment . . . does not prohibit the evidentiary use of speech to establish the elements of a crime or to prove motive or intent. Evidence of a defendant's previous declarations or statements is commonly admitted in criminal trials subject to evidentiary rules dealing with relevancy, reliability, and the like. Nearly half a century ago, in *Haupt* v. *United States*, . . . we rejected a contention similar to that advanced by Mitchell here. Haupt was tried for the offense of treason, which, as defined by the Constitution . . . , may depend very much on proof of motive. To prove that the acts in question were committed out of "adherence to the enemy" rather than "parental solicitude," . . . the

Government introduced evidence of conversations that had taken place long prior to the indictment, some of which consisted of statements showing Haupt's sympathy with Germany and Hitler and hostility towards the United States. We rejected Haupt's argument that this evidence was improperly admitted. Which "[s]uch testimony is to be scrutinized with care to be certain the statements are not expressions of mere lawful and permissible difference of opinion with our own government or quite proper appreciation of the land of birth," we held that "these statements . . . clearly were admissible on the question of intent and adherence to the enemy." . . .

For the foregoing reasons, we hold that Mitchell's First Amendment rights were not violated by the application of the Wisconsin penalty-enhancement provision in sentencing him. The judgment of the Supreme Court of Wisconsin is therefore reversed, and the case is remanded for further proceedings not inconsistent with this opinion.

*Source*: 508 U.S. 476 (1993).

---

## DOCUMENT 65: "Do Hate-Crime Laws Restrict First Amendment Rights?" (1998)

The Supreme Court's decision in *Wisconsin v. Mitchell* was hardly the end of the controversy. As with so many First Amendment issues, debate continues over both the constitutionality of Hate Crimes legislation and its effectiveness. In 1998, a full five years after the *Mitchell* decision, the following essay appeared in *West's Encyclopedia of American Law*.

\* \* \*

The U.S. Supreme Court's upholding of the state "hate-crime" law in *Wisconsin v. Mitchell*, . . . has not stopped some legal commentators from arguing that such laws violate the First Amendment of the U.S. Constitution. Though these critics generally admit that hate crimes are on the rise, they believe that laws that increase the severity of punishment on the basis of the motives of the perpetrator create a dangerous precedent for government interference with freedom of expression and thought. Defenders of hate-crime laws reject these fears, claiming that the laws deal with criminal conduct and are meant to send a message that discrimination will not be tolerated.

Critics of the laws have articulated a number of reasons for their opposition, some constitutional, some practical. The foremost concern is that hate-crime laws violate a person's right to freedom of thought. These statutes enhance the penalties for conduct already punished under state law when the perpetrator is motivated by a type of bigotry the legislature finds offensive. Therefore, if a rich man assaults a homeless person because he hates the poor, the rich man can be charged only with assault, because the legislature has not specifically found bigotry against the poor to be offensive. However, if a man assaults an African American because he hates persons of that race, he can be charged with assault and intimidation, which carries a more severe penalty, or his sentence for assault can be increased, because the legislature has penalized a racially discriminatory motive. For the critics of hate-crime laws, this result reveals that the legislature is regulating the defendant's thoughts, in violation of the First Amendment.

Critics also charge that the focus on motive distorts the traditional rules of criminal law. In the past, criminal law was interested in a defendant's mental state only to the extent that it would reveal whether the defendant had engaged in deliberate conduct. As a general rule, the motive of a crime has never been considered an element that must be proved at trial. Whether a person robbed a bank to buy food for a family or to pay back a gambling debt is considered irrelevant. The key state-of-mind question is whether the person intended to rob the bank.

Some critics also ask what good the additional penalty will do for persons convicted of hate crimes. If a person is filled with prejudices, extra time spent in prison is not likely to help eradicate those beliefs; it may, in fact, reinforce them. These critics do not believe that hate-crime laws seek to deter criminal activity. They feel that instead such laws appear to seek retribution for acts of violence motivated by racism, sexism, anti-Semitism, and homophobia. The critics contend the retribution model is not compatible with the modern goals of the criminal and penal systems.

Another criticism is that hate-crime laws do not address deeper forces within society that create prejudice. Some social psychologists believe that prejudice and the behavior that may accompany it are caused by a combination of social, economic, and psychological conflicts. Adding more punishment for those who act on their prejudice may give the community the illusion it is dealing with the problem, but, in fact, hate-crime laws do little to help change thought and behavior.

Defenders of hate-crime laws reject the idea that they are taking away anyone's First Amendment rights. They note that in *Mitchell* the Supreme Court rejected as "too speculative a hypothesis" the "chilling effect" argument, which maintains that these laws chill, or inhibit, free thought and speech. The Court also cited precedent that permitted the "evidentiary use of speech to establish the elements of a crime or to prove motive or intent." This means that persons are free to express their ideas, no matter how repugnant, but when they engage in unlawful conduct based on these beliefs, they surrender their First Amendment rights.

Defenders also believe that hate-crime laws, like other criminal laws, are aimed at preventing harmful acts. The focus is not on stifling disagreeable and prejudicial beliefs or biases, but on preventing the particularly harmful effects of hate crimes. Even critics of the laws admit that hate-crime violence is often brutal and severe. Defenders argue that increasing the penalties for this type of behavior is therefore justified.

Supporters of hate-crime laws point out, as did the Supreme Court in *Mitchell*, that most of the statutes use the same language as title VII of the Civil Rights Act of 1964 (42 U.S.C.A. § 2000e et seq.). Why, they ask, is it acceptable to penalize employment discrimination that is based on racism and bigotry, but not criminal acts based on similar biases? The courts have long upheld federal and state discrimination laws as acceptable methods of penalizing conduct and promoting nondiscriminatory practices. Intentional employment discrimination requires a person to communicate his or her bias. Supporters conclude that once a person verbalizes a prejudice and acts on it, the state is free to regulate that conduct.

*Source*: "Do Hate-Crime Laws Restrict First Amendment Rights?" *West's Encyclopedia of American Law* (St. Paul, MN: West Group, 1998), 6: 3.

---

## DOCUMENT 66: *Lamb's Chapel and John Steigerwald v. Center Moriches Union Free School District* (1993)

The free-speech guarantees of the First Amendment are not the only provisions that have generated contentious litigation. Ever since the Supreme Court struck down officially imposed school prayer in 1964, the meaning of the religion clauses and particularly the Establishment Clause has been hotly debated. Groups like the Christian Coalition and its legal arm, the American Center for Law and Justice, argue that the courts have become "hostile" to religion. Whatever the merits of these arguments, it is certainly true that the controversy and uncertainty that have surrounded the development of Establishment Clause jurisprudence have caused many schools to be extremely cautious when dealing with any issue implicating religion.

Such overreaction was apparently the problem with the Center Moriches Union Free School District. The district had a policy of allowing groups to use its facilities after school hours for meetings, films, and lectures. It denied Lamb's Chapel's request for space to hold a film series and based that rejection solely upon the religious content of the films Lamb's Chapel intended to screen. Both the American Civil Liberties Union and the American Center for Law and Justice argued that the district's policy violated the free-speech provisions of the First Amendment, and a unanimous Supreme Court agreed.

\* \* \*

Justice WHITE delivered the opinion of the Court.

[Section 414 of the New York Education Law] authorizes local school boards to adopt reasonable regulations for the use of school property for 10 specified purposes when the property is not in use for school purposes. Among the permitted uses is the holding of "social, civic and recreational meetings and entertainments, and other uses pertaining to the welfare of the community; but such meetings, entertainment and uses shall be non-exclusive and shall be open to the general public." . . .

The issue in this case is whether, against this background of state law, it violates the Free Speech Clause of the First Amendment, made applicable to the States by the Fourteenth Amendment, to deny a church access to school premises to exhibit for public viewing and for assertedly religious purposes, a film series dealing with family and child-rearing issues faced by parents today. . . .

. . . The film series involved here no doubt dealt with a subject otherwise permissible under Rule 10, and its exhibition was denied solely because the series dealt with the subject from a religious standpoint. The principle that has emerged from our cases "is that the First Amendment forbids the government to regulate speech in ways that favor some viewpoints or ideas at the expense of others." . . . That principle applies in the circumstances of this case; as Judge Posner said for the Court of Appeals for the Seventh Circuit, to discriminate "against a particular point of view . . . would . . . flunk the test . . . [of] *Cornelius*, provided that the defendants have no defense based on the establishment clause." . . .

The District, as a respondent, would save its judgment below on the ground that to permit its property to be used for religious purposes would be an establishment of religion forbidden by the First Amendment. This Court suggested in *Widmar v. Vincent* . . . that the interest of the State in avoiding an Establishment Clause violation "may be [a] compelling" one justifying an abridgment of free speech otherwise protected by the First Amendment; but the Court went on to hold that permitting use of university property for religious purposes under the open access policy involved there would not be incompatible with the Court's Establishment Clause cases.

We have no more trouble than did the *Widmar* Court in disposing of the claimed defense on the ground that the posited fears of an Establishment Clause violation are unfounded. The showing of this film series would not have been during school hours, would not have been sponsored by the school, and would have been open to the public, not just to church members. The District property had repeatedly been used by a wide variety of private organizations. Under these circumstances, as in *Widmar*, there would have been no realistic danger that the community would think that the District was endorsing religion or any particular creed, and any benefit to religion or to the Church would have been no more than incidental. As in *Widmar*, . . . permitting District property to be used to exhibit the film series involved in this case would not have been an establishment of religion under the three-part test articulated in *Lemon v. Kurtzman*. . . . The challenged governmental action has a secular purpose, does not have the principal or primary effect of advancing or inhibiting religion, and does not foster an excessive entanglement with religion. . . .

*Reversed.*

*Source*: 113 S. Ct. 2141 (1993).

---

## DOCUMENT 67: Communications Decency Act of 1996

It is appropriate that we complete the free-speech parts of this documentary history with a discussion of the Communications Decency Act. As the unfolding history of free-speech jurisprudence has demonstrated, threats to free speech arise whenever a new medium of communication is introduced. The printing press, films, radio, and television—each new technology has been greeted with cries of alarm from those who would control access to ideas they deem dangerous. Cyberspace presents such would-be censors with the greatest challenge to date, because the ability to censor it does not exist. In 1996, Congress passed the Communications Decency Act, which purported to criminalize transmission of "indecent" material over the Internet.

\* \* \*

SEC. 501. SHORT TITLE.

This title may be cited as the "Communications Decency Act of 1996."

SEC. 502. OBSCENE OR HARASSING USE OF
TELECOMMUNICATIONS FACILITIES UNDER THE
COMMUNICATIONS ACT OF 1934.

Section 223 (47 U.S.C. 223) is amended—

(1) by striking subsection (a) and inserting in lieu thereof:

(a) Whoever—

  (1) in interstate or foreign communications—

    (A) by means of a telecommunications device knowingly—

      (i) makes, creates, or solicits, and

      (ii) initiates the transmission of,

    Any comment, request, suggestion, proposal, image, or other communication which is obscene, lewd, lascivious, filthy, or indecent, with intent to annoy, abuse, threaten, or harass another person;

    (B) by means of a telecommunications device knowingly—

      (i) makes, creates, or solicits, and

      (ii) initiates the transmission of,

    Any comment, request, suggestion, proposal, image, or other communication which is obscene or indecent, knowing that the recipient of the communication is under 18 years of age, regardless of whether the maker of such communication placed the call or initiated the communication;

    (C) makes a telephone call or utilizes a telecommunications device, whether or not conversation or communication ensues, without disclosing his identity and with intent to annoy, abuse, threaten, or harass any person at the called number or who receives the communications;

    (D) makes or causes the telephone of another repeatedly or continuously to ring, with intent to harass any person at the called number; or

    (E) makes repeated telephone calls or repeatedly initiates communication with a telecommunications device, during which conversation or communication ensures, solely to harass any person at the called number or who receives the communication; or

  (2) knowingly permits any telecommunications facility under his control to be used for any activity prohibited by paragraph (1) with the intent that it be used for such activity,

shall be fined under title 18, United States Code, or imprisoned not more than two years, or both; and

(2) by adding at the end the following new subsections:

(d) Whoever—

  (1) in interstate or foreign communications knowingly—

    (A) uses an interactive computer service to send to a specific person or persons under 18 years of age, or

    (B) uses any interactive computer service to display in a manner available to a person under 18 years of age,

Any comment, request, suggestion, proposal, image, or other communication that, in context, depicts or describes, in terms patently offensive as measured by contemporary community standards, sexual or excretory activities or organs, regardless of whether the user of such service placed the call or initiated the communication; or

(2) knowingly permits any telecommunications facility under such person's control to be used for an activity prohibited by paragraph (1) with the intent that it be used for such activity,

shall be fined under title 18, Untied States Code, or imprisoned not more than two years, or both.

(e) In addition to any other defenses available by law:

(1) No person shall be held to have violated subsection (a) or (d) solely for providing access or connection to or from a facility, system, or network not under that person's control, including transmission, downloading, intermediate storage, access software, or other related capabilities that are incidental to providing such access or connection that does not include the creation of the content of the communication.

*Source*: Telecommunications Act of 1996, tit. V., Pub. L. 104–104, 110 Stat. 56, 133 (1998).

---

## DOCUMENT 68: *Janet Reno, Attorney General of the United States v. American Civil Liberties Union* (1997)

As the Supreme Court noted in *Reno v. ACLU*, the Internet is an interconnected web consisting of millions of computers located all over the globe. The implications of this technology, which is evolving daily, are awe-inspiring. At the same time, because its technology is so different from that of the print or broadcast media, the Internet's growth raises a host of new issues for the application of First Amendment jurisprudence.

The American Civil Liberties Union is one of a large number of advocacy organizations that maintain sites on the World Wide Web, part of the Internet. Together with several other such organizations, it challenged the provisions of the Communications Decency Act, alleging that the law was far too broad, and could be used to censor material that had never before been considered obscene, including legal and other material posted on the ACLU's Web page. The large class of plaintiffs included several posting information about AIDS and breast cancer, and the Electronic Frontier Foundation, an organization specifically founded to protect civil liberties in cyberspace.

* * *

Justice STEVENS delivered the opinion of the Court.

At issue is the constitutionality of two statutory provisions enacted to protect minors from "indecent" and "patently offensive" communications on the Internet. Notwithstanding the legitimacy and importance of the congressional goal of protecting children from harmful materials, we agree with the three-judge District Court that the statute abridges "the freedom of speech" protected by the First Amendment. . . .

The best known category of communication over the Internet is the World Wide Web, which allows users to search for and retrieve information stored in remote computers, as well as, in some cases, to communicate back to designated sites. In concrete terms, the Web consists of a vast number of documents stored in different computers all over the world. Some of these documents are simply files containing information. However, more elaborate documents, commonly known as Web "pages," are also prevalent. Each has its own address—"rather like a telephone number." Web pages frequently contain information and sometimes allow the viewer to communicate with the page's (or "site's") author. They generally also contain "links" to other documents created by that site's author or to other (generally) related sites. Typically, the links are either blue or underlined text—sometimes images. . . .

Sexually explicit material on the Internet includes text, pictures, and chat and "extends from the modestly titillating to the hardest-core." . . .

Though such material is widely available, users seldom encounter such content accidentally. "A document's title or a description of the document will usually appear before the document itself . . . and in many cases the user will receive detailed information about a site's content before he or she need take the step to access the document. Almost all sexually explicit images are preceded by warnings as to the content." For that reason, the "odds are slim" that a user would enter a sexually explicit site by accident. Unlike communications received by radio or television, "the receipt of information on the Internet requires a series of affirmative steps more deliberate and directed than merely turning a dial. A child requires some sophistication and some ability to read to retrieve material and thereby to use the Internet unattended." . . .

The first [provision of the Act] prohibits the knowing transmission of obscene or indecent messages to any recipient under 18 years of age. . . .

The second provision, § 223(d), prohibits the knowing sending or displaying of patently offensive messages in a manner that is available to a person under 18 years of age. . . .

The breadth of these prohibitions is qualified by two affirmative defenses. . . . One covers those who take "good faith, reasonable, effective, and appropriate actions" to restrict access by minors to the prohibited communications. . . . The other covers those who restrict access to covered material by requiring certain designated forms of age proof, such as a verified credit card or an adult identification number or code. . . .

. . . . In its appeal, the Government argues that the District Court erred in holding that the CDA violated both the First Amendment because it is overbroad and the Fifth Amendment because it is vague. While we discuss the vagueness of the CDA because of its relevance to the First Amendment overbreadth inquiry, we conclude that the judgment should be affirmed without reaching the Fifth Amendment issue. . . .

It is true that we have repeatedly recognized the governmental interest in protecting children from harmful materials. . . . But that interest does not justify an unnecessarily broad suppression of speech addressed to adults. As we have explained, the Government may not "reduc[e] the adult population . . . to . . . only what is fit for children." . . . "[R]egardless of the strength of the government's interest" in protecting children, "[t]he level of discourse reaching a mailbox simply cannot be limited to that which would be suitable for a sandbox." . . .

The District Court found that at the time of trial existing technology did not include any effective method for a sender to prevent minors from obtaining access to its communications on the Internet without also denying access to adults. The Court found no effective way to determine the age of a user who is accessing material through e-mail, mail exploders, newsgroups, or chat rooms. . . . As a practical matter, the Court also found that it would be prohibitively expensive for noncommercial—as well as some commercial—speakers who have Web sites to verify that their users are adults. . . . These limitations must inevitably curtail a significant amount of adult communication on the Internet. By contrast, the District Court found that "[d]espite its limitations, currently available *user-based* software suggests that a reasonably effective method by which *parents* can prevent their children from accessing sexually explicit and other material which *parents* may believe is inappropriate for their children will soon be widely available." . . .

The breadth of the CDA's coverage is wholly unprecedented. Unlike the regulations upheld in *Ginsberg* and *Pacifica*, the scope of the CDA is not limited to commercial speech or commercial entities. Its open-ended prohibitions embrace all nonprofit entities and individuals posting indecent messages or displaying them on their own computers in the presence of minors. The general, undefined terms "indecent" and "patently offensive" cover large amounts of nonpornographic material with serious educational or other value. Moreover, the "community standards" criterion as applied to the Internet means that any communication available to a nation-wide audience will be judged by the standards of the community most likely to be offended by the message. The regulated subject matter includes any of the seven "dirty words" used in the Pacifica monologue, the use of which the Government's expert acknowledged could constitute a felony. . . . It may also extend to discussion about prison rape or safe sexual practices, artistic images that include nude subjects, and arguably the card catalogue of the Carnegie Library. . . .

... Under the CDA, a parent allowing her 17-year-old to use the family computer to obtain information on the Internet that she, in her parental judgment, deems appropriate could face a lengthy prison term. ... Similarly, a parent who sent his 17-year-old college freshman information on birth control via e-mail could be incarcerated even though neither he, his child, nor anyone in their home community, found the material "indecent" or "patently offensive," if the college town's community thought otherwise. ...

We agree with the District Court's conclusion that the CDA places an unacceptably heavy burden on protected speech, and that the defenses do not constitute the sort of "narrow tailoring" that will save an otherwise patently invalid unconstitutional provision. In *Sable*, ... we remarked that the speech restriction at issue there amounted to " 'burn[ing] the house to roast the pig.' " The CDA, casting a far darker shadow over free speech, threatens to torch a large segment of the Internet community. ...

For the foregoing reasons, the judgment of the District Court is affirmed.

*It is so ordered.*

*Source*: 117 S. Ct. 2329 (1997).

---

## DOCUMENT 69: "A Declaration of the Independence of Cyberspace" (John Perry Barlow, 1996)

John Perry Barlow was one of the early pioneers of cyberspace and a founder of the Electronic Frontier Foundation (EFF), an organization devoted to protecting civil liberties in cyberspace. Barlow's declaration of independence for cyberspace, which follows, reflects American understanding of our free-speech heritage at the beginning of a new millennium.

\* \* \*

Governments of the Industrial World, you weary giants of flesh and steel, I come from Cyberspace, the new home of Mind. On behalf of the future, I ask you of the past to leave us alone. You are not welcome among us. You have no sovereignty where we gather.

We have no elected government, nor are we likely to have one, so I address you with no greater authority than that with which liberty itself always speaks. I declare the global social space we are building to be naturally independent of the tyrannies you seek to impose on us. You have no moral right to rule us nor do you possess any methods of enforcement we have true reason to fear.

Governments derive their just powers from the consent of the governed. You have neither solicited nor received ours. We did not invite you. You do not know us, nor do you know our world. Cyberspace does not lie within your borders. Do you not think that you can build it, as though it were a public construction project. You cannot. It is an act of nature and it grows itself through our collective actions.

You have not engaged in our great and gathering conversation, nor did you create the wealth of our marketplaces. You do not know our culture, our ethics, or the unwritten codes that already provide our society more order than could be obtained by any of your impositions.

You claim there are problems among us that you need to solve. You use this claim as an excuse to invade our precincts. Many of these problems don't exist. Where there are real conflicts, where there are wrongs, we will identify them and address them by our means. We are forming our own Social Contract. This governance will arise according to the conditions of our world, not yours. Our world is different.

Cyberspace consists of transactions, relationships, and thought itself, arrayed like a standing wave in the web of our communications. Ours is a world that is both everywhere and nowhere, but it is not where bodies live.

We are creating a world that all may enter without privilege or prejudice accorded by race, economic power, military force, or station of birth.

We are creating a world where anyone, anywhere may express his or her beliefs, no matter how singular, without fear of being coerced into silence or conformity.

Your legal concepts of property, expression, identity, movement, and context do not apply to us. They are based on matter. There is no matter here.

Our identities have no bodies, so, unlike you, we cannot obtain order by physical coercion. We believe that from ethics, enlightened self-interest, and the commonweal, our governance will emerge. Our identities may be distributed across many of your jurisdictions. The only law that all our constituent cultures would generally recognize is the Golden Rule. We hope we will be able to build our particular solutions on that basis. But we cannot accept the solutions you are attempting to impose.

In the United States, you have today created a law, the Telecommunications Reform Act, which repudiates your own Constitution and insults the dreams of Jefferson, Washington, Mill, Madison, DeToqueville [sic], and Brandeis. These dreams must now be born anew in us.

You are terrified of your own children, since they are natives in a world where you will always be immigrants. Because you fear them, you entrust your bureaucracies with the parental responsibilities you are too cowardly to confront yourselves. In our world, all the sentiments and expressions of humanity, from the debasing to the angelic, are parts of a seamless whole, the global conversation of bits. We cannot separate the air that chokes from the air upon which wings beat.

In China, Germany, France, Russia, Singapore, Italy and the United States, you are trying to ward off the virus of liberty by erecting guard posts at the frontiers of Cyberspace. These may keep out the contagion for a small time, but they will not work in a world that will soon be blanketed in bit-bearing media.

Your increasingly obsolete information industries would perpetuate themselves by proposing laws, in America and elsewhere, that claim to own speech itself throughout the world. These laws would declare ideas to be another industrial product, no more noble than pig iron. In our world, whatever the human mind may create can be reproduced and distributed infinitely at no cost. The global conveyance of thought no longer requires your factories to accomplish.

These increasingly hostile and colonial measures place us in the same position as those previous lovers of freedom and self-determination who had to reject the authorities of distant, uninformed powers. We must declare our virtual selves immune to your sovereignty, even as we continue to consent to your rule over our bodies. We will spread ourselves across the Planet so that no one can arrest our thoughts.

We will create a civilization of the Mind in Cyberspace. May it be more humane and fair than the world your governments have made before.

*Source*: John Perry Barlow, "A Declaration of the Independence of Cyberspace," Daros, Switzerland, February 8, 1996. http://www.eff.org/~barlow.

# Part VI

---

# The Free Press:
# A Necessary Irritant

In Parts I through V, we traced the evolution of the idea that liberty depends on man's freedom to communicate free of government interference. We have also seen that the principle of free speech is easier to support in the abstract. A government responsive to majoritarian passions will always exert pressure to suppress ideas the majority finds distasteful, whether those ideas concern sex, religion, disloyalty to the government, or hate—any ideas that run counter to the prevailing orthodoxy. It is the role of the courts to safeguard us against such suppression, but the courts are not always immune to the passions of the times, as the documents in Parts I through V have also demonstrated.

Freedom of the press is a necessary condition to free expression. Without the press to inform, investigate, and opine on matters great and small, public discourse is impoverished. The role of the press is so important that the founders specified the right to a free press in the First Amendment, although such a right would certainly seem to be included in the broader liberty accorded to speech.

In this part, we look again at the evolution of our understanding of First Amendment principles, but this time from a narrower perspective. We will see how the special solicitude extended to a free press has been applied to media unimagined by the founders; how the courts have dealt with media claims to a privileged status in a free society; and how the courts have dealt with the inevitable conflicts between the public's "right to know" and other important interests like privacy, reputation, fair trials, and public school discipline.

The press has been rightfully criticized over the years for its excesses. Members of the media, who are unelected, often exert more power than our elected representatives. Reporting is frequently slanted or otherwise inaccurate. Members of the media are no wiser and often no better informed than the rest of us, yet when they choose to pay attention to one event rather than another, they can distort how the public sees reality.

With all its warts, however, the press as an institution is an irreplaceable element of a democratic society. Its special role was confirmed even before the American Revolution, during the famous trial of John Peter Zenger in 1734–1735. Zenger published a newspaper called the *New York Weekly Journal*, which he founded in 1733. Originally a propaganda vehicle for a New York political faction of the day, its purpose was the presentation of opposition political views. It is often said to be the first example of a politically independent and thus "free" press in America. Zenger published the first American edition of *Cato's Letters* (see Document 3) and his was the first publication in America to argue for the right to criticize the government without being subject to penalty.

While Zenger's name is familiar to most students of American history, he was merely the printer of the *Journal*, which was written and edited primarily by James Alexander, one of the founders of the American Philosophical Society. Alexander was a lawyer, mathematician, journalist and politician who served in the New York General Assembly and as attorney general of New Jersey.

Pioneers often pay a high price, and the *New York Weekly Journal* was no exception. John Peter Zenger was charged under the libel laws his publication had criticized. His acquittal by a jury is today regarded as fundamental to the establishment of a free press in America.

It would not be until the 1920s that the United States Supreme Court would address the meaning of the free speech and free press provisions of the First Amendment; when it finally did so, the legacy of John Peter Zenger provided background and context to those deliberations.

---

## DOCUMENT 70: "The Day Mencken Broke the Law" (Herbert Asbury, 1951)

In the 1920s, H. L. Mencken and his magazine, *American Mercury*, were highly influential. Many of the most esteemed authors of the day were contributors to *American Mercury*, which was widely read. Mencken himself was a noted "muckraker" with a notable lack of respect for authority. (He once compared American presidential campaigns to the marketing of underarm deodorants.)

In 1926, *American Mercury* published an article called "Hatrack" that discussed prostitution in small towns of the Midwest, particularly

Farmington, Missouri. The article took its name from the nickname of a Farmington prostitute whose scrawny figure evidently prompted it. Publication of the article was the last straw for the Massachusetts Watch and Ward Society, Boston's censors. Mencken had been highly critical of the Watch and Ward Society and some of its officers; the magazine containing the "Hatrack" article was duly banned in Boston. What happened next is the subject of the following article by Herbert Asbury, which appeared in *American Mercury* in October 1951.

\* \* \*

At two o'clock on the afternoon of April 5, 1926, a taxicab stopped at the burn on Boston Common, opposite Brimstone Corner at Park and Tremont Streets, and H. L. Mencken, editor of *The American Mercury,* stepped out, a broad grin on his face, several copies of the April 1926 issue of *The Mercury* tucked under his arm, and in his pocket a Boston city license to "peddle and hawk" any commodity except bones, grease, fish, fruit, vegetables, and refuse matter. After him came two lawyers, Arthur Garfield Hays of New York and Herbert E. Ehrmann of Boston. The fact that Mencken would be there had been announced in the newspapers, and a crowd of more than five thousand was on hand, composed mostly of students from Harvard, Boston University, and other colleges. These young men surged boisterously about Mencken, shouting encouragement and snatching at the magazines which he now held firmly clutched in both hands. One enthusiast grabbed Mencken's hat, but the editor retrieved it and jammed it down over his ears.

Some fifteen minutes after Mencken's arrival, the Rev. J. Frank Chase, secretary of the Massachusetts Watch and Ward Society, appeared on the outskirts of the crowd accompanied by an imposing police escort which included Superintendent Michael Crowley, Captain George W. Patterson, Sergeant Thomas O'Donnell, detectives of the Vice Squad, and agents of the Society. Mencken waved his arms and yelled, "Over here, Mr. Chase," and the college boys took up the cry, but it was some time before the police could force a passage through the crowd. Finally, however, Mencken and Chase faced each other. Mencken was still grinning but Chase wore his habitual expression of gloomy determination. From his point of view he was dealing with a low criminal, and it was no time for levity. He pointed to the bundle of magazines in Mencken's hand.

"Will you sell me a copy?" he asked.

"I will," said Mencken, "I will, indeed."

"Just a minute," Hays interrupted. "Are you the Rev. J. Frank Chase?"

"I am."

"Sell him," said the lawyer, tersely.

Mencken thereupon bowed and handed Chase a copy of *The Mercury,* receiving in exchange a half-dollar which Captain Patterson had previously scratched for identification. The crowd cheered wildly as Mencken bit the coin, jiggled it in his palm for a moment, and put it in his pocket. Chase hurriedly riffled the pages of the magazine and glanced at the table of contents. Then he pointed a quivering forefinger at Mencken.

"Arrest that man!" he cried.

Superintendent Crowley motioned to Captain Patterson, who beckoned to Sergeant O'Donnell, who summoned Officer Oliver W. Garrett of the Vice Squad, who tapped Mencken on the shoulder and formally placed him under arrest. Captain Patterson took charge of the magazine which Mencken had sold to Chase, and requested the editor to turn over the half-dollar he had received in payment. The coin was never returned, and in later years Mencken often complained that he had been unjustly deprived of his money.

As the police started to lead Mencken away, he flung the remaining copies of *The Mercury*, which Captain Patterson had not seized, into the crowd. Vice Squad policemen darted after them, but were too late; the magazines were quickly torn to pieces and the pages pocketed as souvenirs. Preceded by Chase, Superintendent Crowley, and Captain Patterson, flanked on either side by an alert Vice Squad detective, and followed by his lawyers and the yelling crowd, Mencken was marched down Tremont Street to Police Headquarters. The students, who were alternately cheering Mencken and booing the police and the Watch and Ward Society, tried to rush into the building, but were pushed back after a hard struggle. Attorney Ehrmann became separated from Mencken and Hays, and excitedly attempted to force his way through the police lines. He was roughly handled, Superintendent Crowley personally pinning him against the wall and shouting, "Will you leave peaceably or will I throw you out?" The lawyer chose peace, and left the building. A little later, however, he was identified and admitted. He hurried to the side of his client, whom he found happily posing for photographers and issuing statements to a swarm of reporters.

After being held in the detention room for an hour or so, Mencken was arraigned before Judge Sullivan of the Boston Municipal Court upon a warrant, which set forth that he "did sell to one Jason F. Chase certain obscene, indecent, and impure printing . . . manifestly tending to corrupt the morals of youth." The police asked for a week's postponement, but Judge Sullivan refused to grant the delay, and set the case down for trial the following morning before Judge James P. Parmenter.

The "impure printing" complained of was an article called "Hatrack," which discussed prostitution in the small towns of the Middle West, particularly in Farmington, Missouri, and was somewhat critical of the attitude of the churches and the virtuous people of Farmington toward their fallen sisters, specifically the town harlot, a scrawny, pathetic creature jokingly called Hatrack because of her figure. I wrote the article, but I was never accused of any crime more serious than bad taste, sacrilege, and trying to imitate Mencken's style.

I was supposed to make the trip to Boston with Mencken and Arthur Garfield Hays, but couldn't get away from my job in New York. I went down on the night of April 5, however, and when the case was heard before Judge Parmenter I testified that Hatrack was an actual person and that the article concerning her was true in every detail. Neither Mencken nor Hays made any suggestions about my testimony, except that Mencken said, "If they ask you if you are a Christian, say yes."

Mencken always insisted that he wasn't excited when he went into court. Well, maybe he wasn't, but I recall that when I walked into the suite at the Hotel Copley-Plaza a few hours before the trial, I found him sitting in the bathtub, furiously smoking a cigar and talking, just as furiously, to a Baltimore newspaper man. I supposed that he was taking a bath, but there was no water in the tub, and he had his hat on.

The hearing before Judge Parmenter was informal, with principals, witnesses, lawyers, and reporters clustered about the bench. The court room was crowded, but the spectators heard little or nothing. I dropped back a few feet after testifying, and several newspaper men began talking to me about the case. A court attendant shushed them, but they paid no attention until Mencken turned and cried, "Shut up, dammit!" Judge Parmenter raised an eyebrow, but said nothing. The reporters shut up.

Judge Parmenter, who was unfamiliar with *The Mercury*, adjourned the trial overnight in order to read the magazine, especially "Hatrack." Mencken, his lawyers, and virtually everyone else expected a conviction. "It's a cinch," said a Boston reporter. "Chase always wins." On the morning of April 7 Judge Parmenter handed down his decision, that "Hatrack" was not obscene and in no way violated the law, and that Mencken had committed no offense in selling the magazine.

Meanwhile, Mencken's lawyers had filed a $50,000 damage suit against Chase and the Watch and Ward Society, which was never tried, and had applied to the United States District Court for an injunction restraining the Society from further molesting *The Mercury*. This injunction was granted on April 14 by Judge James M. Morton, Jr. In New York on April 8, Mencken was informed by the Associated Press that the Post Office Department had barred the April issue of *The Mercury* from the mails, at the request of various religious organizations and the Chamber of Commerce of Farmington, Missouri. This order made no sense, as the April issue had been passed by the Postmaster at Camden, New Jersey, where the magazine was printed, and the entire edition had been mailed to subscribers and distributors before Mencken was arrested. Neither Mencken nor Alfred A. Knopf, then the publisher of *The Mercury*, had been notified that the Post Office contemplated such action, and had no opportunity to offer a defense. After much stalling, the Department finally consented to hear their protests, and on April 15, Mencken, Knopf, and Arthur Garfield Hays met with Post Office officials in Washington. At the conclusion of the hearing, which verged on the farcical, it was announced that the ban would not be lifted. An appeal was immediately taken to the Federal Courts in New York, and on May 12, Judge Julian W. Mack granted a permanent injunction which compelled the Post Office Department to open the mails to the disputed issue. Mencken's victory was complete. The Watch and Ward Society had been shown not to be omnipotent, and its power had been considerably reduced. Since the Hatrack case the censorship situation in Boston has been somewhat more tolerable, though there is still a great deal of room for improvement.

I was working on the *New York Herald Tribune* and occasionally writing mystery and detective fiction when Mencken and George Jean Nathan galloped into the American scene with *The American Mercury* in 1924 and began, as Mencken once put it, "to stir up the animals." The first few issues of the new magazine convinced me that Mencken and Nathan were two of the greatest men the century had yet produced—an opinion which I still hold—and almost overnight to be a *Mercury* contributor became my greatest ambition. After two or three false starts I wrote a reminiscence of my boyhood, which was largely an account of the debasing effects of organized religion as practiced in the Missouri town where I was born and lived for nineteen years. I sent this article to *The Mercury*, and a few days later was asked to have a talk with Nathan. While I was in Nathan's office Mencken came in, and I saw him for the first time. I had expected an imposing giant dripping erudition at every pore; instead, I was introduced to a chunky, moon-faced man of average height, with mild blue eyes and brown hair carefully parted in the middle and slicked down. He had a big cigar in his mouth, and wore a blue suit which was a little untidy and a trifle too small. After I had answered several searching questions, Nathan said *The Mercury* would buy my article. Mencken nodded and said:

"We can't pay much, you know."

"Who writes for money?" I said, scornfully.

Nathan coughed, and Mencken snickered gently. I felt very silly. Mencken never let me forget that unfortunate crack. I don't believe I ever saw him again that he didn't refer to it.

The article was published in the February, 1925, issue of *The Mercury*, after Nathan had retired as co-editor, under the title "Up From Methodism." It produced many violent and abusive letters, and caused a considerable commotion in parts of the Middle West, though nothing compared to the furor raised a year later by the publication of "Hatrack." In the late summer of 1925, at Mencken's suggestion, I expanded "Up

From Methodism" into a book, and Knopf accepted it for publication in September, 1926. I sent a copy of the book manuscript to Mencken, hoping that he could use some of it in *The Mercury*. The story of Hatrack, about three thousand words, was a small section of a chapter called "Diversions of An Abandoned Sinner." Mencken said he would like to lift this section out of the manuscript and publish it as an article.

"I need a piece about that long," he said.

As far as I ever knew that was the only reason he accepted it. I can't recall that he ever expressed an opinion as to the literary merits of the piece, and I still don't know whether he thought it was a good article or just something that would do to fill up space. When he was arrested in Boston, Mencken told the newspaper reporters that "Hatrack" was a "Charming, pretty little thing," but that was obviously for the record, for whatever else Hatrack may have been, it was not that. The article was not advertised, or announced in the previous issue of the magazine, or given an especially good position. The issue in which it appeared was on sale in Boston almost two weeks before any action was taken against it.

Actually, "Hatrack" was not the real cause of the explosion; the article was merely the trigger that set it off. The enmity of the Watch and Ward Society toward Mencken and *The Mercury* began when the magazine, in September, 1925, published an article which exposed and denounced the extra-legal methods by which the Society's secretary, Rev. J. Frank Chase, had established himself as the censor of books and magazines in Massachusetts and, to a large extent, throughout New England. Chase operated by threatening and intimidating book-seller and newsdealers; in no case did he bring a publisher into court and permit him to defend himself or protect his property. If a newsdealer ignored the threats, he was arrested and since the Society, though a Protestant organization, possessed great influence with the Boston police and courts, a conviction was easily obtained. The publisher seldom knew what was going on until he was notified by the distributors, or learned from the newspapers, that his book or magazine had been withdrawn from sale.

After the appearance of this article it soon became common knowledge in Boston and New York that the Watch and Ward Society was gunning for Mencken and *The Mercury*, and would crack down on them at the first opportunity. "Hatrack" provided the opportunity. It is doubtful if even Chase really saw anything obscene in the article, but it could be, and was, construed as an attack upon religion, and it was obvious that any attempt to suppress it would be supported by the churches and religious groups generally, with the cry of blasphemy and sacrilege. Several important newspapers upheld the suppression of *The Mercury* on those grounds. The *New York Herald Tribune*, for example, in an editorial denouncing Mencken as "a professional smart aleck," said that there were "substantial grounds for suppression on the score of sacrilege."

In the latter part of March, the Watch and Ward Society ordered the distributors and newsdealers of Massachusetts to withdraw the April issue of *The Mercury*, and they immediately obeyed as they had always done. One dealer in Cambridge, however, Felix Caragianes by name, sold a copy, and was promptly arrested. His defense was that the customer was a Harvard professor. Some two weeks later Caragianes was brought quietly into court, found guilty, and fined one hundred dollars. On his behalf the case was appealed, and the prosecution was eventually dropped by the state. In New York about April 1 Mencken read in the newspaper that *The Mercury* had been banned in Boston, and a day or so later he was notified of the Society's action by the Boston magazine distributions. I was in Mencken's office on April 4, and he told me that he and Knopf had decided to fight the society, and that he had arranged to sell Chase a copy in Boston and so make a test case.

"Chase and his gang," he said, "have been running wild in Boston for years, and everybody's afraid of them. It's high time somebody fought back. This may be a good chance to clip their wings."

That furor over "Hatrack" began as soon as the Watch and Ward Society had Mencken arrested. Newspapers all over the country printed long news stories and editorials about the case, many of the latter very violent, and several carried accounts of Mencken's trial and acquittal under eight-column headlines. Both Mencken and I received scores of letters, in which we were called the foulest names imaginable. Newsstand stocks of *The Mercury* were soon exhausted, and for several weeks copies of the April issue sold for as much as sixty dollars each. One newsdealer in Oklahoma City made more than fifty dollars by chaining a copy to his stand and charging his customers ten cents a look. A few district attorneys and police officials, trying to grab a little publicity, announced that the sale of *The Mercury* would not be permitted in their jurisdictions. Many libraries removed the magazine from their shelves because of the huge crowds which wanted to see it; several tore out the "Hatrack" pages and destroyed them. Religious organizations held numerous mass meetings at which Mencken and everyone else connected with *The Mercury* were denounced. Methodist preachers usually addressed these gatherings, and many, who should have known better, identified me as the son or grandson of Bishop Francis Asbury. I took great delight in calling their attention to the fact that the Bishop, who died in 1816, was never married, and in expressing my resentment at these slurs upon the character of the greatest figure in American Methodism.

Everywhere except in my home town of Farmington, Missouri, also Hatrack's home town, Mencken was flailed as the chief villain; I was generally looked upon as an unfortunate lad who had succumbed to Mencken's baleful influence. In Farmington, however, I was the evil one.

At a mass meeting called by the Chamber of Commerce, and attended by every clergyman in town as well as by a large number of citizens, I was assailed as one who had fouled his own nest. When the chairman began to read "Hatrack" aloud, he was halted by cries of anguish from the town's leading banker, "Stop! Stop! We must not listen to such an immoral recital!" According to the *United News*, everybody in town was talking about me in the most "dreadful terms." At first the whole town denied that the article was true, or that Hatrack had ever existed, but when the unfortunate woman was found living in a nearby village, with three children in an orphan asylum, the tune was changed somewhat, and I was violently accused of having insulted Farmington womanhood.

I was annoyed for many years, and Mencken and Knopf were also, by people who insisted that the Hatrack affair was a publicity stunt, and that everyone concerned in it had made a great deal of money. Nothing could be farther from the truth. No effort whatever was made to capitalize the publicity that flowed out of the case, and nobody made any more than he would have if the article hadn't been attacked. Knopf, indeed, lost heavily; the legal expenses were very large. Many thousands of additional copies of the April issue of *The Mercury* could have been sold, but not one extra copy was printed. The print order for the May issue, which had been given to the printer before Mencken's arrest, was not increased. When "Up From Methodism" was published in book form in September, 1926, "Hatrack" was returned to its place in the chapter from which Mencken had lifted it, and the fact that it was part of the book was not mentioned in any of Knopf's advertising or promotional matter.

Mencken paid me eighty dollars for the article and I received one hundred dollars in 1944, eighteen years later, when it was used in *The American Mercury Reader*. Since then it has appeared in a few anthologies. The total earnings of the article, over a period of some twenty-five years, do not exceed $250. It was reported in the newspapers that I had sold the dramatic rights, but this is untrue. Two first rate playwrights tried to fashion a play about Hatrack, but failed. Harold Atteridge, a well-known musical comedy writer of the period, who worked mostly for the Shuberts, wanted to do a one-act sketch about Hatrack for the Winter Garden show, a big musical revue. His first idea was for me to make a personal appearance and deliver a little talk about prostitution, a sort of running commentary set against a chorus line of Hatracks. When I told Mencken about this, he said, "that's the damndest idea I ever heard of." I held many conferences with Atteridge and other representatives of the Shuberts, and they were very generous in the matter of theatre tickets, lunches, dinners, and parties. I had a wonderful time, but the whole thing finally petered out and Hatrack was forgotten. *The Mercury* has reprinted the articles twice, in 1936 and 1950. The last printing produced one letter, a brief communication from a man in Georgia, who said, "I have now read your Hatrack article three times, in 1926, in 1936, and in 1950. It still stinks."

Source: Herbert Asbury, "The Day Mencken Broke the Law," American Mercury 73 (October 1951): 62–69.

---

## DOCUMENT 71: *Near v. Minnesota* (1931)

If there is one principle of a free press that everyone knows and to which virtually everyone gives lip service, it is the impropriety of prior restraints on publication. As Chief Justice Charles Evans Hughes noted in his majority opinion in *Near v. Minnesota*, the proscription on prior restraint could be found as far back as *Blackstone's Commentaries*, the best-known history of the doctrines of English common law, published in 1765.

Until the decision in *Near*, however, which was handed down in 1931, the Supreme Court had never been called upon to invalidate attempts to suppress publication. Near and his codefendants were publishers of a periodical in Minneapolis which was said to be malicious and scandalous, among other things; the County Attorney attempted to prevent its publication under a 1925 Minnesota statute. The Court held that such prior restraint could not be justified, a principle which is so familiar to us today that it may come as a surprise to learn that the decision was five to four.

\* \* \*

MR. CHIEF JUSTICE HUGHES delivered the opinion of the Court.

Chapter 285 of the Session Laws of Minnesota for the year 1925 provides for the abatement, as a public nuisance, of a "malicious, scandalous and defamatory newspaper, magazine or other periodical." . . .

Under this statute, . . . the County Attorney of Hennepin County brought this action to enjoin the publication of what was described as a "malicious, scandalous and defamatory newspaper, magazine and periodical," known as "The Saturday Press," published by the defendants in the city of Minneapolis. The compliant alleged that the defendants, on September 24, 1927, and on eight subsequent dates in October and November, 1927, published and circulated editions of that periodical which were "largely devoted to malicious, scandalous and defamatory articles" concerning Charles G. Davis, Frank W. Brunskill, the Minneapolis Tribune, the Minneapolis Journal, Melvin C. Passolt, George E. Leach, the

Jewish Race, the members of the Grand Jury of Hennepin County impaneled in November, 1927, and then holding office, and other persons. . . .

. . . There is no question but that the articles made serious accusations against the public officers named and others in connection with the prevalence of crimes and the failure to expose and punish them. . . .

. . . Judgment was . . . entered adjudging that "the newspaper, magazine and periodical known as The Saturday Press," as a public nuisance, "be and is hereby abated." The judgment perpetually enjoined the defendants "from producing, editing, publishing, circulating, having in their possession, selling or giving away any publication whatsoever which is a malicious, scandalous or defamatory newspaper, as defined by law," and also "from further conducting said nuisance under the name and title of said The Saturday Press or any other name or title. . . ."

. . . It is no longer open to doubt that the liberty of the press, and of speech, is within the liberty safeguarded by the due process clause of the Fourteenth Amendment from invasion by state action. It was found impossible to conclude that this essential personal liberty of the citizen was left unprotected by the general guaranty of fundamental rights of person and property. . . .

". . . Some degree of abuse is inseparable from the proper use of everything, and in no instance is this more true than in that of the press. It has accordingly been decided by the practice of the States, that it is better to leave a few of its noxious branches to their luxuriant growth, than, by pruning them away, to injure the vigour of those yielding the proper fruits. And can the wisdom of this policy be doubted by any who reflect that to the press alone, chequered as it is with abuses, the world is indebted for all the triumphs which have been gained by reason and humanity over error and oppression; who reflect that to the same beneficent source the United States owe much of the lights which conducted them to the ranks of a free and independent nation, and which have improved their political system into a shape so auspicious to their happiness? Had 'Sedition Acts,' forbidding every publication that might bring the constituted agents into contempt or disrepute, or that might excite the hatred of the people against the authors of unjust or pernicious measures, been uniformly enforced against the press, might not the United States have been languishing at this day under the infirmities of a sickly Confederation? Might they not, possibly, be miserable colonies, groaning under a foreign yoke?" . . .

The statute in question cannot be justified by reason of the fact that the publisher is permitted to show, before injunction issues, that the matter published is true and is published with good motives and for justifiable ends. If such a statute, authorizing suppression and injunction on such a basis, is constitutionally valid, it would be equally permissible for the legislature to provide that at any time the publisher of any news-paper could be brought before a court, or even an administrative officer (as the constitutional protection may not be regarded as resting on mere procedural details) and required to produce proof of the truth of his publication, or of what he intended to publish, and of his motives, or stand enjoined. If this can be done, the legislature may provide machin-ery for determining in the complete exercise of its discretion what are justifiable ends and restrain publication accordingly. And it would be but a step to a complete system of censorship. The recognition of au-thority to impose previous restraint upon publication in order to protect the community against the circulation of charges of misconduct, and especially of official misconduct, necessarily would carry with it the ad-mission of the authority of the censor against which the constitutional barrier was erected. The preliminary freedom, by virtue of the very rea-son for its existence, does not depend, as this Court has said, on proof of truth. . . .

. . . we hold the statute . . . to be an infringement of the liberty of the press guaranteed by the Fourteenth Amendment. We should add that this decision rests upon the operation and effect of the statute, without regard to the question of the truth of the charges contained in the par-ticular periodical. The fact that the public officers named in this case, and those associated with the charges of official dereliction, may be deemed to be impeccable, cannot affect the conclusion that the statute imposes an unconstitutional restraint upon publication.

*Judgment reversed.*

*Source*: 283 U.S. 697 (1931).

---

## DOCUMENT 72: "A Letter to the American Society of Newspaper Editors on Free Speech and a Free Press" (Franklin D. Roosevelt, 1941)

Most politicians, and particularly presidents of the United States, have found it expedient to publicly support the independence of the press. No matter how angered they may become at criticism of their policies or invasions of their privacy, they recognize the danger (as someone has aptly put it) of picking a fight with the guys who buy their ink by the barrel.

On April 16, 1941, as the United States was facing an increasing likelihood of involvement in the Second World War, Franklin Delano Roosevelt wrote the following letter to Tom Wallace, editor of the Louisville *Times* and then president of the American Society of Newspaper Editors, assuring him of the president's commitment to freedom of speech and the press.

Despite the ringing endorsement of freedom of the press contained in the President's letter, the Roosevelt administration created an Office of Censorship soon after America's entry into the war. Its stated purpose was to protect national security by controlling the flow of information about the war effort.

\* \* \*

The assurance I would bring to the American Society of Newspaper Editors, if it were possible for me to greet them in person, would be that free speech and a free press are still in the possession of the people of the United States.

Free speech is in undisputed possession of publishers and editors, of reporters and Washington correspondents; still in the possession of magazines, of motion pictures, and of radio; still in the possession of all means of intelligence, comment, and criticism. So far as I am concerned it will remain there for that is where it belongs.

It is important that it should remain there, for suppression of opinion and censorship of news are among the mortal weapons that dictatorships direct against their own peoples and direct against the world. As far as I am concerned there will be no Government control of news unless it be of vital military information.

Like all of our liberties, liberty of speech, and of the press is not a mere phrase, a mere form of words, a constitutional abstraction. It has a living meaning—whatever the press itself gives it. Government juridical process can afford a negative protection against interference with freedom of speech, but its care, its nurture and its use are responsibilities of the press itself, which has never prized it so much as it should prize it now.

How that freedom should be used, what contributions it should make to national defense, national interest, and national morale, are questions for publishers and editors themselves to decide.

It would be a shameful abuse of patriotism to suggest that opinion should be stifled in its service. United national sentiment, which all of us should desire, bears no resemblance to a totalitarian regimentation of opinion and treatment of news.

I cannot better close this message to the American Society of Newspaper Editors than with a final assurance that those who disagree with what is being done, and with the manner in which it is being done, are free to use their freedom of speech.

*Source*: Franklin D. Roosevelt, "A Letter to the American Society of Newspaper Editors on Free Speech and a Free Press," *Public Papers and Addresses, 1941: The Call to Battle Stations* (volume 10) (New York: Russell & Russell, 1950), 120–121.

## DOCUMENT 73: *New York Times Co. v. Sullivan* (1964)

Few cases involving freedom of the press are as important as *New York Times Co. v. Sullivan*. In *Sullivan*, the Supreme Court held that state libel laws could not be used to intimidate or punish publications that were critical of public officials.

The facts of the case provided a textbook example of the dangers inherent in such libel prosecutions. During the height of the civil rights movement, the *New York Times* accepted an advertisement from a group of southern clergymen and others who complained of various official actions directed at student activists and Dr. Martin Luther King. The advertisement contained minor inaccuracies and named no names. Alabama officials brought libel charges, arguing that "everyone knew" who had authority for the criticized activities, and Alabama juries awarded enormous verdicts without any showing of actual damage to anyone's reputation. Under the circumstances, it is hard to believe that there was any motive for the lawsuit other than a desire to punish "outsiders" for publishing opinions critical of Alabama's elected officials.

\* \* \*

MR. JUSTICE BRENNAN delivered the opinion of the Court.

We are required in this case to determine for the first time the extent to which the constitutional protections for speech and press limit a State's power to award damages in a libel action brought by a public official against critics of his official conduct.

Respondent L. B. Sullivan is one of the three elected Commissioners of the City of Montgomery, Alabama. . . .

[His] complaint alleged that he had been libeled by statements in a full-page advertisement that was carried in the New York Times on March 29, 1960. Entitled "Heed Their Rising Voices," the advertisement began by stating that "As the whole world knows by now, thousands of Southern Negro students are engaged in widespread non-violent demonstrations in positive affirmation of the right to live in human dignity as guaranteed by the U.S. Constitution and the Bill of Rights." It went on to charge that "in their efforts to uphold these guarantees, they are being met by an unprecedented wave of terror by those who would deny and negate that document which the whole world looks upon as setting the pattern for modern freedom. . . ." Succeeding paragraphs purported to illustrate the "wave of terror" by describing certain alleged events. The text concluded with an appeal for funds for three purposes: support of the student movement, "the struggle for the right-to-vote," and the legal defense of Dr. Martin Luther King, Jr., leader of the movement, against a perjury indictment then pending in Montgomery. . . .

Of the 10 paragraphs of text in the advertisement, the third and a portion of the sixth were the basis of respondent's claim of libel. They read as follows:

Third paragraph:

"In Montgomery, Alabama, after students sang 'My Country, 'Tis of Thee' on the State Capitol steps, their leaders were expelled from school, and truckloads of police armed with shotguns and tear-gas ringed the Alabama State College Campus. When the entire student body protested to state authorities by refusing to re-register, their dining hall was padlocked in an attempt to starve them into submission."

Sixth paragraph:

"Again and again the Southern violators have answered Dr. King's peaceful protests with intimidation and violence. They have bombed his home almost killing his wife and child. They have assaulted his person. They have arrested him seven times—for 'speeding,' 'loitering' and similar 'offenses.' And now they have charged him with 'perjury'—a *felony* under which they could imprison him for ten years. . . ." . . .

It is uncontroverted that some of the statements contained in the two paragraphs were not accurate descriptions of events which occurred in Montgomery. Although Negro students staged a demonstration on the State Capitol steps, they sang the National Anthem and not "My Country, 'Tis of Thee." Although nine students were expelled by the State Board of Education, this was not for leading the demonstration at the Capitol, but for demanding service at a lunch counter in the Montgomery County Courthouse on another day. Not the entire student body, but most of it, had protested the expulsion, not by refusing to register, but by boycotting classes on a single day; virtually all the students did register for the ensuing semester. . . .

. . . we consider this case against the background of a profound national commitment to the principle that debate on public issues should be uninhibited, robust, and wide-open, and that it may well include vehement, caustic, and sometimes unpleasantly sharp attacks on government and public officials. . . . The present advertisement, as an expression of grievance and protest on one of the major public issues of our time, would seem clearly to qualify for the constitutional protection. The question is whether it forfeits that protection by the falsity of some of its factual statements and by its alleged defamation of respondent. . . .

The constitutional guarantees require, we think, a federal rule that prohibits a public official from recovering damages for a defamatory falsehood relating to his official conduct unless he proves that the statement was made with "actual malice"—that is, with knowledge that it was false or with reckless disregard of whether it was false or not. An oft-cited statement of a like rule, which has been adopted by a number of state courts, is found in the Kansas case of *Coleman* v. *MacLennan*. . . . The State Attorney General, a candidate for re-election and a member of the commission charged with the management and control of the state school fund, sued a newspaper publisher for alleged libel in an article purporting to state facts relating to his official conduct in connection with a school-fund transaction. The defendant pleaded privilege and the trial judge, over the plaintiff's objection, instructed the jury that

"where an article is published and circulated among voters for the sole purpose of giving what the defendant believes to be truthful information concerning a candidate for public office and for the purpose of enabling such voters to cast their ballot more intelligently, and the whole thing is done in good faith and without malice, the article is privileged, although the principal matters contained in the article may be untrue in fact and derogatory to the character of the plaintiff; and in such a case the burden is on the plaintiff to show actual malice in the publication of the article." . . .

We conclude that such a privilege is required by the First and Fourteenth Amendments. . . .

Finally, there is evidence that the Times published the advertisement without checking its accuracy against the news stories in the Times' own files. The mere presence of the stories in the files does not, of course, establish that the Times "knew" the advertisement was false, since the state of mind required for actual malice would have to be brought home to the persons in the Times' organization having responsibility for the publication of the advertisement. With respect to the failure of those persons to make the check, the record shows that they relied upon their knowledge of the good reputation of many of those whose names were listed as sponsors of the advertisement, and upon the letter from A. Philip Randolph, known to them as a responsible individual, certifying that the use of the names was authorized. There was testimony that the persons handling the advertisement saw nothing in it that would render it unacceptable under the Times' policy of rejecting advertisements containing "attacks of a personal character"; their failure to reject it on this ground was not unreasonable. We think the evidence against the Times supports at most a finding of negligence in failing to discover the misstatements, and is constitutionally insufficient to show the recklessness that is required for a finding of actual malice. . . .

*Reversed and remanded.*

MR. JUSTICE BLACK, with whom MR. JUSTICE DOUGLAS joins, concurring. . . .

. . . I base my vote to reverse on the belief that the First and Fourteenth Amendments not merely "delimit" a State's power to award damages to "public officials against critics of their official conduct" but completely prohibit a State from exercising such a power. The Court goes on to hold that a State can subject such critics to damages if "actual malice" can be proved against them. "Malice," even as defined by the Court, is an elusive, abstract concept, hard to prove and hard to disprove. The requirement that malice be proved provides at best an evanescent protection for the right critically to discuss public affairs and certainly does not measure up to the sturdy safeguard embodied in the First Amendment. Unlike the Court, therefore, I vote to reverse exclusively on the ground that the Times and the individual defendants had an absolute, unconditional constitutional right to publish in the Times advertisement their criticisms of the Montgomery agencies and officials. I do not base my vote to reverse on any failure to prove that these individual defendants signed the advertisement or that their criticism of the Police Department was aimed at the plaintiff Sullivan. . . .

. . . There is no reason to believe that there are not more such huge verdicts lurking just around the corner for the Times or any other newspaper or broadcaster which might dare to criticize public officials. In fact, briefs before us show that in Alabama there are now pending eleven libel suits by local and state officials against the Times seeking $5,600,000, and five such suits against the Columbia Broadcasting System seeking $1,700,000. Moreover, this technique for harassing and punishing a free press—now that it has been shown to be possible—is by no means limited to cases with racial overtones; it can be used in other fields where public feelings may make local as well as out-of-state newspapers easy prey for libel verdict seekers.

In my opinion the Federal Constitution has dealt with this deadly danger to the press in the only way possible without leaving the free press open to destruction—by granting the press an absolute immunity for criticism of the way public officials do their public duty. . . .

We would, I think, more faithfully interpret the First Amendment by holding that at the very least it leaves the people and the press free to criticize officials and discuss public affairs with impunity.

*Source*: 376 U.S. 254 (1964).

## DOCUMENT 74: "Libel and the Free Press" (Norman Dorsen, 1964)

Editorial reaction to the result in *New York Times Co. v. Sullivan* was uniformly positive. Much of that reaction was undoubtedly self-serving; the media, after all, had won the day. But even disinterested observers argued, with Norman Dorsen, that the opinion was needed.

\* \* \*

The United States Supreme Court will soon decide a free-speech case in which, for once, the petitioner does not represent the isolated and marginal in American society. It is not the victim of a HUAC inquisition, a Smith Act conviction or a Southern purge of the NAACP. Nor is it a figure on the Right. The petitioner this time is *The New York Times*, that strong, respectable anchor of the Establishment. The *Times* now seeks for itself what its editorial columns have so often sought for others—the protection of the First Amendment to the Constitution. It is appealing from the Alabama Supreme Court a $500,000 judgment rendered against it for an alleged libel.

The libel action stemmed from a full-page advertisement the *Times* published on March 29, 1960, sponsored by the "Committee to Defend Martin Luther King and the Struggle for Freedom in the South." (Another libel action arising out of the advertisement has resulted in a similar jury verdict of $500,000, and yet a third case, involving a claim of $2 million is pending.)

The ad was generated by an indictment handed down early in 1960 by an Alabama grand jury against Dr. King for perjury in connection with the filing of Alabama income tax returns. (Incidentally, he was later acquitted.) The committee to support Dr. King, which included Mrs. Ralph Bunche, A. J. Muste, A. Philip Randolph, Norman Thomas and the late Eleanor Roosevelt, was hastily put together in the belief that the indictment was politically motivated and without foundation. The advertisement, titled "Heed Their Rising Voices" was essentially a political and fundraising appeal. The text began:

As the whole world knows by now, thousands of Southern Negro students are engaged in widespread non-violent demonstration in positive affirmation of the right to live in human dignity as guaranteed by the U.S. Constitution and the Bill of Rights. In their efforts to uphold these guarantees, they are being met by an unprecedented wave of terror by those who would deny and negate that document which the whole world looks upon as setting the pattern for modern freedom. . . .

Without identifying or naming any particular individual, or fixing any particular time, the advertisement then referred to certain specific incidents of claimed repression in Montgomery, Ala., and Orangeburg, S.C. With regard to Montgomery, it said:

> . . . after students sang, "My Country 'Tis of Thee" on the Capitol steps, their Leaders were expelled from school, and truckloads of police armed with shotguns and tear gas ringed the Alabama State College campus. When the entire student body protested to state authorities by refusing to re-register, their dining hall was padlocked in an attempt to starve them into submission. . . .

The advertisement asserted that Martin Luther King "symbolizes the new spirit now sweeping the South," and that his "doctrine of non-violence . . . has inspired and guided the students in their widening wave of sit-ins. . . ." It continued:

> Again and again the Southern violators [of the Constitution] have answered Dr. King's peaceful protests with intimidation and violence. They have bombed his home almost killing his wife and child. They have assaulted his person. They have arrested him seven times—for "speeding," "loitering," and similar "offenses." And now they have charged him with "perjury"—a felony under which they could imprison him for ten years. Obviously, their real purpose is to remove him physically as the leader to whom the students—and millions of others—look for guidance and support, and thereby to intimidate all leaders who may rise in the South. . . .

The conclusion was an appeal for funds.

A wave of anger engulfed Montgomery. John Patterson, then Governor of Alabama, and L. B. Sullivan, one of the three elected Commissioners of Montgomery and plaintiff in the libel suit, demanded a retraction. Although the *Times* believed that no statement in the advertisement referred to either Governor Patterson or Commissioner Sullivan, it published a retraction in the case of the Governor because of his "high office" and the possibility that there was "a reflection on the state of Alabama." The *Times* has conceded that there were certain inaccuracies in the advertisement.

A jury trial of the case resulted in a verdict for Commissioner Sullivan for $500,000 (all damages claimed), under the Alabama rule that a public official is entitled to recover "presumed" and "punitive" damages for a publication critical of a governmental agency under his supervision if a jury thinks that the publication "tends to injure him in his reputation" or "bring him into public contempt as an official." Under this rule, the complainant need not establish actual injury to his reputation.

The case, as presented to the Supreme Court, involves the broad constitutional question of whether the Alabama courts have "abridged" freedom of speech or of the press in rendering this judgment against the *Times*. Obviously, there has in fact been some interference with the practice of free expression: publishers are now considerably more concerned about the contents of both advertising and news copy. The *Times*, in particular, feels this pressure, not only because of the actions stemming from the controversial advertisement, but also because of seven libel suits—again in Alabama—arising from an article by correspondent Harrison Salisbury on racial conflict in that state. At present, the *Times* is not distributed in Alabama, presumably because it fears still more actions.

The threat to free expression is not limited to the cases involving the *Times*. Perhaps because there are fashions in law as elsewhere, there has been a rash of huge libel judgments. John Henry Faulk, a black-listed radio and television commentator, won a judgment for $3 million (later reduced to $550,000) against the publishers of *Red Channels*. General Edwin A. Walker has sued a host of newspapers and radio and television stations, for a total of about $20 million, charging that they disseminated false information about his activities during the riots at the University of Mississippi in 1962. Nor is this style in law suits confined to the political arena. Wally Butts, former football coach at the University of Georgia, recently won a libel judgment that included $3 million (later reduced to $460,000) in punitive damages from the *Saturday Evening Post* for an article it printed charging that he had revealed his team's plays to an opposing coach. Other actions are in the wings.

*The New York Times* thus represents not only its own interests in the Supreme Court. It is the standard-bearer for other defendants and potential defendants. What can the Supreme Court be expected to do?

A decade ago, in the case of *Beauharnais v. Illinois*, Justice Felix Frankfurter declared that "libelous utterances [are] not . . . within the area of constitutionally protected free speech." A sharply divided Court upheld Beauharnais' conviction under a "group libel" statute that prohibited the exposure of citizens of "any race, color, creed or religion to contempt, derision or obloquy." Although it was not essential to the decision, Justice Frankfurter's all-embracing formula has been repeated in later Supreme Court opinions. It rests on the postulate that freedom of speech is merely one of the competing interests in society, and that other important values—national security, the need to curb obscenity or, as here, the protection of personal reputations—may impose limits on free speech. Taken at face value, the opinion delivered by Justice Frankfurter plainly would offer little hope to the *Times*.

At the other end of the spectrum is the view of Justice Hugo Black. In a celebrated interview, he recently argued that the First Amendment "as written and adopted, intended that there should be no libel or defamation law in the United States. . . . absolutely none." This approach is grounded in a philosophy that puts the highest premium on free expression. A major tenet of this philosophy is, in the words of Justice Louis Brandeis, that for "falsehoods and fallacies . . . the remedy to be applied is more speech." If Justice Black's view were to prevail, the Alabama judgments against the *Times* could not stand.

It is not to be supposed, however, that either of these two attitudes will commend itself to a majority of the Court. The Supreme Court has a way of eschewing broad holdings, and the *Times* case will probably be decided on narrower grounds. There appear to be at least two ways in which the Court could reverse the state judgments and give limited constitutional protection to defamatory utterances without having to rule on Justice Black's absolutist position.

The first avenue has been opened by the lawyers for the *Times*. It is implicit in the premises of the First Amendment, they have argued, that "speech or publication which is critical of government or official action may not be repressed upon the ground that it diminishes the reputation of the officers whose conduct it deplores or of the government of which they are a part." In other words, criticism of an elected public official cannot constitutionally be punished, just as concern for the reputation of the bench does not support punishment for criticizing a judge—even with "half-truths" and "misinformation"—unless there is clear danger that justice will be obstructed.

History speaks clearly here. Even before the nation was formed, James Madison maintained that "it is manifestly impossible to punish the intent to bring those who administer the government into disrepute or contempt without striking at the right of freely discussing public characters and measures." Later, when the short-lived Sedition Act of 1798 declared it a crime to defame the government of the United States by bringing its leaders into "contempt or disrepute," Madison and other leaders opposed the Act, and over the years the Supreme Court has often said that the Act was inconsistent with the First Amendment.

One can conclude, therefore, that criticism of governmental conduct may not be prohibited to protect the reputation of the government or its officials. If this were not so, as the *Times* argues, the "daily dialogue of politics would become utterly impossible." This consequences would flow naturally from Alabama law. As pointed out above, certain libels (such as the present one) are by that state *presumed* to be "false and malicious," thus opening the way for unlimited damages both general and punitive—the former for a "presumed" injury to reputation and the latter "not alone to punish the wrongdoer, but as a deterrent to others similarly minded."

This leads directly to a second, and broader, ground for reversing the Alabama courts. The Supreme Court could rule that all *criminal* libels are forbidden by the First Amendment and that, because the jury awarded damages against the *Times* without proof of actual harm to the plaintiff's reputation, the judgment was punitive and therefore equivalent to a fine for criminal libel.

The *Times* has partly argued this position. It contends on appeal that "it is both legally correct and factually realistic to regard the entire verdict as a punitive award." But the *Times* skirts the question of whether all verdicts in civil actions designed to punish rather than to recompense the plaintiff are invalid. Instead it merely contends that the size of the verdict is so "shockingly excessive" that it violates the Constitution.

The first step to the broader approach is to justify a constitutional distinction between civil and criminal libels. This distinction would follow from a recognition that, while an individual's interest in his own reputation requires the availability of a compensatory action for his benefit, society has no comparable interest which would justify criminal penalties for defamation, especially in view of the threat implied in free speech. This distinction could draw upon historic English and American fears, culminating in the First Amendment, that the government would use criminal laws banning "seditious libel" as a means of throttling political opposition. A decision invalidating criminal libel on constitutional grounds would require the overruling of *Beauharnais v. Illinois*, but that case has already been weakened by more recent rulings.

The second step would be to relate punitive damages in civil suits to fines for criminal libel. The argument is along these lines: (1) the purpose of the punitive award is the same as the criminal sanction—to punish the defamer; (2) the effect is the same in that astronomical damages will sharply deter dissemination of news; and (3) punitive damages in civil cases are even more severe than criminal libel because they are inflicted without affording a defendant the protections associated with a criminal trial—indictment by grand jury and proof of the case beyond reasonable doubt.

Of course, the Supreme Court may avoid both the above routes to decision. Other possibilities do not involve the First Amendment. For example, the Court could rule that the Alabama judgments deprived the *Times* of due process of law because the insignificance of that paper's business in Alabama (a total circulation of only 394) did not justify the local courts in assuming jurisdiction over it. If the Court rules according to some such side consideration it will evade an issue of pressing importance. For the chief questions raised by the *New York Times* litigation involve the extent to which defamation laws impose limitations on free speech, and the self-censorship that would hamstring bold journalism if the present vogue of astronomical libel judgments were permitted to become a national custom.

*Source*: Norman Dorsen, "Libel and the Free Press," *Nation*, January 27, 1964, 93–95.

## DOCUMENT 75: *Curtis Publishing Co. v. Butts* (1967)

In *New York Times Co. v. Sullivan*, the Supreme Court erected a legal standard applicable to public *officials*. The question in *Curtis Publishing Co. v. Butts* was whether that same rationale should be extended to public *figures*—unelected and unappointed individuals who nevertheless enjoyed widespread public familiarity. If not, what constitutional theory distinguished the two categories? If so, just how is the status of "public figure" to be defined?

Butts was a football coach at the University of Georgia. He was accused of "fixing" a football game in an article published by the *Saturday Evening Post*. A jury awarded both compensatory and punitive damages. Soon after that award, the Supreme Court handed down *New York Times Co. v. Sullivan*, and Curtis asked for a new trial. The motion was denied on two grounds: that Butts was not a "public official" within the meaning of the new rule; and that there was ample evidence of Curtis's "reckless disregard" for the truth even if the rule did extend to Butts. The appeals court affirmed the denial on technical grounds (it found that Curtis had waived its constitutional arguments). The Supreme Court affirmed the lower court's judgment, but in a flurry of concurring opinions based upon different readings of the principles and precedents involved.

The companion case, *Associated Press v. Walker*, concerned coverage of a riot generated by federal efforts to integrate the University of Mississippi. Press reports had identified a private citizen named Walker as the "ringleader" of the riot. Walker was politically active; according to the Court's sketchy description, he was a person of "some political prominence." At trial, the Associated Press account was found to be inaccurate, but not due to any malice or impropriety of the reporter or his employer. The trial court awarded Walker compensatory, but not punitive, damages, and an appellate court affirmed. The Supreme Court reversed the award of even compensatory damages, holding that he could not recover unless he could prove "highly unreasonable conduct" by the Associated Press.

\* \* \*

We thus turn to a consideration, on the merits, of the constitutional claims raised by Curtis in *Butts* and by the Associated Press in *Walker*. Powerful arguments are brought to bear for the extension of the *New*

*York Times* rule in both cases. In *Butts* it is contended that the facts are on all fours with those of *Rosenblatt* v. *Baer*, . . . since Butts was charged with the important responsibility of managing the athletic affairs of a state university. It is argued that while the Athletic Association is financially independent from the State and Butts was not technically a state employee, as was Baer, his role in state administration was so significant that this technical distinction from *Rosenblatt* should be ignored. Even if this factor is to be given some weight, we are told that the public interest in education in general, and in the conduct of the athletic affairs of educational institutions in particular, justifies constitutional protection of discussion of persons involved in it equivalent to the protection afforded discussion of public officials.

A similar argument is raised in the *Walker* case where the important public interest in being informed about the events and personalities involved in the Mississippi riot is pressed. In that case we are also urged to recognize that Walker's claims to the protection of libel laws are limited since he thrust himself into the "vortex" of the controversy.

We are urged by the respondents, Butts and Walker, to recognize society's "pervasive and strong interest in preventing and redressing attacks upon reputation," and the "important social values which underlie the law of defamation." . . . It is pointed out that the publicity in these instances was not directed at employees of government and that these cases cannot be analogized to seditious libel prosecutions. . . . We are told that "[t]he rule that permits satisfaction of the deep-seated need for vindication of honor is not a mere historic relic, but promotes the law's civilizing function of providing an acceptable substitute for violence in the settlement of disputes." . . .

The fact that dissemination of information and opinion on questions of public concern is ordinarily a legitimate, protected and indeed cherished activity does not mean, however, that one may in all respects carry on that activity exempt from sanctions designed to safeguard the legitimate interests of others. A business "is not immune from regulation because it is an agency of the press. The publisher of a newspaper has no special immunity from the application of general laws. He has no special privilege to invade the rights and liberties of others." . . . Federal securities regulation, mail fraud statutes, and common-law actions for deceit and misrepresentation are only some examples of our understanding that the right to communicate information of public interest is not "unconditional." . . . However, as our decision in *New York Times* makes explicit, while protected activity may in some respects be subjected to sanctions, it is not open to all forms of regulation. The guarantees of freedom of speech and press were not designed to prevent "the censorship of the press merely, but any action of the government by means of which it might prevent such free and general discussion of public matters as seems absolutely essential. . . ." . . . Our touchstones are that acceptable limitations must neither affect "the impartial distribution of news" and ideas, . . . nor because of their history or impact constitute a special burden on the press, . . . nor deprive our free society of the stimulating benefit of varied ideas because their purveyors fear physical or economic retribution solely because of what they choose to think and publish.

The history of libel law leaves little doubt that it originated in soil entirely different from that which nurtured these constitutional values. Early libel was primarily a criminal remedy, the function of which was to make punishable any writing which tended to bring into disrepute the state, established religion, or any individual likely to be provoked to a breach of the peace because of the words. Truth was no defense in such actions and while a proof of truth might prevent recovery in a civil action, this limitation is more readily explained as a manifestation of judicial reluctance to enrich an undeserving plaintiff than by the supposition that the defendant was protected by the truth of the publication. The same truthful statement might be the basis of a criminal libel action. . . .

In *New York Times* we were adjudicating in an area which lay close to seditious libel, and history dictated extreme caution in imposing liability. The plaintiff in that case was an official whose position in government was such "that the public [had] an independent interest in the qualifications and performance of the person who [held] it." . . . [S]uch officials were permitted to recover in libel only when they could prove that the publication involved was deliberately falsified, or published recklessly despite the publisher's awareness of probable falsity. . . .

In the cases we decide today none of the particular considerations involved in *New York Times* is present. . . . Neither plaintiff has any position in government which would permit a recovery by him to be viewed as a vindication of governmental policy. Neither was entitled to a special privilege protecting his utterances against accountability in libel. We are prompted, therefore, to seek guidance from the rules of liability which prevail in our society with respect to compensation of persons injured by the improper performance of a legitimate activity by another. Under these rules, a departure from the kind of care society may expect from a reasonable man performing such activity leaves the actor open to a judicial shifting of loss. In defining these rules, and especially in formulating the standards for determining the degree of care to be expected in the circumstances, courts have consistently given much attention to the importance of defendants' activities. . . . The courts have also, especially in libel cases, investigated the plaintiff's position to determine whether he has a legitimate call upon the court for protection in light of his prior activities and means of self-defense. . . . We note that the public interest in the circulation of the materials here involved, and the publisher's interest in circulating them, is not less than that involved in *New York Times*. And both Butts and Walker commanded a substantial amount of independent public interest at the time of the publications; both, in our opinion, would have been labeled "public figures" under ordinary tort rules. . . . Butts may have attained that status by position alone and Walker by his purposeful activity amounting to a thrusting of his personality into the "vortex" of an important public controversy, but both commanded sufficient continuing public interest and had sufficient access to the means of counterargument to be able "to expose through discussion the falsehood and fallacies" of the defamatory statements. . . .

These similarities and differences between libel actions involving persons who are public officials and libel actions involving those circumstanced as were Butts and Walker, viewed in light of the principles of liability which are of general applicability in our society, lead us to the conclusion that libel actions of the present kind cannot be left entirely to state libel laws, unlimited by any overriding constitutional safeguard, but that the rigorous federal requirements of *New York Times* are not the only appropriate accommodation of the conflicting interests at stake. We consider and would hold that a "public figure" who is not a public official may also recover damages for a defamatory falsehood whose substance makes substantial danger to reputation apparent, on a showing of highly unreasonable conduct constituting an extreme departure from the standards of investigation and reporting ordinarily adhered to by responsible publishers. . . .

Having set forth the standard by which we believe the constitutionality of the damage awards in these cases must be judged, we turn now, as the Court did in *New York Times*, to the question whether the evidence and findings below meet that standard. We find the standard satisfied in No. 37, *Butts*, and not satisfied by either the evidence or the findings in No. 150, *Walker*.

*Source*: 388 U.S. 130 (1967).

---

## DOCUMENT 76: The Fairness Doctrine (1966)

The fairness doctrine, which applied to broadcast media, was promulgated to ensure that both sides to a political contest were given a hearing. The necessity for the rule was premised upon the limited number of bandwidths, or operating frequencies, available; unlike print media, in the days before cable television, digital radio, and similar technologies, there were only so many channels available. That fact was cited to justify both the government's control over licensing and its imposition of rules that would not have withstood constitutional scrutiny if applied to print.

* * *

If any licensee shall permit any person who is a legally qualified candidate for any public office to use a broadcasting station, he shall afford equal opportunities to all other such candidates for that office in the use of such broadcasting station; *Provided*, That such licensee shall have no power of censorship over the material broadcast under the provisions of this section. No obligation is imposed under this subsection upon any licensee to allow the use of its station by any candidate. Appearance by a legally qualified candidate on any—

1. Bona fide newscast.
2. Bona fide news interview.
3. Bona fide news documentary (if the appearance of the candidate is incidental to the presentation of the subject or subjects covered by the news documentary), or
4. On-the-spot coverage of bona fide news events (including but not limited to political conventions and activities incidental thereto).

Shall not be deemed to be use of a broadcasting station within the meaning of this subsection. Nothing in the foregoing sentence shall be construed as relieving broadcasters, in connection with the presentation of newscasts, news interviews, news documentaries, and on-the-spot coverage of news events, from the obligation imposed upon them under this chapter to operate in the public interest and to afford reasonable opportunity for the discussion of conflicting views on issues of public importance.

The charges made for the use of any broadcasting station by any person who is legally qualified for any public office in connection with his campaign for nomination for election, or election to such office shall not exceed—

1. During the forty-five days preceding the date of a primary or primary runoff election and during the sixty days preceding the date of a general or special election in which such person is a candidate, the lowest unit charge of the station for the same class and amount of time for the same period; and
2. At any other time, the charges made for comparable use of such station by other users thereof.

For purposes of this section—

1. The term "broadcasting station" includes a community antenna television system; and

2. The terms "licensee" and "station licensee" when used with respect to a community antenna television system mean the operator of such system.

The Commission shall prescribe appropriate rules and regulations to carry out the provisions of this section.

*Source*: Section 315 of the Communications Act, 47 U.S.C. 315.

---

## DOCUMENT 77: *Red Lion Broadcasting Co., Inc. v. Federal Communications Commission* (1969)

---

The *Red Lion* case involved both the application of the fairness doctrine and its later regulatory clarification. In 1964, a fifteen-minute broadcast by the Reverend Billy James Hargis, called the "Christian Crusade," had included an attack on the patriotism and integrity of the author of a book about Barry Goldwater. The author demanded equal time to respond, and the Federal Communications Commission agreed that he was entitled to that time. The station challenged the constitutionality of the fairness doctrine, attacking it as a violation of freedom of speech and of the press.

The case was consolodated with a challenge to the doctrine by the Radio and Television Broadcasters Association. The Association argued that the "equal time" requirement discouraged them from broadcasting material that could be controversial, and thus subject to demands that response time be made available to those with differing views.

The Supreme Court found the doctrine constitutional in a case that was widely discussed and reported.

* * *

Believing that the specific application of the fairness doctrine in *Red Lion* and the promulgation of the regulations in *RTNDA* [Radio and Television News Director's Association] are both authorized by Congress and enhance rather than abridge the freedoms of speech and press protected by the First Amendment, we hold them valid and constitutional, reversing the judgment below in *RTNDA* and affirming the judgment below in *Red Lion*. . . .

It is strenuously argued, however, that if political editorials or personal attacks will trigger an obligation in broadcasters to afford the opportunity for expression to speakers who need not pay for time and whose views are unpalatable to the licensees, then broadcasters will be irresistibly forced to self-censorship and their coverage of controversial public issues will be eliminated or at least rendered wholly ineffective. Such a result would indeed be a serious matter, for should licensees actually eliminate their coverage of controversial issues, the purpose of the doctrine would be stifled.

At this point, however, as the Federal Communications Commission has indicated, that possibility is at best speculative. The communications industry, and in particular the networks, have taken pains to present controversial issues in the past, and even now they do not assert that they intend to abandon their efforts in this regard. It would be better if the FCC's encouragement were never necessary to induce the broadcasters to meet their responsibility. And if experience with the administration of these doctrines indicates that they have the net effect of reducing rather than enhancing the volume and quality of coverage, there will be time enough to reconsider the constitutional implications. The fairness doctrine in the past has had no such overall effect.

*Source*: 395 U.S. 367 (1969).

---

## DOCUMENT 78: "Fairness Rules of F.C.C. Upheld" (Fred P. Graham, 1969)

The Supreme Court's ruling upholding the Fairness Doctrine was widely reported by the print media, which had never been subjected to similar restrictions. The following article from the *New York Times* notes that the basis of the distinction lies in the issuance of broadcast licenses by the government. Since broadcast licenses are limited in number, the Court has held that their award may be made subject to conditions which cannot be imposed upon print media.

* * *

COURTS SAY CHANCE TO REPLY TO A RADIO OR TV ATTACK ENHANCES
FREE SPEECH

The Supreme Court upheld today the constitutionality of the Federal Communications Commission's "fairness doctrine," which requires radio and television broadcasters to present both sides of important issues.

The Court declared unanimously that the fairness rules "enhance rather than abridge the freedoms of speech and press protected by the first amendment."

"It is the right of the viewers and listeners, not the right of the broadcasters, which is paramount," Justice Byron R. White wrote.

The broadcast industry had contended that the fairness rules curbed their liberty to speak out strongly. Today's ruling was the Court's first on the industry's contention.

The opinion gave little comfort to the broadcast industry in its effort to ease commission rules through litigation. It stressed the duty of those who hold government broadcast licenses to serve the public and hinted that if even heavier demands were put on the broadcasters, they would be upheld.

Specifically at issue were two sub-rules of the fairness doctrine.

The first was the "personal attack" rule, which requires stations to donate free time to any person or group whose honesty, character or integrity has been attacked over the station's facilities.

The second was the "political editorial" rule, which says that if stations endorse or favor a political candidate they must give his opponents a chance to reply.

These requirements do not apply to bona fide news coverage or interviews, commentary or analysis done in the course of news broadcasts. Today's case also did not involve the "equal time" rule passed by Congress, which says that if a broadcaster gives one candidate free time he must do the same for his opponents.

The Supreme Court's resounding endorsement of the fairness concept throws a deep shadow over the tobacco industry's chances in another appeal that is pending.

In that case the argument is made that the F.C.C. has violated the free speech guarantee by requiring broadcasters to carry anti-smoking messages if they broadcast cigarette ads.

One of the two controversies decided in today's opinion concerned the Red Lion Broadcasting Company, owner of radio station WBCG in Red Lion, Pa., and Fred J. Cook, the liberal writer. Mr. Cook demanded time to reply after he had been attacked in a WBCG broadcast by the Rev. Billy James Hargis, the right-wing radio preacher.

The F.C.C. and the Court of Appeals for the District of Columbia ruled that the station must give Mr. Cook time.

In the second suit, the Radio and Television News Directors Association, the Columbia Broadcasting System, the National Broadcasting Company and eight broadcasting companies challenged the rules as they were codified by the F.C.C. in 1967 and 1968.

The United States Court of Appeals for the Seventh Circuit upheld this challenge, declaring that the two rules violated the broadcasters' constitutional rights.

Broadcasters found to have violated the rule are subject to fines of $1,000 for every day of violation plus possible criminal sanctions.

In the appeal, the broadcasters invoked a recent chain of Supreme Court decisions that have struck down governmental restrictions that served to "chill" persons' willingness to speak on important matters.

They contended that the requirement that they provide time for replies discouraged them from carrying controversial material, for fear of having to make costly donations of time to those with opposite views.

Justice White's opinion said that the stations may yet be able to show that some future specific application of the rules offends their free speech rights, but he insisted that in general the fairness doctrine's equal-time requirements encouraged free debate rather than dampened it. He noted that the trend in broadcasting had been toward tart editorial comment.

"A license permits broadcasting, but the licensee has no constitutional right to be the one who holds the license or to monopolize a radio frequency to the exclusion of his fellow citizens," Justice White said.

The Court affirmed the Red Lion decision and reversed the news directors' lower court victory. The vote was 7 to 0. Justice William O. Douglas was absent when the case was argued and did not take part. The Supreme Court has had only eight members since the resignation of Abe Fortas last month.

*Source*: Fred P. Graham, "Fairness Rules of F.C.C. Upheld," *New York Times*, June 10, 1969, p. 1, col. 7; p. 28.

---

## DOCUMENT 79: *New York Times Co. v. United States* (1971)

In a brief *per curiam* opinion, the Supreme Court in 1971 ruled that the government could not prevent the publication by the *New York Times* and the *Washington Post* of government documents that had been leaked to them, detailing the history of the government's Vietnam policy. (*Per curiam* means "by the Court." It is used when no specific justice is identified as the author of the opinion.) This was not a case of libel; it involved a conflict between the government's interest in maintaining the confidentiality of its internal decision-making processes and the public's right to know.

The lengthy concurrence by Justice Hugo Black, with whom Justice William Douglas joined, contains the best analysis of the important interests implicated in the case and the best statement of what is sometimes called the "absolutist" view on prior restraint. In an eloquent essay, Black reminded the Court and the government that "the Founding Fathers gave the free press the protection it must have to fulfill its essential role in our democracy. The press was to serve the governed, not the governors."

* * *

PER CURIAM.

We granted certioraris in these cases in which the United States seeks to enjoin the New York Times and the Washington Post from publishing the contents of a classified study entitled "History of U.S. Decision-Making Process on Viet Nam policy." . . .

"Any system of prior restraints of expression comes to this Court bearing a heavy presumption against its constitutional validity." . . . The Government "thus carries a heavy burden of showing justification for the imposition of such a restraint." . . . The District Court for the Southern District of New York in the *New York Times* case and the District Court for the District of Columbia and the Court of Appeals for the District of Columbia Circuit in the *Washington Post* case held that the Government had not met that burden. We agree.

The judgment of the Court of Appeals for the District of Columbia Circuit is therefore affirmed. The order of the Court of Appeals for the Second Circuit is reversed and the case is remanded with directions to enter a judgment affirming the judgment of the District Court for the Southern District of New York. The stays entered June 25, 1971, by the Court are vacated. The judgment shall issue forthwith.

*So ordered.*

MR. JUSTICE BLACK, with whom MR. JUSTICE DOUGLAS joins, concurring.

I adhere to the view that the Government's case against the Washington Post should have been dismissed and that the injunction against the New York Times should have been vacated without oral argument when the cases were first presented to this Court. I believe that every moment's continuance of the injunctions against these newspapers amounts to a flagrant, indefensible, and continuing violation of the First Amendment. Furthermore, after oral argument, I agree completely that we must affirm the judgment of the Court of Appeals for the District of Columbia Circuit and reverse the judgment of the Court of Appeals for the Second Circuit for the reasons stated by my Brothers DOUGLAS and BRENNAN. In my view it is unfortunate that some of my Brethren are apparently willing to hold that the publication of news may sometimes be enjoined. Such a holding would make a shambles of the First Amendment.

Our Government was launched in 1789 with the adoption of the Constitution. The Bill of Rights, including the First Amendment, followed in 1791. Now, for the first time in the 182 years since the founding of the

Republic, the federal courts are asked to hold that the First Amendment does not mean what it says, but rather means that the Government can halt the publication of current news of vital importance to the people of this country.

In seeking injunctions against these newspapers and in its presentation to the Court, the Executive Branch seems to have forgotten the essential purpose and history of the First Amendment. When the Constitution was adopted, many people strongly opposed it because the document contained no Bill of Rights to safeguard certain basic freedoms. They especially feared that the new powers granted to a central government might be interpreted to permit the government to curtail freedom of religion, press, assembly, and speech. In response to an overwhelming public clamor, James Madison offered a series of amendments to satisfy citizens that these great liberties would remain safe and beyond the power of government to abridge. Madison proposed what later became the First Amendment in three parts, two of which are set out below, and one of which proclaimed: "The people shall not be deprived or abridged of their right to speak, to write, or to publish their sentiments; *and the freedom of the press, as one of the great bulwarks of liberty, shall be inviolable.*" (Emphasis added.) The amendments were offered to *curtail* and *restrict* the general powers granted to the Executive, Legislative, and Judicial Branches two years before in the original Constitution. The Bill of Rights changed the original Constitution into a new charter under which no branch of government could abridge the people's freedoms of press, speech, religion, and assembly. Yet the Solicitor General argues and some members of the Court appear to agree that the general powers of the Government adopted in the original Constitution should be interpreted to limit and restrict the specific and emphatic guarantees of the Bill of Rights adopted later. I can imagine no greater perversion of history. Madison and the other Framers of the First Amendment, able men that they were, wrote in language they earnestly believed could never be misunderstood: "Congress shall make no law . . . abridging the freedom . . . of the press. . . ." Both the history and language of the First Amendment support the view that the press must be left free to publish news, whatever the source, without censorship, injunctions, or prior restraints.

In the First Amendment the Founding Fathers gave the free press the protection it must have to fulfill its essential role in our democracy. The press was to serve the governed, not the governors. The Government's power to censor the press was abolished so that the press would remain forever free to censure the Government. The press was protected so that it could bare the secrets of government and inform the people. Only a free and unrestrained press can effectively expose deception in government. And paramount among the responsibilities of a free press is the duty to prevent any part of the government from deceiving the people and sending them off to distant lands to die of foreign fevers and foreign shot and shell. In my view, far from deserving condemnation for their courageous reporting, the *New York Times*, the *Washington Post*, and other newspapers should be commended for serving the purpose that the Founding Fathers saw so clearly. In revealing the workings of government that led to the Vietnam war, the newspapers nobly did precisely that which the Founders hoped and trusted they would do.

The Government's case here is based on premises entirely different from those that guided the Framers of the First Amendment. The Solicitor General has carefully and emphatically stated:

"Now, Mr. Justice [BLACK], your construction of . . . [the First Amendment] is well known, and I certainly respect it. You say that no law means no law, and that should be obvious. I can only say, Mr. Justice, that to me it is equally obvious that 'no law' does not mean 'no law', and I would seek to persuade the Court that that is true. . . . [T]here are other parts of the Constitution that grant powers and responsibilities to the Executive, and . . . the First Amendment was not intended to make it impossible for the Executive to function or to protect the security of the United States."

And the Government argues in its brief that in spite of the First Amendment, "[t]he authority of the Executive Department to protect the nation against publication of information whose disclosure would endanger the national security stems from two interrelated sources: the constitutional power of the President over the conduct of foreign affairs and his authority as Commander-in-Chief."

In other words, we are asked to hold that despite the First Amendment's emphatic command, the Executive Branch, the Congress, and the Judiciary can make laws enjoining publication of current news and abridging freedom of the press in the name of "national security." The Government does not even attempt to rely on any act of Congress. Instead it makes the bold and dangerously far-reaching contention that the courts should take it upon themselves to "make" a law abridging freedom of the press in the name of equity, presidential power and national security, even when the representatives of the people in Congress have adhered to the command of the First Amendment and refused to make such a law. See concurring opinion of MR. JUSTICE DOUGLAS. . . . To find that the President has "inherent power" to halt the publication of news by resort to the courts would wipe out the First Amendment and destroy the fundamental liberty and security of the very people the Government hopes to make "secure." No one can read the history of the adoption of the First Amendment without being convinced beyond any doubt that it was injunctions like those sought here that Madison and his collaborators intended to outlaw in this Nation for all time.

The word "security" is a broad, vague generality whose contours should not be invoked to abrogate the fundamental law embodied in the First Amendment. The guarding of military and diplomatic secrets at the expense of informed representative government provides no real security for our Republic. The Framers of the First Amendment, fully aware of both the need to defend a new nation and the abuses of the English and Colonial governments, sought to give this new society strength and security by providing that freedom of speech, press, religion, and assembly should not be abridged. This thought was eloquently expressed in 1937 by Mr. Chief Justice Hughes—great man and great Chief Justice that he was—when the Court held a man could not be punished for attending a meeting run by Communists.

"The greater the importance of safeguarding the community from incitements to the overthrow of our institutions by force and violence, the more imperative is the need to preserve inviolate the constitutional rights of free speech, free press and free assembly in order to maintain the opportunity for free political discussion, to the end that government may be responsive to the will of the people and that changes, if desired, may be obtained by peaceful means. Therein lies the security of the Republic, the very foundation of constitutional government."

*Source*: 403 U.S. 713 (1971).

---

## DOCUMENT 80: *Gertz v. Robert Welch, Inc.* (1974)

Because the government exercises control over the activities of broadcasters, the question of "state action" often arises. Individual newspapers or magazines are free, in the exercise of their editorial discretion, to accept or reject advertising of any sort, for virtually any reason. Broadcasters, despite the strictures of operating within the public interest, clearly enjoy a substantial measure of control over their own editorial policies. The First Amendment protects that right. But the First Amendment also prohibits government from infringing the free-speech rights of individual citizens. In an industry as closely regulated as the broadcast industry, when can actions be attributed to the government and when must they be viewed as private?

That was the essential issue in *Columbia Broadcasting System v. Democratic National Committee*. The Democratic National Committee sought a ruling from the FCC that individual broadcasters could not refuse to sell editorial advertising to the DNC. The FCC refused to promulgate such a rule. In a lengthy opinion, by a plurality, the Supreme Court agreed with the FCC.

*Columbia Broadcasting* strengthened the journalistic freedom of broadcasters; at the same time, it clearly limited the availability of important forums to competing views. On the one hand, owners of broadcast stations should enjoy, to the greatest extent possible, the editorial discretion exercised routinely by the print media. On the other hand, broadcasters are in a very real sense the creatures of the government, which allocates channels for their use and licenses them to operate. Should broadcasters who are arguably "government actors" be allowed to act in ways government could not? How far should the Supreme Court uphold the distinctions between broadcast and other forms of media? While the multitude of opinions addressed by the Court in *Columbia* are not included in this volume, and while newer technologies have to some extent eased the conflicts the Court issued in the case, those fundamental issues remain.

Nor has the Supreme Court been able to provide the print media with clear and unambiguous rules governing defamation, as is evident from the attempt, in *Gertz v. Robert Welch, Inc.*, to further refine the rule first enunciated in *New York Times v. Sullivan*.

Gertz sued for defamation. He was clearly not a public official, and the Supreme Court found that he could not plausibly be considered a public figure. The issue was whether his legal representation of the victim's family could be considered "hot news" or news of such general interest that the press was entitled to immunity absent a showing of actual malice or reckless disregard for the truth. The Supreme Court, tacitly acknowledging the impossibility of applying *Rosenbloom*, upheld the right of the states to make and enforce libel laws applicable to such situations. At the same time, however, the Court ruled that punitive damages could not be assessed under such laws.

\* \* \*

MR. JUSTICE POWELL delivered the opinion of the Court.

This Court has struggled for nearly a decade to define the proper accommodation between the law of defamation and the freedoms of speech and press protected by the First Amendment. With this decision we return to that effort. . . .

In 1968 a Chicago policeman named Nuccio shot and killed a youth named Nelson. The state authorities prosecuted Nuccio for the homicide and ultimately obtained a conviction for murder in the second degree. The Nelson family retained petitioner Elmer Gertz, a reputable attorney, to represent them in civil litigation against Nuccio.

Respondent publishes American Opinion, a monthly outlet for the views of the John Birch Society. Early in the 1960's the magazine began to warn of a nationwide conspiracy to discredit local law enforcement agencies and create in their stead a national police force capable of supporting a Communist dictatorship. As part of the continuing effort to alert the public to this assumed danger, the managing editor of American Opinion commissioned an article on the murder trial of Officer Nuccio. For this purpose he engaged a regular contributor to the magazine. In March 1969 respondent published the resulting article under the title "FRAME-UP: Richard Nuccio And The War On Police." The article purports to demonstrate that the testimony against Nuccio at his criminal trial was false and that his prosecution was part of the Communist campaign against the police.

In his capacity as counsel for the Nelson family in the civil litigation, petitioner attended the coroner's inquest into the boy's death and initiated actions for damages, but neither discussed Officer Nuccio with the press nor played any part in the criminal proceeding. Notwithstanding petitioner's remote connection with the prosecution of Nuccio, respondent's magazine portrayed him as an architect of the "frame-up." According to the article, the police file on petitioner took "a big, Irish cop to lift." The article stated that petitioner had been an official of the "Marxist League for Industrial Democracy, originally known as the Intercollegiate Socialist Society, which has advocated the violent seizure of our government." It labeled Gertz a "Leninist" and a "Communist-fronter." It also stated that Gertz had been an officer of the National Lawyers Guild, described as a Communist organization that "probably did more than any other outfit to plan the Communist attack on the Chicago police during the 1968 Democratic Convention."

These statements contained serious inaccuracies. The implication that petitioner had a criminal record was false. Petitioner had been a member and officer of the National Lawyers Guild some 15 years earlier, but there was no evidence that he or that organization had taken any part in planning the 1968 demonstrations in Chicago. There was also no basis for the charge that petitioner was a "Leninist" or a "Communist-fronter." And he had never been a member of the "Marxist League for Industrial Democracy" or the "Intercollegiate Socialist Society."

The managing editor of American Opinion made no effort to verify or substantiate the charges against petitioner. Instead, he appended an editorial introduction stating that the author had "conducted extensive research into the Richard Nuccio Case." And he included in the article a photograph of petitioner and wrote the caption that appeared under it: "Elmer Gertz of Red Guild harasses Nuccio." Respondent placed the issue of American Opinion containing the article on sale at newsstands throughout the country and distributed reprints of the article on the streets of Chicago. . . .

. . . The editor denied any knowledge of the falsity of the statements concerning petitioner and stated that he had relied on the author's rep-

utation and on his prior experience with the accuracy and authenticity
of the author's contributions to American Opinion. . . .

[T]he District Court concluded that the *New York Times* standard
should govern this case even though petitioner was not a public official
or public figure. It accepted respondent's contention that that privilege
protected discussion of any public issue without regard to the status of
a person defamed therein. . . .

The principal issue in this case is whether a newspaper or broadcaster
that publishes defamatory falsehoods about an individual who is neither
a public official nor a public figure may claim a constitutional privilege
against liability for the injury inflicted by those statements. The Court
considered this question on the rather different set of facts presented in
*Rosenbloom* v. *Metromedia, Inc.* Rosenbloom, a distributor of nudist magazines, was arrested for selling allegedly obscene material while making
a delivery to a retail dealer. The police obtained a warrant and seized
his entire inventory of 3,000 books and magazines. He sought and obtained an injunction prohibiting further police interference with his business. He then sued a local radio station for failing to note in two of its
newscasts that the 3,000 items seized were only "reportedly" or "allegedly" obscene and for broadcasting references to "the smut literature
racket" and to "girlie-book peddlers" in its coverage of the court proceeding for injunctive relief. He obtained a judgment against the radio
station, but the Court of Appeals for the Third Circuit held the *New York
Times* privilege applicable to the broadcast and reversed. . . .

Under the First Amendment there is no such thing as a false idea.
However pernicious an opinion may seem, we depend for its correction
not on the conscience of judges and juries but on the competition of other
ideas. But there is no constitutional value in false statements of fact.
Neither the intentional lie nor the careless error materially advances society's interest in "uninhibited, robust, and wide-open" debate on public
issues. They belong to that category of utterances which "are no essential
part of any exposition of ideas, and are of such slight social value as a
step to truth that any benefit that may be derived from them is clearly
outweighed by the social interest in order and morality." . . .

The common law of defamation is an oddity of tort law, for it allows
recovery of purportedly compensatory damages without evidence of actual loss. Under the traditional rules pertaining to actions for libel, the
existence of injury is presumed from the fact of publication. Juries may
award substantial sums as compensation for supposed damage to reputation without any proof that such harm actually occurred. The largely
uncontrolled discretion of juries to award damages where there is no
loss unnecessarily compounds the potential of any system of liability for
defamatory falsehood to inhibit the vigorous exercise of First Amendment freedoms. Additionally, the doctrine of presumed damages invites

juries to punish unpopular opinion rather than to compensate individuals for injury sustained by the publication of a false fact. More to the point, the States have no substantial interest in securing for plaintiffs such as this petitioner gratuitous awards of money damages far in excess of any actual injury. . . .

Petitioner has long been active in community and professional affairs. He has served as an officer of local civic groups and of various professional organizations, and he has published several books and articles on legal subjects. Although petitioner was consequently well known in some circles, he had achieved no general fame or notoriety in the community. None of the prospective jurors called at the trial had ever heard of petitioner prior to this litigation, and respondent offered no proof that this response was atypical of the local population. We would not lightly assume that a citizen's participation in community and professional affairs rendered him a public figure for all purposes. Absent clear evidence of general fame or notoriety in the community, and pervasive involvement in the affairs of society, an individual should not be deemed a public personality for all aspects of his life. It is preferable to reduce the public-figure question to a more meaningful context by looking to the nature and extent of an individual's participation in the particular controversy giving rise to the defamation.

In this context it is plain that petitioner was not a public figure. He played a minimal role at the coroner's inquest, and his participation related solely to his representation of a private client. He took no part in the criminal prosecution of Officer Nuccio. Moreover, he never discussed either the criminal or civil litigation with the press and was never quoted as having done so. He plainly did not thrust himself into the vortex of this public issue, nor did he engage the public's attention in an attempt to influence its outcome. We are persuaded that the trial court did not err in refusing to characterize petitioner as a public figure for the purpose of this litigation.

We therefore conclude that the *New York Times* standard is inapplicable to this case and that the trial court erred in entering judgment for respondent. Because the jury was allowed to impose liability without fault and was permitted to presume damages without proof of injury, a new trial is necessary. We reverse and remand for further proceedings in accord with this opinion.

*It is so ordered.*

*Source:* 418 U.S. 323 (1973).

---

## DOCUMENT 81: Florida Statute on Right of Reply (1973)

In 1974, a unanimous Supreme Court had little difficulty striking down a Florida statute that required newspapers to give a "right of reply" to political candidates who have been criticized or attacked by the papers.

* * *

**§104.38** If any newspaper in its columns assails the personal character of any candidate for nomination or for election in any election, or charges said candidate with malfeasance or misfeasance in office, or otherwise attacks his official record, or gives to another free space for such purpose, such newspaper shall upon request of such candidate immediately publish free of cost any reply he may make thereto in as conspicuous a place and in the same kind of type as the matter that calls for such reply, provided such reply does not take up more space than the matter replied to. Any person or firm failing to comply with the provisions of this section shall be guilty of a misdemeanor of the first degree, punishable as provided in §775.082 or §775.083.

*Source*: Florida Statute §104.38 (1973).

---

## DOCUMENT 82: *Miami Herald Publishing Co., Division of Knight Newspapers, Inc. v. Tornillo* (1974)

The Supreme Court found no distinction between a statue that, in essence, compelled certain speech and the constitutional bar on government action prohibiting speech. In either case, the government is regulating the content of a newspaper in violation of the First Amendment.

While the result may have been predictable, the arguments raised by those defending the statute were intriguing. They based the need for government intervention on the elimination of competing newspapers in many American markets, the consolidation of newspaper ownership, the fact that syndicated columns and other editorial opinion are nationally distributed, and the resulting homogeneity of editorial opinion, commentary, and interpretive analysis. Given the diminution of a true "marketplace of ideas," they argued that the government has a positive duty to encourage the printing of different points of view. The case provides a good example of competing visions of government: the more traditional libertarian view holds that freedom is best guaranteed by limiting the power of the state, while proponents of a more activist role for government believe that the state has a positive role to play in ensuring constitutional liberties.

* * *

MR. CHIEF JUSTICE BURGER delivered the opinion of the Court.

The issue in this case is whether a state statute granting a political candidate a right to equal space to reply to criticism and attacks on his record by a newspaper violates the guarantees of a free press. . . .

. . . The Circuit Court concluded that dictating what a newspaper must print was no different from dictating what it must not print. . . .

On direct appeal, the Florida Supreme Court reversed, holding that § 104.38 did not violate constitutional guarantees. It held that free speech was enhanced and not abridged by the Florida right-of-reply statute, which in that court's view, furthered the "broad societal interest in the free flow of information to the public." It also held that the statute is not impermissibly vague; the statue informs "those who are subject to it as to what conduct on their part will render them liable to its penalties." . . .

Appellant contends the statute is void on its face because it purports to regulate the content of a newspaper in violation of the First Amendment. Alternatively it is urged that the statute is void for vagueness since no editor could know exactly what words would call the statute into operation. It is also contended that the statute fails to distinguish between critical comment which is and which is not defamatory.

The appellee and supporting advocates of an enforceable right of access to the press vigorously argue that government has an obligation to ensure that a wide variety of views reach the public. The contentions of access proponents will be set out in some detail. It is urged that at the time the First Amendment to the Constitution was ratified in 1791 as part of our Bill of Rights the press was broadly representative of the people it was serving. While many of the newspapers were intensely partisan and narrow in their views, the press collectively presented a board range of opinions to readers. Entry into publishing was inexpensive; pamphlets and books provided meaningful alternatives to the organized press for the expression of unpopular ideas and often treated events and expressed views not covered by conventional newspapers. A true marketplace of ideas existed in which there was relatively easy access to the channels of communication.

Access advocates submit that although newspapers of the present are superficially similar to those of 1791 the press of today is in reality very different from that known in the early years of our national existence. In the past half century a communications revolution has seen the introduction of radio and television into our lives, the promise of global community through the use of communications satellites, and the specter of a "wired" nation by means of an expanding cable television network with two-way capabilities.

The printed press, it is said, has not escaped the effects of this revolution. Newspapers have become big business and there are far fewer of them to serve a larger literate population. Chains of newspapers, national newspapers, national wire and news services, and one-newspaper towns, are the dominant features of a press that has become noncompetitive and enormously powerful and influential in its capacity to manipulate popular opinion and change the course of events. Major metropolitan newspapers have collaborated to establish news services national in scope. Such national news organizations provide syndicated "interpretive reporting" as well as syndicated features and commentary, all of which can serve as part of the new school of "advocacy journalism." . . .

. . . In *Columbia Broadcasting System, Inc.* v. *Democratic National Committee*, the plurality opinion as to Part III noted:

"The power of a privately owned newspaper to advance its own political, social, and economic views is bounded by only two factors: first, the acceptance of a sufficient number of readers—and hence advertisers—to assure financial success; and, second, the journalistic integrity of its editors and publishers." . . .

We see that beginning with *Associated Press,* . . . the Court has expressed sensitivity as to whether a restriction or requirement constituted the compulsion exerted by government on a newspaper to print that which it would not otherwise print. The clear implication has been that any such compulsion to publish that which " 'reason' tells them should not be published" is unconstitutional. A responsible press is an undoubtedly desirable goal, but press responsibility is not mandated by the Constitution and like many other virtues it cannot be legislated. . . .

Even if a newspaper would face no additional costs to comply with a compulsory access law and would not be forced to forgo publication of news or opinion by the inclusion of a reply, the Florida statute fails to clear the barriers of the First Amendment because of its intrusion into the function of editors. A newspaper is more than a passive receptacle or conduit for news, comment, and advertising. The choice of material to go into a newspaper, and the decisions made as to limitations on the size and content of the paper, and treatment of public issues and public officials—whether fair or unfair—constitute the exercise of editorial control and judgment. It has yet to be demonstrated how governmental regulation of this crucial process can be exercised consistent with First Amendment guarantees of a free press as they have evolved to this time. Accordingly, the judgment of the Supreme Court of Florida is reversed.

*Source*: 418 U.S. 241 (1974).

## DOCUMENT 83: *Cox Broadcasting Corp. v. Cohn* (1975)

A young woman is brutally raped. Does freedom of the press allow publication of her identity? In *Cox Broadcasting Corp. v. Cohn*, a father sued Cox Broadcasting for reporting the name of his daughter despite the existence of a Georgia statute prohibiting dissemination of the names of rape victims. The Supreme Court, after an examination of the evolving "right-to-privacy" jurisprudence, nevertheless concluded that the Georgia statute could not withstand constitutional scrutiny.

\* \* \*

MR. JUSTICE WHITE delivered the opinion of the Court. . . .

In the course of the proceedings that day, appellant Wassell, a reporter covering the incident for his employer, learned the name of the victim from an examination of the indictments which were made available for his inspection in the courtroom. That the name of the victim appears in the indictments and that the indictments were public records available for inspection are not disputed. Later that day, Wassell broadcast over the facilities of station WSB-TV, a television station owned by appellant Cox Broadcasting Corp., a news report concerning the court proceedings. The report named the victim of the crime and was repeated the following day. . . .

The Court has . . . carefully left open the question whether the First and Fourteenth Amendments require that truth be recognized as a defense in a defamation action brought by a private person as distinguished from a public official or public figure. *Garrison* held that where criticism is of a public official and his conduct of public business, "the interest in private reputation is overborne by the larger public interest, secured by the Constitution, in the dissemination of truth," . . . but recognized that "different interests may be involved where purely private libels, totally unrelated to public affairs, are concerned; therefore, nothing we say today is to be taken as intimating any views as to the impact of the constitutional guarantees in the discrete area of purely private libels." . . . In similar fashion, *Time, Inc. v. Hill* . . . expressly saved the question whether truthful publication of very private matters unrelated to public affairs could be constitutionally proscribed. . . .

Those precedents, as well as other considerations, counsel similar caution here. In this sphere of collision between claims of privacy and those of the free press, the interests on both sides are plainly rooted in the traditions and significant concerns of our society. Rather than address the broader question whether truthful publications may ever be subjected to civil or criminal liability consistently with the First and Fourteenth Amendments, or to put it another way, whether the State may ever define and protect an area of privacy free from unwanted publicity in the press, it is appropriate to focus on the narrower interface between press and privacy that this case presents, namely, whether the State may impose sanctions on the accurate publication of the name of a rape victim obtained from public records—more specifically, from judicial records which are maintained in connection with a public prosecution and which themselves are open to public inspection. We are convinced that the State may not do so. . . .

Appellee has claimed in this litigation that the efforts of the press have infringed his right to privacy by broadcasting to the world the fact that his daughter was a rape victim. The commission of crime, prosecutions resulting from it, and judicial proceedings arising from the prosecutions, however, are without question events of legitimate concern to the public and consequently fall within the responsibility of the press to report the operations of government. . . .

The developing law surrounding the tort of invasion of privacy recognizes a privilege in the press to report the events of judicial proceedings. . . .

. . . [E]ven the prevailing law of invasion of privacy generally recognizes that the interests in privacy fade when the information involved already appears on the public record. . . .

We are reluctant to embark on a course that would make public records generally available to the media but forbid their publication if offensive to the sensibilities of the supposed reasonable man. Such a rule would make it very difficult for the media to inform citizens about the public business and yet stay within the law. The rule would invite timidity and self-censorship and very likely lead to the suppression of many items that would otherwise be published and that should be made available to the public. At the very least, the First and Fourteenth Amendments will not allow exposing the press to liability for truthfully publishing information released to the public in official court records. If there are privacy interests to be protected in judicial proceedings, the States must respond by means which avoid public documentation or other exposure of private information. Their political institutions must weigh the interests in privacy with the interests of the public to know and of the press to publish. Once true information is disclosed in public court documents open to public inspection, the press cannot be sanctioned for publishing it.

*Source*: 420 U.S. 469 (1975).

## DOCUMENT 84: *Federal Communications Commission v. Pacifica Foundation* (1978)

In 1978, the Supreme Court heard one of the most famous of its First Amendment cases, generated by a radio broadcast of comedian George Carlin's monologue on "Filthy Words." Carlin was a popular satirist and social critic. He had performed the monologue in nightclub settings and similar venues; on October 30, 1973, it was broadcast at 2:00 in the afternoon by a New York radio station. Subsequently, the Federal Communications Commission received a complaint from a man who had been riding in a car with his young son when the monologue was aired. The record in the case disclosed no other complaints.

The Federal Communications Commission responded by asserting its right to regulate "indecent" but admittedly nonobscene speech, and a divided Supreme Court, emphasizing the "narrowness" of its opinion, affirmed. The case is a classic confrontation between those on the Court of a more paternalistic bent and those who would, in Justice William Brennan's words, "place the responsibility and the right to weed worthless and offensive communications from the public airways where it belongs and where, until today, it resided: in a public free to choose those communications worthy of its attention from a marketplace unsullied by the censor's hand."

* * *

MR. JUSTICE STEVENS delivered the opinion of the Court. . . .

This case requires that we decide whether the Federal Communications Commission has any power to regulate a radio broadcast that is indecent but not obscene. . . .

When the issue is narrowed to the facts of this case, the question is whether the First Amendment denies government any power to restrict the public broadcast of indecent language in any circumstances. For if the government has any such power, this was an appropriate occasion for its exercise.

The words of the Carlin monologue are unquestionably "speech" within the meaning of the First Amendment. It is equally clear that the Commission's objections to the broadcast were based in part on its content. The order must therefore fall if, as Pacifica argues, the First Amendment prohibits all governmental regulation that depends on the content of speech. Our past cases demonstrate, however, that no such absolute rule is mandated by the Constitution. . . .

. . . If there were any reason to believe that the Commission's characterization of the Carlin monologue as offensive could be traced to its political content—or even to the fact that it satirized contemporary attitudes about four-letter words—First Amendment protection might be required. But that is simply not this case. These words offend for the same reasons that obscenity offends. Their place in the hierarchy of First Amendment values was aptly sketched by Mr. Justice Murphy when he said: "[S]uch utterances are no essential part of any exposition of ideas, and are of such slight social value as a step to truth that any benefit that may be derived from them is clearly outweighed by the social interest in order and morality." . . .

Although these words ordinarily lack literary, political, or scientific value, they are not entirely outside the protection of the First Amendment. Some uses of even the most offensive words are unquestionably protected. . . . Indeed, we may assume, *arguendo*, that this monologue would be protected in other contexts. Nonetheless, the constitutional protection accorded to a communication containing such patently offensive sexual and excretory language need not be the same in every context. It is a characteristic of speech such as this that both its capacity to offend and its "social value," to use Mr. Justice Murphy's term, vary with the circumstances. Words that are commonplace in one setting are shocking in another. To paraphrase Mr. Justice Harlan, one occasion's lyric is another's vulgarity. . . .

We have long recognized that each medium of expression presents special First Amendment problems. . . . And of all forms of communication, it is broadcasting that has received the most limited First Amendment protection. . . .

The reasons for these distinctions are complex, but two have relevance to the present case. First, the broadcast media have established a uniquely pervasive presence in the lives of all Americans. Patently offensive, indecent material presented over the airwaves confronts the citizen, not only in public, but also in the privacy of the home, where the individual's right to be left alone plainly outweighs the First Amendment rights of an intruder. . . . Because the broadcast audience is constantly tuning in and out, prior warnings cannot completely protect the listener or viewer from unexpected program content. To say that one may avoid further offense by turning off the radio when he hears indecent language is like saying that the remedy for an assault is to run away after the first blow. One may hang up on an indecent phone call, but that option does not give the caller a constitutional immunity or avoid a harm that has already taken place.

Second, broadcasting is uniquely accessible to children, even those too

young to read. Although Cohen's written message might have been incomprehensible to a first grader, Pacifica's broadcast could have enlarged
a child's vocabulary in an instant. Other forms of offensive expression
may be withheld from the young without restricting the expression at
its source. Bookstores and motion picture theaters, for example, may be
prohibited from making indecent material available to children. We held
in *Ginsberg* v. *New York* . . . that the government's interest in the "well-
being of its youth" and in supporting "parents' claim to authority in
their own household" justified the regulation of otherwise protected expression. . . . The ease with which children may obtain access to broadcast material, coupled with the concerns recognized in *Ginsberg*, amply
justify special treatment of indecent broadcasting.

It is appropriate, in conclusion, to emphasize the narrowness of our
holding. This case does not involve a two-way radio conversation between a cab driver and a dispatcher, or a telecast of an Elizabethan com-
edy. We have not decided that an occasional expletive in either setting
would justify any sanction or, indeed, that this broadcast would justify
a criminal prosecution. The Commission's decision rested entirely on a
nuisance rationale under which context is all-important. The concept requires consideration of a host of variables. The time of day was emphasized by the Commission. The content of the program in which the
language is used will also affect the composition of the audience, and
differences between radio, television, and perhaps closed-circuit trans-
missions, may also be relevant. As Mr. Justice Sutherland wrote, a "nuisance may be merely a right thing in the wrong place,—like a pig in the
parlor instead of the barnyard." . . . We simply hold that when the Commission finds that a pig has entered the parlor, the exercise of its regulatory power does not depend on proof that the pig is obscene. . . .

MR. JUSTICE BRENNAN, with whom MR. JUSTICE MARSHALL join, dissenting. . . .

"The ability of government, consonant with the Constitution, to shut
off discourse solely to protect others from hearing it is . . . dependent
upon a showing that substantial privacy interests are being invaded in
an essentially intolerable manner. Any broader view of this authority
would effectively empower a majority to silence dissidents simply as a
matter of personal predilections." . . . I am in wholehearted agreement
with my Brethren that an individual's right "to be let alone" when engaged in private activity within the confines of his own home is encom-
passed within the "substantial privacy interests" to which Mr. Justice
Harlan referred in *Cohen*, and is entitled to the greatest solicitude. . . .
However, I believe that an individual's actions in switching on and listening to communications transmitted over the public airways and directed to the public at large do not implicate fundamental privacy

interests, even when engaged in within the home. Instead, because the radio is undeniably a public medium, these actions are more properly viewed as a decision to take part, if only as a listener, in an ongoing public discourse.... Although an individual's decision to allow public radio communications into his home undoubtedly does not abrogate all of his privacy interests, the residual privacy interests he retains vis-à-vis the communication he voluntarily admits into his home are surely no greater than those of the people present in the corridor of the Los Angeles courthouse in *Cohen* who bore witness to the words "Fuck the Draft" emblazoned across Cohen's jacket. Their privacy interests were held insufficient to justify punishing Cohen for his offensive communication.

Even if an individual who voluntarily opens his home to radio communications retains privacy interests of sufficient moment to justify a ban on protected speech if those interests are "invaded in an essentially intolerable manner," ... the very fact that those interests are threatened only by a radio broadcast precludes any intolerable invasion of privacy; for unlike other intrusive modes of communication, such as sound trucks, "[t]he radio can be turned off," ... —and with a minimum of effort. As Chief Judge Bazelon aptly observed below, "having elected to receive public air waves, the scanner who stumbles onto an offensive program is in the same position as the unsuspecting passers-by in *Cohen* and *Erznoznik* ...; he can avert his attention by changing channels or turning off the set." ... Whatever the minimal discomfort suffered by a listener who inadvertently tunes into a program he finds offensive during the brief interval before he can simply extend his arm and switch stations or flick the "off" button, it is surely worth the candle to preserve the broadcaster's right to send, and the right of those interested to receive, a message entitled to full First Amendment protection. To reach a contrary balance, as does the Court, is clearly to follow MR. JUSTICE STEVENS' reliance on animal metaphors, *ante*, ... "to burn the house to roast the pig." ...

... For my own part, even accepting that this case is limited to its facts, I would place the responsibility and the right to weed worthless and offensive communications from the public airways where it belongs and where, until today, it resided: in a public free to choose those communications worthy of its attention from a marketplace unsullied by the censor's hand.

*Source*: 438 U.S. 726 (1978).

---

# DOCUMENT 85: *Landmark Communications, Inc. v. Virginia* (1978)

---

At the time *Landmark Communications, Inc. v. Virginia* came before the Supreme Court, Virginia and forty-eight other jurisdictions had en-

acted laws to protect the confidentiality of judicial disciplinary proceedings. There are important policy reasons undergirding such
protections: the reputation of the judiciary is an important element of
respect for the legal system as a whole. Furthermore, it is unlikely that
people will come forward to press complaints if their identities and the
particulars of their charges are widely publicized.

The Virginia statute imposed criminal penalties on those who violated the confidentiality of a judicial disciplinary proceeding. The *Virginian Pilot*, a Landmark Communications newspaper, published an
article that accurately reported the deliberations of the Virginia Judicial
Inquiry and Review Commission. Sanctions were imposed and upheld
by the Virginia courts. The Supreme Court overruled. While the Court
explicitly recognized the importance of the state's interest, it nevertheless held that the imposition of sanctions against the *Virginian Pilot*
violated First Amendment free-press guarantees.

\* \* \*

MR. CHIEF JUSTICE BURGER delivered the opinion of the Court. . . .

On October 4, 1975, the Virginian Pilot, a Landmark newspaper, published an article which accurately reported on a pending inquiry by the
Virginia Judicial Inquiry and Review Commission and identified the
state judge whose conduct was being investigated. The article reported
that "[n]o formal complaint has been filed by the commission against
[the judge], indicating either that the five-man panel found insufficient
cause for action or that the case is still under review." A month later, on
November 5, a grand jury indicted Landmark for violating Va. Code §
2.1–37.13 (1973) by "unlawfully divulg[ing] the identification of a Judge
of a Court not of record, which said Judge was the subject of an investigation and hearing" by the Commission. . . .

. . . Landmark was found guilty and fined $500. . . . The Supreme
Court of Virginia affirmed. . . . That court characterized the case as involving "a confrontation between the First Amendment guaranty of freedom of the press and a Virginia statute which imposes criminal sanctions
for breach of the confidentiality of proceedings before the Judicial Inquiry and Review Commission." . . .

At the present time it appears that 47 States, the District of Columbia,
and Puerto Rico have established, by constitution, statute, or court rule,
some type of judicial inquiry and disciplinary procedures. All of these
jurisdictions, with the apparent exception of Puerto Rico, provide for the
confidentiality of judicial disciplinary proceedings, although in most the
guarantee of confidentiality extends only to the point when a formal
complaint is filed with the State Supreme Court or equivalent body. . . .

The substantial uniformity of the existing state plans suggests that confidentiality is perceived as tending to insure the ultimate effectiveness of

the judicial review commissions. First, confidentiality is thought to encourage the filing of complaints and the willing participation of relevant
witnesses by providing protection against possible retaliation or recrim-
ination. Second, at least until the time when the meritorious can be
separated from the frivolous complaints, the confidentiality of the proceedings protects judges from the injury which might result from publication of unexamined and unwarranted complaints. And finally, it is
argued, confidence in the judiciary as an institution is maintained by
avoiding premature announcement of groundless claims of judicial misconduct or disability since it can be assumed that some frivolous complaints will be made against judicial officers who rarely can satisfy all
contending litigants. . . .

. . . Unlike the generalized mandate of confidentiality, the imposition
of criminal sanctions for its breach is not a common characteristic of the
state plans. . . .

The narrow and limited question presented, then, is whether the First
Amendment permits the criminal punishment of third persons who are
strangers to the inquiry, including the news media, for divulging or publishing truthful information regarding confidential proceedings of the
Judicial Inquiry and Review Commission. . . .

The operation of the Virginia Commission, no less than the operation
of the judicial system itself, is a matter of public interest, necessarily engaging the attention of the news media. The article published by
Landmark provided accurate factual information about a legislatively
authorized inquiry pending before the Judicial Inquiry and Review Commission, and in so doing clearly served those interests in public scrutiny
and discussion of governmental affairs which the First Amendment was
adopted to protect. . . .

It can be assumed for purposes of decision that confidentiality of Commission proceedings serves legitimate state interests. The question, however, is whether these interests are sufficient to justify the encroachment
on First Amendment guarantees which the imposition of criminal sanctions entails with respect to nonparticipants such as Landmark. The
Commonwealth has offered little more than assertion and conjecture to
support its claim that without criminal sanctions the objectives of the
statutory scheme would be seriously undermined. While not dispositive,
we note that more than 40 States having similar commissions have not
found it necessary to enforce confidentiality by use of criminal sanctions
against nonparticipants.

. . . As Mr. Justice Black observed in *Bridges* v. *California* . . . :

"The assumption that respect for the judiciary can be won by shielding judges
from published criticism wrongly appraises the character of American public
opinion. . . . [A]n enforced silence, however limited, solely in the name of pre-

serving the dignity of the bench, would probably engender resentment, suspicion, and contempt much more than it would enhance respect." . . .

Accordingly, the judgment of the Supreme of Court of Virginia is reversed, and the case remanded for further proceedings not inconsistent with this opinion.

*Source*: 435 U.S. 829 (1978).

---

## DOCUMENT 86: Public Broadcasting Act (1967)

In 1967, Congress established the Corporation for Public Broadcasting and decreed that it should be both noncommercial and nonpolitical. Originally, the act also prohibited any editorializing, but that language, as the case following the excerpt from the statute will show, was struck down as too restrictive.

\* \* \*

### §399. Support of political candidates prohibited

No noncommercial educational broadcasting station may support or oppose any candidate for political office.

### §399b. Offering of certain services, facilities, or products by public broadcast station

(a) "Advertisement" defined

For purposes of this section, the term "advertisement" means any message or other programming material which is broadcast or otherwise transmitted in exchange for any remuneration, and which is intended—

(1) to promote any service, facility, or product offered by any person who is engaged in such offering for profit;

(2) to express the views of any person with respect to any matter of public importance or interest; or

(3) to support or oppose any candidate for political office.

(b) Offering of services, facilities, or products permitted; advertisements prohibited

(1) Except as provided in paragraph (2), each public broadcast station shall be authorized to engage in the offering of services, facilities, or products in exchange for remuneration.

(2) No public broadcast station may make its facilities available to any person for the broadcasting of any advertisement.

(c) Use of funds from offering services, etc.

Any public broadcast station which engages in any offering specified in subsection (b)(1) of this section may not use any funds distributed by the Corporation under section 396(k) of this title to defray any costs associated with such offering. Any such offering by a public broadcasting station shall not interfere with the provision of public telecommunications services by such station.

(d) Development of accounting system

Each public broadcast system which engages in the activity specified in subsection (b)(1) of this section shall, in consultation with the Corporation, develop an accounting system which is designed to identify any amounts received as remuneration for, or costs related to, such activities under this section, and to account for such amounts separately from any other amounts received by such station from any source.

*Source*: 47 U.S.C. §399, 399(b), November 7, 1967.

---

## DOCUMENT 87: *Federal Communications Commission v. League of Women Voters of California* (1984)

In 1984, the Supreme Court considered a challenge to provisions of the Public Broadcasting Act that barred local Public Broadcasting Service stations from editorializing. Justice William Brennan wrote the majority opinion, striking down the regulations as violative of the First Amendment. There are a number of interesting aspects to this opinion. Originally, the Justice Department had declined to defend the challenged provisions; only after the election of President Ronald Reagan and the installation of a new staff at the Justice Department did the government decide to defend the statute. Some of the language of Justice Brennan's majority opinion is particularly ironic in light of the subsequent sustained political attacks on the Corporation for Public Broadcasting. (In response to concerns that affiliate editorials might anger Congress, Brennan suggested that Congress was far more likely to become angered by nationally distributed programs addressing controversial issues than by editorials that were likely to be focused on issues of local interest. Time has proved Brennan prescient.) Justice William Rehnquist strongly dissented, opining, as he did in *Rust v. Sullivan* (see Document 61) and other cases, that government can constitutionally control what it funds, even if those controls might otherwise be deemed unconstitutional.

\* \* \*

JUSTICE BRENNAN delivered the opinion of the Court.

Moved to action by a widely felt need to sponsor independent sources of broadcast programming as an alternative to commercial broadcasting, Congress set out in 1967 to support and promote the development of noncommercial, educational broadcasting stations. A keystone of Congress' program was the Public Broadcasting Act of 1967, . . . which established the Corporation for Public Broadcasting, a nonprofit corporation authorized to disburse federal funds to noncommercial television and radio stations in support of station operations and educational programming. Section 399 of that Act . . . forbids any "noncommercial educational broadcasting station which receives a grant from the Corporation" to "engage in editorializing." . . . In this case, we are called upon to decide whether Congress, by imposing that restriction, has passed a "law . . . abridging the freedom of speech, or of the press" in violation of the First Amendment of the Constitution. . . .

Appellee Pacifica Foundation is a nonprofit corporation that owns and operates several noncommercial educational broadcasting stations in five major metropolitan areas. . . .

The District Court granted summary judgment in favor of appellees, holding that § 399's ban on editorializing violated the First Amendment. . . . The court rejected the Federal Communication Commission's contention that "§ 399 serves a compelling government interest in ensuring that funded noncommercial broadcasters do not become propaganda organs for the government." . . . Noting the diverse sources of funding for noncommercial stations, the protections built into the Public Broadcasting Act to ensure that noncommercial broadcasters remain free of governmental influence, and the requirements of the FCC's fairness doctrine which are designed to guard against one-sided presentation of controversial issues, the District Court concluded that the asserted fear of Government control was not sufficiently compelling to warrant § 399's restriction on speech. . . . The court also rejected the contention that the restriction on editorializing as [sic] necessary to ensure that Government funding of noncommercial broadcast stations does not interfere with the balanced presentation of opinion on those stations. . . . The FCC appealed from the District Court judgment directly to this Court pursuant to 28 U.S.C. § 1252. We . . . now affirm. . . .

At first glance, of course, it would appear that the District Court applied the correct standard. Section 399 plainly operates to restrict the expression of editorial opinion on matters of public importance, and, as we have repeatedly explained, communication of this kind is entitled to the most exacting degree of First Amendment protection. . . . Were a similar ban on editorializing applied to newspapers and magazines, we would not hesitate to strike it down as violative of the First Amendment. . . . But, as the Government correctly notes, because broadcast regulation involves unique considerations, our cases have not followed precisely the same approach that we have applied to other media and have never gone so far as to demand that such regulations serve "compelling" governmental interests. At the same time, we think the Government's argument loses sight of concerns that are important in this area and thus misapprehends the essential meaning of our prior decisions concerning the reach of Congress' authority to regulate broadcast communication. . . .

In seeking to defend the prohibition on editorializing imposed by § 399, the Government urges that the statute was aimed at preventing two principal threats to the overall success of the Public Broadcasting Act of 1967. According to this argument, the ban was necessary, first, to protect noncommercial educational broadcasting stations from being coerced, as a result of federal financing, into becoming vehicles for Government propagandizing or the objects of governmental influence; and, second, to keep these stations from becoming convenient targets for capture by private interest groups wishing to express their own partisan viewpoints. By seeking to safeguard the public's right to a balanced presentation of public issues through the prevention of either governmental or private bias, these objectives are, of course, broadly consistent with the goals identified in our earlier broadcast regulation cases. But, in sharp contrast to the restrictions upheld in *Red Lion* or in *CBS, Inc. v. FCC*, which left room for editorial discretion and simply required broadcast editors to grant others access to the microphone, § 399 directly prohibits the broadcaster from speaking out on public issues even in a balanced and fair manner. The Government insists, however, that the hazards posed in the "special" circumstances of noncommercial educational broadcasting are so great that § 399 is an indispensable means of preserving the public's First Amendment interests. We disagree. . . .

Indeed, what is far more likely than local station editorials to pose the kinds of dangers hypothesized by the Government are the wide variety of programs addressing controversial issues produced, often with substantial CPB funding, for national distribution to local stations. Such programs truly have the potential to reach a large audience and, because of the critical commentary they contain, to have the kind of genuine national impact that might trigger a congressional response or kindle governmental resentment. The ban imposed by § 399, however, is plainly not directed at the potentially controversial content of such programs; it is, instead, leveled solely at the expression of editorial opinion by local station management, a form of expression that is far more likely to be aimed at a smaller local audience, to have less national impact, and to be confined to local issues. In contrast, the Act imposes no substantive restrictions, other than normal requirements of balance and fairness, on those who produce nationally distributed programs. Indeed, the Act is designed in part to encourage and sponsor the production of such programs and to allow each station to decide for itself whether to accept such programs for local broadcast.

Furthermore, the manifest imprecision of the ban imposed by § 399 reveals that its proscription is not sufficiently tailored to the harms it seeks to prevent to justify its substantial interference with broadcasters' speech. . . . [T]he Government never explains how, say, an editorial by local station management urging improvements in a town's parks or museums will so infuriate Congress or other federal officials that the future of public broadcasting will be imperiled unless such editorials are suppressed. Nor is it explained how the suppression of editorials alone serves to reduce the risk of governmental retaliation and interference when it is clear that station management is fully able to broadcast controversial views so long as such views are not labeled as its own. . . .

In sum, § 399's broad ban on all editorializing by every station that receives CPB funds far exceeds what is necessary to protect against the risk of governmental interference or to prevent the public from assuming that editorials by public broadcasting stations represent the official view of government. The regulation impermissibly sweeps within its prohibition a wide range of speech by wholly private stations on topics that do not take a directly partisan stand or that have nothing whatever to do with federal, state, or local government. . . .

. . . Since the breadth of § 399 extends so far beyond what is necessary to accomplish the goals identified by the Government, it fails to satisfy the First Amendment standards that we have applied in this area. . . .

. . . [T]he Government argues that by prohibiting noncommercial educational stations that receive CPB grants from editorializing, Congress has, in the proper exercise of its spending power, simply determined that it "will not subsidize public broadcasting station editorials." . . .

In this case, however, unlike the situation faced by the charitable organization in *Taxation With Representation*, a noncommercial educational station that receives only 1% of its overall income from CPB grants is barred absolutely from all editorializing. Therefore, in contrast to the appellee in *Taxation With Representation*, such a station is not able to segregate its activities according to the source of its funding. The station has no way of limiting the use of its federal funds to all noneditorializing activities, and, more importantly, it is barred from using even wholly private funds to finance its editorial activity. . . .

In conclusion, we emphasize that our disposition of this case rests upon a narrow proposition. We do not hold that the Congress or the FCC is without power to regulate the content, timing, or character of speech by noncommercial educational broadcasting stations. Rather, we hold only that the specific interests sought to be advanced by § 399's ban on editorializing are either not sufficiently substantial or are not served

in a sufficiently limited manner to justify the substantial abridgment of important journalistic freedoms which the First Amendment jealousy protects. Accordingly, the judgment of the District Court is
  *Affirmed.*

*Source*: 468 U.S 364 (1984).

---

## DOCUMENT 88: *Reverend Jerry Falwell v. Larry C. Flynt* (1986)

In 1988, the Supreme Court upheld the free-speech rights of Larry Flynt, publisher of *Hustler*, in a suit brought by the Reverend Jerry Falwell of Moral Majority fame. Flynt's magazine had carried a highly derogatory and sexually explicit parody of Falwell. It is worth noting that the original suit brought by Falwell charged Flynt with libel, invasion of privacy, and intentional infliction of emotional distress. At no level—district court, appellate court, or Supreme Court—did Falwell prevail on the libel or invasion-of-privacy theories. However, on the count alleging intentional infliction of emotional distress, the court of appeals upheld the district-court verdict awarding Falwell damages.

While the award of damages was affirmed (indeed, Flynt himself testified that the parody was intended to inflict emotional distress on Falwell), the decision confirmed the "actual malice" standard for libel of a public figure established in *New York Times v. Sullivan*. It also distinguished between libel and intentional infliction of emotional distress, and clarified the boundaries between those theories.

The 1986 opinion of the court of appeals follows. If free speech is indeed "freedom for the thought we hate," in Justice Oliver Wendell Holmes's memorable phrase, Larry Flynt and *Hustler* may prove the point.

\* \* \*

CHAPMAN, Circuit Judge: . . .

The "ad parody" which gives rise to the instant litigation attempts to satirize an advertising campaign for Campari Liqueur. In the real Campari advertisement celebrities talk about their "first time." They mean, their first encounter with Campari Liqueur, but there is double entendre with a sexual connotation. In the *Hustler* parody, Falwell is the celebrity in the advertisement. It contains his photograph and the text of an interview which is attributed to him. In this interview Falwell allegedly details an incestuous rendezvous with his mother in an outhouse in Lynchburg, Virginia. Falwell's mother is portrayed as a drunken and immoral woman and Falwell appears as a hypocrite and habitual drunkard. At the bottom of the page is a disclaimer which states "ad parody—not to be taken seriously." The parody is listed in the table of contents as "Fiction; Ad and Personality Parody."

Falwell was first shown the ad parody by a reporter in the fall of 1983. Shortly thereafter, he filed suit against Flynt, Hustler and FDC in the United States District Court for the Western District of Virginia. Falwell alleged three theories of liability: libel, invasion of privacy under Va. Code § 8.01–40 (1984), and intentional infliction of emotional distress. Hustler then republished the parody in its March 1984 issue.

In June 1984, Falwell's counsel took Larry Flynt's deposition, which was recorded on video tape. During the deposition Flynt identified himself as Christopher Columbus Cornwallis I. P. Q. Harvey H. Apache Pugh and testified that the parody was written by rock stars Yoko Ono and Billy Idol. It also contained the following colloquy concerning the parody:

Q. Did you want to upset Reverend Falwell?

A. Yes. . . .

Q. Do you recognize that in having published what you did in this ad, you were attempting to convey to the people who read it that Reverend Falwell was just as you characterized him, a liar?

A. He's a glutton.

Q. How about a liar?

A. Yeah. He's a liar, too.

Q. How about a hypocrite?

A. Yeah.

Q. That's what you wanted to convey?

A. Yeah.

Q. And didn't it occur to you that if it wasn't true, you were attacking a man in his profession?

A. Yes.

Q. Did you appreciate, at the time that you wrote "okay" or approved this publication, that for Reverend Falwell to function in his livelihood, and in his commitment and career, he has to have an integrity that people believe in? Did you not appreciate that?

A. Yeah.

Q. And wasn't one of your objectives to destroy that integrity, or harm it, if you could?

A. To assassinate it. . . .

The jury returned a verdict for the defendants on the libel claim, finding that no reasonable man would believe that the parody was describing actual facts about Falwell. On the emotional distress claim, the jury returned a verdict against Flynt and *Hustler*, but not F.D.C. The jury awarded $100,000 in actual damages, $50,000 in punitive damages against Flynt, and $50,000 in punitive damages against *Hustler*.

## II

The defendants make two constitutional arguments. First, they assert that since Falwell is admittedly a public figure the actual malice standard of *New York Times v. Sullivan* . . . must be met before Falwell can recover for emotional distress. They argue that the actual malice standard has not been met. Second, the defendants contend that since the jury found that the parody was not reasonably believable, the statements contained therein cannot be statements of fact but must be opinion and are, therefore, completely shielded by the first amendment. . . .

In *New York Times*, the Supreme Court determined that libel actions brought by public officials against the press can have a chilling effect on the press inconsistent with the first amendment. Therefore, when a public official sues for libel based upon a tortious publication, the defendant is entitled to a degree of first amendment protection. This protection has been extended to cases in which the plaintiff is a public figure. . . . It is not the theory of liability advanced, but the status of the plaintiff, as a public figure or official and the gravamen of a tortious publication which give rise to the first amendment protection prescribed by *New York Times*.

In the case at bar, Falwell is a public figure, and the gravamen of the suit is a tortious publication. The defendants are, therefore, entitled to the same level of first amendment protection in the claim for intentional infliction of emotional distress that they received in Falwell's claim for libel. To hold otherwise would frustrate the intent of *New York Times* and encourage the type of self censorship which it sought to abolish.

The issue then becomes what form the first amendment protection should take in an action for intentional infliction of emotional distress. The defendants argue that Falwell must prove that the parody was published with knowing falsity or reckless disregard for the truth. This is the actual malice standard of *New York Times v. Sullivan*. While we agree that the same level of protection is due the defendants, we do not believe that the literal application of the actual malice standard which they seek is appropriate in an action for intentional infliction of emotional distress.

The actual malice standard originated as a remedy for the first amendment problem that arises under common law defamation. Historically, the individual's interest in a good reputation has been regarded as so significant that the law has held one who intentionally published defamatory material to a standard of strict liability. But recognizing that people in a free society must have ready access to information and ideas if that society is to endure, the established common law attempted to reconcile these divergent interests by holding a publisher strictly liable for his publication unless he could prove that the publication was either true or subject to a conditional privilege. There was no privilege for a good faith mistake of fact. . . .

The Supreme Court changed the law in *New York Times v. Sullivan.* The court held that defendants could be held liable for defamation of public officials only if the defamatory falsehood was published with actual malice. The effect of *New York Times* and its progeny is to increase the level of fault necessary for a public figure to prevail in an action for defamation. Where the defendant was once held strictly liable for a false publication, he is now held liable only for his knowing or reckless misconduct. *New York Times* gives the press protection from honest mistakes, but it is not a license to lie.

The use of calculated falsehood, however, would put a different cast on the constitutional question. Although honest utterance, even if inaccurate, may further the fruitful exercise of the right of free speech, it does not follow that the lie, knowingly and deliberately published about a public official, should enjoy a like immunity. . . . Hence the knowingly false statement and the false statement made with reckless disregard of the truth, do not enjoy constitutional protection. . . .

The first of the four elements of intentional infliction of emotional distress under Virginia law requires that the defendant's misconduct be intentional or reckless. This is precisely the level of fault that *New York Times* requires in an action for defamation. The first amendment will not shield intentional or reckless misconduct resulting in damage to reputation, and neither will it shield such misconduct which results in severe emotional distress. We, therefore, hold that when the first amendment requires application of the actual malice standard, the standard is met when the jury finds that the defendant's intentional or reckless misconduct has proximately caused the injury complained of. The jury made such a finding here, and thus the constitutional standard is satisfied.

The defendants also argue that since the jury found that a reader could not reasonably believe that the parody was describing actual facts about Falwell, it must be an opinion and therefore is protected by the first amendment. At common law the dichotomy between statements of fact and opinion was often dispositive in actions for defamation. An action for intentional infliction of emotional distress concerns itself with intentional or reckless conduct which is outrageous and proximately causes severe emotional distress, not with statements per se. We need not consider whether the statements in question constituted opinion, as the issue is whether their publication was sufficiently outrageous to constitute intentional infliction of emotional distress. The defendants' argument on this point is, therefore, irrelevant in the context of this tort.

## III

. . . The elements of libel and intentional infliction of emotional distress are different and the facts in the instant case will independently support the latter tort. We are convinced, therefore, that Falwell's failure to recover for libel does not, as a matter of law, prevent him from recovering for intentional infliction of emotional distress. . . .

In his deposition, Flynt testified that he intended to cause Falwell emotional distress. If the jury found his testimony on this point to be credible, then it could have found that Falwell satisfied the first element. Evidence of the second element, outrageousness, is quite obvious from the language in the parody and in the fact that Flynt republished the parody after this lawsuit was filed. The final elements require the plaintiff to prove that the defendant's conduct proximately caused severe emotional distress. At trial, when Falwell was asked about his reaction to the parody, he testified as follows:

A. I think I have never been as angry as I was at that moment. . . . My anger became a more rational and deep hurt. I somehow felt that in all of my life I had never believed that human beings could do something like this. I really felt like weeping. I am not a deeply emotional person; I don't show it. I think I felt like weeping.

Q. How long did this sense of anger last?

A. To this present moment.

Q. You say that it almost brought you to tears. In your whole life, Mr. Falwell, had you ever had a personal experience of such intensity that could compare with the feeling that you had when you saw this ad?

A. Never had. Since I have been a Christian I don't think I have ever intentionally hurt anybody. I am sure I have hurt people but not with intent. I certainly have never physically attacked anyone in my life. I really think that at that moment if Larry Flynt had been nearby I might have physically reacted.

. . . We find . . . that the evidence is sufficient to sustain the jury's verdict against the defendants for intentional infliction of emotional distress. . . .

## V

At the close of evidence, the district court dismissed Falwell's action for invasion of privacy pursuant to Va. Code § 8.01–40 (1985) on the grounds that the ad parody which appeared in *Hustler* did not constitute a use of Falwell's name and likeness "for purposes of trade" within the meaning of the statute. Falwell has filed a cross appeal alleging that the district court erred in this ruling. We disagree.

The Virginia statute reads, in pertinent part:

> Any person whose name, portrait, or picture is used without having first obtained the written consent of such person . . . for advertising purposes or for the purposes of trade, such persons may maintain a suit in equity against the person, firm, or corporation so using such person's name, portrait, or picture to prevent and restrain the use thereof; and may also sue and recover damages for any injuries sustained by reason of such use. And if the defendant shall have knowingly used such person's name, portrait or picture in such manner as is forbidden or declared to be unlawful by this chapter, the jury, in its discretion, may award exemplary damages. . . .

Because the jury found that the parody in the instant case was not reasonably believable and because it contained a disclaimer, publication of the parody did not constitute a use of Falwell's name and likeness for purposes of trade. The district court properly dismissed this claim. For these reasons, the decision of the district court is affirmed.

AFFIRMED.

*Source*: 797 F.2d 1270 (4th Cir. 1986).

---

# DOCUMENT 89: *Hazelwood School District v. Kuhlmeier* (1988)

If *Tinker v. Des Moines* (Document 47) represents a symbolic "high point" in students' rights, *Hazelwood School District v. Kuhlmeier* represents one of several lows. The Supreme Court, no less than various legislative bodies, has more difficulty with First Amendment freedoms when there is reason to believe that exercise of those freedoms may harm children. The Court has also been famously reluctant to extend the protection of the Bill of Rights to minors. While that reluctance has been most obvious in the Fourth Amendment area, the First Amendment has taken its share of lumps as well.

*Hazelwood* is one of those lumps. The case concerns the rights of high-school journalism students to include articles in the school paper despite the disapproval of their content by the school's principal (Kuhlmeier was the Superintendent of Public Instruction). Such conflicts are common, and their resolution generally depends upon the way in which teachers and administrators see their pedagogical duty. Is that duty one of protecting students from inappropriate influences and improper, possibly hurtful, publications? Or is their job to instruct young people on the responsible use of the freedoms they will enjoy as adult Americans?

* * *

JUSTICE WHITE delivered the opinion of the Court.

This case concerns the extent to which educators may exercise editorial control over the contents of a high school newspaper produced as part of the school's journalism curriculum. . . .

Spectrum was written and edited by the Journalism II class at Hazelwood East. The newspaper was published every three weeks or so during the 1982–1983 school year. More than 4,500 copies of the newspaper were distributed during that year to students, school personnel, and members of the community.

The Board of Education allocated funds from its annual budget for the printing of Spectrum. These funds were supplemented by proceeds from sales of the newspaper. The printing expenses during the 1982–1983 school year totaled $4,668.50; revenue from sales was $1,166.84. The other costs associated with the newspaper—such as supplies, textbooks, and a portion of the journalism teacher's salary—were borne entirely by the Board.

The Journalism II course was taught by Robert Stergos for most of the 1982–1983 academic year. Stergos left Hazelwood East to take a job in private industry on April 29, 1983, when the May 13 edition of Spectrum was nearing completion, and petitioner Emerson took his place as newspaper adviser for the remaining weeks of the term.

The practice at Hazelwood East during the spring 1983 semester was for the journalism teacher to submit page proofs of each Spectrum issue to Principal Reynolds for his review prior to publication. On May 10, Emerson delivered the proofs of the May 13 edition to Reynolds, who objected to two of the articles scheduled to appear in that edition. One of the stories described three Hazelwood East students' experiences with pregnancy; the other discussed the impact of divorce on students at the school.

Reynolds was concerned that, although the pregnancy story used false names "to keep the identity of these girls a secret," the pregnant students still might be identifiable from the text. He also believed that the article's references to sexual activity and birth control were inappropriate for some of the younger students at the school. In addition, Reynolds was concerned that a student identified by name in the divorce story had complained that her father "wasn't spending enough time with my mom, my sister and I" prior to the divorce, "was always out of town on business or out late playing cards with the guys," and "always argued about everything" with her mother. . . . Reynolds believed that the student's

parents should have been given an opportunity to respond to these remarks or to consent to their publication. He was unaware that Emerson
had deleted the student's name from the final version of the article.

Reynolds believed that there was no time to make the necessary
changes in the stories before the scheduled press run and that the newspaper would not appear before the end of the school year if printing
were delayed to any significant extent. He concluded that his only op-
tions under the circumstances were to publish a four-page newspaper
instead of the planned six-page newspaper, eliminating the two pages
on which the offending stories appeared, or to publish no newspaper at
all. Accordingly, he directed Emerson to withhold from publication the
two pages containing the stories on pregnancy and divorce. He informed
his superiors of the decision, and they concurred.

Respondents subsequently commenced this action in the United States
District Court for the Eastern District of Missouri seeking a declaration
that their First Amendment rights had been violated, injunctive relief,
and monetary damages. After a bench trial, the District Court denied an
injunction, holding that no First Amendment violation had occurred. . . .

The District Court concluded that school officials may impose restraints on students' speech in activities that are " 'an integral part of the
school's educational function' "—including the publication of a school-
sponsored newspaper by a journalism class—so long as their decision
has " 'a substantial and reasonable basis.' " . . .

The Court of Appeals for the Eighth Circuit reversed. . . . The court
held at the outset that Spectrum was not only "a part of the school
adopted curriculum," . . . but also a public forum, because the newspaper
was "intended to be and operated as a conduit for student viewpoint."
. . . The court then concluded that Spectrum's status as a public forum
precluded school officials from censoring its contents except when " 'necessary to avoid material and substantial interference with school work
or discipline . . . or the rights of others.' " . . .

. . . we now reverse. . . .

School officials did not deviate in practice from their policy that production of Spectrum was to be part of the educational curriculum and a
"regular classroom activit[y]." . . .

The evidence relied upon by the Court of Appeals in finding Spectrum
to be a public forum . . . is equivocal at best. . . . Accordingly, school officials were entitled to regulate the contents of Spectrum in any reasonable manner. . . . It is this standard, rather than our decision in *Tinker*,
that governs this case.

### B

The question whether the First Amendment requires a school to tol-
erate particular student speech—the question that we addressed in

*Tinker*—is different from the question whether the First Amendment requires a school affirmatively to promote particular student speech . . .

. . . a school must be able to take into account the emotional maturity of the intended audience in determining whether to disseminate student speech on potentially sensitive topics, which might range from the existence of Santa Claus in an elementary school setting to the particulars of teenage sexual activity in a high school setting. A school must also retain the authority to refuse to sponsor student speech that might reasonably be perceived to advocate drug or alcohol use, irresponsible sex, or conduct otherwise inconsistent with "the shared values of a civilized social order." . . .

Accordingly, we conclude that the standard articulated in *Tinker* for determining when a school may punish student expression need not also be the standard for determining when a school may refuse to lend its name and resources to the dissemination of student expression. Instead, we hold that educators do not offend the First Amendment by exercising editorial control over the style and content of student speech in school-sponsored expressive activities so long as their actions are reasonably related to legitimate pedagogical concerns. . . .

In sum, we cannot reject as unreasonable Principal Reynolds' conclusion that neither the pregnancy article nor the divorce article was suitable for publication in Spectrum. Reynolds could reasonably have concluded that the students who had written and edited these articles had not sufficiently mastered those portions of the Journalism II curriculum that pertained to the treatment of controversial issues and personal attacks, the need to protect the privacy of individuals whose most intimate concerns are to be revealed in the newspaper, and "the legal, moral, and ethical restrictions imposed upon journalists within [a] school community" that includes adolescent subjects and readers. Finally, we conclude that the principal's decision to delete two pages of Spectrum, rather than to delete only the offending articles or to require that they be modified, was reasonable under the circumstances as he understood them. Accordingly, no violation of First Amendment rights occurred. . . .

*Reversed.*

*Source*: 484 U.S. 260 (1988).

---

## DOCUMENT 90: "The Wrong Lesson" (Tom Wicker, 1988)

Most journalists were convinced that the Supreme Court had erred in *Hazelwood*. The following editorial by Tom Wicker of the *New York Times* is representative of the media response.

\* \* \*

The Supreme Court, as Justice William J. Brennan Jr. wrote in dissent, taught "young men and women" the wrong civics lesson when it upheld the right of a principal to impose prior restraint on a student newspaper. So it did, and that damaging lesson may well be absorbed far beyond the corridors of high school.

Most specifically, the Court's 5-to-3 decision in the Hazelwood school case may now be invoked in efforts to limit freedom of expression in student publications, theatrical presentations and the like at state universities. Despite the differences in high schools and colleges, it's hard to see why the rationale of the decision—that public education officials may censor any activity "reasonably related to legitimate pedagogical concerns"—could not be cited by university administrators.

What, moreover, are "legitimate pedagogical concerns"? Justice Byron R. White's opinion for the majority went so far as to say that schools could legitimately censor expression that might "associate the school with any position other than neutrality on matters of public controversy." What kind of support is that for the supposedly American values of robust debate and the "marketplace" of ideas?

Besides, the Hazelwood principal did far more than dissociate his school from articles to which he objected in its student newspaper. He quashed the printing of two pages of the paper, effectively silencing speech—not just in the two articles to which he objected, but in four others on the pages. The Court found this action "not unreasonable," owing to the nature of his objections to the two articles, to the fact that the student publication, in the Court's view, was not a "public forum" and that its contents were a "legitimate pedagogical" matter over which the principal had jurisdiction.

In so finding, the Court nevertheless upheld a "prior restraint"—the prevention of publication of something someone finds offensive. In the Pentagon Papers case and others, prior restraints have been held unconstitutional except in the most exceptional cases. Now the Court not only holds that prior restraint may be imposed almost routinely on student publications; but it adds substance to the view that in some cases, for some forms of expression, prior restraint is constitutional after all.

A high school newspaper partially financed by the school board, and which is published as part of the curriculum, may not be technically, as Justice White insisted, a "public forum." But it may be the only forum the students have; if school officials can censor it, student rights of expression previously established by the Supreme Court have been limited. If student speech is not fully protected by the first Amendment, are there other classes of citizens who might be so limited?

The decision well may drive some students to "underground" publications—and to the logical conclusion that what schools teach about free speech is not what schools practice. Isn't *that* a legitimate pedagogical concern?

The Hazelwood principal's reasons for objecting to the articles in question seem reasonable—he thought one might violate some students' privacy and that the other was unfair to a person mentioned in it. But whatever his good intentions, he had open to him other remedies than prior restraint.

It's not even clear why he couldn't have insisted upon changes he thought necessary. Page proofs were shown to him on May 10; publication was not scheduled until May 13.

But if there really was no time for editing, the principal could have specified his objections and warned against future problems, he could have ordered a change in procedure to make sure he had adequate time to read page proofs and work out agreed-upon changes with the student editors. Perhaps a stronger, or a better understood, set of rules for publication could have been worked out to prevent future conflicts.

All of these possible courses of action, it will be objected, would have resulted in publication of the articles to which the principal objected. But some expressions will always be found offensive or unjustifiable or incorrect by some in the audience; and it is inherent in a free press that privacy will sometimes be violated, not always necessarily, and that some stories may be unfair.

If such excesses could be prevented by authority, the press, in the nature of the case, would not be free. The Hazelwood lesson is that some authorities can prevent some publications. As Justice Brennan observed, that's the wrong lesson.

*Source*: Tom Wicker, "The Wrong Lesson," *New York Times*, January 18, 1988, A19.

---

## DOCUMENT 91: "Freedom for All: Can Public Records Be Too Public?" (Chris Feola, 1996)

It seems fitting to conclude a part devoted to freedom of the press with some words from a magazine aimed at working members of the media. *Quill Magazine* is the publication of the Society for Professional Journalists, and just as quill pens have been displaced by computers in the nation's newsrooms, the subjects addressed in the publication reflect modern concerns of the working press. Debates about the place of the media in American political and social life have not abated during our nation's history. As quickly as the courts have clarified rules in one area, new issues have arisen. That is true of the subjects addressed in the following articles, and it will continue to be true so long as inventive minds create new modes of communication. The law governing communication will never be tidy, because the subject matter is the very fabric of social intercourse and the ongoing debate over our right as citizens to choose what we shall read, listen to, view, or download, free of the paternalistic or censorious interference of government.

\* \* \*

Ah, the Freedom of Information Act. The living law that ensures public records are open to the public. A veritable pillar of our democracy.

Who can forget the never-ending battles to open records? The multi-faceted fight of The New York Times to publish the Pentagon Papers; the seemingly endless effort to get cameras in courtrooms; Aaron Nabil spending $222 for the Oregon Department of Motor Vehicles database, which he posted on the World Wide Web; the White House records. . . .

Sorry, what was that? Go back one? Who the hell is Aaron Nabil, and how dare he post Oregon's driver records where just anyone can look at them?

Quickie quiz: When you think public records, do you mean the public actually should have access to them? Or do you mean that journalists should have access and decide what the public sees?

Can public records be too public?

Would the news media then be an unelected, self-appointed arm of government?

Think of this: After all the *sturm und drang* erupted over the posting of the DMV records, Nabil posted a list of others who had purchased access to the list. Surprise! All the newspapers and televisions stations had access.

So is it our position that the public has a right to public records only after they've been cleared through us?

Theoretically, everyone has had access to public records. In practice, though, we've most aware of access by journalists, lawyers, and those of similar ilk—who else spends all day hanging out at Town Hall poring through paper records?

Now computers threaten to turn theory into practice. Oh sure, we could stuff the genie back into the bottle, as far as the groundlings are concerned. But here's a flash. Privacy is an illusion in the Age of Information. The big data-mining companies don't need DMV records to obtain your driver's license information. They already have it. If you've ever filled out a hotel registration slip, loan application or been subjected to a credit evaluation—which happens to you hundreds of times a year without you knowing—or applied for a mortgage . . . you get the picture.

The question is who will have access to the information, not whether it will be available.

Like it or not, the United States increasingly is dividing into a country of information haves and have-nots. This always has been true to a certain extent. But for most of this century, it mattered less. In 1960, high school dropouts earned just less than half the salary of a college graduate. By 1987, high-school dropouts found their college-educated friends earning three times their salaries. The trend is accelerating.

Time was you could graduate from high school, get a job at the local factory pushing a broom, become an apprentice, and retire 40 years later as a master machinist.

No more. Today's master machinists are using Computer-Assisted Design/Computer-Assisted Manufacturing equipment.

What does any of this have to do with freedom of information?

Everything and nothing. It is not an issue of legal access. It is a question of right, and wrong, and where journalism and journalists will stand.

Will it be with the politicians and bureaucrats, the lawyers and conglomerates? Or will it be with those who have no voice because their pocketbook won't stretch far enough to allow them to join fully the Information Age?

There was a time when journalism defined itself with the notion of comforting the afflicted and afflicting the comfortable. Now, much of journalism has become comfortable.

Besides the philosophical question, there is a practical one. Is there a role in the Information Age for journalists if those with the financial resources to be conversant in Information Age technology have the same access as journalists?

So, are we at risk on two flanks? On one side, losing commitment and purpose, on the other, becoming unnecessary.

All is not despair. Before the Freedom of Information Act, journalism existed because journalists were willing to take risks—sometimes even with their lives—to report the truth, a truth unvarnished by the likes of Dick Morris.

Times of peril also are times of opportunity. A few decades ago, anyone with a small printing press could be a publisher. Then came metros and Goss Metroliners and fleets of trucks and capital costs and chain ownership.

Computers have changed that. A determined person with a PC can now do what once took legions of printers or, if print isn't the vehicle of choice, give birth to a new publication on the Net.

Obviously, you say, new laws are needed for this new age.

Let us say for the sake of the argument that we as a society decide everyone and their brother should not have access to those Oregon drivers records.

So what?

Even if it is illegal in the United States, there is nothing to prevent some Gibsonesque nightmare where illegal records are held in offshore data havens for sale to the highest bidder. What do national boundaries and the laws they contain matter on the Net?

The Net will change society in ways we can't fathom yet. Alexander Graham Bell might have envisioned international phone calls. But it's doubtful he imagined 800 numbers, cell phones, fax machines, and voice mail—any way we can put that genie back?—caller ID, and digital data transmission.

The Net already is changing access to records public and private—whether we like it or not. Better that we think it through now than deal with some future fait accompli.

Back to the question: Where will journalism and journalists stand?

*Source*: Chris Feola, "Freedom for All: Can Public Records Be Too Public?" *Quill Magazine* 84, no. 8 (October 1996): 77.

---

## DOCUMENT 92: "Public Information Is a Public Issue" (Maggie Balough, 1996)

What exactly does freedom of information mean? Not enough people realize how different their lives would be if President Johnson had let July 4, 1966 pass without his signature.

That's the problem, and that's why this issue of *Quill* is devoted to information and access issues.

Thirty years ago, a few members of Congress joined forces with the news media to hammer home a piece of legislation that at least began the process of giving citizens the rights to acquire information about the operation of the federal government.

Freedom of information efforts in the states put news media and citizens groups together to work for legislation that set ground rules for the public's business.

The news media led the way in requesting information and prepared for the public stories that detailed what government records showed—or failed to show. When the spotlight was shone on decisions that the public questioned, reform legislation or budgetary changes frequently followed.

Watchdogs realized they had a new tool to use in the check-and-balance system of government. Citizen groups with special interests—environmental, health, safety and others—began requesting information as did business and commerce, realizing that data in government records could enhance their positions.

President Johnson noted: "This legislation springs from one of our most essential principles: a democracy works best when the people have all the information that the security of the nation permits. No one should be able to pull curtains of secrecy around decisions which can be revealed without injury to the public interest."

For most of 25 years, the processes of opening records rocked along, sometimes forward, sometimes backward, always searching to put definition to public interest. Successes were incremental, failures weren't fatal.

About five years ago, the equation changed.

Access to information came to mean access to money in an era when information is the commodity of trade. Uncle Sam gathers much data that big business now wants to buy, reprocess and sell. The problem is that the potential consumer for this information is the same citizenry that already has footed the bill—as taxpayers.

Privacy concerns have moved front and center as some citizens feel violated. Social Security numbers, debts and medical records have come into the public arena as the fodder of databases.

Journalists are on the point, fighting for the public's right to know, a right some of the public isn't sure it wants. And, in the world of politics and strange bedfellows, communications companies frequently are joined by—or are—the folks with visions of dollar signs in their heads.

What should journalists do?

First, educate ourselves about information access and privacy issues. Information is our stock in trade. Too few of us understand and use the laws. All too often journalists accept a refusal for information without questioning the legality of that decision. Information won't be free unless we make it so.

Second, be pragmatic and mindful of what interests the public. Our agendas and the public's aren't always in sync. Give the public information about issues of concern. Remind the public this information was available because of laws that ensure access to government information.

Journalists, in the rush to prove points of principle, sometimes forget points of practicality. The public doesn't. Journalists too are custodians of public trust and public interest.

Third, make sure we understand how the information is used after it is made available. This is thorny. When we free information, we free information. The news media may use that information responsibly. Others may not. What the public remembers is the latter.

The challenge for journalists is to help the public understand that freedom of information is like freedom of speech. It is a right given to all. We must make the point that the solution is not to close the information, but to pressure those who abuse the system until they stop.

This country is just around the corner from complete information access at our fingertips. We must ensure that when we perfect the technology, the information is there.

Freedom of information is not just the news media's issue. But, it's up to us to make sure the public understands.

*Source*: Maggie Balough, "Public Information Is a Public Issue," *Quill Magazine* 84, no. 8 (October 1996): 3.

# Part VII

# The Right to Assemble and Petition: Haranguing, Picketing, and Public Order

The final part of this documentary history considers the special problems presented by First Amendment expressive activities that, by their very nature, intrude on others. That intrusion may be great or minimal, but it virtually guarantees that the exercise of these rights will be contentious. Rallies, pickets, marches, and the like are too visible to be ignored; that is one reason why they are deemed valuable by those who wish to force an issue into the public consciousness.

The title of this part is misleading in one respect: cases included in Parts III, IV, and V demonstrate that not every exercise of the right to assemble is public and intrusive, nor are petitions to one's government always delivered with the fanfare of a march or other public display. The documents in this part are concerned only with those instances where a legitimate concern for public order is implicated. The central issue in such cases is whether government can ever use those concerns as a justification for suppression of the speech involved—allowing what has been aptly called "the heckler's veto" of otherwise protected speech.

## DOCUMENT 93: Alabama Statute on Loitering and Picketing (1923)

As recently as 1940, when *Thornhill v. Alabama* (see Document 94) reached the Supreme Court, several states had statutes outlawing peaceful picketing. Most such statutes, like the statute considered in *Thornhill v. Alabama*, equated picketing with "loitering," an all-purpose term infamous for its adaptability. (Loitering, being largely in the eye of the beholder, is a handy charge for police to use when they want to arrest people who have apparently not been considerate enough to violate any other laws.) The Supreme Court found the Alabama statute void on its face.

\* \* \*

**Section 3448.** Loitering or picketing forbidden.—Any person or persons, who, without a just cause or legal excuse therefore, go near to or loiter about the premises or place of business of any other person, firm, corporation, or association of people, engaged in a lawful business, for the purpose, or with the intent of influencing, or inducing other persons not to trade with, buy from, sell to, have business dealings with, or be employed by such persons, firm, corporation, or association, or who picket the works or place of business of such other persons, firms, corporations, or associations of persons, for the purpose of hindering, delaying, or interfering with or injuring any lawful business or enterprise of another, shall be guilty of a misdemeanor; but nothing herein shall prevent any person from soliciting trade or business for a competitive business.

*Source*: §3448 of the Alabama State Code of 1923.

## DOCUMENT 94: *Thornhill v. Alabama* (1940)

Byron Thornhill was convicted of violating Alabama's Statute on Loitering and Picketing by engaging in the peaceful picketing of a business in the course of a labor dispute. The Supreme Court paid little attention to the facts of the underlying dispute, finding the statute constitutionally defective on its face. Alabama argued that Thornhill could express his opinions freely elsewhere, and that the statute simply removed the street as a venue for his expression. In response, the Court declared public streets a "natural and proper" forum for the expression of opinions, and ruled that government cannot excuse improper restrictions on speech by arguing that other venues are available to the speaker.

\* \* \*

Mr. Justice Murphy delivered the opinion of the Court.
Petitioner, Byron Thornhill, was convicted in the Circuit Court of Tus-

caloosa County, Alabama, of the violation of § 3448 of the State Code of 1923.

... the charge is that petitioner "did picket" the works of the Company "for the purpose of hindering, delaying or interfering with or injuring [its] lawful business." Petitioner demurred to the complaint on the grounds, among others, that § 3448 was repugnant to the Constitution of the United States in that it deprived him of "the right of peaceful assemblage[.]" ...

... Those who won our independence had confidence in the power of free and fearless reasoning and communication of ideas to discover and spread political and economic truth. Noxious doctrines in those fields may be refuted and their evil averted by the courageous exercise of the right of free discussion. Abridgment of freedom of speech and of the press, however, impairs those opportunities for public education that are essential to effective exercise of the power of correcting error through the processes of popular government. ... Mere legislative preference for one rather than another means for combating substantive evils, therefore, may well prove an inadequate foundation on which to rest regulations which are aimed at or in their operation diminish the effective exercise of rights so necessary to the maintenance of democratic institutions. It is imperative that, when the effective exercise of these rights is claimed to be abridged, the courts should "weigh the circumstances" and "appraise the substantiality of the reasons advanced" in support of the challenged regulations. ...

... The power of the licensor against which John Milton directed his assault by his "Appeal for the Liberty of Unlicensed Printing" is pernicious not merely by reason of the censure of particular comments but by reason of the threat to censure comments on matters of public concern. It is not merely the sporadic abuse of power by the censor but the pervasive threat inherent in its very existence that constitutes the danger to freedom of discussion. ... The existence of such a statute, which readily lends itself to harsh and discriminatory enforcement by local prosecuting officials, against particular groups deemed to merit their displeasure, results in a continuous and pervasive restraint on all freedom of discussion that might reasonably be regarded as within its purview. It is not any less effective or, if the restraint is not permissible, less pernicious than the restraint on freedom of discussion imposed by the threat of censorship. ...

*Third.* Section 3448 has been applied by the state courts so as to prohibit a single individual from walking slowly and peacefully back and forth on the public sidewalk in front of the premises of an employer, without speaking to anyone, carrying a sign or placard on a staff above his head stating only the fact that the employer did not employ union men affiliated with the American Federation of Labor; the purpose of the described activity was concededly to advise customers and prospective customers of the relationship existing between the employer and its employees and thereby to induce such customers not to patronize the employer. . . . The statute as thus authoritatively construed and applied leaves room for no exceptions based upon either the number of persons engaged in the proscribed activity, the peaceful character of their demeanor, the nature of their dispute with an employer, or the restrained character and the accurateness of the terminology used in notifying the public of the facts of the dispute. . . .

. . . In sum, whatever the means used to publicize the facts of a labor dispute, whether by printed sign, by pamphlet, by word of mouth or otherwise, all such activity without exception is within the inclusive prohibition of the statute so long as it occurs in the vicinity of the scene of the dispute.

*Fourth.* We think that § 3448 is invalid on its face. . . .

. . . "[The] streets are natural and proper places for the dissemination of information and opinion; and one is not to have the exercise of his liberty of expression in appropriate places abridged on the plea that it may be exercised in some other place." . . .

*Reversed.*

Source: 310 U.S. 88 (1940).

## DOCUMENT 95: *Marsh v. Alabama* (1946)

*Marsh v. Alabama*, decided in 1946, is a deceptively simple case. It addresses the question whether a state may allow a "company town" to restrict the distribution of literature on its streets in a manner that would be patently unconstitutional if the town were a conventional political subdivision of the state. A "company town" is one where a local business, rather than the taxpayers, erects, maintains, and regulates the use of the town's buildings, streets, and sidewalks.

The Supreme Court noted that only the ownership of the land differentiated the town from others; no "gates" limited access, and travelers and other business and residential visitors made use of the facilities just as they would anywhere else. Reasoning that the right to disseminate and receive information was of even more importance in a community "owned" by one company, the Court held that the restrictions violated the First Amendment.

With the gradual disappearance of "company towns" it might seem that *Marsh* is of limited relevance today, but the reasoning of the case has been applied to literature distribution in shopping malls, which are their modern equivalent. Like "company towns," today's malls are usually under a single ownership; they even function like town centers in many communities. The reasoning in *Marsh* is thus aptly applied when such malls attempt to restrict pamphlet distribution, leafleting, and similar expressive activities.

\* \* \*

MR. JUSTICE BLACK delivered the opinion of the Court.

In this case we are asked to decide whether a State, consistently with the First and Fourteenth Amendments, can impose criminal punishment on a person who undertakes to distribute religious literature on the premises of a company-owned town contrary to the wishes of the town's management. . . .

In short the town and its shopping district are accessible to and freely used by the public in general and there is nothing to distinguish them from any other town and shopping center except the fact that the title to the property belongs to a private corporation.

Appellant, a Jehovah's Witness, came onto the sidewalk we have just described, stood near the post office and undertook to distribute religious literature. In the stores the corporation had posted a notice which read as follows: "This Is Private Property, and Without Written Permission, No Street, or House Vendor, Agent or Solicitation of Any Kind Will Be Permitted." Appellant was warned that she could not distribute the literature without a permit and told that no permit would be issued to her. She protested that the company rule could not be constitutionally applied so as to prohibit her from distributing religious writings. When she was asked to leave the sidewalk and Chickasaw she declined. . . .

Had the title to Chickasaw belonged not to a private but to a municipal corporation and had appellant been arrested for violating a municipal ordinance rather than a ruling by those appointed by the corporation to manage a company town it would have been clear that appellant's conviction must be reversed. Under our decision in *Lovell* v. *Griffin*, and others which have followed that case, neither a State nor a municipality can completely bar the distribution of literature containing religious or political ideas on its streets, sidewalks and public places or make the right to distribute dependent on a flat license tax or permit to be issued by an official who could deny it at will. We have also held that an ordinance completely prohibiting the dissemination of ideas on the city streets cannot be justified on the ground that the municipality holds legal title to them. And we have recognized that the preservation of a free society is so far dependent upon the right of each individual citizen to receive such literature as he himself might desire that a municipality could not, without jeopardizing that vital individual freedom, prohibit door to door distribution of literature. From these decisions it is clear that had the people of Chickasaw owned all the homes, and all the stores, and all the streets, and all the sidewalks, all those owners together could not have set up a municipal government with sufficient power to pass an ordinance completely barring the distribution of religious literature. Our question then narrows down to this: Can those people who live in or come to Chickasaw be denied freedom of press and religion simply because a single company had legal title to all the town? For it is the State's contention that the mere fact that all the property interests in the town are held by a single company is enough to give that company power, enforceable by a state statute, to abridge these freedoms. . . .

We do not think it makes any significant constitutional difference as to the relationship between the rights of the owner and those of the public that here the State, instead of permitting the corporation to operate a highway, permitted it to use its property as a town, operate a "business block" in the town and a street and sidewalk on that business block. Whether a corporation or a municipality owns or possesses the town the public in either case has an identical interest in the functioning of the community in such manner that the channels of communication remain free. As we have heretofore stated, the town of Chickasaw does not function differently from any other town. The "business block" serves as the community shopping center and is freely accessible and open to the people in the area and those passing through. The managers appointed by the corporation cannot curtail the liberty of press and religion of these people consistently with the purposes of the Constitutional guarantees, and a state statute, as the one here involved, which enforces such action by criminally punishing those who attempt to distribute religious literature clearly violates the First and Fourteenth Amendments to the Constitution.

Many people in the United States live in company-owned towns. These people, just as residents of municipalities, are free citizens of their State and country. Just as all other citizens they must make decisions which affect the welfare of community and nation. To act as good citizens they must be informed. In order to enable them to be properly informed their information must be uncensored. There is no more reason for depriving these people of the liberties guaranteed by the First and Fourteenth Amendments than there is for curtailing these freedoms with respect to any other citizen.

*Reversed and remanded.*

*Source*: 326 U.S. 501 (1946).

---

## DOCUMENT 96: Arthur Terminiello's Speech (1949)

Chicago, Illinois, had an ordinance that forbade any "breach of the peace" that "stirs the public to anger, invites dispute, brings about a condition of unrest, or creates a disturbance." Arthur Terminiello was charged and convicted under the ordinance for making a speech at a rally called by an organization named the Christian Veterans of America. The Supreme Court noted that the speech contained vicious criticisms of political and racial groups and was attended by large and noisy crowds both within and outside the auditorium. There were disturbances among the crowd members. The following is excerpted from Justice Jackson's dissent to *Terminiello v. City of Chicago*, in which some "relatively innocuous passages" were deleted. The Justice added italics for emphasis, which we have not reproduced here.

\* \* \*

Now, I am going to whisper my greetings to you, Fellow Christians. I will interpret it. I said, "Fellow Christians," and I suppose there are some of the scum got in by mistake, so I want to tell a story about the scum:

... And nothing I could say tonight could begin to express the contempt I have for the slimy scum that got in by mistake.

... The subject I want to talk to you tonight about is the attempt that is going on right outside this hall tonight, the attempt that is going on to destroy America by revolution. ...

My friends, it is no longer true that it can't happen here. It is happening here, and it only depends upon you, good people, who are here tonight, depends upon all of us together, as Mr. Smith said. The tide is changing, and if you and I turn and run from that tide, we will all be drowned in this tidal wave of Communism which is going over the world.

... I am not going to talk to you about the menace of Communism, which is already accomplished, in Russia, where from eight to fifteen million people were murdered in cold blood by their own country men, and millions more through Eastern Europe at the close of the war are being murdered by these murderous Russians, hurt, being raped and sent into slavery. That is what they want for you, that howling mob outside.

I know I was told one time that my winter quarters were ready for me in Siberia. I was told that. Now, I am talking about the fifty-seven varieties that we have in America, and we have fifty-seven varieties of pinks and reds and pastel shades in this country; and all of it can be traced back to the twelve years we spent under the New Deal, because that was the build-up for what is going on in the world today. ...

Now, Russia promised us we would ga [*sic*] back to the official newspaper of Russia. Primarily, it was back about 1929. They quoted the words of George E. Dimitroff, who at that time was the Executive Secretary of the Communist International. I only quote you this one passage.

I could quote thousands of paragraphs for you. Let me quote you: "The worldwide nature of our program is not mere talk, but an all embracing blood-soaked reality." That is what they want for us, a blood-soaked reality but it was promised to us by the crystal gazers in Washington; and you know what I mean by the "crystal gazers," I presume.

First of all, we had Queen Eleanor. Mr. Smith said, "Queen Eleanor is now one of the world's communists. She is one who said this—imagine, coming from the spouse of the former President of the United States for twelve long years—this is what she said: "The war is but a step in the revolution. The war is but one step in the revolution, and we know who started the war."

Then we have Henry Adolph Wallace, the sixty million job magician. You know we only need fifty-four million jobs in America and everybody would be working. He wants sixty million jobs, because some of the bureaucrats want two jobs apiece. Here he is, what he says about revolution: "We are in for a profound revolution. Those of us who realize the inevitableness of the revolution, and are anxious that it be gradual and bloodless instead of somewhat bloody. Of course, if necessary, we will have it more bloody."

And then Chief Justice Stone had this to say: "A way has been found for the effective suppression of speeches and press and religion, despite constitutional guarantee,"—from the Chief Justice, from the Chief Justice of the United States.

Now, my friends, they are planning another ruse; and if it ever happens to this cou-try [sic], God help America. They are going to try to put into Mr. Edgar Hoover's position a man by the name of George Swarzwald. I think even those who were uneducated on so-called sedition charges, that the majority of the individuals in this department, that Christ-like men and women who realize today what is going on in this country, men who are in this audience today, who want to know the names of those people, before they are outside, they want to know the names if any. Did you hear any tonight that you recognize? Most of them probably are imported. They are imported from Russia, certainly. If you know the names, please send them to me immediately. . . .

. . . Didn't you ever read the Morgenthau plan for the starvation of little babies and pregnant women in Germany? Whatever could a child that is born have to do with Hitler or anyone else at the beginning of the war? Why should every child in Germany today not live to be more than two or three months of age? . . .

*Source: Terminiello v. Chicago, 337 U.S. 1 (1949).*

---

## DOCUMENT 97: *Terminiello v. Chicago* (1949)

Justice William D. Douglas, writing in the majority opinion in *Terminiello v. Chicago* that the Chicago ordinance could not stand, held that one purpose of speech in a free country is to invite dispute, and that any attempt by government to curtail speech on the grounds that it upsets people must fail. While it is not apparent from the text of the majority opinion, contemporaneous documents suggest that Terminiello was engaged in racist and anti-Semitic rhetoric; it is thus an irony worth noting that his victory in this case would later be successfully invoked to protect the rights of black civil rights activists.

\* \* \*

MR. JUSTICE DOUGLAS delivered the opinion of the Court.

Petitioner after jury trial was found guilty of disorderly conduct in violation of a city ordinance of Chicago and fined. The case grew out of an address he delivered in an auditorium in Chicago under the auspices of the Christian Veterans of America. The meeting commanded considerable public attention. The auditorium was filled to capacity with over eight hundred persons present. Others were turned away. Outside of the auditorium a crowd of about one thousand persons gathered to protest against the meeting. A cordon of policemen was assigned to the meeting to maintain order; but they were not able to prevent several disturbances. The crowd outside was angry and turbulent.

Petitioner in his speech condemned the conduct of the crowd outside and vigorously, if not viciously, criticized various political and racial groups whose activities he denounced as inimical to the nation's welfare.

The trial court charged that "breach of the peace" consists of any "misbehavior which violates the public peace and decorum"; and that the "misbehavior may constitute a breach of the peace if it stirs the public to anger, invites dispute, brings about a condition of unrest, or creates a disturbance, or if it molests the inhabitants in the enjoyment of peace and quiet by arousing alarm." . . .

The argument here has been focused on the issue of whether the content of petitioner's speech was composed of derisive, fighting words, which carried it outside the scope of the constitutional guarantees. . . . We do not reach that question, for there is a preliminary question that is dispositive of the case. . . .

. . . a function of free speech under our system of government is to invite dispute. It may indeed best serve its high purpose when it induces a condition of unrest, creates dissatisfaction with conditions as they are, or even stirs people to anger. Speech is often provocative and challenging. It may strike at prejudices and preconceptions and have profound unsettling effects as it presses for acceptance of an idea. That is why freedom of speech, though not absolute, . . . is nevertheless protected against censorship or punishment, unless shown likely to produce a clear and present danger of a serious substantive evil that rises far above public inconvenience, annoyance, or unrest. . . . There is no room under our

Constitution for a more restrictive view. For the alternative would lead to standardization of ideas either by legislatures, courts, or dominant political or community groups.

The ordinance as construed by the trial court seriously invaded this province. It permitted conviction of petitioner if his speech stirred people to anger, invited public dispute, or brought about a condition of unrest. A conviction resting on any of those grounds may not stand. . . .

*Reversed.*

*Source*: 337 U.S. 1 (1949).

---

## DOCUMENT 98: *Feiner v. New York* (1951)

Barely two years after *Terminiello*, the Supreme Court handed down its decision in *Feiner v. New York*, in which it reached almost precisely the opposite conclusion. In *Feiner*, Chief Justice Fred M. Vinson, writing for the majority, upheld the actions of police officers who arrested Irving Feiner for "inciting." The majority opinion was characterized by unquestioning acceptance of the prosecution's version of the underlying facts, although an ordinary citizen would find at least some of the assertions very difficult to square with common sense and experience. Justice Hugo Black authored a stinging and eloquent dissent, emphasizing that the duty of the police in the event of a genuine disturbance was to protect the speaker from the crowd, not the crowd from the speaker.

* * *

MR. CHIEF JUSTICE VINSON delivered the opinion of the Court.

Petitioner was convicted of the offense of disorderly conduct, a misdemeanor under the New York penal laws, in the Court of Special Sessions of the City of Syracuse and was sentenced to thirty days in the county penitentiary. The conviction was affirmed by the Onondaga County Court and the New York Court of Appeals. . . .

On the evening of March 8, 1949, petitioner Irving Feiner was addressing an open-air meeting at the corner of South McBride and Harrison Streets in the City of Syracuse. At approximately 6:30 p.m., the police received a telephone complaint concerning the meeting, and two officers were detailed to investigate. One of these officers went to the scene immediately, the other arriving some twelve minutes later. They found a crowd of about seventy-five or eighty people, both Negro and white, filling the sidewalk and spreading out into the street. Petitioner, standing on a large wooden box on the sidewalk, was addressing the crowd through a loud-speaker system attached to an automobile. Although the purpose of his speech was to urge his listeners to attend a meeting to be held that night in the Syracuse Hotel, in its course he was making derogatory remarks concerning President Truman, the American Legion, the Mayor of Syracuse, and other local political officials.

The police officers made no effort to interfere with petitioner's speech, but were first concerned with the effect of the crowd on both pedestrian and vehicular traffic. They observed the situation from the opposite side of the street, noting that some pedestrians were forced to walk in the street to avoid the crowd. Since traffic was passing at the time, the officers attempted to get the people listening to petitioner back on the sidewalk. The crowd was restless and there was some pushing, shoving and milling around. One of the officers telephoned the police station from a nearby store, and then both policemen crossed the street and mingled with the crowd without any intention of arresting the speaker.

At this time, petitioner was speaking in a "loud, high-pitched voice." He gave the impression that he was endeavoring to arouse the Negro people against the whites, urging that they rise up in arms and fight for equal rights. The statements before such a mixed audience "stirred up a little excitement." Some of the onlookers made remarks to the police about their inability to handle the crowd and at least one threatened violence if the police did not act. There were others who appeared to be favoring petitioner's arguments. Because of the feeling that existed in the crowd both for and against the speaker, the officers finally "stepped in to prevent it from resulting in a fight." One of the officers approached the petitioner, not for the purpose of arresting him, but to get him to break up the crowd. He asked petitioner to get down off the box, but the latter refused to accede to his request and continued talking. The officer waited for a minute and then demanded that he cease talking. Although the officer had thus twice requested petitioner to stop over the course of several minutes, petitioner not only ignored him but continued talking. During all this time, the crowd was pressing closer around petitioner and the officer. Finally, the officer told petitioner he was under arrest and ordered him to get down from the box, reaching up to grab him. Petitioner stepped down, announcing over the microphone that "the law has arrived, and I suppose they will take over now." In all, the officer had asked petitioner to get down off the box three times over a space of four or five minutes. Petitioner had been speaking for over a half hour. . . .

We are not faced here with blind condonation by a state court of arbitrary police action. Petitioner was accorded a full, fair trial. The trial judge heard testimony supporting and contradicting the judgment of the police officers that a clear danger of disorder was threatened. After weighing this contradictory evidence, the trial judge reached the conclusion that the police officers were justified in taking action to prevent a breach of the peace.... Petitioner was thus neither arrested nor convicted for the making or the content of his speech. Rather, it was the reaction which it actually engendered....

We are well aware that the ordinary murmurings and objections of a hostile audience cannot be allowed to silence a speaker, and are also mindful of the possible danger of giving overzealous police officials complete discretion to break up otherwise lawful public meetings. "A State may not unduly suppress free communication of views, religious or other, under the guise of conserving desirable conditions." ... But we are not faced here with such a situation. It is one thing to say that the police cannot be used as an instrument for the suppression of unpopular views, and another to say that, when as here the speaker passes the bounds of argument or persuasion and undertakes incitement to riot, they are powerless to prevent a breach of the peace. Nor in this case can we condemn the considered judgment of three New York courts approving the means which the police, faced with a crisis, used in the exercise of their power and duty to preserve peace and order. The findings of the state courts as to the existing situation and the imminence of greater disorder coupled with petitioner's deliberate defiance of the police officers convince us that we should not reverse this conviction in the name of free speech.

*Affirmed.*

\* \* \*

MR. JUSTICE BLACK, dissenting.

The record before us convinces me that petitioner, a young college student, has been sentenced to the penitentiary for the unpopular views he expressed on matters of public interest while lawfully making a street-corner speech in Syracuse, New York. Today's decision, however, indicates that we must blind ourselves to this fact because the trial judge fully accepted the testimony of the prosecution witnesses on all important points. Many times in the past this Court has said that despite findings below, we will examine the evidence for ourselves to ascertain whether federally protected rights have been denied; otherwise review here would fail of its purpose in safeguarding constitutional guarantees. Even a partial abandonment of this rule marks a dark day for civil liberties in our Nation.

But still more has been lost today. Even accepting every "finding of fact" below, I think this conviction makes a mockery of the free speech guarantees of the First and Fourteenth Amendments. The end result of the affirmance here is to approve a simple and readily available technique by which cities and states can with impunity subject all speeches, political or otherwise, on streets or elsewhere, to the supervision and censorship of the local police. I will have no part or parcel in this holding which I view as a long step toward totalitarian authority.

Considering only the evidence which the state courts appear to have accepted, the pertinent "facts" are: Syracuse city authorities granted a permit for O. John Rogge, a former Assistant Attorney General, to speak in a public school building on March 8, 1948 on the subject of racial discrimination and civil liberties. On March 8th, however, the authorities canceled the permit. The Young Progressives under whose auspices the meeting was scheduled then arranged for Mr. Rogge to speak at the Hotel Syracuse. The gathering on the street where petitioner spoke was held to protest the cancellation and to publicize the meeting at the hotel. In this connection, petitioner used derogatory but not profane language with reference to the city authorities, President Truman and the American Legion. After hearing some of these remarks, a policeman, who had been sent to the meeting by his superiors, reported to Police Headquarters by telephone. To whom he reported or what was said does not appear in the record, but after returning from the call, he and another policeman started through the crowd toward petitioner. Both officers swore they did not intend to make an arrest when they started, and the trial court accepted their statements. They also said, and the court believed, that they heard and saw "angry mutterings," "pushing," "shoving and milling around" and "restlessness." Petitioner spoke in a "loud, high pitched voice." He said that colored people "don't have equal rights and they should rise up *in arms* and fight for them." One man who heard this told the officers that if they did not take that "S . . . O . . . B . . ." off the box, he would. The officers then approached petitioner for the first time. One of them first "asked" petitioner to get off the box, but petitioner continued urging his audience to attend Rogge's speech. The officer next "told" petitioner to get down, but he did not. The officer finally "demanded" that petitioner get down, telling him he was under arrest. Petitioner then told the crowd that "the law had arrived and would take over" and asked why he was arrested. The officer first replied that the charge was "unlawful assembly" but later changed the ground to "disorderly conduct."

The Court's opinion apparently rests on this reasoning: The policeman, under the circumstances detailed, could reasonably conclude that serious fighting or even riot was imminent; therefore he could stop petitioner's speech to prevent a breach of peace; accordingly, it was "disorderly conduct" for petitioner to continue speaking in disobedience of the officer's request. As to the existence of a dangerous situation on the street corner, it seems far-fetched to suggest that the "facts" show any imminent threat of riot or uncontrollable disorder. It is neither unusual nor unexpected that some people at public street meetings mutter, mill about, push, shove, or disagree, even violently, with the speaker. Indeed, it is rare where controversial topics are discussed that an outdoor crowd does not do some or all of these things. Nor does one isolated threat to assault the speaker forebode disorder. Especially should the danger be discounted where, as here, the person threatening was a man whose wife and two small children accompanied him and who, so far as the record shows, was never close enough to petitioner to carry out the threat.

Moreover, assuming that the "facts" did indicate a critical situation, I reject the implication of the Court's opinion that the police had no obligation to protect petitioner's constitutional right to talk. The police of course have power to prevent breaches of the peace. But if, in the name of preserving order, they ever can interfere with a lawful public speaker, they first must make all reasonable efforts to protect him. Here the policemen did not even pretend to try to protect petitioner. According to the officers' testimony, the crowd was restless but there is no showing of any attempt to quiet it; pedestrians were forced to walk into the street, but there was no effort to clear a path on the sidewalk; one person threatened to assault petitioner but the officers did nothing to discourage this when even a word might have sufficed. Their duty was to protect petitioner's right to talk, even to the extent of arresting the man who threatened to interfere. Instead, they shirked that duty and acted only to suppress the right to speak.

Finally, I cannot agree with the Court's statement that petitioner's disregard of the policeman's unexplained request amounted to such "deliberate defiance" as would justify an arrest or conviction for disorderly conduct. On the contrary, I think that the policeman's action was a "deliberate defiance" of ordinary official duty as well as of the constitutional right of free speech. For at least where time allows, courtesy and explanation of commands are basic elements of good official conduct in a democratic society. Here petitioner was "asked" then "told" then "commanded" to stop speaking, but a man making a lawful address is certainly not required to be silent merely because an officer directs it. Petitioner was entitled to know why he should cease doing a lawful act. Not once was he told. I understand that people in authoritarian countries must obey arbitrary orders. I had hoped that there was no such duty in the United States.

In my judgment, today's holding means that as a practical matter, minority speakers can be silenced in any city. Hereafter, despite the First and Fourteenth Amendments, the policeman's club can take heavy toll of a current administration's public critics. Criticism of public officials will be too dangerous for all but the most courageous. This is true regardless of the fact that in two other cases decided this day, . . . a majority, in obedience to past decisions of this Court, provides a theoretical safeguard for freedom of speech. For whatever is thought to be guaranteed in *Kunz* and *Niemotko* is taken away by what is done here. The three cases read together mean that while previous restraints probably cannot be imposed on an unpopular speaker, the police have discretion to silence him as soon as the customary hostility to his views develops.

In this case I would reverse the conviction, thereby adhering to the great principles of the First and Fourteenth Amendments as announced for this Court in 1940 by Mr. Justice Roberts:

"In the realm of religious faith, and in that of political belief, sharp differences arise. In both fields the tenets of one man may seem the rankest error to his neighbor. To persuade others to his own point of view, the pleader, as we know, at times, resorts to exaggeration, to vilification of men who have been, or are, prominent in church or state, and even to false statement. But the people of this nation have ordained in the light of history, that, in spite of the probability of excesses and abuses, these liberties are, in the long view, essential to enlightened opinion and right conduct on the part of the citizens of a democracy." . . .

I regret my inability to persuade the Court not to retreat from this principle.

*Source*: 340 U.S. 315 (1951).

---

## DOCUMENT 99: *Edwards v. South Carolina* (1963)

It was during the civil rights movement in the American South that the Supreme Court was faced most directly with the issue of public demonstrations and the various devices used by government officials to deny First Amendment freedoms to those who were "agitating" for rights those officials did not wish to grant. The two cases that follow, *Edwards v. South Carolina* and *Cox v. Louisiana*, may seem unbelievable to students in the 1990s; the legal "theories" advanced to keep black citizens from expressing their positions seem ludicrous to us today. But the civil rights movement did not seem so inevitable to those living in the 1960s and especially not to those living in states with long histories of segregation and disparate treatment. Faced with clear evidence of excesses by local governments, the Supreme Court persistently applied the reasoning and rule of *Terminiello* and "distinguished or ignored" *Feiner* to reach a result consistent with common sense, morality, and the Bill of Rights. It is impossible to read these cases without appreciating anew the dignity and courage of those who took to the streets and lunch counters to demand equal treatment and the protection of the First Amendment.

\* \* \*

MR. JUSTICE STEWART delivered the opinion of the Court.

The petitioners, 187 in number, were convicted in a magistrate's court in Columbia, South Carolina, of the common-law crime of breach of the peace. . . .

There was no substantial conflict in the trial evidence. Late in the morning of March 2, 1961, the petitioners, high school and college students of the Negro race, met at the Zion Baptist Church in Columbia. From there, at about noon, they walked in separate groups of about 15 to the South Carolina State House grounds, an area of two city blocks open to the general public. Their purpose was "to submit a protest to the citizens of South Carolina, along with the Legislative Bodies of South Carolina, our feelings and our dissatisfaction with the present condition of discriminatory actions against Negroes, in general, and to let them know that we were dissatisfied and that we would like for the laws which prohibited Negro privileges in this State to be removed."

Already on the State House grounds when the petitioners arrived were 30 or more law enforcement officers, who had advance knowledge that the petitioners were coming. Each group of petitioners entered the grounds through a driveway and parking area known in the record as the "horseshoe." As they entered, they were told by the law enforcement officials that "they had a right, as a citizen, to go through the State House grounds, as any other citizen has, as long as they were peaceful." During the next half hour or 45 minutes, the petitioners, in the small groups, walked single file or two abreast in an orderly way through the grounds, each group carrying placards bearing such messages as "I am proud to be a Negro" and "Down with segregation."

During this time a crowd of some 200 to 300 onlookers had collected in the horseshoe area and on the adjacent sidewalks. There was no evidence to suggest that these onlookers were anything but curious, and no evidence at all of any threatening remarks, hostile gestures, or offensive language on the part of any member of the crowd. The City Manager testified that he recognized some of the onlookers, whom he did not identify, as "possible trouble makers," but his subsequent testimony made clear that nobody among the crowd actually caused or threatened any trouble. There was no obstruction of pedestrian or vehicular traffic within the State House grounds. No vehicle was prevented from entering or leaving the horseshoe area. Although vehicular traffic at a nearby street intersection was slowed down somewhat, an officer was dispatched to keep traffic moving. There were a number of bystanders on the public sidewalks adjacent to the State House grounds, but they all moved on when asked to do so, and there was no impediment of pedestrian traffic. Police protection at the scene was at all times sufficient to meet any foreseeable possibility of disorder.

In the situation and under the circumstances thus described, the police authorities advised the petitioners that they would be arrested if they did not disperse within 15 minutes. Instead of dispersing, the petitioners engaged in what the City Manager described as "boisterous," "loud," and "flamboyant" conduct, which, as his later testimony made clear, consisted of listening to a "religious harangue" by one of their leaders, and loudly singing "The Star Spangled Banner" and other patriotic and religious songs, while stamping their feet and clapping their hands. After 15 minutes had passed, the police arrested the petitioners and marched them off to jail. . . .

. . . it is clear to us that in arresting, convicting, and punishing the petitioners under the circumstances disclosed by this record, South Carolina infringed the petitioners' constitutionally protected rights of free speech, free assembly, and freedom to petition for redress of their grievances. . . .

This, therefore, was a far cry from the situation in *Feiner* v. *New York*, . . . where two policemen were faced with a crowd which was "pushing, shoving and milling around," . . . where at least one member of the crowd "threatened violence if the police did not act," . . . where "the crowd was pressing closer around petitioner and the officer," . . . and where "the speaker passes the bounds of argument or persuasion and undertakes incitement to riot." . . . And the record is barren of any evidence of "fighting words." . . .

. . . These petitioners were convicted of an offense so generalized as to be, in the words of the South Carolina Supreme Court, "not susceptible of exact definition." And they were convicted upon evidence which showed no more than that the opinions which they were peaceably expressing were sufficiently opposed to the views of the majority of the community to attract a crowd and necessitate police protection. . . .

As Chief Justice Hughes wrote in *Stromberg* v. *California*, "The maintenance of the opportunity for free political discussion to the end that government may be responsive to the will of the people and that changes may be obtained by lawful means, an opportunity essential to the security of the Republic, is a fundamental principle of our constitutional system. A statute which upon its face, and as authoritatively construed, is so vague and indefinite as to permit the punishment of the fair use of this opportunity is repugnant to the guaranty of liberty contained in the Fourteenth Amendment. . . ." . . .

For these reasons we conclude that these criminal convictions cannot stand.

*Reversed.*

*Source*: 372 U.S. 229 (1963).

## DOCUMENT 100: *Cox v. Louisiana* (1965)

MR. JUSTICE GOLDBERG delivered the opinion of the Court. . . .

On December 14, 1961, 23 students from Southern University, a Negro college, were arrested in downtown Baton Rouge, Louisiana, for picketing stores that maintained segregated lunch counters. This picketing, urging a boycott of those stores, was part of a general protest movement against racial segregation, directed by the local chapter of the Congress of Racial Equality, a civil rights organization. The appellant, an ordained Congregational minister, the Reverend Mr. B. Elton Cox, a Field Secretary of CORE, was an advisor to this movement. On the evening of December 14, appellant and Ronnie Moore, student president of the local CORE chapter, spoke at a mass meeting at the college. The students resolved to demonstrate the next day in front of the courthouse in protest of segregation and the arrest and imprisonment of the picketers who were being held in the parish jail located on the upper floor of the courthouse building.

The next morning about 2,000 students left the campus, which was located approximately five miles from downtown Baton Rouge. Most of them had to walk into the city since the drivers of their busses were arrested. Moore was also arrested at the entrance to the campus while parked in a car equipped with a loudspeaker, and charged with violation of an antinoise statute. Because Moore was immediately taken off to jail and the vice president of the CORE chapter was already in jail for picketing, Cox felt it his duty to take over the demonstration and see that it was carried out as planned. He quickly drove to the city "to pick up this leadership and keep things orderly."

When Cox arrived, 1,500 of the 2,000 students were assembling at the site of the old State Capitol building, two and one-half blocks from the courthouse. Cox walked up and down cautioning the students to keep to one side of the sidewalk while getting ready for their march to the courthouse. The students circled the block in a file two or three abreast occupying about half of the sidewalk. The police had learned of the proposed demonstration the night before from news media and other sources. Captain Font of the City Police Department and Chief Kling of the Sheriff's office, two high-ranking subordinate officials, approached the group and spoke to Cox at the northeast corner of the capitol grounds. Cox identified himself as the group's leader, and, according to Font and Kling, he explained that the students were demonstrating to protest "the illegal arrest of some of their people who were being held in jail." The version of Cox and his witnesses throughout was that they came not "to protest just the arrest but ... [also] to protest the evil of discrimination." Kling asked Cox to disband the group and "take them back from whence they came." Cox did not acquiesce in this request but told the officers that they would march by the courthouse, say prayers, sing hymns, and conduct a peaceful program of protest. The officer repeated his request to disband, and Cox again refused. Kling and Font then returned to their car in order to report by radio to the Sheriff and Chief of Police who were in the immediate vicinity; while this was going on, the students, led by Cox, began their walk toward the courthouse.

They walked in an orderly and peaceful file, two or three abreast, one block east, stopping on the way for a red traffic light. In the center of this block they were joined by another group of students. The augmented group now totaling about 2,000 turned the corner and proceeded south, coming to a halt in the next block opposite the courthouse.

As Cox, still at the head of the group, approached the vicinity of the courthouse, he was stopped by Captain Font and Inspector Trigg and brought to Police Chief Wingate White, who was standing in the middle of St. Louis Street. The Chief then inquired as to the purpose of the demonstration. Cox, reading from a prepared paper, outlined his program to White, stating that it would include a singing of the Star Spangled Banner and a "freedom song," recitation of the Lord's Prayer and the Pledge of Allegiance, and a short speech. White testified that he told Cox that "he must confine" the demonstration "to the west side of the street." White added, "This, of course, was not—I didn't mean it in the import that I was giving him any permission to do it, but I was presented with a situation that was accomplished, and I had to make a decision." Cox testified that the officials agreed to permit the meeting. James Erwin, news director of radio station WIBR, a witness for the State, was present and overheard the conversation. He testified that "My understanding was that they would be allowed to demonstrate if they stayed on the west side of the street and stayed within the recognized time," and that this was "agreed to" by White.

The students were then directed by Cox to the west sidewalk, across the street from the courthouse, 101 feet from its steps. They were lined up on this sidewalk about five deep and spread almost the entire length of the block. The group did not obstruct the street. It was close to noon and, being lunch time, a small crowd of 100 to 300 curious white people, mostly courthouse personnel, gathered on the east sidewalk and courthouse steps, about 100 feet from the demonstrators. Seventy-five to eighty policemen, including city and state patrolmen and members of the Sheriff's staff, as well as members of the fire department and a fire truck were stationed in the street between the two groups. Rain fell throughout the demonstration.

Several of the students took from beneath their coats picket signs similar to those which had been used the day before. These signs bore legends such as "Don't buy discrimination for Christmas," "Sacrifice for Christ, don't buy," and named stores which were proclaimed "unfair." They then sang "God Bless America," pledged allegiance to the flag, prayed briefly, and sang one or two hymns, including "We Shall Overcome." The 23 students, who were locked in jail cells in the courthouse building out of the sight of the demonstrators, responded by themselves singing; this in turn was greeted with cheers and applause by the demonstrators. Appellant gave a speech, described by a State's witness as follows:

"He said that in effect that it was a protest against the illegal arrest of some of their members and that other people were allowed to picket ... and he said that they were not going to commit any violence, that if anyone spit on them, they would not spit back on the person that did it."

Cox then said:

"All right. It's lunch time. Let's go eat. There are twelve stores we are protesting. A number of these stores have twenty counters; they accept your money from nineteen. They won't accept it from the twentieth counter. This is an act of racial discrimination. These stores are open to the public. You are members of the public. We pay taxes to the Federal Government and you who live here pay taxes to the State."

In apparent reaction to these last remarks, there was what state witnesses described as "muttering" and "grumbling" by the white onlookers.

The Sheriff, deeming, as he testified, Cox's appeal to the students to sit in at the lunch counters to be "inflammatory," then took a power microphone and said, "Now, you have been allowed to demonstrate. Up until now your demonstration has been more or less peaceful, but what you are doing now is a direct violation of the law, a disturbance of the peace, and it has got to be broken up immediately." The testimony as to what then happened is disputed. Some of the State's witnesses testified that Cox said, "don't move"; others stated that he made a "gesture of defiance." It is clear from the record, however, that Cox and the demonstrators did not then and there break up the demonstration. Two of the Sheriff's deputies immediately started across the street and told the group, "You have heard what the Sheriff said, now, do what he said." A state witness testified that they put their hands on the shoulders of some of the students "as though to shove them away."

Almost immediately thereafter—within a time estimated variously at two to five minutes—one of the policemen exploded a tear gas shell at the crowd. This was followed by several other shells. The demonstrators quickly dispersed, running back towards the State Capitol and the downtown area; Cox tried to calm them as they ran and was himself one of the last to leave. . . .

Our conclusion that the record does not support the contention that the students' cheering, clapping and singing constituted a breach of the peace is confirmed by the fact that these were not relied on as a basis for conviction by the trial judge, who, rather, stated as his reason for convicting Cox of disturbing the peace that "[i]t must be recognized to be inherently dangerous and a breach of the peace to bring 1,500 people, colored people, down in the predominantly white business district in the City of Baton Rouge and congregate across the street from the courthouse and sing songs as described to me by the defendant as the CORE national anthem carrying lines such as 'black and white together' and to urge those 1,500 people to descend upon our lunch counters and sit there until they are served. That has to be an inherent breach of the peace, and our statute 14:103.1 has made it so." . . .

For all these reasons we hold that appellant's freedoms of speech and assembly, secured to him by the First Amendment, as applied to the States by the Fourteenth Amendment, were denied by his conviction for disturbing the peace. The conviction on this charge cannot stand. . . .

We now turn to the issue of the validity of appellant's conviction for violating the Louisiana statute, . . . which provides:

### "Obstructing Public Passages

"No person shall wilfully obstruct the free, convenient and normal use of any public sidewalk, street, highway, bridge, alley, road, or other passageway, or the entrance, corridor or passage of any public building, structure, watercraft or ferry, by impeding, hindering, stifling, retarding or restraining traffic or passage thereon or therein.

"Providing however nothing herein contained shall apply to a bona fide legitimate labor organization or to any of its legal activities such as picketing, lawful assembly or concerted activity in the interest of its members for the purpose of accomplishing or securing more favorable wage standards, hours of employment and working conditions." . . .

. . . The rights of free speech and assembly, while fundamental in our democratic society, still do not mean that everyone with opinions or beliefs to express may address a group at any public place and at any time. The constitutional guarantee of liberty implies the existence of an organized society maintaining public order, without which liberty itself would be lost in the excesses of anarchy. The control of travel on the streets is a clear example of governmental responsibility to insure this necessary order. A restriction in that relation, designed to promote the public convenience in the interest of all, and not susceptible to abuses of discriminatory application, cannot be disregarded by the attempted exercise of some civil right which, in other circumstances, would be entitled to protection. One would not be justified in ignoring the familiar red light because this was thought to be a means of social protest. Nor could one, contrary to traffic regulations, insist upon a street meeting in the middle of Times Square at the rush hour as a form of freedom of speech or assembly. . . .

We have no occasion in this case to consider the constitutionality of the uniform, consistent, and nondiscriminatory application of a statute forbidding all access to streets and other public facilities for parades and meetings. Although the statute here involved on its face precludes all street assemblies and parades, it has not been so applied and enforced by the Baton Rouge authorities. City officials who testified for the State clearly indicated that certain meetings and parades are permitted in Baton Rouge, even though they have the effect of obstructing traffic, provided prior approval is obtained. This was confirmed in oral argument before this Court by counsel for the State. He stated that parades and meetings are permitted, based on "arrangements . . . made with officials." The statute itself provides no standards for the determination of local officials as to which assemblies to permit or which to prohibit. Nor are there any administrative regulations on this subject which have been called to our attention. From all the evidence before us it appears that the authorities in Baton Rouge permit or prohibit parades or street meetings in their completely uncontrolled discretion.

The situation is thus the same as if the statute itself expressly provided that there could only be peaceful parades or demonstrations in the unbridled discretion of the local officials. The pervasive restraint on freedom of discussion by the practice of the authorities under the statute is not any less effective than a statute expressly permitting such selective enforcement. . . .

This Court has recognized that the lodging of such broad discretion in a public official allows him to determine which expressions of view will be permitted and which will not. This thus sanctions a device for the suppression of the communication of ideas and permits the official to act as a censor. . . .

*Reversed.*

*Source*: 379 U.S. 536 (1965).

---

## DOCUMENT 101: *Gregory v. City of Chicago* (1969)

Taken together, *Gregory v. City of Chicago* and *Coates v. City of Cincinnati* offer a good overview of current Supreme Court doctrine on public assembly issues. Gregory was one of approximately eighty-five protesters who marched to the home of Chicago Mayor Richard Daly to demonstrate against continued racial segregation in the city schools. Accompanied by over one hundred police officers, they arrived at the mayor's home around eight in the evening, and marched around the block for approximately half an hour, singing and chanting slogans. After 8:30, they marched quietly but continued to display signs critical of the mayor. A large crowd of white onlookers gathered and grew increasingly hostile. When Gregory refused to lead the marchers out of the area, they were arrested and charged with violating Chicago's disorderly conduct ordinance, which prohibited, among other things, gathering in groups "to the annoyance or disturbance of other persons."

The Court's opinion, handed down in 1969, begins with the statement that "this is a simple case," and in a very real sense, it was. But as Justice Black's concurrence demonstrates, the implications go to the very heart of a constitutional system: the right of every citizen to know in advance what conduct the law forbids, and the limits of police discretion and authority. As Justice Black put it, "To let a policeman's command become equivalent to a criminal statute comes dangerously near making our government one of men rather than of laws." That danger is to be avoided by crafting ordinances and statutes that give citizens adequate warning of the nature of the conduct that is forbidden.

When a law is so vague that it fails to give people of reasonable intelligence fair guidance, it cannot pass constitutional scrutiny. That was the situation in *Coates*; the ordinance in question made it a criminal offense for "three or more persons" to assemble and conduct themselves in a manner "annoying to persons passing by." The record showed only that Coates was a student engaged in a demonstration while his co-defendants were pickets involved in a labor dispute. Justice Stewart, noting the lack of any other information, wrote pointedly that "The details of the offense could no more serve to validate this ordinance than could the details of an offense charged under an ordinance suspending unconditionally the right of assembly and free speech." The Court held that "The city is free to prevent people from blocking sidewalks, obstructing traffic, littering streets, committing assaults or engaging in countless other forms of antisocial conduct. It cannot constitutionally do so through enactment and enforcement of an ordinance whose violation may entirely depend upon whether or not a policeman is annoyed."

\* \* \*

MR. CHIEF JUSTICE WARREN delivered the opinion of the Court.

This is a simple case. Petitioners, accompanied by Chicago police and an assistant city attorney, marched in a peaceful and orderly procession

from city hall to the mayor's residence to press their claims for desegregation of the public schools. Having promised to cease singing at 8:30
p.m., the marchers did so. Although petitioners and the other demonstrators continued to march in a completely lawful fashion, the onlookers
became unruly as the number of bystanders increased. Chicago police,
to prevent what they regarded as an impending civil disorder, demanded that the demonstrators, upon pain of arrest, disperse. When this
command was not obeyed, petitioners were arrested for disorderly conduct. . . .

The opinion of the Supreme Court of Illinois suggests that petitioners
were convicted not for the manner in which they conducted their march
but rather for their refusal to disperse when requested to do so by Chicago police. . . . However reasonable the police request may have been
and however laudable the police motives, petitioners were charged and
convicted for holding a demonstration, not for a refusal to obey a police
officer. As we said in *Garner* v. *Louisiana*: "[I]t is as much a denial of due
process to send an accused to prison following conviction for a charge
that was never made as it is to convict him upon a charge for which
there is no evidence to support that conviction." . . .

Finally, since the trial judge's charge permitted the jury to convict for
acts clearly entitled to First Amendment protection, *Stromberg* v. *California* . . . independently requires reversal of these convictions.

The judgments are

*Reversed.*

\* \* \*

MR. JUSTICE BLACK, with whom MR. JUSTICE DOUGLAS joins, concurring.

This I think is a highly important case which requires more detailed
consideration than the Court's opinion gives it. It in a way tests the
ability of the United States to keep the promises its Constitution makes
to the people of the Nation. Among those promises appearing in the
Preamble to the Constitution are the statements that the people of the
United States ordained this basic charter "in Order to form a more perfect Union, establish Justice, insure domestic Tranquillity . . . and secure
the Blessings of Liberty to ourselves and our Posterity. . . ." Shortly after
the original Constitution was adopted, again undoubtedly in an attempt
to "secure the Blessings of Liberty," the Bill of Rights was added to the
Constitution, in which the First Amendment, later made applicable to
the States by the Fourteenth Amendment, provides that: "Congress shall
make no law . . . abridging the freedom of speech, or of the press; or the
right of the people peaceably to assemble, and to petition the Government for a redress of grievances."

In 1954 our Court held that laws segregating people on the basis of race or color in the public schools unconstitutionally denied Negroes equal protection of the laws. Negroes, and many others who sympathized with them, cooperatively undertook to speed up desegregation. These groups adopted plans under which they marched on the streets carrying placards, chanting, and singing songs, all designed to publicize their grievances and to petition the various units of government, state and national, for a redress of these grievances. Their activities along these lines quite obviously aroused highly emotional feelings both on their part and on the part of others who opposed the changes in local laws and customs which the "picketers" and "demonstrators" advocated. Agitation between groups brought about sharp conflicts and clashes, threats, fights, riots, and near-riots. This Court, to be sure, has had its difficulties and sharp differences of opinion in deciding the precise boundaries dividing what is constitutionally permissible and impermissible in this field. There have also been sharp disputes over whether the Court can hold laws unconstitutional because the Court deems them to be "unreasonable," "arbitrary," or contrary to fundamental standards of ethics, morals, or conscience. Fortunately, however, these differences need not concern us here. For while we have pointed out in many cases that the States and their subordinate units do have constitutional power to regulate picketing, demonstrating, and parading by statutes and ordinances narrowly drawn so as not to abridge the rights of speech, press, assembly, or petition, neither Chicago nor Illinois at the time these petitioners were demonstrating had passed any such narrowly drawn laws. . . .

I agree with the Illinois Supreme Court that the "record shows a determined effort by the police to allow the marchers to peacefully demonstrate and at the same time maintain order." I also think the record shows that outside of the marching and propagandizing of their views and protests, Gregory and his group while marching did all in their power to maintain order. Indeed, in the face of jeers, insults, and assaults with rocks and eggs, Gregory and his group maintained a decorum that speaks well for their determination simply to tell their side of their grievances and complaints. Even the "snake" and "snake pit" invectives used by Gregory and his demonstrators, unlike some used by their hecklers, remained within the general give-and-take of heated political argument. Thus both police and demonstrators made their best efforts faithfully to discharge their responsibilities as officers and citizens, but they were nevertheless unable to restrain the hostile hecklers within decent and orderly bounds. These facts disclosed by the record point unerringly to one conclusion, namely, that when groups with diametrically opposed, deep-seated views are permitted to air their emotional grievances, side by side, on city streets, tranquility and order cannot be maintained even by the joint efforts of the finest and best officers and of those who desire to be the most law-abiding protestors of their grievances.

It is because of this truth, and a desire both to promote order and to safeguard First Amendment freedoms, that this Court has repeatedly warned States and governmental units that they cannot regulate conduct connected with these freedoms through use of sweeping, dragnet statutes that may, because of vagueness, jeopardize these freedoms. In those cases, however, we have been careful to point out that the Constitution does not bar enactment of laws regulating conduct, even though connected with speech, press, assembly, and petition, if such laws specifically bar only the conduct deemed obnoxious and are carefully and narrowly aimed at that forbidden conduct. The dilemma revealed by this record is a crying example of a need for some such narrowly drawn law. It is not our duty and indeed not within our power to set out and define with precision just what statutes can be lawfully enacted to deal with situations like the one confronted here by police and protestors, both of whom appear to us to have been conscientiously trying to do their duties as they understood them. Plainly, however, no mandate in our Constitution leaves States and governmental units powerless to pass laws to protect the public from the kind of boisterous and threatening conduct that disturbs the tranquility of spots selected by the people either for homes, wherein they can escape the hurly-burly of the outside business and political world, or for public and other buildings that require peace and quiet to carry out their functions, such as courts, libraries, schools, and hospitals. . . .

The so-called "diversion tending to a breach of the peace" here was limited entirely and exclusively to the fact that when the policeman in charge of the special police detail concluded that the hecklers observing the march were dangerously close to rioting and that the demonstrators and others were likely to be engulfed in that riot, he ordered Gregory and his demonstrators to leave, and Gregory—standing on what he deemed to be his constitutional rights—refused to do so. The "diversion" complained of on the part of Gregory and the other marchers was not any noise they made or annoyance or disturbance of "other persons" they had inflicted. Their guilt of "disorderly conduct" therefore turns out to be their refusal to obey instanter an individual policeman's command to leave the area of the Mayor's home. Since neither the city council nor the state legislature had enacted a narrowly drawn statute forbidding disruptive picketing or demonstrating in a residential neighborhood, the conduct involved here could become "disorderly" only if the policeman's command was a law which the petitioners were bound to obey at their peril. But under our democratic system of government, lawmaking is not entrusted to the moment-to-moment judgment of the policeman on his beat. Laws, that is valid laws, are to be made by representatives chosen to make laws for the future, not by police officers whose duty is to enforce laws already enacted and to make arrests only for conduct already made criminal. One of our proudest boasts is that no man can be convicted of crime for conduct, innocent when engaged in, that is later made criminal. . . . To let a policeman's command become equivalent to a criminal statute comes dangerously near making our government one of men rather than of laws. . . . There are ample ways to protect the domestic tranquility without subjecting First Amendment freedoms to such a clumsy and unwieldy weapon.

*Source:* 394 U.S. 111 (1969).

---

## DOCUMENT 102: *Coates v. City of Cincinnati* (1971)

MR. JUSTICE STEWART delivered the opinion of the Court. . . .

Beyond this, the only construction put upon the ordinance by the state court was its unexplained conclusion that "the standard of conduct which it specifies is not dependent upon each complainant's sensitivity." . . . But the court did not indicate upon whose sensitivity a violation does depend—the sensitivity of the judge or jury, the sensitivity of the arresting officer, or the sensitivity of a hypothetical reasonable man.

We are thus relegated, at best, to the words of the ordinance itself. If three or more people meet together on a sidewalk or street corner, they must conduct themselves so as not to annoy any police officer or other person who should happen to pass by. In our opinion this ordinance is unconstitutionally vague because it subjects the exercise of the right of assembly to an unascertainable standard, and unconstitutionally broad because it authorizes the punishment of constitutionally protected conduct.

Conduct that annoys some people does not annoy others. Thus, the ordinance is vague, not in the sense that it requires a person to conform his conduct to an imprecise but comprehensible normative standard, but rather in the sense that no standard of conduct is specified at all. As a result, "men of common intelligence must necessarily guess at its meaning." . . .

It is said that the ordinance is broad enough to encompass many types of conduct clearly within the city's constitutional power to prohibit. And so, indeed, it is. The city is free to prevent people from blocking sidewalks, obstructing traffic, littering streets, committing assaults, or engaging in countless other forms of antisocial conduct. It can do so through the enactment and enforcement of ordinances directed with reasonable specificity toward the conduct to be prohibited. . . . It cannot constitutionally do so through the enactment and enforcement of an ordinance whose violation may entirely depend upon whether or not a policeman is annoyed.

But the vice of the ordinance lies not alone in its violation of the due process standard of vagueness. The ordinance also violates the constitutional right of free assembly and association. Our decisions establish that mere public intolerance or animosity cannot be the basis for abridgement of these constitutional freedoms. . . . The First and Fourteenth Amendments do not permit a State to make criminal the exercise of the right of assembly simply because its exercise may be "annoying" to some people. If this were not the rule, the right of the people to gather in public places for social or political purposes would be continually subject to summary suspension through the good-faith enforcement of a prohibition against annoying conduct. And such a prohibition, in addition, contains an obvious invitation to discriminatory enforcement against those whose association together is "annoying" because their ideas, their lifestyle, or their physical appearance is resented by the majority of their fellow citizens.

The ordinance before us makes a crime out of what under the Constitution cannot be a crime. It is aimed directly at activity protected by the Constitution. We need not lament that we do not have before us the details of the conduct found to be annoying. It is the ordinance on its face that sets the standard of conduct and warns against transgression. The details of the offense could no more serve to validate this ordinance than could the details of an offense charged under an ordinance suspending unconditionally the right of assembly and free speech.

The judgment is reversed.

*Source*: 402 U.S. 611 (1971).

---

## DOCUMENT 103: *Smith, President of the Village of Skokie, Illinois v. Collin* (1978)

There have been few cases in American jurisprudence with the emotional impact of *Village of Skokie v. Collin*. In March 1977, the American Nazi party announced its intention to march down the main street of Skokie, Illinois. The residents of the village of Skokie included the largest number of Holocaust survivors in the United States. It was clear that the Nazis had chosen Skokie because the impact on onlookers would be greatest there. Nevertheless, the Illinois Supreme Court held that the Nazis had a constitutional right to march.

The Supreme Court refused to hear the appeal in *Village of Skokie.* As the dissent from the Supreme Court's denial of certiorari indicates, the case had aroused intense passions. The American Civil Liberties Union, which represented the Nazis, lost nearly 50,000 members who resigned in protest. Civil libertarians pointed out that free speech is an indivisible right; that a government with power to censor the Nazis is a government with power to censor civil rights marchers. Those trying to prohibit the march retorted that society should be able to draw some lines, and this was one that should be drawn. Perhaps no other First Amendment case has so sorely tried America's commitment to the principle that the First Amendment provides "freedom for the thought we hate."

\* \* \*

MR. JUSTICE BLACKMUN, with whom MR. JUSTICE WHITE joins, dissenting.

It is a matter of regret for me that the Court denies certiorari in this case, for this is litigation that rests upon critical, disturbing, and emotional facts, and the issues cut down to the very heart of the First Amendment.

The village of Skokie, Ill., a suburb of Chicago, in 1974 had a population of approximately 70,000 persons. A majority were Jewish; of the Jewish population a substantial number were survivors of World War II persecution. In March 1977, respondents Collin and the National Socialist Party of America, which Collin described as a "Nazi organization," publicly announced plans to hold an assembly in front of the Skokie Village Hall. On May 2, the village enacted three ordinances. The first established a permit system for parades and public assemblies and required applicants to post public liability and property damage insurance. The second prohibited the dissemination of material that incited racial or religious hatred with intent so to incite. The third prohibited public demonstrations by members of political parties while wearing military-style uniforms.

On June 22, respondent Collin applied for a permit under the first ordinance. His application stated that a public assembly would take place on July 4, would consist of persons demonstrating in front of the Village Hall, would last about a half hour, and would not disrupt traffic. It also stated that the participants would wear uniforms with swastikas and would carry placards proclaiming free speech for white persons, but would not distribute handbills or literature. The permit was denied.

Skokie's Village Hall stood on a street that was zoned commercial.

There were residential areas, however, adjoining to the North, South, and West. The front of the Village Hall was visible from dwellings in those areas.

Upon the rejection of the permit application, respondents filed a complaint in the United States District Court for the Northern District of Illinois against the president of the village of Skokie, its manager, its corporation counsel, and the village itself. Respondents asked that the ordinances be declared void and their enforcement enjoined. The District Court, after receiving evidence, ruled that the ordinances were unconstitutional on their face, and granted the requested declaratory and injunctive relief. It filed a comprehensive opinion. The United States Court of Appeals for the Seventh Circuit, with one judge dissenting in part, affirmed.

A permit then was issued to respondents for a demonstration on the afternoon of June 25, 1978, in front of the Village Hall. Respondents, however, shifted their assembly from Skokie to Chicago where activities took place on June 24 and July 9.

Other aspects of the controversy already have reached this Court. In April 1977, the Circuit Court of Cook County, Ill., entered an injunction against respondents prohibiting them, within the village, from parading in the National Socialist uniform, displaying the swastika, or displaying materials that incite or promote hatred against persons of the Jewish or any other faith. The Illinois Appellate Court denied an application for stay pending appeal. The Supreme Court of Illinois, in turn, denied a stay and also denied leave for an expedited appeal. Relief was sought here. This Court, *per curiam* but by a divided vote, reversed the denial of a stay and remanded the case for further proceedings.

On remand, the Illinois Appellate Court reviewed and modified the injunction the Circuit Court had entered and this time upheld only that portion thereof that prevented the display of swastikas "in the course of a demonstration, march, or parade." The Supreme Court of Illinois denied an application for stay pending expedited review. MR. JUSTICE STEVENS, as Circuit Justice, denied a stay of the injunction as so modified. The Illinois Supreme Court ultimately reversed the remaining injunctive feature, "albeit reluctantly," and with one justice dissenting.

Thereafter, the village and its codefendants in the present federal litigation filed an application to stay the Seventh Circuit's mandate or, in the alternative, to stay enforcement of the injunction entered by the District Court. This Court, with two Justices dissenting, denied the application.

These facts and this chronology demonstrate, I believe, the pervading sensitivity of the litigation. On the one hand, we have precious First Amendment rights vigorously asserted and an obvious concern that, if those asserted rights are not recognized, the precedent of a "hard" case might offer a justification for repression in the future. On the other hand, we are presented with evidence of a potentially explosive and dangerous situation, enflamed by unforgettable recollections of traumatic experiences in the second world conflict. Finally, Judge Sprecher of the Seventh Circuit observed that "each court dealing with these precise problems (the Illinois Supreme Court, the District Court and this Court) feels the need to apologize for its result."

Furthermore, in *Beauharnais v. Illinois*, this Court faced up to an Illinois statute that made it a crime to exhibit in any public place a publication that portrayed "depravity, criminality, unchastity, or lack of virtue of a class of citizens, of any race, color, creed or religion," thereby exposing such citizens "to contempt, derision, or obloquy." The Court, by a divided vote, held that, as construed and applied, the statute did not violate the liberty of speech guaranteed as against the States by the Due Process Clause of the Fourteenth Amendment.

I stated in dissent when the application for stay in the present litigation was denied, that I feel the Seventh Circuit's decision is in some tension with *Beauharnais*. That case has not been overruled or formally limited in any way.

I therefore would grant certiorari in order to resolve any possible conflict that may exist between the ruling of the Seventh Circuit here and *Beauharnais*. I also feel that the present case affords the Court an opportunity to consider whether, in the context of the facts that this record appears to present, there is no limit whatsoever to the exercise of free speech. There indeed may be no such limit, but when citizens assert, not casually but with deep conviction, that the proposed demonstration is scheduled at a place and in a manner that is taunting and overwhelmingly offensive to the citizens of that place, that assertion, uncomfortable though it may be for judges, deserves to be examined. It just might fall into the same category as one's "right" to cry "fire" in a crowded theater, for "the character of every act depends upon the circumstances in which it is done."

*Source*: 439 U.S. 916 (1978).

---

## DOCUMENT 104: *Nazis in Skokie: Freedom, Community, and the First Amendment* (Donald Alexander Downs, 1985)

The debate over the application of the First Amendment to the situation in Skokie continued long after the incident itself had played out. In 1984, Donald Downs published a thoughtful book in which he analyzed free-speech doctrine in the context of such assaultive and intentionally hurtful expression and suggested a formula for abridging free speech in certain specified circumstances.

* * *

Our analysis leaves us with the following components of abridgeable speech concerning race in the public forum: 1) assaultive, intimidating speech content, either explicit or symbolic-implicit; 2) the targeting of such expression; 3) the unprovoked intent to target such expression in order to harm. In sum, I suggest the following legal formulation as a first step in the direction of reform. Speech in the public forum involving race or ethnicity may be abridged

1) When such expression is accompanied by the advocacy of death or violence perpetrated against that group as determined by a reasonable person; *or*, when such expression explicitly demeans or vilifies through reference to race or ethnicity as determined by a reasonable person; *or*, when such expression so vilifies or demeans in a symbolic or implicit manner as determined by a reasonable person; *and*

2) such expression and harm are intended by the speaker and are unjustifiable due to the lack of significant provocation; *and*

3) such expression is directed at an individual, home, neighborhood, or community in such a way as to single out an individual or specified group as the definite target of the expression.

The Skokie case raised another point which must be addressed: the fact that the survivors were, in the words of the survivor at the Board of Trustees meeting on April 25, 1977, "a special breed of animal." That is, they were more vulnerable to the NSPA provocation than were other Jews because of the wounds caused by their past experiences (their propitious sociological circumstances notwithstanding). Frank Collin knew of this vulnerability and took advantage of it. Yet our analysis has demonstrated that targeted racial or ethnic vilification is *inherently* traumatic; accordingly, special vulnerability of a target group need not be a factor in determining the perpetration of a harm sufficient to justify the abridgement of speech, as harm is presumed in any case. However, any special vulnerability of the target(s), as well as any knowledge of such vulnerability on the part of the speaker may be factors the court may consider in its determination of intent and culpability. These considerations are especially important if the jury exercises discretion in arriving at its decision; as Arkes pointed out above, juries will often consider factors of circumstance and character in their deliberations concerning guilt. The degree of vulnerability would also be a consideration in the decision to prosecute, which is always discretionary. By providing for special vulnerability in this fashion, uncertainty is not eliminated, but is placed in areas of criminal law in which discretion and concomitant uncertainty have always existed. In this respect, my policy is an improvement upon the tort of the intentional infliction of emotional trauma (in which harm must be proved in court, and in which legal provision is made for special vulnerability) because it does not require the actual presence of harm to be determined in court. The sheer existence of the speech act is enough to constitute guilt because harm is presumed. . . .

Before we conclude, three potential problems must be addressed: the problem of chilling effect, the problem of intent, and the issue of the vilification of groups or individuals who do not belong to a racial or ethnic minority.

### A. Slippage and the Problem of Chilling Effect

U.S. District Judge Decker predicated his decision in *Collin v. Smith* on the assumption that assaultive racial slurs cannot be separated in practice from controversial yet legitimate speech about racial issues. I have shown that they are analytically distinguishable, and that assaultive expression should be abridgeable despite the fact that it may be "mixed" with worthy or even truthful speech. This position lessens the weight of the "mixed utterance" doctrine Decker endorses.

But critics may still argue that my policy would jeopardize free speech because it introduces a "slippery slope" problem in two respects: 1) courts would misapply the doctrine, thereby in practice abridging speech which my policy does not analytically cover; 2) even if the court could implement the doctrine without affecting worthy speech, the mere threat of faulty enforcement of the law could "chill" legitimate speech.

My answer to the criticism of misapplication is straightforward. Yes, there may be misapplication. But misapplication is not a sufficient argument against my policy unless it could be shown that misapplication would have *undue* effect on the exercise of free speech. The threat of misapplication has not prevented the Supreme Court from upholding the constitutionality of the death penalty. Is racialist speech more precious than life itself? Nor has the potential problem of misapplication caused the Supreme Court to abandon its normative exclusion of obscenity from First Amendment protection. In *Young v. American Mini Theatres, Inc.*, Justice Stevens acknowledged that "slippage" could occur in the implementation of Detroit's zoning ordinance concerning pornographic shops. Yet Stevens held that this slippage was not a major problem because the affected expression was of only marginal value to society in terms of the social value norm found in *Chaplinsky*:

The only vagueness in the ordinances relates to the amount of sexually explicit activity that may be portrayed before the material can be said to be "characterized by an emphasis" on such matter. For most films the question will be readily answerable; to the extent that an area of doubt exists, we see no reason why the statute is not "readily subject to a narrowing construction by the state courts." *Since there is surely a less vital interest in the uninhibited exhibition of material that is on the border line between pornography and artistic expression than in the free dissemination of ideas of social and political significance,* and since the limited amount of uncertainty in the statute is easily susceptible of a narrowing construction, we think this is an inappropriate case in which to adjudicate the hypothetical claims of persons not before the court.

Steven's [*sic*] logic is appropriate in the regulation of targeted racial vilification, as well. Even if my proposals were to "slip" and "chill" some racialist expression, this slippage would affect only expression of low value (as low as obscenity). Yet to accept this position, one must take seriously *Chaplinsky's* norm of social value in the adjudication of speech. That is, the *ends* of free speech (their relation to substantive justice) would have to be considered.

### B. The Problem of Intent

Libertarian speech theorists assert that free speech interests would be harmed if courts took the intent of speakers into consideration in determining the validity of free speech claims. Yet the courts explicitly consider intent (on the part of government or private citizens, depending on the case) in many vital areas of law, including constitutional law and First Amendment cases. The prosecution must demonstrate a defendant's specific intent to break a law in most serious criminal cases (acts *mala in se*). In constitutional law, the plaintiff must show the intent to discriminate on the part of the government in a suit concerning the equal protection clause, and the Supreme Court even considers intent in such First Amendment areas as commercial speech and libel suits brought by public officials. In-person solicitation by lawyers may be prohibited because its "aim and effect" is often to compel people in distress to use a particular lawyer, making its commercial aspect and intent more important than its "speech" value. Likewise, libel of public officials made with "malice" is constitutionally tortious according to the Court in the *Sullivan* case (a watershed pro–free speech decision). The consideration of intent in the area of targeted racial vilification, therefore, is valid, *a fortiori*.

### C. The Vilification of Majority Groups

Finally, readers will ask about the proper policy concerning minority groups' vilification of majority group members. My discussion of the *Gooding* and *Lewis* cases in Chapter One foreshadowed my position on this issue, as I criticized how these decisions in favor of angry black defendants watered down *Chaplinsky's* fighting words doctrine.

Thought it is true that racism directed against minorities is especially vicious because of the history of racial oppression in this country (a factor in making racial classifications "inherently suspect," as pointed out in the last chapter), I recommend that my policy reforms apply across the board to all forms of targeted racial vilification. First, whites who are targeted for vilification because of their race may feel just as intimidated as blacks, Jews, or other minorities. Second, the very act of *targeting* adds to the assaultive nature of the expression, so whites may be expected to feel unjustifiably assaulted in these instances. Third, it seems unfair to treat races differently in this area of law, especially because the basic values at stake concern the *fundamental principle that people should not be unduly abused on account of their race*. Whites who target racial vilification at blacks may be punished for violating this principle. Is it sensible to then turn around and allow blacks to commit the same harm against whites? I think not. Finally, such a double standard seems to constitute a subtle, new form of patronizing racism—it assumes that some minorities must be treated differently because they are less able to control themselves. Such assumptions undermine the constitutional principles of equality and individual responsibility.

For these reasons, I endorse an evenhanded policy of application and enforcement in terms of race (subject, as above, to legitimate police and prosecutorial discretion). Richard Delgado espouses a similar approach in the tort area. His conclusion may be applied to my policy:

The cause of action outlined is intended primarily to protect members of racial minority groups traditionally victimized. However, in some situations racial insults may cause harm when directed at members of the majority. The best example of such a situation would be the insult "You dumb honkey" directed at a white child by a black teacher in a predominantly black school. The potential for psychological harm in such a situation is obvious. And although the basis for the tort, the legacy of slavery and race discrimination, might seem to limit the class of those who can bring such actions to members of traditionally victimized minorities, it is the use of race to make invidious distinctions that is the ultimate evil the tort is designed to combat. . . .

In the Skokie litigation the courts ignored the intent and latent meaning of the NSPA's proposed speech act. Their limited view was a function of both their doctrinal commitment to the content neutrality rule and to their refusal to consider evidence pertaining to the NSPA's actions and statements leading up to Skokie. As a result, the legal decisions appeared out of touch with the facts and, therefore, out of touch with justice.

The Skokie decisions were the result of a free speech jurisprudence which is excessively libertarian. They upheld the NSPA's speech right despite the harms such speech caused (and would cause) the Skokie survivor community. The delicate balance of liberty and social value which the Supreme Court practiced in *Chaplinsky* was absent. My analysis of the Skokie case (both empirical and normative) has demonstrated that it is time the Supreme Court took the *Chaplinsky* social value principle and fighting words doctrine seriously once again. Such reconsideration would reconnect the First Amendment with substantive justice and the civility and protective functions of the just community.

The method of free speech adjudication I have proposed in this chapter would require the courts to consider community values. The present method of adjudication is anti-communitarian for two reasons: (1) It does not allow the courts to consider the *context* of political speech or its concrete application. Yet context and concreteness are important values of community or *gemeinschaft*. (2) By forbidding courts to consider all relevant evidence in order to ascertain the intent and therefore the full meaning of speech, the method resembles the anti-community principle (or principle of "analysis") which Roberto Unger criticizes in *Knowledge and Politics*. Simply stated, the principle of analysis involves the dissection of "wholes" into constituent parts which then stand isolated from their former contextual meaning. This nominalism results in "the proposition that in the acquisition of knowledge the whole is the sum of its parts." The relation between the principle of analysis and the principle of libertarian individualism is apparent: each focuses on individual entities in isolation from the contexts or environments within which they are embedded. Unger contrasts the principle of analysis with the principle of "synthesis," which maintains that we cannot understand facts or individuals outside of their place in larger wholes. In social terms, the principle or synthesis recognizes the individual as a social person.

If Unger is right, it is no accident that First Amendment jurisprudence concerning political speech in the public forum exalts an individualism abstracted from the community at the same time as it practices a method which is analytical in nature: the context, intent, and associated expression that give meaning to any individual speech act are ignored in honor of the individual's particular right at a particular time to exercise uninhibited free speech. It was this type of jurisprudence which prohibited the judicial consideration of wider context in the *Gooding, Lewis, Collin* and *Skokie* cases. Nor is it an accident that the courts downplayed *Chaplinsky's* deeper "social value" principle in reaching these results.

But man is a political, communal animal in addition to being an individual. Indeed, his development and growth require adequate socialization and learning from his culture. And the acts of individuals have important consequences, as the science of ecology teaches us in a different realm. Accordingly, the most prudent jurisprudence should *balance* individualism and community, the principles of analysis and synthesis. Alexander Meiklejohn achieves this balance in his theory of free speech. Though he is often considered an extreme libertarian, Meiklejohn justifies free speech in terms of its contribution to the political and communal practice of self-government. His theory is incomprehensible outside of this teleological context. Significantly, Meiklejohn asserts that the citizens who practice self-government must possess "self-control" and virtue, and that selfishness and inconsideration (incivility) are inimical to freedom, properly understood. Meiklejohn's theory is consistent with both *Chaplinsky's* civility principle and its definitional (two-level) approach to free speech adjudication that emphasizes social value. By these means, a propitious balance is struck between individualism and communitarianism. Frank Collin's abuse of free speech at Skokie and similar precedents have upset this delicate balance. It is time courts set the balance aright.

*Source*: Donald Alexander Downs, *Nazis in Skokie: Freedom, Community, and the First Amendment* (Notre Dame, IN: University of Notre Dame Press, 1985), 163–169 (notes omitted).

---

## DOCUMENT 105: "The Speech We Hate" (*Progressive*, 1992)

Most free-speech advocates recognized the issues raised by Downs and others, but concluded that the dangers of abridgment of free speech outweighed any temporary benefit to community that might be achieved. The *Progressive* magazine supported the ACLU during the Skokie litigation; in 1992, at the height of the anti-hate-speech movement on college campuses, it revisited *Skokie* and reaffirmed its commitment to the importance of free expression of all ideas, even (or perhaps especially) "the speech we hate."

\* \* \*

Back in the mid-1970s, a ragtag band of self-styled American Nazis threatened to stage a march through the streets of Skokie, a predominantly Jewish suburb of Chicago. Skokie residents—among them survivors of German concentration camps—were furious, and so were many good people all over the United States. Local and state authorities did their best to block the Nazi march. But the American Civil Liberties Union argued that the march was a form of political expression and that the First Amendment to the U.S. Constitution applied even—and perhaps *especially*—to hateful speech. Protecting First Amendment freedoms, the ACLU contended, had to take precedence over protecting the wounded feelings of Skokie residents.

For taking that position, the ACLU suffered a drastic drop in membership from which it took years to recover. For supporting the ACLU's stance, *The Progressive* lost subscribers and financial support. It was clear that many liberals and progressives and radicals—though certainly not all—shared the Right's predilection for attempting to suppress speech they found difficult or dangerous or dead wrong.

The ACLU eventually prevailed in the courts and the Nazis got their parade permit—which they never used, because they had been deprived of the opportunity they sought: the confrontation and publicity attendant to mounting an *illegal* protest. But the issues raised in the Skokie controversy are with us still, and the threats to freedom of speech are multiplying. Today, the most severe assaults on the First Amendment seem to originate with those whose intentions (as distinct from their good sense) are beyond question.

On a number of college and university campuses, for example, administrators, faculty members, and students have collaborated in drafting "hate speech" codes that would impose penalties on those who express hostile or contemptuous views based on race, ethnicity, sex or sexual orientation, disability, or other presumably vulnerable status. Though such regulations have been held unconstitutional in Michigan and Wisconsin, they continue to proliferate; the University of Wisconsin, for example, has come up with tortuous and vague new language in an attempt to adopt a hate-speech rule that will pass constitutional muster.

What is particularly troublesome is that such regulations often have the support of minority groups, feminists, gays and lesbians, and political activitists of sundry persuasions. Canetta Ivy, a black student leader at Stanford, spoke for altogether too many of her classmates when she said, "We don't put as many restrictions of freedom of speech as we should."

Well, what's wrong with that? Why not curb speech that promotes a hostile and intimidating climate, that fosters hate, that reflects the worst instincts of those who utter it and those who hear it?

What's wrong, first of all, is that any restriction on speech, no matter how narrowly drawn or well intended, is certain to lead to further restraints that will be broader and distinctly less benign. The precedent of today's ban on hateful speech is bound to be invoked tomorrow to justify constraints on other forms of expression. And when those constraints are imposed, their first victims are likely to be the very same groups who now call for rules and regulations—racial and ethnic minorities, women, lesbians and gays, political dissidents.

What's wrong is that the appropriate response to bad speech is not censorship or punishment but good speech. If those of us who believe in full and equal rights for all cannot prevail in open dispute with the forces of hate and bigotry, we might as well abandon all hope for a just, rational, humane, and democratic society; the struggle is already lost.

What's wrong is that the attempt to ban or punish hateful speech does nothing at all to empower the presumed victims of bigotry. Instead, it compels them to seek the protection of authorities whose own commitment to justice is often, to put it mildly, less than vigorous. Restraining speech increases the dependency of minorities and other victims of hate and oppression. Instead of empowering them, it enfeebles them.

What's wrong, finally, is that curtailing speech is a cheap, easy, and utterly meaningless way to address the deep-seated bigotry that pervades our society. As constitutional scholar Steven Rhode has pointed out, "A university campus, whether public or private, must be a place of robust, wide-open, and free discussion. Students bring to college all their prejudices, their fears, their doubts, their misconceptions. If they spend four years cooped up under repressive regulations, they might well dutifully obey the rules, offend no one, and leave with all their prejudices, fears, doubts, and misconceptions firmly intact."

The vogue of hate-speech regulation has spread from the campuses to local and state law. Increasingly, statutes and ordinances attempt to curtail expressions of animosity toward women and various minorities. Fortunately, even today's ultraconservative Supreme Court seems to retain sufficient respect for traditional First Amendment principles to rule against such legislation.

In a case from St. Paul, Minnesota, decided in June, the Court overturned that city's Bias-Motivated Crime Ordinance, which stated, "Whoever places on public or private property a symbol, object, appellation, characterization, or graffiti, including but not limited to a burning cross or Nazi swastika, which one knows or has reasonable grounds to know arouses anger, alarm, or resentment in others on the basis of race, color, creed, religion, or gender, commits disorderly conduct and shall be guilty of a misdemeanor."

Justice Antonin Scalia, writing for the Court, made it clear that he understood what law is supposed to do for speech that "arouses anger, alarm, or resentment." It is supposed to protect it, not suppress it. "The First Amendment," he wrote, "does not permit St. Paul to impose special prohibitions on those speakers who express views on disfavored subjects."

Whether the Court's decision will put an end to the wave of speech constraints now washing over the United States remains to be seen. First reactions to *R.A.V. v. City of St. Paul* were not encouraging. Authors of various hate-speech rules and statutes—including the new regulations at the University of Wisconsin—scrambled to insist that their language was, on one or another technicality, immune to the constitutional test enunciated by the Justices in *St. Paul*. But if the lower courts are diligent about applying the Supreme Court's *St. Paul* ruling, they will go a long way toward slowing down, if not halting and reversing, the pernicious process of chipping away at First Amendment freedoms in the name of protecting society from the speech we hate.

*Source*: "The Speech We Hate," *Progressive* 56, no. 8 (August 1992): 8–9.

---

**DOCUMENT 106:** *Paul Schenck and Dwight Saunders v. Pro-Choice Network of Western New York* **(1997)**

---

It is one thing to hold, as the Supreme Court has repeatedly held, that observers and passersby cannot exercise a "heckler's veto" over one who is exercising his or her right to free speech. But what does the Constitution require when the speech of one group interferes with the privacy of others? That was the situation the Court faced in *Schenck v. Pro-Choice Network*.

Abortion clinics in New York State had been targeted by some of the most radical antichoice organizations. The lower courts found— and the Supreme Court accepted—that the protesters' actions had interfered with the exercise of women's constitutional right to obtain abortions. The district court had entered an injunction prohibiting certain aspects of the picketing. The question before the Supreme Court was whether those restrictions went too far. Did the district court's order restrict speech of the protesters more than was absolutely necessary to protect the rights of the women who wished to enter the clinics?

*Schenck* was not a case about the protesters' rights to picket and demonstrate. All sides agreed that they had such a right. The issue was how far the courts might go in circumscribing the rights of the protesters in order to protect other, equally important rights. It is instructive that even the American Civil Liberties Union was divided on this question: the national office submitted a brief urging the Court to affirm the entire district-court injunction; the ACLUs of Florida, Indiana, and the National Capital Area submitted a joint brief urging reversal of the so-called buffer-zone provisions. The majority opinion adopted the argument advanced by these state ACLU affiliates.

\* \* \*

Chief Justice REHNQUIST delivered the opinion of the Court.

The question presented is whether an injunction that places restrictions on demonstrations outside abortion clinics violates the First Amendment. We uphold the provisions imposing "fixed bubble" or "fixed buffer zone" limitations, as hereinafter described, but hold that the provisions imposing "floating bubble" or "floating buffer zone" limitations violate the First Amendment.

I

Respondents include three doctors and four medical clinics (two of which are part of larger hospital complexes) in and around Rochester and Buffalo in upstate New York. These health care providers perform abortions and other medical services at their facilities. The eighth respondent is Pro-Choice Network of Western New York, a not-for-profit corporation dedicated to maintaining access to family planning and abortion services. . . .

In February 1992, after hearing 12 additional days of testimony, the District Court issued the injunction, parts of which are challenged here. . . . while the TRO [Temporary Restraining Order] banned "demonstrating . . . within fifteen feet of any person" entering or leaving the clinics, the injunction more broadly banned "demonstrating within fifteen feet from either side of edge of, or in front of, doorways or doorway entrances, parking lot entrances, driveways and driveway entrances of such facilities" ("fixed buffer zones"), or "within fifteen feet of any person or vehicle seeking access to or leaving such facilities" ("floating buffer zones"). In addition, the injunction clarified the "cease and desist" provision, specifying that once sidewalk counselors who had entered the buffer zones were required to "cease and desist" their counseling, they had to retreat 15 feet from the people they had been counseling and had to remain outside the boundaries of the buffer zones. . . .

In analyzing defendants' assertion that the injunction violated their First Amendment right to free speech, the court applied our standard "time, place, and manner analysis," asking whether the speech restrictions in the injunction (i) were content neutral, (ii) were narrowly tailored to serve a significant government interest, and (iii) left open ample alternative channels for communication of the information. . . . The court held that the injunction served three significant governmental interests— public safety, ensuring that abortions are performed safely, and ensuring that a woman's constitutional rights to travel interstate and to choose to have an abortion were not sacrificed in the interest of defendants' First Amendment rights.

. . . the court held that the injunction left open ample alternative channels for communication, because defendants could still "picket, carry signs, pray, sing or chant in full view of people going into the clinics." . . .

The test . . . , we held [in *Madsen v. Women's Health Center*], is "whether the challenged provisions of the injunction burden no more speech than necessary to serve a significant government interest." . . .

Petitioners challenge three aspects of the injunction: (i) the floating 15-foot buffer zones around people and vehicles seeking access to the clinics; (ii) the fixed 15-foot buffer zones around the clinic doorways, driveways, and parking lot entrances; and (iii) the "cease and desist" provision that forces sidewalk counselors who are inside the buffer zones to retreat 15 feet from the person being counseled once the person indicates a desire not to be counseled. Because *Madsen* bears many similarities to this case and because many of the parties' arguments depend on the application of *Madsen* here, we review our determination in that case. . . .

We now apply *Madsen* to the challenged provisions of the injunction and ask whether they burden more speech than necessary to serve a significant governmental interest. . . .

An injunction tailored to respondents' claims for relief may nonetheless violate the First Amendment. In making their First Amendment challenge, petitioners focus solely on the interests asserted by respondents in their complaint. But in assessing a First Amendment challenge, a court looks not only at the private claims asserted in the complaint, but also inquires into the governmental interests that are protected by the injunction, which may include an interest in public safety and order. . . .

Given the factual similarity between this case and *Madsen*, we conclude that the governmental interests underlying the injunction in *Madsen*—ensuring public safety and order, promoting the free flow of traffic on streets and sidewalks, protecting property rights, and protecting a woman's freedom to seek pregnancy-related services . . . —also underlie the injunction here, and in combination are certainly significant enough to justify an appropriately tailored injunction to secure unimpeded physical access to the clinics.

C

We strike down the floating buffer zones around people entering and leaving the clinics because they burden more speech than is necessary to serve the relevant governmental interests. The floating buffer zones prevent defendants—except for two sidewalk counselors, while they are tolerated by the targeted individual—from communicating a message from a normal conversational distance or handing leaflets to people entering or leaving the clinics who are walking on the public sidewalks. This is a broad prohibition, both because of the type of speech that is restricted and the nature of the location. Leafletting and commenting on matters of public concern are classic forms of speech that lie at the heart of the First Amendment, and speech in public areas is at its most protected on public sidewalks, a prototypical example of a traditional public forum. . . .

. . . attempts to stand 15 feet from someone entering or leaving a clinic and to communicate a message—certainly protected on the face of the injunction—will be hazardous if one wishes to remain in compliance with the injunction. Since there may well be other ways to both effect such separation and yet provide certainty (so that speech protected by the injunction's terms is not burdened), we conclude that the floating buffer zones burden more speech than necessary to serve the relevant governmental interests.

*Source*: 117 S. Ct. 855 (1997).

# Glossary

*Affirm.* An appellate court decision confirming the result reached in a case by the lower court.

*Amicus curiae.* Literally, "friend of the court." One who is not a party to the litigation, but who submits a brief directed to issues in a case.

*Appeal.* To appeal is to ask a higher court to review the decision of the trial court. Generally, a party losing at trial may appeal once to an appellate court as a matter of right. Review of appellate court decisions is generally within the discretion of the State or U.S. Supreme Courts.

*Appellant.* The party filing an appeal.

*Appellee.* The party against whom the appeal is filed; the party that won in the lower court.

*Certiorari, writ of.* A writ issued from the Supreme Court, at its discretion and at the request of a petitioner, to order a lower court to send the record of a case to the Court for its review.

*Civil law.* The body of law dealing with the private rights of individuals, as distinguished from criminal law.

*Class action.* A lawsuit brought by one person or group on behalf of all persons similarly situated.

*Common law.* The collection of principles and rules, particularly from unwritten English law, derived from decisions in previous cases, or from long-standing usage and custom.

*Compelling state interest.* A test used to justify government action challenged under First Amendment and equal protection doctrines.

*Concurring opinion.* An opinion by a justice agreeing with the result reached by the Court in a case but disagreeing with the Court's rationale or reasoning for its decision.

*De facto.* In fact, in reality.

*Defendant.* In a civil action, the party denying or defending itself against charges brought by a plaintiff. In a criminal action, the person charged with the commission of an offense.

*De jure.* As a result of law, as a result of official action.

*Dissenting opinion.* An opinion by a justice that disagrees with the result reached by the Court in a case.

*Due process.* Fair and regular procedures. At a minimum, notice and opportunity to be heard. The Fifth and Fourteenth Amendments guarantee persons that they will not be deprived of life, liberty, or property by the government without due process of law.

*Ex parte.* From only one side. Application to a court for some ruling or action on behalf of only one party, without giving the other party an opportunity to respond.

*Federalism.* The interrelationships among the states and the relationship between the states and the national government.

*Habeas corpus.* Literally, "you have the body"; a writ issued to inquire whether a person is lawfully imprisioned or detained. The writ demands that the person's holding the prisoner justify the detention or release the body.

*Injunction.* A court order prohibiting a person from performing a particular act.

*In re.* In the affair of, concerning; often used in judicial proceedings where the matter (such as a bankrupt's estate) requires judicial action.

*Judicial review.* The power to review and strike down any legislation or other government action that is inconsistent with federal or state constitutions.

*Jurisdiction.* The power of a court to hear a case or controversy, which exists when the proper parties are present and when the point to be decided is among the issues authorized to be handled by a particular court.

*Moot.* A moot question is no longer material, or has already been resolved, and has thus become hypothetical.

*Motion.* A written or oral application to a court or judge to obtain a rule or order.

*Per curiam.* "By the court"; an unsigned opinion of the court.

*Petitioner.* One who files a petition with a court seeking action or relief, including a plaintiff or appellant. When a writ of certiorari is granted by the Supreme Court, the party seeking review is called the petitioner, and the party responding is called the respondent.

*Remand.* To send back. After a decision in a case, the case may be sent back to the trial court for further action consistent with the higher court's decision.

*Respondent.* The party that is compelled to answer claims or questions brought to the court by a petitioner.

*Reverse.* In an appellate court, to reach a decision that disagrees with the result reached in a case by a lower court.

*Separation of powers.* The division of the powers of the national government according to the three branches of government: the legislative, which is empowered to make laws; the executive, which is required to carry out the laws; and the judicial, which has the power to interpret, uphold or invalidate legislation and to adjudicate legal disputes.

*Sovereignty.* Supreme political authority; the absolute and uncontrollable power by which an independent nation-state is governed.

*Standing.* Having the necessary legal characteristics to bring a case; this generally requires that one have a personal interest and stake in the outcome.

*Stare decisis.* "Let the decision stand." The principle of adherence to precedent, the doctrine that principles of law established in earlier cases should be accepted as authoritative in similar subsequent cases.

*State action.* Actions undertaken by state government or its political subdivisions and those done "under the color of the state law"; that is, those actions required or sanctioned by a state. The term is sometimes used to mean any action by government.

*Subpoena.* An order to present oneself before a grand jury, court, or legislative hearing.

*Subpoena duces tecum.* An order to present specified documents or papers to a grand jury, court or legislative body.

*Vacate.* To make void, annul, or rescind the decision of a lower court.

*Writ.* An order commanding someone to perform or not to perform acts specified in the order.

# Selected Bibliography

*American Voices: Prize-winning Essays on Freedom of Speech, Censorship, and Advertising Bans.* New York: P. Morris, USA, 1987.

Cox, Archibald. *Freedom of Expression.* Cambridge, MA: Harvard University Press, 1981.

Criley, Richard. *The FBI v. the First Amendment.* Los Angeles: First Amendment Foundation, 1990.

Farish, Leah. *The First Amendment: Freedom of Speech, Religion, and the Press.* Springfield, NJ: Enslow, 1998.

———. *Tinker v. Des Moines: Student Protest.* Springfield, NJ: Enslow, 1997.

Frohnmayer, John. *Out of Tune: Listening to the First Amendment.* Golden, CO: North American Press, 1995.

Gefland, Ravina. *The Freedom of Speech in America.* Minneapolis: Lerner Publications Co., 1967.

Glasser, Ira. *Visions of Liberty: The Bill of Rights for All Americans.* New York: Arcade, 1991.

Godwin, Mike. *Cyber Rights: Defending Free Speech in the Digital Age.* New York: Times Books, 1998.

Gora, Joel M., David Goldberger, Gary M. Stern, and Morton H. Halperin. *The Right to Protest: The Basic ACLU Guide to Free Expression.* Carbondale: Southern Illinois University Press, 1991.

Gurstein, Rochelle. *The Repeal of Reticence.* New York: Hill & Wang, 1996.

Hamlin, David. *The Nazi/Skokie Conflict: A Civil Liberties Battle.* Boston: Beacon Press, 1981.

Hentoff, Nat. *The First Freedom: The Tumultuous History of Free Speech in America.* New York: Delacorte Press, 1988.

———. *Free Speech for Me—But Not for Thee: How the American Left and Right Relentlessly Censor Each Other.* New York: HarperCollins, 1992.

Hixson, Richard F. *Pornography and the Justices: The Supreme Court and the Intractable Obscenity Problem.* Carbondale: Southern Illinois University Press, 1996.

Kalven, Harry, Jr. *A Worthy Tradition: Freedom of Speech in America*. New York: Harper & Row, 1988.

Kennedy, Sheila Suess. *What's a Nice Republican Girl like Me Doing in the ACLU?* Amherst, NY: Prometheus Books, 1997.

King, David C. *Freedom of Assembly*. Brookfield, CT: Millbrook Press, 1997.

Levy, Leonard W. *Blasphemy: Verbal Offense against the Sacred, from Moses to Salman Rushdie*. New York: Alfred A. Knopf, 1993.

———. *Freedom of Speech and Press in Early American History: Legacy of Suppression*. New York: Harper & Row, 1963.

Lipschultz, Jeremy Harris. *Broadcast Indecency: F.C.C. Regulation and the First Amendment*. Boston: Focal Press, 1997.

Marcus, Laurence R. *Fighting Words: The Politics of Hateful Speech*. Westport, CT: Praeger, 1996.

McCarthy, Eugene J. *The Ultimate Tyranny: The Majority over the Majority*. New York: Harcourt Brace Jovanovich, 1980.

McWhirter, Darien A. *Freedom of Speech, Press, and Assembly*. Phoenix, AZ: Oryx, 1994.

Meiklejohn, Alexander. *Free Speech and Its Relation to Self-Government*. New York: Harper, 1948.

Middleton, Kent, and Roy M. Mersky. *Freedom of Expression: A Collection of Best Writings*. Buffalo, NY: William S. Hein & Company, 1981.

Neier, Aryeh. *Defending My Enemy: American Nazis, the Skokie Case, and the Risks of Freedom*. New York: Dutton, 1979.

O'Neil, Robert M. *Free Speech in the College Community*. Bloomington: Indiana University Press, 1997.

Rabban, David M. *Free Speech in Its Forgotten Years*. Cambridge: Cambridge University Press, 1997.

Smolla, Rodney A. *Free Speech in an Open Society*. New York: Alfred A. Knopf, 1992.

Steins, Richard. *Censorship: How Does It Conflict with Freedom?* New York: Twenty-First Century Books, 1995.

Van Alstyne, William W. *Interpretations of the First Amendment*. Durham, NC: Duke University Press, 1984.

Walker, Samuel. *Hate Speech: The History of an American Controversy*. Lincoln: University of Nebraska Press, 1994.

Zeinert, Karen. *Free Speech: From Newspapers to Music Lyrics*. Springfield, NJ: Enslow, 1995.

# Index

**About the Editor**

SHEILA SUESS KENNEDY is Assistant Professor of Law and Public Policy at Indiana University.

**Primary Documents in American History and Contemporary Issues**